Thank You M. Monnet

Essays on the History of European Integration

Richard T. Griffiths

Thank You M. Monnet

Essays on the History of European Integration

LEIDEN UNIVERSITY PRESS

Cover design: Studio Ron Van Loon
Lay-out: CO2 Premedia b.v.

ISBN 978 90 8728 171 7
e-ISBN 978 94 0060 107 9 (e-pdf)
e-ISBN 978 94 0060 108 6 (e-pub)
NUR 697

Contents

Introduction

When the history of the 20th century is written, the process of European integration will figure as a major feature in the development of Western Europe. It will not be because it prevented a future war – the looming presence of the Soviet Union was sufficient to stop any local adventure in that direction – but because it anchored an era of unparalleled prosperity and because it lay the foundation for the democratic transformation of East Central Europe once the Cold War was over. The term 'European integration' has been used to describe these events, as though there was a single unbroken trail of successes, and the occasional setback, leading to the European Union of today. And since there appears to be a sequence to these developments, there is always a 'process' to explain them. History is rarely so tidy.

Alongside the early treaties founding the European Coal and Steel Community (1951) and the European Economic Communities (1957) there existed other regional experiments at integration (in the sense of growing together, or becoming more interdependent), including the Organisation for European Economic Cooperation (1948) and the European Free Trade Association (1960), which have tended to fade from view, as well as the ill-fated attempt by the original six Coal and Steel Community members to create a European defence community and a European political community (1952-1955).

History is written in different ways and in different waves at different times. Almost before the dust has settled on a particular episode of the past a rash of publications appears that capture, analyse, explain and place in context what has just happened, very often before the outcome is known and the full impact appreciated. These are mostly based on the open record and after the initial splash the output gradually eddies until public interest wanes altogether. This is what we may call 'contemporaneous history'. There is nothing wrong with it, and when spiced up with a dollop of theory, many have become classics of their kind.

A second wave then begins to emerge as the participants in the events, or their biographers or ghost-writers, start to place themselves into the flow of history to demonstrate how their presence in the story may have nudged the tide in this direction or that. This is a history from the participant's perspective – which is exactly what we want from an ego-document – but we must remember that it is not always the perspective that the historian would necessarily choose. The eyewitness' perspectives will have identified what, for them, were the important events. They will have seen them from their own position as a participant, and they will have placed other actors accordingly. And they will have also rationalised, or perhaps even justified, the positions that they took at the time.

The third wave begins as the documentation that informed the decision-making process begins to emerge into the public domain. This moment varies from country to country, but in Western Europe the documents are made available to the public most commonly after thirty years have passed. Governments judge that sufficient time has elapsed to nullify any dangers to national security, and potential damage to the reputation and careers of the participants has been diminished. Unfortunately, by then it also leaves precious little time for historians to match the written record with the testimony of surviving eyewitnesses. The records most eagerly sought by historians fall into three main categories: records of international negotiations, diplomatic records from embassies abroad, and documentation relating to domestic decision-making. And from these perspectives, they do indeed shed new light on questions from the past. However, they do not tell the whole story. The documents, too, were written from a particular perspective and if their judgements were wrong at the time, they are likely to be wrong today. Moreover, the documents do not tell a story; they help answer questions and these questions are framed from the historians' own perspectives.

After a flurry of activity as historians access the newly released archive record, the volume of published research again wanes. Occasionally interest is reignited as the approach of a new anniversary rekindles interest (and, if you are lucky, also provides funding) or if a particular 'crisis' prompts some historical reflection. For the rest, it is slowly assimilated into the textbook accounts of events.

The essays in this volume were written at different stages over the past thirty years, mostly coinciding with the opening of the archival record of the events described. Thus, in the 1980s, historians were becoming able to access the records related to the founding treaties establishing the forerunners to the present-day European Union. They also cover the history of other integration experiments dating from the time. Most appeared in edited volumes bringing together different perspectives on historical topics. It was in this way that the history of European integration was driven forward. In those days, to have published in the established journals would have been tantamount to 'losing' the article for the relevant audience. However, as the internet has opened up journal articles to researchers and has facilitated the searching of article databases, it is the book chapters that are difficult to find and to locate. For this reason, I appreciate the initiative of Leiden University Press in bringing some of them together in this volume.

We decided against 'upgrading' the annotations since that would be tantamount to falsifying the writing of history. Instead, at the end of each contribution there will be a brief indication of where and why it was written (and published) followed by a short discussion of the most important literature to have appeared since.

Richard T. Griffiths, Leiden, March 2013

1

The European Integration Experience, 1945-1958[1]

In 1945 Western Europe counted the cost of yet another Continental conflict: the third within seventy years involving France and Germany. Yet in 1958 France and Germany formed the core of a new supranational 'community'. Between these two dates intra-state relations had been transformed. It represented a development to which many in 1945 would have aspired, but which few would have dared hope to see realised so quickly. This evolution marked the beginning of what is commonly referred to as 'the process of European integration'.

It is worth pausing at the double connotation of the word 'integration' since the expression is used to imply both a set of institutional steps (all involving the surrender of sovereignty) and the enmeshing of economies and societies that is supposed to flow from the measures adopted. To be more precise, the word 'integration' is applied to the European Coal and Steel Community (ECSC), founded by France, Germany, Italy and the Benelux countries in 1952, and to the European Economic Community (EEC) and Euratom, both founded by the same six states in 1958. The term excludes a great deal, as indeed is its intention. Nonetheless, we must realise that it sidelines many other institutional changes on the grounds that they are 'inter-governmental', and do not involve sovereignty surrender. It also marginalises other sources, institutional or otherwise, of Europe's growing 'interdependence'.

The 'process of integration' is given pride of place in the memoirs of those most closely identified with it. This is because they were convinced of the historical importance of their achievements, but also because they were eager to win a propaganda war against the existing intergovernmental alternatives which they saw as weak, impotent and incapable of sustaining further development.[2] The institutions and workings of the new supranational communities were pushed further into the limelight by the writings of a generation of political scientists, attracted by the novelty of their provisions and the dynamic inherent in their operations. These attitudes have subsequently been back-projected onto the past in a series of histories which concentrate on the struggle for supranational, even federal, institutions but which virtually exclude developments elsewhere. However, the EEC came onto the scene relatively late in the day and although the ECSC had been created earlier, it was limited in its economic impact. Insofar as the economic boom of the 1950s and the trade expansion that accompanied it had an institutional explanation, it lay elsewhere. The EEC's creation witnessed the end of the Continent's financial and commercial rehabilitation, and not the beginning.

Since the late 1970s, a new generation of historians, trudging in the wake of the so-called 'thirty-year rule' referring to the period lapsed before (some) national governments grant access to their archives, has been rewriting the history of this period. Much of this work has still to be assimilated into mainstream accounts but, once it has been, its main achievement will have been to widen the perspective and context of analysis and to rediscover the complexity of the past. This, in itself, has often constituted a challenge to the simplistic 'high politics' analysis (and sometimes straight federalist propaganda) of existing accounts. Historians, however, have been less successful in agreeing on a coherent 'alternative' explanation.

One casualty of the new history has been 'American hegemony theory', at least in its early chronology. The 'hegemonic leadership' theory argues that the existence of a hegemony allowed for the reconciliation of lesser level, national differences. Thus, at the height of its relative economic, political, military and moral power the United States is supposed to have used its good offices to establish a liberal world order and, more particularly, to have supported 'integrative' solutions that mirrored its own history and that seemed to underpin its own success and prosperity. The new literature has demonstrated the limits of hegemonic power and has raised awareness of the degree to which Europe could resist American wishes. Equally, it has underscored the 'European' as opposed to American motives in seeking to 'change the rules' through institutional innovation or reform.

Secondly, the historians have stumbled into the 'actor-agency' dilemma already familiar to political scientists. Initially, much of the literature focused on the actors: the ideas that drove them, their positions of political power and role in networks of key players, and the political processes which they adapted or invented to accomplish their ends. The need to find peace in Western Europe and to build a bulwark against totalitarianism formed the 'real world' components in this analysis. Subsequently, historians working usually in governmental archives have found a more prosaic subtext to events. Far from a heroic, visionary quest for a better future, they recount a story of entrenched defence of perceived national positions. This version of history is often juxtaposed against the earlier approaches but the two are not necessarily irreconcilable. The international agreements that underpin the integration 'process' were usually submitted to parliamentary scrutiny, and the threat of rejection placed constraints on a too-cavalier surrender on issues of public concern. Moreover, the whole idea of 'supranationality' is to adapt rules for future political behaviour, to determine the 'how' of the political process. It may remain a primary goal even if it requires a surrender of consistency or elegance in the short-term.

This version of 'perceived national interest' is itself the outcome of domestic political processes and is susceptible to changes in balance within governments and between governments. It is some way removed from the concept of national interest as formulated by 'realist' or 'neo-realist' scholars. They would argue that the state is a unitary actor, intent on maximising its interests, and whose foreign policy behaviour can be deduced from an objective reading of its relative geo-political position. Within the integration literature, this made its appearance in the early 1960s[3] and has recently been revived. In its current version, the viability or survival of post-war, mass-democratic states lay in their ability to satisfy a 'consensus' built around welfare, growth and agricultural protection. Only when these goals could not be met in any other way did governments agree to surrender sovereignty and emerge stronger as a result.[4] Aside from postulating an implausible degree of coherence in collective decision-making, this version of events exaggerates both the dangers confronting European states in what was, after all, the middle of the greatest economic boom in modern history, and the importance of supranational mechanisms in resolving residual commercial challenges.

—

Despite the awesome destructive power of modern weaponry, Europe's post-war productive capacity was not as damaged as is often claimed. Although the image of utter devastation still persists, the physical damage was concentrated on infrastructural investment (mainly transport and housing) and much less on productive capital. Most historians now accept that Europe's industrial capacity was larger than it had been in 1938 and, in some respects, better adapted to the needs of the post-war era. Without taking this into account, it is impossible to understand Europe's rapid industrial recovery. Already in 1947, most Western European countries had surpassed their pre-war levels of industrial output. Germany, the main exception, was not to do so until 1950, by which point Western Europe as a whole was producing almost 25 per cent more than in the pre-war years. Although the expansion of manufacturing was remarkable, serious problems still remained. Basic industries, such as coal and steel, struggled to recapture pre-war production levels and the neglect and destruction of transport also caused major bottlenecks. Agricultural production was not severely weakened within Western Europe but recovery was much slower than it had been for industry. Although a poor harvest in 1947 reinforced a more negative image, this was a serious but isolated incident and output rebounded quickly. Even so, it was not until 1950 that production recovered its prewar levels.[5]

The impact of all these changes was to widen the productivity gap between Europe and the USA. Taking industry alone, the USA emerged from the war with double the output of 1938 and, despite the dislocation of adjustment to peacetime conditions and a short-lived recession, had added to that position by 1950. Without closing the gap, it was felt that Europe would be unable to repair the trade imbalance with the USA nor sustain acceptable standards of welfare for its peoples. This problem was aggravated by the impact of the war on Europe's trading relationships, both with other European countries and with the rest of the world.

American wartime planning had aspired to a world multilateral trade and payments system. The Bretton Woods Conference, held in July 1944, decided in favour of the restoration of the gold exchange standard (based on gold and convertible reserve currencies) but with two important safeguards. Firstly, it created the International Monetary Fund (IMF) to aid countries against speculative attack. Secondly it agreed a set of 'rules' to govern international monetary behaviour. In December 1945, the USA proposed complementing the arrangements for world monetary order by the creation of the International Trade Organisation (ITO) to ease trade conditions and coordinate national countercyclical policies. In a much watered down form its constitution was agreed in Havana in 1948. However, the ITO never came into existence, as the US Congress, unwilling to surrender so much control over its protectionist arsenal, refused its ratification. This left the (temporary) far less embracing General Agreement on Tariffs and Trade (GATT), agreed in 1947, as the main regulatory body for commodity trade. It is important to note that in both areas, the agenda for action was a global one. There was little place for new regional discrimination and every intention to eradicate existing preference areas, usually founded on a colonial-metropole axis.[6]

Instead of a multilateral trading system, Europe's trade and payments had returned to the pattern of bilateralism and autarky that had characterised the 1930s. Indeed, the pervasiveness of frontier controls, through countries and across products, surpassed anything that had been seen in peacetime since the start of the free trade movement a century earlier. Europe's commercial problems stemmed from several different sources. The effect of the dislocation to many economies made it difficult to divert production to exports at the expense of investment or already low levels of consumption. Moreover, the liquidation or destruction of foreign investments, earnings from which even by 1950 were still in real terms 75 per cent less than they had been in 1938, removed an important source for covering import requirements. These two developments aggravated trade imbalances, but the problem was complicated by shifts in the direction of trade. Germany had provided many countries with imports of fuel and raw materials, semi-manufactures and investment goods upon which their own industries had depended. Because German recovery was inhibited by the occupying Allies, this source of supply was much diminished. Moreover, agricultural goods, and particularly grain, were no longer available in the same quantities from Eastern Europe. Indeed the only area capable of compensating for this shortfall in supply was North America. Thus the deficit with the dollar area increased enormously compared with before the war, at a time when the disruption of colonial economies also meant that Europe was no longer able to earn dollars from triangular trade. The scarcity of hard currencies forced countries to restrict imports and to control trade through bilateral agreements, augmented with quantitative restrictions and exchange controls. The effects of these problems, and the measures chosen to cope with them, reduced the relative levels of intra-trade in peacetime in Western Europe to possibly their lowest point in the 20th century. The share of intra-trade in Europe's total imports and exports fell from virtually 48 per cent in 1938 to under 35 per cent ten years later.[7]

It was against this background that, early in 1947, there occurred a sharp deterioration in Western Europe's dollar deficit. It was probably occasioned primarily by ambitious inflationary investment plans initiated in the interests of domestic reconstruction, but it was aggravated by the impact of poor harvests on Europe's terms of trade. Yet it was this second factor, with its associated images of hunger, high prices and social discontent, which formed the prime public legitimisation of a major dollar investment programme announced by the American secretary of state, General George Marshall, at a speech in Harvard in June 1947. The announcement of the Marshall Plan has often been associated with the Truman Doctrine of March 1947 pledging American help to the Greeks in their struggle against communists in the Civil War. Together, they have come to symbolise the start of the Cold War. Yet Marshall Aid marks another fundamental shift in American policy. It represented a recognition that Europe's reconstruction could not be managed within a global multilateral framework, but rather that the Continent's rehabilitation was a prerequisite for the functioning of wider arrangements.[8]

The failure of a global strategy was underlined within months of the announcement of Marshall Aid. When, in 1945, the Anglo-American loan agreement had been signed, one of its clauses had stipulated that the United Kingdom would reintroduce sterling convertibility by mid-1947. This would allow countries to use their sterling reserves for multilateral settlements and thus reduce the pressures on the dollar. On the appointed day, supported by new loans, the British government duly announced the return of convertibility and found itself immediately confronted with a run on reserves. Within seven weeks, the experiment was abruptly curtailed. Nothing else could have demonstrated as eloquently that it was not currency or liquidity that the system needed, but one currency in particular (the US dollar) and in one area (Western Europe).

Of course there was realisation that special transitional arrangements would be needed to assist recovery from wartime destruction. In November 1943, for example, forty-four governments created the United Nations Relief and Rehabilitation Administration (UNRAA) for the provision of immediate relief in the form of food, clothing and shelter, as well as raw materials and machinery to restart agriculture and industry. In mid-1946 it decided to wind up its operations by spring of 1947. Before then, in June 1946, another Bretton Woods institution, the International Bank for Reconstruction and Development (the IBRD or World Bank) was due to commence operations, although it was a full year before it made its first loan. Marshall Aid, however, was an acknowledgment that its funds would be no match for the task at hand.

The United States began its active intervention in Europe's structural problems with the European Recovery Program (ERP). In comparison with the $4 billion that the United States had contributed to European reconstruction in the first two years following the war through the UNRAA and other programmes, over the four years of its operation Marshall Aid amounted to about $12.5 billion:

$10 billion in grants, $1 billion in loans and $1.5 billion in 'conditional aid' used to lubricate the limited intra-European payments agreement of 1948. Not only were the sums larger than had been previously considered necessary, ERP was important in committing to provide financial aid and other assistance on a four-year (rather than an *ad hoc*) basis which enabled countries to adopt longer and more secure planning frameworks for their investment strategies. On the American side, the Economic Cooperation Administration (ECA) ran the scheme. In Europe, sixteen Western states formed the Committee for European Economic Cooperation (CEEC) to decide on accepting the aid and, in 1948, continued their existence as the Organisation for European Economic Cooperation (OEEC).

The dollars were made available for vital import requirements. Only 17 per cent was spent directly on imports of 'machinery and vehicles', the rest on raw materials and agricultural products. The importers, however, paid the equivalent in domestic currency to their governments, which were free to use the money on capital projects. This mechanism freed domestic funds for capital formation and, since ECA approval was required before the funds could be spent, it allowed US planners to influence directly the direction of economic change. In addition, for example by refusing funds to Italian firms that dealt with non-'free' (i.e. communist) trade unions, it also permitted their intrusion into the politics and societies of European states.

The macroeconomic impact of the ERP on the European economies has recently been questioned. Certainly it did not save the Continent from ruin and starvation since, by the time its funds came on stream in mid-1948, that moment had long passed. Instead, it contributed to the maintenance of already high investment levels, with the greatest relative impact in the first two years. However, funding was not on a scale sufficient to explain the super-growth of the 1950s. It is true that in 1948 and 1949 the contribution of ERP funds to gross domestic capital formation touched 30 per cent in Germany and Italy, but in both countries the global figures were particularly low. The more usual level was around 10 per cent, as it was also for Italy and Germany in 1950 and 1951: a useful, but not a decisive, contribution. New calculations suggest that direct aid contributed only 0.5 per cent per annum to growth in this period. Indirectly, the flow of funds for raw materials itself released resources for investment, while secure planning horizons might also have contributed to raising investment and output targets. The ERP also reduced the tension of the costs of structural adjustment. At a time when demand exceeded supply by 7.5 per cent, an addition of 2.5 per cent to GNP reduced the potential conflict over the distribution of income between labour and capital.[9]

Not unnaturally, the Americans were reluctant to see their funds siphoned off into competing national schemes, each presumably demanding further measures of national protection. They insisted from the start, therefore, that the funds be allocated according to pan-European criteria and in the service of a pan-European plan. The European criterion for aid assessment was adopted. It was taken as the size of the dollar gap rather than any estimate of size of income or degree of damage. The European plan also emerged, aimed at the previously prescribed goal of balance-of-payments equilibrium by 1952. However, a closer reading demonstrated that the European plan was little more than the aggregation of separate national plans. The Americans had more success, however, in encouraging measures for the freeing of trade and payments from national constraints and protectionism. Although the causes of the economic growth of the 1950s, and the even more spectacular expansion of trade that accompanied it, are many and complex, at an institutional level it was the ERP, through the OEEC, that laid the foundations.

—

In October 1949, the ECA administrator, Paul Hoffman, made a major speech to the OEEC in which he called repeatedly for 'integration' as the price for a continued, generous level of dollar aid. 'The substance of such integration', he went on, 'would be the formation of a single large market in which quantitative restriction on the movement of goods, monetary barriers to the flow of payments and, eventually, all tariffs are permanently swept away.' Although the OEEC had experimented in 1948 and 1949 with some limited multilateral payments schemes and was at that moment considering a (modest) start to a programme of quota removal, the Hoffman speech concentrated minds wonderfully.

In case the OEEC was in doubt about the direction of American thinking, another ECA official, Richard Bissell, produced an outline for a European Payments Union (EPU) for a discriminatory soft-currency zone that in its detail went far beyond the usual policy advice. The Americans also pledged themselves to providing a sum of $350 million for the EPU's working capital. It is noteworthy that the EPU was a recognition that another American creation, the IMF, was incapable of the task of supervising Europe's transition to convertibility. However, its rules and objectives were oriented towards the attainment of full, non-discriminatory convertibility. The sterling crisis of 1947 had demonstrated that any such move would have rapidly drained the IMF of its loanable funds. All the IMF could do was recognise the serious structural problems facing the Continent and sanction the discriminatory currency practices that were already commonplace.

The European Payments Union (EPU) embraced all OEEC members and came into operation in September 1950. The OEEC is commonly known as an 'intergovernmental' institution but, as such, the structure adopted for the EPU formed an interesting innovation. To decide conflicts there existed a Special Restricted Committee of five persons chosen by lot from a list nominated by each of the members. None of the members could be from the countries involved in the dispute. The committee reported to the OEEC Council, which then pronounced judgement. The managing board of the EPU, comprising seven representatives and one American observer, worked on majority vote. This, too, was at odds with standard OEEC procedure, but since the board was responsible to the OEEC Council, any serious disputes were likely to end up there anyway.

Of the initial $350 million granted to the EPU, some $80 million was immediately allocated to countries with 'structural' payment problems and the remainder provided the working capital of the Union. This money was necessary to bridge the gap in the arrangements for debtors and those for creditors. The way the system worked was that a margin of deficit (equivalent to 15 per cent of the value of trade) was calculated for each country that would receive (some) automatic credit on its intra-European transactions. This pay-out was divided into five steps. In the first step, the debtor received 100 per cent credit; in the second, he received 80 per cent credit but had to pay the rest in gold or dollars. The scale of hard currency payment was increased until the fifth step, when only 20 per cent was covered by credit and the rest in hard currency. Beyond that, all transactions took effect in hard currency. Overall, within the EPU allocation, a debtor could rely on credit covering 60 per cent of the deficit. A similar situation prevailed for creditors within the Union but, although the overall position was the same (60:40), the steps were not synchronised with the effect that creditors received hard currency from the Union earlier than the debtors were paying it in. It was to cover this gap that the dollar funding was intended.[10]

No sooner had the EPU been installed than it was put to the test. The German economy already had a huge deficit in autumn 1950 and it rapidly deteriorated. With the exhaustion of its quota in sight, the EPU extended an extra credit line and in February 1951 acknowledged the need for a reintroduction of quotas and the creation of state-monopoly import agencies. By the summer of 1952, the crisis had been weathered, and an upturn in German exports allowed it to reopen its markets. Similar, though less violent, crises hit the United Kingdom and France in these early years and it was the EPU that provided the means whereby countries were not forced to adopt violent deflationary measures. Moreover, although in every case there was some backsliding in the commitment to hold back levels of import quotas, the fact that EPU and the OEEC's 'trade liberalisation' scheme (of which more below) were in existence acted as a control over a more drastic and dislocating return to (temporary) protection.

From a low point in June 1952, when the combined reserves of the OEEC states stood at $7.8 billion, the position steadily improved until mid-1955 when they reached $13.4 billion. Against this background, the conditions within the EPU were gradually hardened. In place of a ratio 60:40 between credit and gold, in mid-1954 the coverage was changed to 50:50 and in 1955 to only 25:75. By this stage much of the EPU's work had been done and many countries had introduced *de facto* convertibility on current transactions. However, this step was not formally taken until December 1958. Meanwhile the EPU main customer was France and, although the job could equally have been done by the IMF, the operation held France within the European institutional orbit at a time of political upheavals caused by colonial unrest, and at a time when more 'integrationist' experiments were being discussed.

The mirror of American concern on payments was its determination to remove quotas on intra-European trade. The evident multilateral forum for dealing with the issue was the General Agreement on Tariffs and Trade (GATT) agreed in Havana in 1948. Yet the GATT was fatally flawed. It was dependent for its existence on a regular renewal by its members. Moreover, the rejection of the ITO had signalled that the US Congress was wary about agreeing to anything that might affect levels of protection for US industry. At a time when the major dysfunctional element in the world economy was seen to be the inability to pay for dollar imports through the sale of goods on the American market, it was inconceivable to envisage a reciprocal tariff negotiation that did not require for its success concessions by the United States. Although at Geneva, in 1947, the GATT partners negotiated cuts of 19 per cent in their registered tariffs on manufactured goods, at Annecy, two years later, the meagre harvest was estimated at 2 per cent and at Torquay, in 1950-1951, it reached a scarcely more credible 3 per cent. In both cases a major factor was the reluctance of the USA to negotiate reciprocal tariff reductions. With success on tariffs beyond them, the members of GATT perhaps wisely refrained from tackling the enforcement of prohibitions on quotas, which were seen as even more harmful to trade than tariffs. It was for this reason that the USA accepted a regional solution to the removal of quantitative restrictions (QRs) or quotas on intra-European trade.[11]

At the end of 1949, the OEEC adopted the target for removing import quotas, directed against each other, on 50 per cent of their 'private' trade by the end of the year. This target applied separately also to each of the three groups: food and feeding stuffs, raw materials and manufactured goods. Under prompting from ECA officials, who argued that something a little more spectacular was necessary to convince Congress to continue aid on a high level, the target was raised first to 60 per cent and subsequently to 75 per cent. The 'trade liberalisation scheme' as it became known had several drawbacks that made the commitments, and the achievements, less than initially suggested. Firstly, the operation referred to 'private trade' and exempted, therefore, imports on government account. This had been done so as not to interfere in 'domestic' political decisions but the effect was to remove from the operation of the scheme entire swathes of trade (mostly in agriculture but sometimes also in fuel) controlled by government monopoly purchasing agencies. This 'skew' in the operation was compounded by the fact that the initial obligation to remove QRs evenly over broad product categories was dropped once the targets were further raised. An overperformance in raw materials, for example, could and usually did compensate for an underachievement in agriculture. Furthermore, the Liberalization Code allowed countries with balance-of-payments difficulties to reimpose unilaterally restrictions if necessary, causing a rebound effect on its trading partners and undermining the EPU's 'discipline' in the process. Finally, the whole operation excluded tariffs, considered the preserve of GATT, so that QR removal was often accompanied by the (re)imposition of (partially) suspended tariffs. The initial agreement bore all the hallmarks of the compromises necessary to secure its passage through the OEEC Council.

In October 1950, the OEEC Council agreed that by February 1951 members should remove QRs on 75 per cent of imports from other members, but there progress stalled. The crisis atmosphere engendered by the payments problems in Germany, the UK and France meant that for them even the 75 per cent target had to be temporarily shelved. Such circumstances obviously inhibited the pressure for further advance. Discussions were also constrained by increasing disenchantment by the 'low tariff' countries (the Benelux, Scandinavia and Switzerland) towards the failure to tackle tariffs, and therefore to deal with *all* frontier barriers to trade. Finally, as QR removal advanced it threatened to touch the hard core of protectionism around sectors deemed by governments to be politically, socially or strategically vital to the national interest.

By the mid-1950s, reflecting their less-strained balance-of-payments positions, most OEEC countries had satisfied their 75 per cent targets. Many had also relaxed their quota regimes towards the dollar area, although not to the same extent. Yet when the decision was taken, in January 1955, to progress towards 90 per cent liberalisation, the 'low tariff' countries had made their agreement conditional upon action being taken by the organisation to deal with high tariffs. Although they did not get their way, the target was nonetheless renewed and when, in December 1958, France finally attained it, private trading within Western Europe had, to all intents and purposes, been purged of quantitative restrictions. There remained residual quota discrimination against the USA and, of course, state trading in agriculture was widespread. Nonetheless, for an experiment with such tentative beginnings, the achievement was remarkable.

—

Hoffman's call for 'integration' back in October 1949 acted as a catalyst for a pan-European programme of action on trade and payments. Yet, even at the time, there was an awareness that there existed another path to 'integration' and that it might even be preferable. Whereas Hoffman sought to increase Europe's degree of multilateral cooperation in carefully defined but meaningful areas, Secretary of State Dean Acheson preferred a strengthening of political mechanisms that would weaken the ability of national veto rights to sideline desirable initiatives. In fairness, one should add that he preferred his path because he considered that it would be easier for European countries to comply than it would be for them to accept a more concrete programme. For both men, the ultimate goal was a 'Europe' that mirrored more closely the political model of the United States of America. The 'new' continent could still show the old how to throw off the last shackles of its *ancien régime.*

The articulation of the concept of 'integration' in political or institutional terms had also entered the mainstream of debate in Western Europe. During the Second World War, resistance movements had been forced, partly by the pan-European model espoused by the fascists, to produce a cogent alternative that also transcended national frontiers. Their thinking was shaped by several factors that pointed the way towards international institutional reform. The failure of the Treaty of Versailles and the League of Nations to prevent reassertion of aggressive nationalism suggested that the foreign policies of nation states required stronger constraints. Similarly, the 'beggar-thy-neighbour' policies that characterised separate national responses towards the onset of the Great Depression suggested that there, too, some higher disciplinary force was necessary. These ideas had inspired the original surge of post-war institution-building, but for many observers the strengthening of intergovernmental organisations was not enough. They argued that national units were too small to guarantee security and prosperity in the modern world and too uncontrollable to guarantee freedom from assault. Their solution lay in the pooling of national sovereignties, thereby effectively proscribing the use of national means for waging economic or military aggression.

After the war almost every country witnessed the creation of national 'European' movements, even though they often disagreed on both aims and tactics. Some dedicated themselves to the task of opinion leadership; others aspired to the status of mass movement. Some saw progress as a ripple effect from a core of commitment; others wanted a swift adoption of new political structures. And some saw it as good for other nations, but not necessarily for themselves. Various nationalist federalist groups, characterised by a certain 'constitutionalism' in approach and more geared towards mobilising mass opinion, formed the European Union of Federalists in 1946. Another organisation formed at this time intent on mobilising support for a new form of European political organisation was the Socialist Movement for a United States of Europe. However, the leader in galvanising public opinion was the United Europe Movement, inspired by Winston Churchill's Zurich speech in September 1946 calling for a United States of Europe, and founded by his son-in-law Duncan Sandys. It was this body that, in May 1948, sponsored the Congress of the European Movement, held in The Hague.[12]

The Hague Congress created the Council of Europe, which was supposed to be the start of a new momentum towards higher goals. Instead, its own creation was the high point of its achievement. Whether the British government, or Churchill in opposition, had ever held more than a fleeting interest in actively associating themselves with the construction of a European federation is highly questionable. Embroiled now in an organisation with that goal as an inspiration, the government proceeded to distance itself from the 'integration' of others, and became in the process the focus of opposition. The Council of Europe became torn between the 'federalists' who wanted to move quickly towards new constitutional arrangements, and the 'functionalists' who believed that new arrangements would only be workable if sovereignty surrender were functionally necessary. The latter envisaged that progress would be decided on a step-by-step basis but, when one remembers that the UK was the leading exponent of the functionalist school, it took little to imagine that the position boiled down to one of no progress at all.

These developments quickly paralysed the developments in the Council of Europe and certainly robbed the European movement, in its various guises, of direct political influence. Only in Italy, under the leadership of Altiero Spinelli, was there an attempt to convert the federalist cause into a mass movement, the Movimento Federalista Europeo. Spinelli became disenchanted with the MFE but his enthusiasm for supranationalism remained undimmed. When the head of the Italian government, Alcide De Gasperi, asked him to draft a federalist plan for controlling European institutions, Spinelli seized the chance. These efforts resulted in the introduction of the 'federalist' clause 38 into the European Defence Community Treaty (see below). This, however, represented the pinnacle achievement. As the European Defence Community (EDC) faded, so too did the movement's influence ebb.[13]

Whilst popular movements cannot claim credit for initiating 'the process of integration', they nonetheless provided a pool of new ideas and vocabulary that decision-makers could draw upon when confronted by immediate political problems. This occurred most dramatically when, in May 1950, the French foreign minister, Robert Schuman, announced his plan to form a coal and steel pool embracing Germany. When this call was answered by the Benelux countries and Italy as well, the way was cleared for 'the Six' to embark on a series of institutional experiments built around the concepts of supranationality and sovereignty surrender.

—

It was not preordained that six countries would become irrevocably associated with each other in a series of supranational communities, nor was the fact that those six would be France, Germany, Italy, the Netherlands, Belgium and Luxembourg. To appreciate how the Six reached that stage, we have to go back to the creation of Benelux, and the reaction of France, especially, to that development.

Benelux was the oldest of the post-war experiments in regional integration in Western Europe. It linked Belgium and Luxembourg (whose own economic union, the BLEU, dated back to 1921) to the Netherlands first through a monetary agreement concluded in 1943, and second by a customs union treaty signed a year later by the three governmentsinexile in London. Before the war the BLEU and the Netherlands had conducted approximately 10 per cent of their trade with each other, although there was an increasing imbalance in favour of the former. The greater wartime damage in the Netherlands served to accentuate the Dutch deficit, which doubled between 1947 and 1951. Despite manifold difficulties, the customs union came into force in January 1948, when all tariffs were abolished and a common external tariff was created. However, trade was still impeded by the widespread imposition of quotas, especially on the side of the Dutch. To remove these, even if only towards the BLEU, threatened merely to aggravate the deficit. Progress was only made possible by two further measures. Firstly, Belgium granted ever greater credit extensions (which it was willing to do if it meant securing the Dutch market from Germany while the latter's industry was still kept artificially low) and eventually the problem was subsumed into the European Payments Union. Secondly, the Dutch were able to secure preferential access to the Belgian agricultural market. They had wanted completely free access, since this would have helped remedy the deficit, but they had to make do with a provision which left Belgium's domestic protectionism intact.[14]

From its inception, the Benelux experiment attracted considerable attention from policy-makers in France. This should be no surprise, since before the war Belgium had been France's largest European trading partner. Just as Belgium hoped to supplant Germany in Dutch markets, so France too needed to expand into the German vacuum to justify its own modernisation plans. However, as the Benelux tariffs lay close to each other at the lower end of the range when they agreed to a common external tariff, it was realised that a union with France would be behind highly protectionist walls. Moreover, the Dutch required the German market for their agrarian exports and to earn their traditional shipping services. This required a reciprocal ability to purchase German imports; something that would be impossible if they agreed to the arrangements proposed by the French.

From 1944 onwards there was continuous French pressure to break open Benelux. It was headed off by the creation of a joint consultative body, known as the Conseil Tripartite, which arranged raw material swaps in the early post-war months, which attempted to coordinate policy towards Germany (difficult given the different national provisions) and provided a forum for French attempts for a customs union. These efforts to break open the Benelux were countered by a demand that the move could only be considered if West Germany were to be included; a demand that ran counter to the reason for the French wanting the union in the first place. In 1947 the French used the CEEC conference in Paris to bluff the Benelux partners into daring to turn down the customs union option. They had hoped to use the leverage of the Americans, who themselves wanted to use dollar aid as a means to encourage closer regional integration, as a means of securing their ends. Instead the study group for a pan-European customs union was created to deflect some of the pressure. This deliberated until the end of 1948 but ultimately failed because no decision had yet been taken on the future of the German economy and its position in any scheme. More immediately, the French found their challenge to move to the immediate formation of a customs union accepted only by the Italians. The fact that the primary goal remained the Benelux was reflected in two further approaches in 1948 to persuade them to join. Both were refused.[15]

By December 1947 the first feasibility study for the Franco-Italian Customs Union was ready. It was surprisingly optimistic and a second commission was established to investigate how it could be implemented. In March 1949 Sforza and Schuman signed a treaty that would effectuate a customs union over a number of stages. A tariff union was already envisaged in 1950 and full economic union about six years later. Because of the fear of Italian competition, particularly in agriculture, the French Conseil Économique (a tripartite advisory body representing labour, industry and agriculture) thrice rejected the treaty. The government drew the inevitable conclusion and demurred from presenting it to parliament for ratification.[16]

It was whilst the Franco-Italian customs union issue was still alive that the French economy was confronted by a serious but highly localised problem – a balance-of-payments deficit with Belgium. From such unpromising beginnings was born FRITALUX. The French solution had been a devaluation against the Belgian franc and the help of Belgium in managing the 'broken exchange rates' that this move implied. From there the idea developed to a mini 'payments union' with a flexible exchange rate mechanism. Thinking in this direction was reinforced by the prospect that US dollars would be available to sponsor regional integration initiatives. This served to lubricate the discussions long after the exchange rate realignments of September 1949 had resolved the original French problems. Given the advanced stage that the talks between France, Italy and Belgium had reached and the implications all of this would have had for the Benelux, it is amazing that only in September 1949 were the Dutch informed of what had been happening. They immediately declared that they disliked the idea and would consider it only if it was supplemented by a customs union. That customs union would also embrace the newly sovereign West German state. The French, whilst not rejecting the idea out of hand, argued that the union would better be created first and that Germany could join later. The Dutch feared that this would never materialise and that German entry, if ever agreed, would be surrounded by so many exemptions and escape clauses that it might be unwilling or even unable to join. There the negotiations stuck until the spring of 1950 when it became clear that the Americans had decided to do something else with their cash. They used it to provide the initial capital for the EPU.[17]

With the exception of the Benelux itself, all the episodes discussed in this section ended in failure. Yet they reveal several imperatives guiding policy in the immediate post-war period. The first was the motivation in all the modernisation programmes to utilise the breathing space, while German recovery was being controlled by the Allies, to supplant the German position in both domestic and in foreign markets. The second was the fear of unrestricted German competition. Towards the end of 1949 Allied controls were already being relaxed and the powers of the new supervisory authorities were ill-defined and as yet untested. With or without the Dutch complication of surrendering frontier controls against Germany, which a customs union would imply, the re-emergence of German industry was already a certainty. It was upon meeting that challenge, either politically or economically, that the entire commercial future of Europe depended.

—

The coal and steel sectors of Western Europe took time to recover from the war. These were key industries and figured prominently in governmental recovery programs, like the Monnet Plan in France. It was not accidental that the first major broad-based sectoral integration plan was the European Coal and Steel Community (ECSC). Coal and steel were important traded goods and essential industrial inputs. Since they were largely homogeneous products, they were easy to control and had a long history of international cooperation. Neither the timing nor the authorship of the first integration proposals was accidental either. The French initiative stemmed from an acceptance that they would otherwise be unable to establish some sort of control over German re-industrialisation. French steel reconstruction plans had been based on an attempt to secure previous German markets and also upon guaranteed access to German coal supplies. In 1950, the US policy of relaxing controls threatened to release excess German steel capacity upon a market that showed signs of becoming glutted. If, at the same time, German coal was redirected towards German mills and coal supplies to France were priced relatively unfavourably, the adverse effects on France would be compounded. The Benelux countries and, to a lesser extent Italy, were pulled into the arrangements because they could not afford to remain aloof from a powerful producer bloc being created on its borders.

The Schuman Plan, as it was known, had been prepared in the French Planning Commission by the staff of Jean Monnet. It was launched on 9 May 1950, on the eve of talks with the Americans and the British on the future of controls of the Ruhr industry, and it was clearly aimed at seizing the policy agenda. The British had been neither consulted nor informed of the proposals beforehand but quickly ascertained that they implied an entanglement in continental Europe of a nature that was inconsistent with other obligations and that the organisational form implied too great a surrender of sovereignty. Attempts by France, whose sincerity had been questioned, to persuade them to participate were quickly abandoned and in the summer of 1950 the negotiations began. The Treaty of Paris, establishing the European Coal and Steel Community, was signed in March 1951 and came into effect in July 1952.[18]

The stated goal of the treaty was to rationalise the production and sale of coal and steel. To this end, all import and export duties, subsidies and other discriminatory measures on the trade of coal and steel were immediately abolished. Although rules for pricing were established, in 'normal' circumstances the market was supposed to be competitive. The Community also managed funds for subsidising and providing for firms hurt by the creation of the ECSC and for retraining workers. These were aimed particularly at the Belgian coal industry, some sectors of which were penalised by a combination of thin seams and high labour costs. Over a transitional period, efficient producers paid a levy to facilitate Belgian mines in their adjustment to lower prices. Moreover, because of the heavy weight of fixed costs, the industry was extremely vulnerable to fluctuations in demand and therefore many of the remaining provisions were intended to come into effect in 'abnormal' circumstances; namely, to mitigate the impact of price falls in times of recession. It is curious that although cartel practices were prohibited within the community, the ECSC's marketing policies in the rest of the world were identical to those which would have been followed by a private cartel.

The innovation in the treaty, and the reason why it inspired such interest among proponents of deeper 'integration', lay not in the settlement of a potential political and commercial problem but in the manner of its resolution. The ECSC was administered by an organisational structure which bore many outward similarities to that of the future EEC. It was controlled by the High Authority (HA), a supranational organisation comprised of nine independent members assigned by the member nations. It had freedom to initiate action in specific areas of competencies and rights of initiative at extremes in the business cycle.

The HA cooperated with a Consultative Committee recruited from producer, labour, consumer and distributive interests. It also worked closely with a Special Council of Ministers, in which each country would have one vote, whose role was designed to increase as decisions on coal and steel impinged on wider economic and security issues. The HA was ultimately responsible to a Common Assembly comprising 78 members drawn from national parliaments. Although the HA was the most powerful governing body, the Council could block certain decisions and the Assembly could force the resignation of HA members.[19]

It is hard to judge the immediate economic impact of the ECSC. The immediate removal of trade controls, without the transitional periods common in most European agreements, was a success. However, for coal and steel, traditional trade barriers were less important in regulating trade than they had been in the past or than they were for other sectors of the economy. The coal trade was covered by international agreements in which tariffs did not really play a role; Italy, with a rate of 15 per cent, was something of an exception. For steel, both France and Germany had already suspended tariffs before the treaty was signed and the Benelux tariff was anyway fairly low. Again, only in Italy, where an *ad valorem* tariff of 11-23 per cent had been levied (and which was allowed anyway to remain intact over a transition period) did tariffs have a protectionist intent.

More important was the impact of the ECSC on pricing. The ECSC eliminated the practice of dual pricing and created a base-point pricing system. Although price controls and subsidies were not fully abolished, even small progress on this front eased trade. Moreover, discriminatory transport price policies of the ECSC members were eliminated. By volume, coal and steel were among the most important traded goods, so reduction of cross-border rates of about 30 per cent made a major impact in decontrolling transport. The opening of the coal and steel trade also expanded imports of steel products into France and the Saar. They jumped from 27.7 thousand tons in 1952 to 117.6 thousand in 1953 – a period of low demand with trade barriers in effect for the first few months. In fact, throughout the 1950s, total intra-Community trade grew much faster than production or trade with non-members; intra-ECSC trade in treaty products increased 171 per cent from 1952 to 1957, while production increased only 43 per cent and extra-ECSC trade only 51 per cent. In addition to these concrete effects, the ECSC set the pace and structure of the debate over the next initiative undertaken by the Six. That initiative took place in the area of defence and security policy.

—

Although they were soon to be overshadowed by the Cold War with the Soviet Union and its satellites, it is important to remember that security and defence problems had initially focused on the need to inhibit future German aggression. The Treaty of Dunkirk, signed in March 1947, was a long-term Franco-British alliance directed against Germany. When, a year later with the Brussels Pact, the

Benelux countries joined the alliance, they modified its exclusive orientation towards Germany by a commitment to ward off aggression from whatever source.[20] In the intervening twelve months, the announcement of the Truman Doctrine had highlighted a more immediate and more dangerous threat to peace and security. Yet the sad fact remained that, had the Soviets invaded, the new alliances were ill-placed to stand in their way. Some have even argued that their very frailty was intended to demonstrate the necessity for a commitment of American troops and equipment, backed by nuclear weapons if necessary, to Europe's defence. Indeed, the secret so-called 'Pentagon Talks', which embraced the USA and Canada, started soon afterwards. These discussions came into the open in the summer of 1948 and were widened in scope, culminating in April 1949 with the signing of the Atlantic Pact, which formed the North Atlantic Treaty Organisation (NATO).[21]

American strategic planning in this period recognised that it would be impossible, even with the US troops already in Europe, to defend Europe from Soviet aggression. In the event of an attack, the best scenario was a withdrawal behind the Pyrenees to Spain and across the Channel to the United Kingdom, from which points the reconquest of Europe could begin. A plausible defence line at the Rhine or the Alps was not envisaged before 1957 at the earliest. The only way to bring that date forward was to increase the European defence effort and to employ the latent military strength of West Germany. Two events accelerated thinking in this direction: the victory of the Communists in China and, more importantly, the loss of the nuclear monopoly signified by the detection of the first Soviet atomic test in autumn 1949. These plans were made public in the crisis atmosphere surrounding the Communist invasion of South Korea and the start of the Korean War. In September 1950, Acheson demanded the rearming of West Germany within NATO whilst pledging an increase in US troops stationed in Europe and assistance for an arms build-up elsewhere.

The European reaction to events in Korea was rather more sanguine than that of the USA, and few really saw any link with an increased threat to security in Europe. Given the fact that the hike in raw material prices, which had accompanied the outbreak of war, had undermined their balance-of-payments positions and weakened their recoveries, they were reluctant to undermine progress further by increased defence budgets. Still less did they see any immediate necessity for German rearmament. In France especially, this reaction was acute. If the idea of facing a resurgent industry had filled French policy-makers with dismay, their reaction to the prospect of a reconstituted German army was much worse. Since much of the French army was involved in Indo-China, Germany would soon have the largest army in Western Europe. Within the French planning ministry, however, an alternative strategy was hurriedly put together. If supranationality had provided a vehicle for controlling German industry, could it not equally serve to control its rearmament as well? In October 1950, therefore, Prime Minister René Pleven announced that France would accept German rearmament only in the context of a European army under the control of a single minister of defence. The Americans were initially horrified at the delay in the formation of German divisions that acceptance of the French proposals would imply. Although talks on the Pleven Plan started in February 1951, parallel efforts continued to find a formula for integration of a German army into NATO. When these failed, in summer 1951, the USA not only tolerated the French scheme but became an enthusiastic advocate. A European Defence Community (EDC) would become the agent for carrying forward the integration process in Europe.[22]

At this point, only five of the six ECSC countries were involved as full participants in the negotiations. After the switch in the American position, the Netherlands finally joined, its change of heart prompted by a fear of losing American goodwill (and cash), and the hope of securing a defence line (the IJssel Line) that would not abandon most of the country to advancing Soviet forces. In May 1952 the treaty establishing the EDC was signed in Paris. It was not particularly elegant in design, nor particularly equal in intent. To neutralise the danger of independent German armed action, the army was to be made up of national units of battalion size only. Having thus fragmented German military capacity, the French went on to remove their colonial armed forces from Community control. Then, by defining Germany as a potential war zone, it proscribed the manufacture of certain war equipment on German soil. Despite the modifications made in the negotiations, it did not make much military sense either. Nor did it much appeal to the other members of the Six. But its greatest failure lay in its primary task of making German remilitarisation acceptable to French public opinion. Successive French governments shrank from presenting the treaty to Parliament for ratification and when they eventually did so, in August 1954, it was rejected.

The EDC is an interesting example of the limits of American hegemonic leadership. American pressure was instrumental in securing a higher priority for European defence spending and for obtaining recognition that German troops were necessary. Yet the American administration had to defer to the French political agenda. Moreover, having done so, they failed to secure French acceptance of its own creation, despite the fact that Europe's defence was impossible without the USA. Certainly, this point was repeatedly made and never more clearly than when Secretary of State John Foster Dulles threatened an 'agonising reappraisal' of the American defence commitment to Europe if the issue was not resolved quickly. Moreover, French security objectives, albeit in the colonies, were utterly dependent on US assistance. From 1950 to the fall of Dien Bien Phu, the United States covered 70 per cent of the costs of the French colonial war in Indo-China. Despite all the possibilities of leverage, the United States still failed to secure the acceptance of a policy with which it had become increasingly identified.[23]

Part of the problem with the EDC was the question of control. To whom would the European minister of defence be responsible? Who would decide how and when the European army would be used? Who would decide the foreign policy that the existence of the army was supposed to support? The treaty had indeed envisaged an Assembly and its first task would be to design a new, democratic model for political control. The existence of these clauses were a triumph for Spinelli's federalist movement and had been introduced on the insistence of Alcide De Gasperi. In September 1952, the foreign ministers decided not to wait for the ratification of the EDC Treaty but to move ahead immediately with the preparations for a 'European Political Community'. Bang on schedule, six months later the *ad hoc* Assembly produced a draft treaty for the EPC. Meanwhile the increase in Gaullist representation in the French parliament had led to the coalition government dispensing with the services of Schuman as foreign minister. This, more than anything, symbolised the abandonment of supranationality as the leitmotif of French foreign policy. Within the new environment, however, the EPC merely complicated an already difficult situation. For the socialists, the EDC was only acceptable if the democratic elements of control were strengthened. But any concessions in this direction would only antagonise the Gaullists and others for whom the treaty was only acceptable (if at all) if the elements of national control were reinforced. Thus the French made desperate efforts to add protocols to the EDC Treaty in the utterly vain hope of finding the combination that might allow the French parliament to ratify it.[24]

Within the Netherlands, the EDC had created problems of a different nature. The European army had been accepted only reluctantly and the government was not interested in increasing its entanglement with premature experiments in political federation. Thus, when the EPC was launched, the Dutch made their acceptance conditional on the EPC being given specific economic tasks. Thus their foreign minister, Johan Willem Beyen, attempted to get the EPC Treaty to include provisions for the automatic creation of a customs union. In the subsequent intergovernmental talks on the EPC which lasted from the autumn of 1953 until the summer of 1954, the Beyen Plan received only qualified endorsement. In theory, it was acceptable to Belgium and Germany only if widened to embrace a complete common market and only if provisions were added for economic policy coordination. The Italians were willing to accept the idea of creating a common market as one of the tasks of the EPC (which left open the option that the EPC might do nothing) but were not willing to countenance it as a separate protocol. But the French were unwilling to accept it at all. With an economy lurching into deficit because of colonial wars and abandoning many of the 'liberalisation' measures adopted earlier, the time was evidently unripe for discussing the automatic removal of protectionism.[25]

The EDC was never a very stable construction. It was utterly inadequate to carry, in addition, the ambitions of the European federalists and the Dutch designs for a permanent and fair removal of trade barriers. When the EDC collapsed in August 1954, on the French refusal to ratify, it seemed to dash at the same time all hopes for further integration among the Six.

—

In the wake of the EDC's collapse, there was an intense surge of diplomatic activity to resolve outstanding sources of Franco-German conflict. One success of this was the decision, based on a UK initiative, to create a German army under the umbrella of NATO and the auspices of the Western European Union (WEU), which was now to embrace all six ECSC countries as well as the UK itself. Ironically, it was a solution that could have been had almost four years earlier. A second potential thorn in the flesh in relations between the two countries had been the disputed status of the Saar, pre-war German territory under French administration and incorporated into a customs union with France. The French government had wanted to give the area a 'European' status but, under a new agreement, France agreed to be bound by a plebiscite to be held in October 1955. In the event the populace rejected the European option and the territory was transferred back to Germany in January 1957. Another source of inconvenience, if not tension, had been the French desire to secure markets for agricultural produce in Germany. This question had become trapped in the so-called 'green pool' negotiations for the creation of some form of European agricultural organisation, but after their failure and the transfer of the agricultural brief to the OEEC in January 1955, the first bilateral agreement to emerge was the Franco-German wheat agreement. Possibly the next in importance among the other agreements dating from this period was that to canalise the Moselle, thereby improving trade between the two countries. France's partners reacted to this flurry of activity with some ambivalence. While they could see the potential gains in easing relations between the two countries, they could also see the danger that if France no longer needed 'integration' to control Germany, their own interests could easily become utterly marginalised in the ensuing rounds of bilateral dealing. Under these circumstances, the Benelux governments began to consider ways of relaunching the 'European agenda'.

At the headquarters of the ECSC in Luxembourg, Jean Monnet was also concerned by the drift in events. Unaware that the French government was indifferent to his fate, he decided to make his continuance as chairman of the High Authority contingent upon progress on the European front. Rather than start afresh, or pick over the wreckage of the EDC disaster to see what could be salvaged, he considered that the best approach would be to build outwards from the one and only existing community. This could be into inland transport in general, into other classical energy forms (particularly electricity generation) and – and this was to be the key to its success – into atomic power. Nuclear energy was seen as an exciting new prospect which had had little time for entrenched interests to emerge, and yet the developing costs of which were too heavy for a single country to bear. This last consideration, however, had not prevented most industrial nations from embarking on experimental programmes of their own. The French government, especially, was extremely keen on developing nuclear cooperation and they particularly wanted to jointly construct an isotope separation plant, a necessary but expensive component in developing enriched uranium for future reactors, and for nuclear bombs. Unknown at the time, it was in December 1954 that the French nuclear energy agency began to implement a five-year programme to manufacture a French nuclear bomb.[26]

The question of a nuclear community, Euratom, was one of the items on the agenda when the foreign ministers met in Messina in June 1955, and it was adopted for further study alongside a patchwork of other initiatives (the main one of which was a common market, discussed further below). The first results envisaged that Euratom would acquire a monopoly of all nuclear material and its transformation into fissionable products. It would also build and control its own isotope separation plant and other nuclear installations, financed from a common budget. Further, it would run a common market in all these materials and equipment. The one point it did not touch on was the relation of this structure to national military programmes, such as that already underway in France. At this juncture the French suggested a moratorium on the manufacture and testing of nuclear weapons for five years, which did not affect the French programme because it would not be ready for such tests until then. The military programme was part of a wider programme that already, midway through the negotiations, was beginning to sap Euratom's rationale. It was never envisaged that Euratom would represent the sole European programme, merely that it would assist and facilitate (and to some extent control) parallel national programmes.[27]

Euratom's future was further enfeebled by the intervention of the United States. Back in 1946, the McMahon Act had tried to limit the spread of nuclear technology by classifying US atomic knowledge as secret. Instead, by prohibiting collaboration of any kind, it had effectively prevented the Americans from exercising any control over developments that were taking place anyway. In his famous 'atoms for peace' speech to the United Nations in December 1953, Eisenhower had signalled a change in US policy which held out the prospect of the United States providing 'fissionable material' for projects designed to promote the peaceful use of nuclear energy. In February 1956 the USA offered 20 tons of enriched uranium to Euratom at half the cost at which any European venture could hope to supply it. Aside from the noble aim of promoting peace (and deflecting attention from the fact that the 'new look' strategy could turn much of central and western Europe into a nuclear battlefield), the offer would displace UK competition and provide an outlet for the surplus of three US separator plants. It would also show American backing for a new supranational initiative. Finally, it would ensure that Euratom would not build its own separation plant.

If Euratom were not to build a separation plant – and right to the bitter end France tried to ensure that it should – the French were determined to keep a separate national programme and to keep both peaceful and military options open. Moreover, it was only willing to surrender the sovereignty necessary to run a parallel operation (which was not much). The only limitation on its freedom of action was a four-year moratorium on testing. Parallel to these developments was a move in the OEEC for a cooperative nuclear cooperation. Thus, when Euratom was formed, robbed already of most its substance and denuded of much supranational responsibility, one of its first acts, which also absorbed much of its operational budget, was to pay the subscription of the Six for joining the OEEC's 'Dragon' scheme for an experimental reactor.

Euratom had carried all the hopes of, and had been the target of favourable propaganda by, the Action Committee for a United States of Europe, founded by Monnet in October 1955. It was a 'success' only in the sense that a treaty was signed at all. The other treaty signed in Rome in March 1957 was that establishing the European Economic Community (EEC). It was lucky to get onto the Messina agenda at all and, ironically, it was Euratom that helped keep it there.

During the EDC negotiations, the Beyen Plan for the creation of a customs union had received varying degrees of support from five of the six governments. The Beyen Plan had at its core the creation of a customs union according to a rigid timetable over a period of 10 to 12 years. In order to accommodate countries in economic difficulties, the plan contained provisions for temporary escape clauses whose implementation and execution rested with the institutions of the EPC. There would also be an adjustment fund to assist countries with structural problems. Although the Beyen Plan failed because the French Assembly rejected the EDC Treaty, the discussions on its merits had served to test the range of political opinion and to anticipate many of the technical problems. Firstly, the step-by step approach to tariff cuts was condemned as too inflexible, the very inflexibility making it more likely that countries would have difficulties in following the schedules. A less rigid programme, albeit with intermediate and end targets, was preferable. Secondly, the safeguard clauses were thoroughly disliked by Germany and Belgium, in particular. They argued that repeated backsliding followed by justification and appeals procedures would eventually destroy the Community. Instead, they urged far-reaching measures of policy coordination to prevent economies from moving too far out of step, thereby removing the occasion for invoking the clauses. Thirdly, although the Dutch were fixated on commodity trade, it became apparent that progress would be impossible unless capital and labour mobility were also dealt with. These were valuable insights, and all would eventually find their way into the Treaty of Rome. But there was one more insight in the summer of 1954: French politicians were implacably opposed to the idea in whatever shape or form.[28]

The Dutch government was inclined, rightly or wrongly, to ascribe the trenchant French opposition to the complexion of the government then in power. Once the Mendès France cabinet had fallen, it considered the main obstacle to persisting with the initiative, and indeed to expanding it by incorporating agriculture, to have been removed. Thus, when the idea of a 'relaunch' of European integration gathered momentum, the Dutch government made its support for the Benelux memorandum conditional upon the inclusion of a customs union in the list of demands presented at Messina. However Monnet, especially, was reluctant to risk an immediate rejection of a new European initiative because it introduced an immediate challenge to French protectionism. Curiously, the German government had had similar reservations and its delegation to Messina came armed with negative instructions on the customs union in order not to isolate the French. In the event, after a particularly indecisive meeting, an agreement was reached to establish study groups under the overall direction of Spaak, to investigate *all* the components of the Benelux memorandum.[29]

Once the talks commenced, it became obvious that the French were primarily interested in atomic energy. However, having been willing to back the French at a critical moment, the Germans entered the common market negotiations with conviction, as too did the Belgians. Various moments have been offered by historians for the moment at which France decided to take the common market issue seriously but the most credible seems to be January 1956, when a new socialist-led coalition led by Guy Mollet came to power. And to dispel any tendency towards backsliding, from that moment the German delegation insisted whenever appropriate on a 'Junktim' between the common market treaty and that for atomic energy. Another moment of truth during this early phase of negotiations concerned the position of the United Kingdom. Surprised at having been invited at all, the UK had joined the initial talks without a prepared position, other than to express a loose preference for a free trade area over a customs union. Opinion within the cabinet soon afterwards veered to a rejection of a closer European entanglement, and when in November 1955 Spaak announced that the talks had proceeded sufficiently to start preparing a final report, the UK delegation elected not to take any further part, but to judge the report when it appeared. In reality, the decision had been taken to reject the common market option and, at the prompting of the Americans (and to avoid being saddled with any blame when negotiations failed) the announcement was made the following month. But the common market negotiations did not collapse.[30]

The 'Spaak Report' was approved by the ministers of the Six in May 1956 and negotiations proper were able to start. But the French government's conversion to the common market did not mean that it did not have to placate potential parliamentary opposition when the treaty came up for ratification. Thus a great deal of time and emotion was expended on what turned out to be peripheral items of the treaty. For example, France demanded that elements of its own expensive social legislation (equal pay for men and women, overtime pay for work beyond forty hours a week) be incorporated into the treaty to equalise competitive conditions. Once these demands had been conceded, the French delegation returned with a proposal for sharing some of its (ex)colonial development costs in return for access to their markets. Even with these concessions in place, the French negotiated special provisions to allow the country to commence lowering its own tariff barriers later than the rest whilst still enjoying the benefits of market access elsewhere. None of these provisions added to the elegance of the treaty, but they all helped to condition acceptance by the French Assembly.

A second circumstance also helped shape the negotiations, although not as decisively as some authors have suggested. In October 1956, together with the

British and in collusion with the Israelis, the French launched an attack on Egypt in order to wrest control of the Suez Canal from the nationalists. The invasion outraged public opinion and attracted the condemnation of both the USSR and the USA. On the brink of achieving the military objectives, the British cancelled operations, leaving both powers tasting the bitter ashes of a political defeat. In a gesture loaded with symbolism, Adenauer travelled to Paris for talks with Mollet, during which both leaders announced the outlines of the compromise (that had largely been hammered into place before the Suez Crisis) that would set the common market treaty back on its tracks. Suez did not rescue the common market, nor did it finally convince the French government to accept it. But it did have one other consequence. Spaak became convinced that the days of the French government were numbered. If any treaty were to be certain of ratification, it had to be concluded and presented quickly. As a result, many questions that had not been resolved or that looked unlikely to be resolved quickly were left for the community itself to work out later. This accounts for the odd mixture in the treaty of detailed provisions on some issues and more procedural outlines on others.

At the core of the common market treaty lay the creation of a customs union, in three steps of four years, with the possibility of a three-year overrun. Spelled out in precise detail, each phase would be marked by the completion of part of the removal of tariffs on intra-area trade and the erection of a common external tariff. With the exception of some troublesome items (list G), the new tariff schedule had also been calculated. By contrast, the details of the agricultural clauses concerned the way in which the steps towards a common policy were to be achieved but little about the shape of the policy itself. This reflected a realisation by the Dutch that if they pressed for more concrete clauses, they would not likely be happy with the outcome. Yet the move was also viewed favourably by federalists who saw the entrusting of future tasks to community institutions as a positive step towards supranationality. Few at the time paid much attention to the clause at the beginning of the treaty that linked progress towards a common agricultural policy at each stage to further progress towards the common market. Yet this link was to form a 'Junktim' of its own and to underpin the implementation of both elements in the treaty.

In order to manage the community and steer its future development, the Treaty of Rome modified the supranational structure agreed for the ECSC. A European Commission, headed by independent commissioners chosen by the member states, would have sole rights of initiative across a wide range of policy issues. Only when these had been approved by the European parliament could the

Council of Ministers take decisions. Moreover, after the second stage, the treaty foresaw that the ministers would reach decisions by majority vote rather than by unanimity.

The Treaty of Rome, signed in March 1957, was the product of a society that had already reduced many of the cruder barriers to international trade, that wished to get rid of them altogether and that wanted to ensure that they would not re-emerge in the event of a subsequent recession. In addition it reflects an ambition to deal with other competitive distortions (state aid, restrictive practices and other invisible trade barriers) by eliminating them at source. This required a more sophisticated institutional structure than previous intergovernmental organisations. This implication was willingly accepted because the treaty was seen as more than a simple economic agreement; for some, at least, it carried the hopes for a future federal European state.

POSTSCRIPT

This essay first appeared in 1995 as one of two historical introductory chapters (the other covered the years 1958-1973) in Keith Middlemas, *Orchestrating Europe: The Informal Politics of the European Union, 1973-95* (London, 1995). The book itself was a monumental contribution to the contemporary history of the European Union. It pieced together the relationship between the various institutions, formal and informal, involved in making European policy, and the networks that bound them together. I was surprised he asked me, since it was not an approach which I employed, either then or since, but it provided me a challenge to knit the early history into a cohesive narrative.

For those looking for general introductions to the history of the European Union, the best available in English are Desmond Dinan, *Europe Recast: A History of European Union* (Houndmills, 2004), and Martin Gilbert, *European Integration: A Concise History* (Lanham, 2011). For those who can manage French, I can recommend Pierre Gerbet, *La Construction de L'Europe* (Paris, 2004). Finally, if you want a different medium, may I tentatively suggest my own *History of the European Union: An Audio Course on the Development of the EU* (Home Academy, The Hague, 2004). A useful survey of different approaches to European integration history can be found in W. Kaiser and A. Vasori (eds.), *European Union History: Themes and Debates* (Houndmills, 2010).

2
The Founding Fathers

To approach history through the lens of personalities, as this essay does, carries with it serious implications of historical interpretation. This is particularly true when we look at the so-called 'founding fathers' of what became the European Union. We cannot resolve these issues here, but we will explore the implications so that the reader is aware of the choices that this particular perspective may involve.

One of the most persistent debates in political science literature concerns the dichotomy between structure and agency: the difference between the circumstances shaping history and the agencies or actors enacting change, or not as the case may be. To talk of the 'founding fathers' places the discussion squarely in the agency camp. This does not necessarily mean, however, that one has to accept a 'heroic' interpretation of the past when great men bent the future to their will. Historians who choose this direction concentrate on the influences that moulded these personalities. Moreover, if we do decide to retain this focus, there are plenty of routes from which to choose. For example, much has been made of the fact that many of the actors had grown up in border areas and were presumably less attached to the concepts of nation states – Robert Schuman in Luxembourg, when it was part of the German Zollverein, Alcide De Gasperi in the Southern Tyrol when it was part of the Austro-Hungarian Empire and Konrad Adenauer in the Rhineland. Schuman became foreign minister of France, De Gasperi became prime minister of Italy and, of course, Adenauer became chancellor of West Germany. Another line of thought links their shared Roman Catholicism as a factor binding them together, though quite how this translates into their subsequent adoption of the European cause is less clear. Another link lies less through their religious faith as through the religious-based mass political parties that emerged after the war and the network of contacts that these allowed, which enabled the growth of a shared rhetoric and experience.

There is a more direct route to their shared political goals towards Europe and that is through political ideology. Since the espoused goal of the European Union is ever closer union, the most obvious place to start (though not necessarily the correct one) is the European federalist movement which found its roots in the United States between the wars but which gathered momentum and influence in the immediate post-war years. Alternatively, since the European federalist model was based on the earlier American one, one could skip the European movement altogether and seek the common factor in the inspiration, or alternatively the pressure, of American policy-makers and officials in Europe – a treasured gift from the New World for the Old. However, if Americans 'made Europe' (which they did not) we would need a whole new list of founding fathers.

Placing the 'founding fathers' at the crossroads of history is an easier task. They were all highly placed policy-makers, or their influential advisors, in a Europe emerging from five years of war, death and destruction. All were concerned with the tasks of economic and political reconstruction and with avoiding the mistakes that had precipitated the war in the first place – the economic depression, the accompanying trade wars, and the nationalistic, authoritarian and aggressive militaristic regimes that they had spawned and nurtured. In addition, looming from the East was the emergence of new Communist states, backed by the armed might of the Soviet Union. Thus, in the late 1940s and early 1950s, the 'founding fathers' were in positions of political power and able to take decisions that would help resolve current problems of Europe and shape the future course of history. And, by this route, we arrive at the structural side of the agency/structure debate.

One of the immediate problems facing post-war planners was the position of Germany. The initial policy of the occupying forces was to keep down Germany's industrial and military potential, by destroying plants and imposing restrictions on industrial production. This, however, entailed large costs for the occupiers and prolonged the economic dislocation in Europe that was dependent on German markets and supplies. At some point, Germany would have to be reintegrated into the normal economic and political life of the Continent, but under what terms? What was to prevent Germany in the future from adopting nationalistic trading policies and an aggressive, militaristic foreign policy?

In answering this question some historians have adopted a meta-stance, focusing on the German problem as some exogenous issue of equal concern to all and resolved by some creating institutional formulae, such as the institutions that eventually became the European Union. These historians have usually been able to align their analysis with the various agency approaches. Other historians, however, have stressed the different degrees to which states were affected by Germany's rehabilitation and they have concentrated on the domestic positions which each attempted to protect. Aggressively adopting a 'national interest' label, they shattered the consensus that had hitherto prevailed in mainstream writings on the origins of European integration.

It would be nice to report that there had been a debate between the two approaches, and possibly a reinterpretation, but nothing could be further from the truth. Generally, both sides have studiously ignored each other's findings and, as the 'national interest school' retired from the field, the old consensus had emerged virtually unchallenged. However, the dichotomy was a false one from the start. The national interest school has approached negotiations towards international agreements as attempts to secure (domestic) national interests. The fact that such interests were secured is then transmuted to becoming the main driving force behind the agreement. On the other hand, if an international agreement is to be achieved (and ratified!) every party must be able to endorse it – an impossible feat, if vital national interests have not been secured. Thus, assuming that satisfaction of substantive issues is a precondition for agreement, one can then concentrate on the form and the thinking behind the institutional architecture adopted – whether it be a faith in the rule of law, or a belief in federalism or supranationality – which brings the question back to the agents of change and, in our case, the founding fathers.

The following sections will be designed around the three main supranational treaties that were signed in the years 1951-1957 – the European Coal and Steel Community, the European Defence Community and the European Economic Community. Through these contexts, the main protagonists, the 'founding fathers', will be introduced, each accompanied by a necessarily short description of his career to date. This might lead to a more complicated history, but hopefully one that is closer to reality.

THE EUROPEAN COAL AND STEEL COMMUNITY

Jean Monnet (1888-1979) was the architect of the European Coal and Steel Community (ECSC) which came into existence in 1952 and which is often viewed as the first European supranational institution. Monnet, the son of a Cognac merchant, made his career as an international banker. After a brief spell with the League of Nations following the First World War, he spent most of the interwar period in the United States. It goes without saying that he was well aware of the American federal political system. He also built up an impressive network of political contacts that served him well later on. During the war itself, he helped the British negotiate aircraft contracts with the Americans, before joining the Free French forces in Algiers. In 1946 General De Gaulle created the Commissariat du Plan to oversee the economic reconstruction of the country and named Jean Monnet as its director. In this position, Monnet was responsible for planning the priorities for the French economy and allocating the necessary resources. One of his targets was to realise a substantial increase in French heavy industry, making full use of the opportunity afforded by the elimination by the occupation authorities of German competition. In 1949, the assumptions underpinning this strategy were beginning to unravel.

In 1949, the control of German heavy industry was placed in the hands of the International Ruhr Authority in which the Western Occupation Authorities were joined by the Benelux countries and in which Germany would also eventually take its place. The limits of its power and authority were still untested. In September 1949 Germany partially regained its sovereignty with its own democratically elected parliament and its own chancellor, Konrad Adenauer. The Allies still maintained some control over the country through an agreement to maintain Occupation Statutes until the German government replaced them with its own legislation. Again, it was uncertain how effective these measures would be on an ostensibly sovereign country. These were not idle concerns.[1] Already in early 1950 German steel production surpassed its supposed ceiling – not by much, but there were still seven million tons of idle capacity ready to enter an already glutted market. Because of international shortages, German coal was being sold abroad at prices above those charged to domestic industry. Moreover, the practice of differential transport prices also served to distort the market in favour of domestic output. In addition, the break-up of vertical ownership of coal mines by steel mills, a long-held goal of Allied policy, had still not materialised. As long as this situation prevailed, producers could withhold supplies altogether, supplies upon which French steel production depended. A final problem lay in the future of the disputed Saar region, at that point linked to France by a customs union, and its coal mines under French state control. The Saar helped alleviate the French coal shortage and should it revert to Germany, French dependence on German supplies would increase uncomfortably. It is little wonder that early in 1950 Jean Monnet became concerned with the future of Germany.

Jean Monnet was not a prolific writer, nor a great reader for that matter. He also had a poor memory, so his memoirs were largely reconstructed by close associates and should be read as a political statement rather than an accurate work of historical record.[2] References to his political ideas in the period before 1950 are scarce. In his writings in the desert during the war, there are a couple mentions of federalist solutions for the future of Europe and the need for a joint organisation for the Continent's heavy industry. Apart from that there is nothing; not, at least, until 1950. Monnet's original idea to control German heavy industry was to place French heavy industry alongside it and under the same regime. That regime would be depoliticised insofar as supervision of the industry would be entrusted to a panel, to be known as the High Authority (HA), of technical experts, operating independently from their nationalities. The plan was modified early in the negotiations so that the institutional architecture acquired many of the organs associated with a neo-federalist structure – an assembly, a court and a council of ministers in addition to the High Authority originally envisaged – but that did not necessarily mean that it was inspired by federalist thinking. The original structure had far more in common with the Tennessee Valley Authority, inaugurated in 1933 as part of the New Deal, allowing for the development of the river system in a desperately poor part of the USA, which was only possible if states surrendered part of their sovereignty over this one shared resource. The original plan was not quite as high-minded as later federalists would suggest, for within the working document Monnet prepared for the launch of the negotiations was a clause suggesting that all other controls over Germany would be respected for as long as they were kept intact. Moreover, there exists a memorandum to Foreign Minister Schuman setting out quite clearly how the arrangements would help control Germany, and Monnet did have a considerable interest in controlling Germany. So too did the French Foreign Ministry. At the same time that Monnet's staff was preparing draft after draft of his proposals, the Foreign Ministry wanted to increase the powers of the International Ruhr Authority when the ministers met in London on 12 May 1950, but these efforts were unlikely to succeed. Time, therefore, was of the essence. On 28 April 1950 Monnet finally had his alternative plan ready, but he was not a government minister. He took a copy of the plan to Prime Minister Georges Bidault, who promptly ignored it. He also arranged for a copy to be received by Foreign Minister Robert Schuman. It was Schuman who introduced the scheme to the cabinet.

Robert Schuman (1886-1963) was born in Luxembourg, and after the war he was elected parliament deputy for Moselle. He was placed under house arrest by the Germans before escaping to non-occupied France and working for the resistance. After the war, he returned to mainstream politics on behalf of the Christian democrat MRP and became foreign minister in July 1948. Schuman was an ardent federalist, but thought that, in the light of public opinion, it was premature to strive for a political federation in Europe, and certainly not one that included Germany. At the time, Monnet's more limited sectoral approach was more appealing. It was Schuman, therefore, who steered the plan through cabinet, who secured the backing of both the United States and West Germany for the scheme, and thus secured a majority even before the 12 May London conference had opened. On 9 May 1950, five years after the end of the war and almost ten years to the day after the German invasion of his country, Schuman made the dramatic radio announcement calling for the pooling of German and French heavy industry under a common High Authority and inviting all nations willing to accept the scheme to join. The plan would end the means and will to wage war, and would lay the foundations for a future federal Europe. The Benelux countries and Italy all responded positively.

For the plan to succeed, it required Germany's approval. That, in turn, depended upon Konrad Adenauer (1876-1967). Had the Social Democrats been in power, the response would probably have been very different since they were to hold aloof from entanglements in tests that might jeopardise German reunification. Educated as a lawyer, Adenauer became mayor of Cologne in 1919 until the Nazis came to power in 1933. He was periodically imprisoned by them, but after the war he returned to his position as mayor of the first German city liberated by the Allies, that is until the British sacked him. He then became leader of a reconstituted Christian Democratic Party and, at the age of 73, became the first chancellor of West Germany. Adenauer was genuinely pleased with the Schuman Plan and positively endorsed it before the German public. He publically ignored the unequal treatment that lay in the detail but from the start, he was determined that if Germany submitted to control, it would only do so once – other forms of control, such as the International Ruhr Authority, would have to lose their powers. It was almost the last issue to be resolved in the subsequent negotiations.

The negotiations on the Schuman Plan were dominated by Monnet and his team. They chaired the most important committees and staffed the secretariat. Although Monnet had wanted a quick negotiation establishing the HA and its areas of competencies, he accepted the need for some political control over it. He was also forced to respect the demands, especially by the Benelux countries, not only to define the areas of HA competences, but also to define the competences themselves – what price systems, what tariffs, when intervention etc. What emerged was a HA with considerable freedom of action, within the rules prescribed, over the coal and steel sectors. The Council of Ministers would be involved only when industrial policy conflicted with other policy areas, such as wages or defence strategies. The Court would arbitrate in cases of interpretation over the treaty and there would be an Assembly, with extremely limited powers. The Treaty of Paris was signed in April 1951 and the ECSC itself came into force in August 1952. Jean Monnet was nominated as its first president.

THE EUROPEAN DEFENCE COMMUNITY

As the negotiations for the ECSC were starting, another problem was emerging. The successful atomic test by the Soviet Union in August 1949 had scuppered the American hope that the USA could for much longer base its defence strategy on its nuclear monopoly. The president ordered the National Security Council to review the options and its report, NSC-68, completed in April 1950, painted a scenario of a defenceless Europe falling within months to a Soviet attack and, thereafter, posing a serious threat to Atlantic communications. Having surveyed various alternatives, the report concluded that the only solution was, with American help, to increase European defence capabilities, and to rearm Germany. Soon after the report was delivered to the president, the Korean War started, and the decision was made to press ahead with the demand for German rearmament.

If the idea of the re-emergence of German heavy industry had worried French policy-makers, it was nothing like the impact the prospect of a rearmed Germany had upon the French population. Schuman frankly told US policy-makers that the suggestion was completely unacceptable to French public opinion and the French Assembly. However, if supranationality could control German heavy industry, could not the same mechanism be used to control a German army? In haste, Monnet instructed his staff to prepare a scheme for a European army into which German forces would be integrated. Launched in October 1950, the Pleven Plan as it became known, named after the prime minister, became the French alternative to the US scheme.[3] It set out the principle of a European army, with a single budget and a single minister of defence. However, Article 38 left the details of its exact institutional framework to be elaborated later, after ratification, by a parliamentary assembly. Although the Pleven Plan endorsed supranationality, it was not a particularly even treaty that emerged. It contained clauses that disadvantaged Germany and privileged France: there was to be no German army or German high command (unlike other nations, German troops would enlist directly into the European army); Germany unilaterally renounced the possession of nuclear weapons; there was to be no advanced military industry in strategically vulnerable areas (with a defence line initially envisaged along the Rhine, which meant most of Germany). The German Social Democrats were vehemently opposed to the plan, and opposed to rearmament generally. As with the ECSC, for the plan to work, it required Adenauer's endorsement. It is interesting that throughout the long, torturous and ultimately futile negotiations for a European Defence Community, the Germans never tried to claw back these provisions.

Eventually the Americans withdrew their scheme and threw their backing behind the Pleven Plan. Negotiations involving all six ECSC members produced a treaty, which was signed in Paris in May 1952. All that remained was to secure its ratification. Meanwhile, the Italian prime minister, Alcide De Gasperi (1881-1954), convinced Schuman that the period before ratification could usefully be employed if the Assembly envisaged in Article 38 were to start its work beforehand. De Gasperi was a local Catholic politician in his native Austrian South Tyrol. When, in 1919, the area devolved to Italy, he went to Rome as one of its parliamentary deputies. He was imprisoned for eighteen months by the fascists, and upon his release he retired from public life to work in the Vatican Library. After the overthrow of Mussolini he returned to politics. In 1944 he founded Italy's Christian Democratic Party and became Italy's foreign minister. Three years later he became the country's prime minister, a post which he held until his death. He was an ardent federalist, though it is doubtful whether he anticipated the effect of his actions in establishing a provisional assembly to give effect to Article 38. He certainly supported the outcome.

At the time, the ECSC had just come into effect and its Assembly, drawn from members of the Consultative Assembly of the Council of Europe, had yet to meet. Aside from reviewing association agreements, respectfully following the work of the High Authority and keeping an organic link with the Council of Europe, its powers were strictly limited. Under Article 38, this body, with its composition slightly amended to reflect the different composition of the ECSC and European Defence Community (EDC) assemblies, would design an institutional framework to contain both existing treaties.[4] In September 1952 the '*ad hoc* Assembly' was given six months to prepare a draft text. The chairman of the Assembly was former Belgian foreign minister, Paul-Henri Spaak (1899-1972). A socialist politician, he became his country's foreign minister in 1936 and briefly prime minister. He spent the Second World War in exile in London. After the war, he had two short stints as prime minister, but in 1949 he and his party were in opposition. As a member of parliament, he joined the newly formed Consultative

Assembly of the Council of Europe and was elected its first chairman. However, he quickly chafed under the restrictions imposed on the Assembly's mandate and in December 1951 resigned as its chairman. Although he initially opposed the more radical elements of the federalist movement, whilst fighting for more powers for the Consultative Assembly, he fell increasingly under their sway and turned his attention to the Six as a means of pioneering the constitutional reform of the Continent. In March 1952, even before the agreement to activate Article 38, he convened a group of lawyers to prepare the groundwork for the European Communities. When the *ad hoc* Assembly was convened, Spaak was elected its chairman.

By this stage, Spaak was heavily under the influence of the radical Italian federalist, Altiero Spinelli (1907-1986). A communist political journalist, Spinelli fell afoul of the Italian fascist authorities and spent most of the period after 1927 in prison. Whilst in prison, he broke with Stalin and fell under the influence of UK federalist writings. He became convinced that a federal Europe would not come about if it were entrusted to national politicians. What was needed was the immediate creation of a democratically elected constituent assembly that would design the constitution for a new Europe. With political legitimacy would come power and authority, and not the other way round – piecemeal surrenders of sovereignty leading to democratic responsibility. In 1943, immediately after the fall of Mussolini, he founded the European Federalist Movement, espousing this radical brand of federalism. Forced to compromise at the 1984 Congress in The Hague, which created the Council of Europe, and as a member of its Consultative Assembly, he witnessed firsthand as his misgivings were confirmed. Now, together with Spaak, he formed part of the secretariat empowered to lead the *ad hoc* Assembly in designing a new constitution. The design went straight back to basic federalist principles, with a strict functional split between federal (i.e. European) and state (i.e. national) levels, and with a full panoply of institutions at the federal level – a court, a two-chamber legislature, an executive council and a council of (national) ministers (with the latter consigned to a subsidiary role). It was little less than an attempted coup d'état.

Meanwhile, the situation was further complicated by the Dutch demand for inclusion in the new community of a customs union. The Netherlands was a highly trade-dependent economy, always strongly reliant on Germany for both markets and supplies. Since the war, and still smarting from the experience during the Great Depression, successive governments had struggled to reduce trade barriers, to control their re-erection in case of economic difficulties and to obtain Germany's re-entry into the European trading network. They had used any and every available forum to push their cause.[5] It was only a matter of time before they devised a scheme for the six ECSC countries. The task fell to the new foreign minister, Jan-Willem Beyen (1987-1976). Beyen was an international financier who had worked with the Bank of International Settlements before the war and with the IMF after the war. He had no party allegiance and was brought into the government by Prime Minister Drees to counteract the pro-integration drift within his cabinet. It was a big mistake. Drees had not wanted a European army nor was he enamoured by yet another layer of European institutions. It was not difficult to get him to tie Dutch demands for a customs union to Dutch acceptance of the latter. But what might have started as opportunism on Beyen's part, soon transmuted to warm support for European integration.

While all these developments were taking place, the French political landscape was shifting radically. New elections increased the representation of Gaullist parliamentarians in the French Assembly and although the MRP remained in government, Robert Schuman's support for supranationality was no longer sustainable. In January 1953 he lost his post as minister of foreign affairs to his party colleague Georges Bidault. He remained in parliament and continued to support the European Defence Community. In 1955 he returned to government for a short time as minister for justice, before becoming once more a parliamentarian, president of the European Movement and president of the Assembly of the EEC. Meanwhile, events in Strasbourg were now moving far ahead of the original French design – a simple construction to contain German rearmament. They now embraced a nascent federal structure and a move towards economic integration. When the *ad hoc* Assembly presented a draft treaty to the ECSC ministers for an intergovernmental conference in March 1953, the French government started to empty the draft treaty of its content while, at the same time, demanding additional safeguards to the EDC Treaty itself. Only De Gasperi stayed true to the original design. In August 1954 the French government made a final set of demands on the EDC Treaty signatories, including abandoning everything that had happened since the acceleration of Article 38 and starting the institutional design anew. When these demands were refused, the French Assembly rejected the EDC Treaty. De Gasperi died on the eve of that vote. Spinelli continued to fight actively for a federal Europe and in 1979 he became a member of the European Parliament. In this capacity, he single-mindedly set in motion a campaign for greater powers for the parliament that led to its adoption in 1984 of a Draft Treaty of European Union. The draft was taken up by European governments but by the time it re-emerged as the Single European Act, most of the increased parliamentary powers had disappeared.

EUROPEAN ECONOMIC COMMUNITY

The rejection of the EDC Treaty by the French Assembly made clear that, without a change in government, it was pointless to pursue any new integrationist schemes. The High Authority, still led by Jean Monnet, remained Europe's sole supranational institution. It had indeed overseen the creation of a single market in coal and steel, but was being criticised for being weak in the face of steel barons and supine before the foot-dragging of the German government when it came to taking measures to dismantle the national coal cartel.[6] Monnet was a 'do-er'; he was not suited to administering what was basically a supranational regulator. He was impatient for action. When, in February 1955 the Mendès France government, responsible for the EDC failure, collapsed, he accelerated his plans for a European 'relaunch'.

Monnet originally had two aims. The first was to remain as president of the High Authority but on condition that negotiations would start, hopefully under his leadership, that would mark the next steps towards European integration. The second was to determine the direction that those steps would take. To start with the second, Monnet considered that one should build on the experience of the High Authority and expand into areas that flanked its existing competences – all coal consumption, 'traditional energy' or rail traffic. Viable and worthy though these initiatives seemed, they were not the stuff to set the world alight. What Monnet thought would clinch the deal was atomic energy. It was new, so there were few entrenched interests; it was expensive, so it paid to work together; it was exciting, so it would capture the public's imagination; and the French wanted it. By this time, Monnet was beginning to get signals that the French, in particular, were far from keen to have him run any new negotiations and that any 'relaunch' emanating from the HA might be a liability. If there were to be a new initiative, it would have to come from elsewhere and therefore Monnet turned to Spaak, once more his country's foreign minister, to see whether the Benelux countries would be prepared to front the initiative. At this point, Beyen made it clear that if there was to be a Benelux memorandum, it would have to include a customs union. Beyen's argument was that in the negotiations around the draft treaty, five countries had been willing to countenance a move to further economic integration, even if not exactly in the form the Dutch were proposing. The only exception had been France, but therein lay the problem. Monnet was not opposed to a customs union, but he was wary of tying the new initiative to something that the French had already rejected and therefore inviting a further rebuff. Beyen's insistence ensured that economic integration remained on the table. Monnet also allowed his own candidature for HA president, and his offer to run the subsequent negotiations, to go forward, despite clear signals that this would be unacceptable to the French. Monnet's logic was that the French might start the new negotiations with one veto; they were unlikely to use two.

In May 1955 the ECSC ministers met in Messina in Italy.[7] Monnet's candidature was the first item on the agenda and it was, as expected, refused. His chosen successor was the Belgian René Mayer. Monnet resigned his post shortly afterwards and created the Action Committee for the United States of Europe, which he ran until forced by ill-health to retire in 1975. Through this means he tried to mobilise support, especially from trade unions, for European integration and employed his considerable network of contacts in the higher echelons of the American administration to bolster support for the new communities. The Messina meeting did go on to accept virtually the whole raft of proposals as a basis for further negotiation, but significantly, it downplayed any mention of federalism or of supranationality. Spaak was chosen to lead the negotiations.

From the start, Spaak treated the common market and atomic energy as the twin prongs of his efforts, aided by the Germans who insisted throughout that the two treaties be negotiated and signed together. His efforts were greatly assisted by a change in government in France in January 1956, which produced a more positive approach towards economic integration, though still a cautious one (France was becoming increasingly embroiled in Algeria and its balance-of-payments position was precarious). The 'Spaak Report' became the basis for negotiations that led to the signing of the Treaty of Rome in March 1957. Beyen was not one of the signatories. He had lost his cabinet post in October 1956 and ended his career as Dutch ambassador to Paris. Spaak went on to become secretary-general of NATO in May 1957, and never returned to advocate the federalist cause.

REFLECTIONS

There are several observations that one can make following this review of the 'founding fathers'. The first is that we can debunk the common assertion that from the start the founding fathers intended to achieve a political goal (European integration) by economic means (the ECSC and EEC). On the contrary, they intended to obtain political goals by political means. There are surely few things more political than linking armed forces and, by implication, foreign policy. These ambitions went further than anything attempted since, and it was the crushing failure to realise them that left the economic route as one of the few alternatives available.

The second fallacy that we can disprove is that there is a Darwinian link between the ECSC and the EEC. It is true that the institutional architecture is similar, but the constellation of power is radically different. The Messina meeting did not endorse the pattern of earlier integration, but decisively rejected it, and its embodiment, Jean Monnet. In place of a powerful, independent and technocratic HA, the Treaty of Rome placed most of the decision-making in the hands of the states, represented by the Council of Ministers. The powers of initiative granted to the Commission were, in reality, severely circumscribed by the degree of support among the states.

The third observation lies in the working methods. Each of the three treaties was negotiated in a different way. For Monnet, the secret to success in the ECSC negotiations was to sideline the politicians, while technocrats worked together to solve practical problems. Spaak, by contrast, while directing the EEC negotiations, believed that it required a strong direction from a political personality to push innately conservative officials forward. Contrasting most with these were the negotiations for the new institutional framework for the ECSC and EDC treaties, which were initiated and directed by a parliamentary assembly or, rather, by its secretariat. Whether working methods are instrumental to success is difficult to sustain; successful outcomes almost by definition have successful methods. However, the parliamentary method does seem a questionable one. The *ad hoc* Assembly advanced so far outside the limits of acceptability of the member states that it was almost fifty years before the idea was tried again, in a modified form, in the European Convention leading to the treaty establishing a Constitution for Europe that was rejected by referenda in France and the Netherlands in May/June 2005. The European Assembly's unsolicited draft constitution in 1984 was similarly stripped of most of its content by member states. If history can teach us little about the methods for success in intergovernmental conferences, it does suggest that the more democratic approach has not triumphed.

Looking back at the period covered in this chapter, there would be few at that time who would have believed the progress towards European integration made over the next fifty years. This is often heralded as a vindication of the 'Monnet method', a gradual step-by-step functional approach involving concrete projects. Spinelli's one-step institutional approach to the creation of a federation was relegated to the history of ideas. Interestingly, the Monnet and Spinelli approaches clashed directly at the Conference of the European Union of Federalists early in 1956, at which Spinelli rejected a compromise resolution to support both approaches simultaneously. He established his own organisation, European Federalist Action, whose 650,000 adherents, however, proved insufficient to attract government backing. Although the mantle of history belongs to the Monnet method, it is difficult, with hindsight, to refute Spinelli's analysis that member states, left to themselves, would be slow to surrender their powers to democratic bodies, let alone to federalist institutions. The 'democratic deficit' is part of the price paid by the success of Monnet's approach.

At the start of this chapter, we introduced the structure/agent debate and suggested that history is best served by conflating the two approaches. This serves to pay attention to the constraints under which historical actors operated, and the problems that had to be overcome, while holding on to some vision of a future. The founding fathers were not 'European saints' or visionaries,[8] but practical politicians dealing with real problems, and trying to solve them in institutional forms that would prove more attractive and more durable than those that had ended in economic depression, autarky, militarism and war. This makes their personal achievements more real than if we were to portray them as heroes of myth and legend.

POSTSCRIPT

This essay was published in Erik Jones, Anand Menon and Stephen Weatherill, *The Oxford Handbook on the European Union* (Oxford, 2012), 181-192. For those looking for introductions to the main personalities involved in the early history of European integration, the best point of entry is Pierre Gerbet, Gérard Bossuat and Thierry Grobois (eds.), *Dictionnaire historique de l'Europe unie* (Brussels, 2009). For the period after 1958, one could do worse than consult Michel Dumoulin (ed.), *The European Commission: History and Memories*, European Commission (2007) and, of course, the other chapters in *The Oxford Handbook*.

3

The Marshall Plan and Western European Reconstruction

When the Marshall Plan was conceived in 1947, much of Western Europe was midway through a process of economic reconstruction, though it seemed that further progress was being choked by a lack of hard currency reserves. By the time the next four years had passed, recovery had been such that output had surged past its pre-war peak and programs were in place to foster economic collaboration and interdependence. Parallels between the situation in the Soviet Union and Eastern Europe at their own critical junctures in their transitions to democratic market economies at the end of the Cold War were suggestive. Just as the Marshall Plan had facilitated the rebuilding of post-World War II Europe, so the idea was revived as the means for facilitating the transformation of post-Cold War Europe.

For many policy-makers and commentators the Marshall Plan was nothing more (and nothing less) than a metaphor for a deep-rooted feeling that the West should be doing more for its ex-adversaries on the other side of the Iron Curtain. The Cold War had suddenly been won, with very little anticipation and without NATO having to fire a shot. And when the arch-enemy, the Soviet Union, then proceeded to dissolve itself and embrace Western, capitalist standards and values, it almost defied belief. With the West anticipating a large 'peace dividend' there were many that felt that a generous, structured commitment of assistance would not be out of place. It is one of the greatest tributes that can be paid to the Truman administration that, over forty years since its conception, the Marshall Plan should still symbolise these noble ideals and become the means for articulating them. In both Eastern Europe and Russia, there were repeated calls for a 'Marshall Plan' to assist these countries' economic reconstruction and, implicitly, their political transformation.

These appeals all fell on deaf ears and, to date, there has been no concerted transfer of official resources on a scale to match that of the Marshall Plan. This did not mean that there have been no official resource transfers. The main official resource has been the World Bank and the International Monetary Fund, whose assistance, however, was offered under strict, and often unacceptable conditions. Their argument, however, was that there was a tidal wave of private funding available if only the target countries could establish economic and institutional conditions sufficiently attractive to pull it in. In addition, a plethora of bilateral assistance schemes have cropped up offering both funding and expertise to address specific economic, technical and social problems.

One of the unique factors of the Marshall Plan, in retrospect, was that it channelled aid outside the existing international framework. As we shall see, international private investment was not a feasible option in 1947, but the IMF was created to resolve balance-of-payments crises and the International Bank for Reconstruction and Development (later the World Bank) was intended for structural development aid. Both these organisations were bypassed. This choice reflected a recognition that the newly created institutions did not have the funds to exercise the task and that Europe had to be exempted from their 'rules' if ever the one-world system so dear to post-war American planners was to come into existence. Europe and its dependencies were too important a part of the international system to be ignored. It could not recover within the rules of the international system and the international system could never operate without European participation. Thus European recovery was allowed to take place within a framework of plans and controls and with an accent on domestic capital accumulation. For Russia no similar suspension of the 'rules' was envisaged. Instead the route chosen was IMF support during the first phase of reconstruction, followed by foreign capital. This may well have reflected Russia's peripheral position in the international economy, but a parallel with post-war Europe might have suggested a more 'controlled' transition to free markets. This was presumably ruled out because it would imply reinforcing the Communist bureaucracies that the West was intent on replacing. The fact remained that the much-vaunted flows of private investment in Russia never materialised, and its domestic capital became concentrated in the hands of the old bureaucracy and security apparatus, with little experience in market production. This pattern of asset concentration and the (exaggerated) reports of the criminalisation of the Russian economy may well have contributed to this failure. To this extent, the Russian experience with foreign investment diverges from that of much of Eastern Europe, but also from that of China. And the experience of China suggests another route for attracting capital: that of an authoritarian, though market-oriented, rule. Russia's revolution, and the Western fear of working too closely with the old regime or encouraging its persistence, left the economy exposed to the rigours of the transition to market capitalism, with fewer of the benefits.

When we examine the Marshall Plan, we shall see that one of the guiding motives was to establish social and political stability as a prerequisite for economic growth and that economic growth, in its turn, was to be the key to cementing support of democratic, capitalist institutions. The core assumption, though, was that the bulk of the populace had to identify with the Western free-market system rather than drift towards communist alternatives. These are not staggering assumptions. Much of today's IMF and World Bank rhetoric assumes that social stability and good governance underpin both domestic and international investment. Yet if one examines the Western approach to Russian reconstruction efforts, one is struck by the apparent indifference towards public opinion. As elsewhere in Eastern Europe, the main concern seems to have been with the political position of the elite. This might have been justified by the consideration that the new leaders were inexperienced with democracy and lacked the networks of power available to longer-established democracies. It may also have been a reflection of their concern that whilst political power had been democratised, economic power was in the hands of the old bureaucracies, which had profited disproportionately from the privatisation polices and were perceived to be enriching themselves by flagrant asset-stripping rather than by production. It could even be that they felt the decay of Communism was a reflection of a revolution from below, and that the masses, disenchanted with their previous system had nowhere else to go. Whatever the reason, this key difference between the US approach to post-war Europe and the West's approach towards post-Communist Russia was to have terrible consequences for Russian's attempts at economic reconstruction.

A final important difference both in approach and in results in the two cases was that, from the first, post-war Europe was considered a region with an important internal economic dynamic and integrated into the world economy. This was reflected in the US insistence that the region as a whole created institutions to present a unified programme for Congress, and later in the US pressure for regional trade and payments arrangements. By contrast, Eastern Europe and the successor states of the Soviet Union in the 1990s were considered a collection of individual economies, each to be separately integrated into the world market by price liberalisation and currency stabilisation and convertibility. All possibilities for regional integration were deliberately neglected. Even within each economy, and this was clear from the Russian example, there was little conception of a *national* economy. The financial *system* appears to have been the main focus for concern. One consequence was that the complex interrelationships that had built up within and between East European and former Soviet economic spheres, and even within the Russian federation itself, were allowed to disintegrate with enormous losses in economic capital. In this disintegrated world the ability of most countries to deal with economic reconstruction and to establish a high level of competitiveness for their economies was almost a hopeless task. In countries such as Georgia or Kazakhstan, where economic collapse was aggravated by ethnic tensions, the consequences were devastating. Even in Russia, the destruction of industrial apparel came close to the levels suffered during World War II.

It would have been pleasing if all the attention paid to a structural adjustment plan conceived and implemented almost fifty years earlier had contributed to a deeper public appreciation of what the Marshall Plan actually involved. Instead, the opposite seems to have been the case. In Russia, the refusal of Western governments to stump up the cash to assist their former adversaries reinforced the belief, already propagated through generations of textbooks, that the Marshall Plan was indeed a weapon of the Cold War designed to consolidate an alliance against Communism and to secure American hegemony over Western Europe.

In the West, especially as the fiftieth anniversary of the Marshall Plan approached in 1997, there was an almost universal acclaim for the benefits that it had bestowed on Western Europe by promoting virtually a quarter-century of unprecedented economic growth and prosperity. On both sides of the former Iron Curtain, it was almost as if the entire output of research and debate had been swept aside in favour of the original, immediate post-war stereotypes. As is the nature of stereotypes, they usually contain only a partial caricature of the truth and, by misinterpreting the past, they might miss some of the valuable lessons that it has to offer. In this chapter we will address the following questions on the Marshall Plan:

- Why was it conceived?
- How was it run?
- What was the 'Plan'?
- What were its achievements?

WHY WAS THE MARSHALL PLAN CONCEIVED?

Invited to give the commencement address at Harvard University on 5 June 1947, Secretary of State George C. Marshall addressed the problems of post-war European reconstruction. Among the problems he listed were the physical destruction of plants and infrastructure, the backlog of replacement investment, the disruption of commercial ties, the weakness of domestic currencies and the uncertainty surrounding the future of Germany (and Austria). Moreover, the lack of industrial goods on the market was retarding the recovery of domestic agriculture, resulting in deprivation in the cities and a drain on scarce reserves of foreign currency:

> *The truth of the matter is that Europe's requirements for the next three or four years of foreign food and other essential products – principally from America – are so much greater than her present ability to pay that she must have substantial additional help or face economic, social, and political deterioration of a very grave character.*

He then committed the United States to doing whatever was possible, on a longer-term basis, to alleviate the situation. What was needed was to provide 'a cure rather than a mere palliative'. He then invited the European nations to take initiative and draft a joint, European programme of their requirements, which the United States would subsequently consider.[1]

The Marshall Plan linked economic aid 'against hunger, poverty, desperation and chaos' to 'the emergence of political and social conditions in which free institutions can exist'. Only three months earlier President Truman had based his appeal to Congress for aid for Greece and Turkey on a commitment 'to help free peoples to maintain their free institutions and their national integrity against aggressive movements that seek to impose upon them totalitarian regimes'.[2] The Truman Doctrine, as it became known, is one of the defining political statements of Cold War. It is not surprising, therefore, that the academic discussion on the Marshall Plan inevitably became entangled in the same traditionalist/revisionist debates that characterised the Cold War controversies. Neither debate could completely disassociate itself from the immediate realities in which the participants found themselves. In social sciences, as in the real world, what you are likely to see depends to a large extent on where you are standing at the time.

The academic debate on the Marshall Plan has been around sufficiently long for it to have travelled through the whole cycle of 'traditional', 'revisionist' and 'post-revisionist' interpretations. The questions centred on the motives behind the launch of Marshall Aid and the impact of Marshall Aid on European recovery. The main standpoints in the debate have been summarised in Table 3.1.

TABLE 3.1: THE DEBATE ON MARSHALL AID

Interpretation	*Motivation*	*Effects*
Traditional	• Defensive action in the Cold War • To save Europe from collapse	• Saved Europe • Laid the basis for future prosperity
Revisionist	• Offensive action in the Cold War • To save the USA from impending economic crisis	• Too little and too late to 'save' Europe • Marginal economic importance
Post-revisionist	• Projecting US norms and values • Enlightened self-interest	• Creating an institutional framework for the promotion of prosperity

Many of the early publications on the Marshall Plan were written in the shadow of the events they describe, often by those directly involved with the development and implementation of the programmes themselves. With the Cold War and the arms race in full swing, it is not surprising that most of the literature generally supported, implicitly or explicitly, current American policy. One pioneer work in this 'heroic' or 'traditional' genre was the study of Harry Price in 1955. Although Price did not deny a connection between the Marshall Plan and the Cold War, he interpreted American policy as both reactive and defensive. He viewed the main achievements of Marshall Aid in terms of the salvation of Western Europe from economic and political (i.e. communist) disaster and its major contribution to the unparalleled economic growth of the 1950s. Illustrative of the Cold War climate was his conclusion that one of the uncompleted tasks of the Marshall Plan lay in keeping Communist forces in check in the less developed parts of the Continent.[3] Writing in 1987, the eminent economic historian (and former Marshall Plan planner) Charles Kindleberger addressed himself the question of whether American dollars saved the world and, depending on how the word 'save' should be interpreted, came out with a resoundingly positive reply.[4]

It should not be surprising that such an uncritical assessment would eventually be challenged, and this occurred originally in the context of the 'revisionist' and 'post-revisionist' contributions to Cold War literature. It also coincided with a growing disillusion with the American government as a result of its disastrous involvement in the war with Vietnam and revelations of the abuse of executive power by the Nixon administration. The revisionist standpoint can be summarised as follows. From the moment that the Truman Doctrine committed the West to the 'containment' of communism and assistance to Greece and Turkey, the United States carried the major share of the blame for the start and intensification the Cold War. Given the fact that Marshall made his speech a mere three months after that of President Truman, it took little imagination to interpret the Marshall Plan as the launching of the Cold War on the economic front, rather than as a defensive measure.[5] The revisionists also argued that there was a direct link between the offer of American aid and the growing stocks of food and raw materials in the United States as a result of a slow-down in American economic growth. In this view, the Marshall Plan was an attempt to avoid further domestic economic problems by attacking the threat of these supplies hanging over a saturated market.[6] Although the question of whether US policy in the Cold War was offensive or defensive is still open to debate, few historians now make the link between Marshall Aid and the crisis of American capitalism. It is perhaps interesting to note, however, that recent research in Soviet archives suggested that Kremlin leaders at the time did believe in it.[7]

By the turn of the 1980s a new 'post-revisionist' consensus was emerging among historians and political scientists who had begun to research the immediate post-war period on the basis of newly released government archives. They emphasised that American political leaders had goals other that the containment of communism and that they had also committed themselves to European economic integration and stimulating a growth of productivity and efficiency. The central work in this genre is that of Michael Hogan, who saw in the Marshall Plan the projection onto Europe of the American ideal embodied in the New Deal of the 1930s.[8] A second important contribution was that of Charles Maier, who considered that the Marshall Plan was a reflection of the American capitalist model of mass consumption, whereby a continuous ride in productivity would remove the distributional conflicts that underlay the class struggle in Western Europe.[9] It fell to Immanuel Wexler to tie this more positive image of Marshall Aid with a more optimistic evaluation of the economic results. He argued that the Plan should be judged a success since most of the goals that the Plan had set itself had been met.[10] This last view was later challenged by historians who either downplayed the direct causal link between Marshall Aid and concurrent economic developments it was supposed to have brought about or who traced that link through completely different channels. However, we will return to this question later in this chapter.

Was the Marshall Plan solely or primarily directed against the Soviet Union and the forces of Communism? Was it an altruistic gesture of aid to former allies whilst recognising, of course, that in the long-run the United States might benefit? And was it then conceived with the idea that the adoption of values and institutions closer to those of the New World would benefit the development and prosperity of the Old? Most historians now agree that there was no definite 'plan' in existence when Marshall made his speech in June 1947. Most would go further and state that there was no clear strategy either. On the other hand, most historians would agree that there was a prevailing atmosphere of anxiety among top policy-makers about the intentions of the Soviet Union and an openness towards the idea that 'something' should be done for Europe. But why?

From the archives, we can identify several documents that shaped the US administration's thinking in the early months of 1947, before the launching of the Marshall Plan itself. These are internal policy-making documents which were not intended for publication. That should not be taken to mean that they reflect the 'real feelings' of the writers. Arguments presented may have been shaped to reflect those that policy-makers most wanted to hear and they will almost certainly have been shaped to benefit the standing (and funding) of the section of the administration from which they emerged. On the other hand, they get closer to the mood prevailing in Washington than the public debate that followed, where anti-communist rhetoric held sway. The shriller tone of the debate in Washington, as the original Marshall Plan mutated into the European Recovery Act passed by both chambers of Congress, reflected both the deteriorating political position in Eastern Europe and the decision of the administration to shape the aid question in terms of 'high politics' to increase the chances of achieving bi-partisan support for the measures proposed. Let us look at these policy-making documents in the chronological order of their appearance.

The first document to appear was from the State-War-Navy Coordinating Committee, charged with studying the question of assistance to Europe. On 21 April 1947 it submitted a report outlining the countries which, for the security and national interest of the United States, seemed eligible for assistance. It defined those interests primarily as ensuring the stability and security of free nations, although it did add that the administration should be extra alert to these considerations in countries with strategic materials important for the USA. The aid itself would be in the form of a 'timely provision of moderate amounts of assistance, to avoid the development of crises which will demand urgent, much larger expenditures.' It argued that, since any programme would probably exceed the immediate funds available, it would be necessary to establish priorities. The European countries it identified in the first rank were Greece, Turkey, Italy, France ('for political and not economic reasons'), Austria and Hungary. Those countries it considered as having no immediate requirements, but which might in the future develop some, were Britain, Belgium and Luxembourg, the Netherlands, Portugal, Czechoslovakia and Poland. The Committee observed that the dollar deficit was inconsistent with 'the type of world trading system' the USA sought to bring about and was also undermining US political objectives in several of the countries under consideration. Under these circumstances, it urged the formulation of a programme aimed at making scarce commodities (grain, fertilizer, fuel, steel and equipment) available.[11]

On 29 April the Joint Chiefs of Staff published their report based on a review by a subcommittee (the Joint Strategic Survey Committee). Like the previous report it tried to establish priorities for countries eligible to receive aid in the interests of national security. It set out that the first priority was for the United States to defend its seaboard (including waters of North and South America, Australasia and Greenland) from a threat which would come from or through Europe. Since the Atlantic was of the utmost importance, it was vital that the USA had allies in Europe, and these were most usefully, and traditionally, in Western Europe. If France were to fall in a future conflict, the UK was in danger and if the UK fell, North America would be at risk. This was seen as the first strategic priority. The Joint Chiefs of Staff then went one important step further. They suggested that without Germany, Western Europe would have difficulty in resisting a Soviet advance. Thus, although it was recognised that it would encounter strong French resistance, German revival was also seen as being in the American best interest, with the additional advantage that such a decision would also reduce the heavy occupation costs to the Allies. The priorities of the Joint Chiefs of Staff on the grounds of national security and on grounds of need (with those of the SWNCC for comparison) are presented in Table 3.2.

TABLE 3.2: THE PRIORITIES OF THE JOINT CHIEFS OF STAFF AND THE STATE-WAR-NAVY COORDINATING COMMITTEE FOR US ASSISTANCE, APRIL 1947

National Security	*Urgency of Need*	*Overall*	*(SWNCC)*
1. Britain	1. Greece	1. 1. Britain	1. Greece
2. France	2. Turkey	2. France	2. Turkey
3. Germany	3. Italy	3. Germany	3. Austria
4. Belgium	4. France	4. Italy	4. France
5. Netherlands	5. Austria	5. Greece	5. Italy
6. Austria	6. Hungary	6. Turkey	6. Britain
7. Italy	7. Britain	7. Austria	7. BLEU
8. Turkey	8. BLEU	8. Belgium	8. Netherlands
9. Greece	9. Netherlands	9. Netherlands	9. Portugal
10. Spain	10. Portugal	10. Spain	10. Czechoslovakia
	11. Czechoslovakia		11. Poland
	12. Poland		

In their final piece of advice, the Joint Chiefs of Staff decided against extending aid to Eastern Europe on the grounds that the American effort should not be spread too thinly, and that any aid given would probably be insufficient to offset Soviet influence. The assistance to each country should be sufficient for their continued independence, for national defence and to assist the United States in the ideological warfare to come.[12]

In April 1947, George Kennan, former US ambassador to Russia and newly appointed head of the Policy Planning Staff, returned from Moscow after a fruitless Council of Foreign Ministers meeting and a grim private discussion with Stalin. Marshall charged him with the task of preparing a document on European recovery. On 16 May he was ready with his first thoughts. He elucidated five principles to guide any future programme:

1. There should be a master programme for four or five years.
2. It should be formulated in cooperation with the Europeans.
3. Europe would need to subscribe to anti-communist measures.
4. When there are no prospects for repayment, the aid should be in the form of grants.
5. There should be encouragement of a 'regional political association', which should include both Germany and Austria.

Finally, he urged that the administration take incisive, early action to galvanise the entire process.[13] A more detailed review on the question of aid to Western Europe followed a week later. He now suggested that the USA should launch an aid programme concentrated on specific bottlenecks, which would resolve the short-term problem of confidence, whilst leaving time for a longer-term programme to be worked out, in conjunction with European countries. For a man who is accredited with having virtually invented the strategy of 'containment' of communism, he then made an interesting statement. 'The Policy Planning Staff', he wrote, 'does not see communist activities as the root of the difficulties of western Europe', but rather the effects of wartime disruption (aggravated by the division of the Continent). It was this crisis that the Communists were able to exploit and any US plan should, therefore address the European problem, which was making Western Europe vulnerable to Communist manipulation. In the longer term, he suggested a programme drawn up in cooperation with the Europeans, but that the Europeans, in their turn, should produce a joint approach and not a series of isolated appeals for assistance. Their aim should be a tolerable standard of living on a financially self-supporting basis. The Unites States should clearly be involved, possibly using UN machinery but only if it could ensure that there would be no Russian interference. He felt that the administration should set the record straight about the 'Truman Doctrine'. It should avoid giving the impression that if there were no communist threat the USA would do nothing, or that, as long as a country was facing a threat of communism, it could expect a blank cheque from the USA.[14]

On 27 May Clayton recommended a programme in the form of grants of goods worth $6 to $7 billion per annum for three years on the basis of a plan worked out by the Europeans themselves. He argued his case on the grounds of the physical distress in Europe, which he attributed more to the economic dislocation than the physical destruction of the war. He also pushed this argument over that of the Russian threat. He argued against any long-winded study. US resources were sufficient as long as US citizens were prepared to make (fiscal) sacrifices, and he was confident they would do so as long as the administration was frank about its policy. Aid should be distributed on a European plan, centred on a European federation. Whilst other countries could be allowed to help, there should not be another UNRAA: 'The United States must run the show.'[15]

HOW WAS THE MARSHALL PLAN RUN?

On the American side, the ECA was constructed as an independent body headed by an administrator with cabinet status and direct access to the president. This was partly a reflection of the Democrats' preference for public/private constructions that had characterised much of the New Deal legislation of the 1930s and partly a recognition that the State Department was not equipped to undertake the kind of day-to-day decision-making that the programme would require. Under the administrator would be a special representative in Europe, with ambassadorial status and teams of experts in the embassies in each of the participating states. Overseeing the entire operation would be two advisory committees.[16] The top appointments all reflected the desire to have prominent businessmen controlling the ECA's administration. The first administrator was Paul G. Hoffman, the president of the Studebaker automobile corporation and a proponent of responsible capitalism. Although a Republican, he had been closely associated with the government's wartime planning. His counterpart in Europe was Averill W. Harriman, a prominent Wall Street merchant banker and US commerce secretary at the time. In 1950, Hoffmann was succeeded as administrator by the steel magnate William C. Foster, who had previously served as Harriman's deputy in Europe. Harriman himself was later appointed to run the Mutual Defence Assistance Program which replaced the ERP in 1951.

On the European side, the requests for aid were coordinated by the Organisation for European Economic Cooperation (OEEC), created in June 1948, representing all participating states. At its top would be a ministerial Executive Council, meeting at regular intervals, with the day-to-day running of affairs entrusted to a smaller seven-member Executive Committee of senior civil servants and the secretary-general, who was in charge of the organisation's secretariat. The smaller Executive Committee was created with a view to expediting the efficiency of decision-making, and ensuring the relative dominance of the British and French within the organisation. The position of the secretary-general was a bone of contention between the US administration, who wanted the post filled by someone with the same semi-independent executive powers as that of the ECA's administrator, and the Europeans, who preferred to maintain national control over developments by subordinating the post firmly under the Executive Council. It was the latter view that prevailed.[17] The chairmanship of the Executive Council was entrusted to the Benelux states and the position was filled first by Belgian foreign minister Paul-Henri Spaak and later by his Dutch colleague Dirk Stikker. The chairmanship of the Executive Council was held by the British and filled by a senior foreign office official, Edmund Hall-Patch. The post of secretary-general was held by a French civil servant, Robert Marjolin, whose subsequent memoirs reveal how much he chafed at the restrictions imposed on his mandate.[18]

The OEEC had been preceded by the Committee for European Economic Cooperation, created in Paris in July 1947. Aside from deciding the future constitution of the OEEC, it was charged with preparing a joint four-year programme for American assistance. This was easier said than done. Firstly, national planning priorities depended upon existing levels of development, degrees of war damage, structures of foreign trade and balance-of-payments problems. These differed sharply from country to country. Apart from the difficulties inherent in standardising and integrating different national plans, it was almost impossible to gauge future dollar requirements as long as there was uncertainty over the permitted levels of German output and the structure of any European trade and payments agreements that might emerge. By August 1947, a confrontation of the various national bids for aid had yielded a total of $29.2 billion, double the total amount of aid from all sources in the two years following the end of the war, and considered in Washington as far too high for Congress to swallow. US authorities suggested that the targets be re-examined in the light of achieving overall payments equilibrium with the United States within four years. The scale of demands, they suggested, could be reduced by eliminating 'competitive' requests for capital goods, by pruning back excessively optimistic or unrealistic requests, by incorporating measures to prune back inflationary financial policies that were leading to increased import demands, and by investigating measures for European cooperation in investment planning and multilateral payments arrangements. At the end of September the OEEC produced its long-awaited joint report which reduced the total requested assistance to $19.3 billion (still above the $16 billion that the US administration thought was feasible) but which otherwise fell far short of the integrated planning for which the administration had been hoping. This amount was based on assumptions about the likely dollar deficit over the four years of the plan, and not on any basis of investment requirements or other considerations. Meanwhile, to alleviate the deteriorating financial position in some of the participating European countries while this wrangling had been going on, the administration submitted demands to Congress for interim aid to bridge the gap before the ERP could begin operation. These sums, which amounted to $522 million were granted to France, Italy and Austria without any of the conditions the USA was requesting for the overall programme.[19] In the event, the Foreign Assistance Act approved a four-year, $17 billion programme with $6,5 billion in the first fifteen months, starting April 1948. In today's values, these sums were equivalent to $135 billion for the whole programme and $50 billion for the first fifteen months. Further tranches, approved annually, eventually brought the total for the three years or so in which the ERP was operational to approximately $11 billion.

The ERP did not distribute aid in the form of cash, but in goods (and services). Once Congress had authorised and appropriated the aid, it was allotted by the ECA in the first tranche, and by the ECA and OEEC thereafter, to the individual countries. Each quarter, the ECA put at the disposal of each state the funds necessary and they in turn submitted requests for goods. The ECA then, within a month, issued a procurement authorisation and released the funds to make the necessary purchases in the next quarter. The Europeans then issued an import licence and the ECA located a purchaser. Initially, the entire process had to be concluded within a period of three months, or else the ECA considered the authorisation cancelled and the process could begin anew. This process was dictated by the desire of the ECA to maintain strict control over the programme, but the cumbersome nature of the procedure and the lack of routine of the US authorities soon combined to make the system almost unworkable. Gradually the system was modified until, in November 1949, the ECA created an automatic six months margin of delay which acted to break the bottleneck.[20] Of course, authorisation and procurement of the goods did not signify any improvement for the recipient countries. The goods had to be shipped and it is only when they arrived in Europe that any effect was felt. Of the aid allocated, a small percentage was reserved to cover administrative costs in the USA. Another factor 'reducing' the value of aid was a congressional stipulation that at least half of the goods be carried in US ships, and at US freight rates. This represented a form of tied aid, but it scarcely reduced Europe's dollar deficit since the task could equally have been performed by European merchant ships which, by this provision, lost the market to the American fleet.

The goods were given to the member states, but they were not given to the end-user. The states were obliged by the ECA to sell the goods through to the end-users. Even if the act had not contained this provision, most states would probably have chosen to do so anyway since to not do so would have discriminated unfairly between those obliged to employ 'free market' goods and those enjoying 'free' ECA goods. It was what happened to these funds that adds an extra dimension to the ERP. At the time of allocation, states were required to deposit an equivalent amount in local currency into a special account known as 'counterpart funds'. Since they had to do this from their own budgets at this early point in the procedure, while they could not expect to receive any income from their sales, the system was initially deflationary, especially in the early stages when delays and cancellations were relatively common. At that stage it was an expensive budgetary operation to pre-fund ERP imports. Eventually, though, governments could expect an income from the sales, though how much depended on the prices charged. The main point of counterpart funds was that their subsequent expenditure had to be agreed jointly between local ECA officials and the member state government (after reserving a small percentage for meeting local ECA expenditures, that is). In this way, ECA officials hoped to have some influence in the direction of local currency expenditure for reconstruction.

Enumerating all these points of administrative detail is not intended as part of a campaign to detail the minutiae of history – they become important when assessing the impact of the Marshall Plan and judging its success or failure. But first we have to address the question of what the Marshall Plan actually was.

WHAT WAS THE MARSHALL PLAN?

When the Marshall Plan was launched, back in 1947, it is obvious that the US administration had no clear ideas about how the scheme was to operate. Although an operational model quickly evolved, it would be wrong to think of the Marshall Plan as a single blueprint for European recovery. Indeed, over its short lifespan, there evolved a series of shifting priorities that reflected the changing environments and the experience accumulated in running the programme, and the need to assuage the doubts expressed within Congress.

At the beginning the first aim of the ERP was to close the dollar deficit. This was evident from the fact that one of the overall aims was the reestablishment of balance-of-payments equilibrium between the United States and the OEEC as a whole by 1952. It was also a fact that the main criterion for aid distribution among the OEEC member states was their individual balance-of-payments position. It was somewhat ironic, therefore, that much of the effort in preparing for the first tranche of aid was directed at trying to realise a programme of integrated production planning. As we saw, the first OEEC General Report fell considerably short of satisfying these demands. Subsequent negotiations with US authorities brought some adjustments, but the end result still fell far short of the ideal.

The Marshall Plan also had its own goals for cementing social peace in Western Europe. One part of this strategy was an anti-communist offensive. Communists were forced out of coalition governments and concerted efforts were made to encourage free trade unions, or to form them where none existed.[21] But social peace could not be bought by institutional reform alone; it required a mechanism for increasing the size of the economic cake and ensuring its more equitable distribution. The key to resolving 'distributional conflicts' lay in promoting European productivity and transplanting the American model to resolve the class conflict latent in Western European society.[22] An experiment had already been conducted in 1948 in the form of creating an Anglo-American productivity council and this experiment was soon expanded to cover all participating countries, through the medium of a series of bilateral agreements and the use of counterpart funds. This productivity drive was accelerated in 1951, when, in the aftermath of the outbreak of the Korean War, the US administration realised that a call to increase European defence expenditure could undo much of the progress sustained to date.[23] Only increased productivity could resolve the classic dilemma of 'guns or butter'.

From the start, the US authorities had tried to encourage the development of more efficient trade and payments mechanisms within Europe, both as a contribution to its overall goal of encouraging a greater measure of European 'unification' and as part of the effort to reduce dependence on dollar imports. Success was limited. A European Customs Union Study Group was created, as much as an attempt to deflect immediate US pressure as to make genuine progress towards its realisation. It eventually fizzled out without success in 1950.[24] A second approach was that the USA granted some countries what was called 'conditional aid': sums of dollars designed to compensate for the 'soft currency' that surplus countries would otherwise earn in trading with chronic-deficit countries. Most of this aid, however, was employed bilaterally and did little to ease the settlements problem.[25] In 1949, the ECA made more concerted efforts to achieve a multilateral trade and payments regime in Western Europe, allocating $350 million of ERP funds to establish a European Payments Union,[26] and promoting a 'trade liberalisation scheme' directed at the gradual removal of quotas on intra-European trade.[27]

WAS THE MARSHALL PLAN SUCCESSFUL?

As part of the fiftieth anniversary commemorations of the Marshall Plan, one eminent historian, Immanuel Wexler, who had written a study of the Plan back in 1983, reflected upon the question of whether the Marshall Plan had been successful in the light of the original goals. He listed these outcomes as follows:

- The achievement of a healthy economy independent of extraordinary economic assistance
- A strong production effort
- An expansion of foreign trade
- The creation and maintenance of internal financial stability
- The development of economic cooperation

He concluded that the record was mixed. Although the first goal of economic viability had not been achieved by 1952, the European economies did record considerable economic growth. Agriculture, however, lagged behind. Equally, Europe had notched up major achievements in the area of foreign trade, especially in trade among themselves. On the other hand, progress in controlling inflation that had been made before 1950 was undermined thereafter, and many economies were marked by serious balance-of-payments disequilibria. As for the goal of economic integration, he considered that most of the progress had come later, and had stemmed from European rather than American initiatives. Overall he judges the Marshall Plan only a qualified success, but claimed that it laid the basis for Europe's subsequent development.[28]

Although Wexler makes an effort towards a nuanced judgement, this kind of checklist approach to history has serious shortcomings, most noticeably a failure to link the ends to the means, or to consider alternative factors that might, coincidently, have produced the same results. It is impossible to rectify this within the confines of this chapter, but nonetheless we will attempt to link the mechanisms of the ERP with some of the 'results' observed. It will provide data for the ERP recipients as a whole and, because Europe displayed a range of problems, it will offer individual data for the five larger economies – France, Italy, West Germany, Netherlands and the United Kingdom.

HOW MUCH AID?

Even before the Marshall Plan, Western Europe was the recipient of foreign aid. These sums of aid were in both relative and absolute terms far greater than the sums advanced under the Marshall Plan (see Table 3.3 and they would have been equivalent to between $120 billion and $150,billion in today's purchasing power. However, the literature on post-war relief, or the UNRAA, is almost non-existent, and certainly none of the semi-mythical sphere surrounds it as does the literature on the Marshall Plan. We shall offer an explanation for the second part of this puzzle later in this chapter.

TABLE 3.3: POST-WAR CREDITS AND RELIEF, MAY 1945-AUTUMN 1947 ($ MILLION)

	UNRAA	*USA*	*Other*	*Total*
France	-	1920	1202	3122
Italy	505	325	136	966
West Germany	-	670	480	1150
Netherlands	-	413	502	915
UK	-	4400	2926	7326
OEEC Total	1088	8436	5845	15369

Source: J. Killick, *The United States and European Reconstruction, 1945-1960*, Edinburgh, 1998, 45, Table 5.2.

Before we look at the Marshall Aid programme itself, we have to confront our first counterfactual. The question posed by Harold B. Cleveland, himself a participant in the ERP programme, was that Western Europe might have financed its capital requirements by borrowing on the New York capital markets, whilst Germany's special requirements would continue to be met through a continuation of the GARIOA (military occupation) expenditures.[29] The idea that private capital would be preferable to government aid has become increasingly popular since in the 1990s, and has often been employed to argue against inaugurating large government programmes for Eastern Europe and the former Soviet Union. Indeed, private investment flows to developing and emerging economies since

1990 have taken place on a scale that dwarves that of the ERP, even when allowing for inflation. However, the 1940s are not the 1990s. US markets were inexperienced in foreign lending and, for contemporary policy-makers, a look at the boom-and-bust of Weimar Germany and much of East-Central Europe in the early 1930s would have made them wary of basing their own recovery programmes on the notorious volatility of American loans.[30] Besides, American investors looking at Western Europe were understandably nervous of the prospects for safe and profitable investment. In the two years after the war, for example, Western Europe managed to raise exactly $140 million this way as opposed to the $15 billion that was raised in foreign aid.[31]

A second counterfactual is more easily disposed of. The question could be posed why Europe did not obtain assistance from the International Monetary Fund (IMF) or the International Bank for Reconstruction and Development (IBRD). Aside from the well-documented answers that the IMF probably did not have the funds, and that the IBRD proved too cumbersome and slow, the US authorities blocked both routes. There were several reasons for this choice. First, American officials had by 1947 begun to resent the lack of control over the UNRAA and were determined not to repeat the mistake. Second, all UN organisations, including the IMF and the World Bank, also embraced the Soviet Union and the Eastern European countries and, with the clouds of the Cold War gathering, the US administration was reluctant to make the aid programme hostage to Soviet approval, even if the initial offer of Marshall Aid was ostensibly open to them as well. Finally, the Americans realised that considerable leverage would be sacrificed if Europeans had alternative routes to dollar funds, which might allow the possibility for playing different agencies against each other. If the United States was to provide aid, the ERP would be its only conduit.

The amounts of aid disbursed by the United States under the ERP were large, but historians disagree about exactly how large they were. Since the programme was prematurely terminated, the sums did not reach the total set in the original Act. Most of the numbers cluster between $13 billion, which is presumably derived from the various acts of Congress[32] and $10.4 billion, which reflects the amounts actually approved for shipment either in June 1951, when the ERP was effectively assimilated into the mutual security programme, or $11.4 billion by June 1952, if account is taken of the shipments that trickled in during the subsequent twelve months.[33] The gap is not unimportant; it is equivalent to 1.9 per cent of Western Europe's GNP in 1948, the starting year of the programme, or 1.6 per cent of its GNP in 1951, the year in which it terminated.[34] Rather more important than the total sum of assistance is its timing. As we observed above, there is a large difference between the allocation of aid and its conversion into goods ready for shipment. These backlogs were especially large at the start of the programme and, moreover, they varied from country to country. For example, although $4 billion of aid had been allocated by the end of 1948, only $2.1 billion had actually been shipped. Expressed as a percentage of Western Europe's GNP in that year, this represents a difference between 3 per cent of GNP and 1.5 per cent. By 1949 the aid amounts had increased and discrepancy between allocation and shipment was smaller. Assuming that both figures for the last three months of the year reflect the average for the first nine, the figures for allocation ($4.6 billion) were equivalent to 6.2 per cent of GNP in that year, whilst those for goods shipped ($4.7 billion) amounted to 6.3 per cent. The year 1949 represented the peak of the Marshall Plan effort, measured both in quantitative terms and in their relative impact on the European economies. In next eighteen months $2.6 billion was allocated and $3.8 billion was shipped.

TABLE 3.4: CUMULATIVE ERP ALLOCATIONS ($ MILLION) AND SHIPMENTS (%)

	Dec. 1948	*Sept. 1949*	*June 1951*	*Dec. 1948*	*Sept. 1949*	*June 1951*
France	951	1506	2401	52%	76%	88%
Italy	494	799	1294	40%	68%	82%
West Germany	405	697	1297	34%	59%	92%
Netherlands	372	644	978	42%	69%	94%
UK	1094	1897	2713	70%	83%	99%
OEEC Total	4045	6976	11310	51%	78%	94%

Source: C. Spagnolo, *The Marshall Plan and the Stabilization of Western Europe*, PhD thesis, European University Institute, 1998, 209.

EUROPEAN RECONSTRUCTION

The timing of the arrival of Marshall Aid goods in Western Europe is vital in explaining its economic impact. It is evident that they did not fully come on-stream until 1949, some eighteen months after the perception of the 'crisis' which the programme was intended to resolve. By 1949, Europe's economic recovery was already in full swing. Discounting West Germany, whose industrial recovery was being restricted by the Allied occupation authorities, Europe's industrial output had overtaken its pre-war levels already by 1947, and was considerably above that level by 1948. Agriculture lagged somewhat behind, reflecting the fact that it was harder to redress the wartime damage in that sector, but also the fact that export markets, especially that of Germany, were still restricted.

TABLE 3.5: INDICES OF WESTERN EUROPE'S PRODUCTION

	1947	1948	1949	1950	1951
Industrial Production	87	99	112	124	135
Industrial Production (minus Germany)	105	119	130	138	145
Agricultural Output	81 (47/48)	95 (48/49)	104 (49/50)	111 (50/51)	

1938=100

Source: B. Eichengreen and M. Uzan, 'The Marshall Plan: Economic Effects and Implications for Eastern Europe and the Former USSR', *Economic Policy*, 14 (1992): 203, 205.

The discrepancy between timing of the first deliveries of ERP goods and the tempo of European recovery prompted historians to question a direct link between Marshall Aid and economic growth. Milward suggests that the 1947 crisis was a foreign exchange crisis occasioned by an unbridled investment boom. The effect of ERP, when it eventually arrived was simply to allow the boom to continue.[35] Charles Maier was one of the first historians to question the quantitative impact of Marshall Aid on European reconstruction. He observed that ERP was the equivalent of 10 to 20 per cent of capital formation in the first two years of the plan, and subsequently fell below 10 per cent.[36] With investment rates running at over 20 per cent of GNP in most of the participating states, that still left considerable scope for economic growth, even without the extra impetus provided by ERP.

TABLE 3.6: US AID AS A PERCENTAGE OF GDCF

	1948	1949	1950	1951
UK	9	11	10	2
France	14	12	10	7
West Germany	31	22	11	7
Italy	27	34	10	9

Source: C.S. Maier, 'The Two Postwar Eras and the Conditions for Stability in Twentieth-Century Western Europe', *American Historical Review*, 86, 2 (1981): 342.

Milward also examines the impact of Marshall Aid on reconstruction. He provides an assessment of importance of aid by taking account not only of the direct aid channelled through the ECAS, but also of the second category advantage obtained by trading credits advanced to deficit countries through dollar-financed clearing agreements. This provides a higher assessment for all countries, but especially the Netherlands, which was able to fund a large part of its deficit with Belgium from this source, and which was also the reason why Belgium received the credits in the first place. If we take these figures and superimpose them on the savings rates for the period 1948-1951 calculated by Eichengreen and Uzan, the effects are considerably larger, but only for this one year.

TABLE 3.7: ERP AID AFTER OPERATION OF DRAWING RIGHTS AS PERCENTAGE OF GNP AND AS A PERCENTAGE OF SAVINGS

	ERP/GNP 7/48-6/49	*ERP/GNP 1949 (i)*	*ERP/ GNP 1949 (ii)*	*Savings Rates 1948-51*	*ERP/Savings 1949*
France	6.5	9.9	11.5	18%	55-63%
Italy	5.3	8.8	9.6	18%	48-53%
Netherlands	10.8	16.1	23.1	20%	70-115%
UK	2.4	5.2	7.5	13%	40-57%
West Germany	2.9	4.7	5.9	19%	26-31%

1949 (i) measured at pre-devaluation exchange rates

1949 (ii) measured at post-devaluation exchange rates

Source: Milward (1987), 96-97; B. Eichengreen and M. Uzan, 'The Marshall Plan: Economic Effects and Implications for Eastern Europe and the Former USSR', Economic Policy, 14 (1992): 23.

These figures, it must be stressed, are equivalents. They do not mean that aid actually did increase investment; it could equally have permitted an increase in consumption, which also occurred in most countries in 1949. Overall, Milward suggests that for most countries, the impact of Marshall Aid was 'marginal'.[37] Eichengreen and Uzan come to a similar conclusion. If Marshall Aid amounted to 2 per cent of GNP for Western Europe as a whole, it would have raised investment's share of GNP by 0.7 per cent the following year and raised domestic output by 0.3 per cent. At 2.5 per cent of GNP, Marshall Aid would have raised growth by half a percentage point. 'While helpful,' they conclude, 'this is hardly the dramatic stimulus trumpeted by champions of the Marshall Plan.'[38] This conclusion was broadly endorsed by De Long and Eichengreen who considered the contribution of ERP to growth 'valuable' but 'too little to make the difference between prosperity and stagnation'.[39]

THE BALANCE OF PAYMENTS

many historians who downplay the 'real' nature of Europe's crisis in 1947, that had provoked the US response in the form of Marshall Aid, nonetheless admit to the existence of a profound payments crisis. They may disagree among themselves about its exact cause, with explanations ranging from a sharp deterioration in the terms of trade, whether caused by a change in US policy towards its strategic reserves[40] or a failure in world harvests,[41] to an inflationary import boom reflecting the domestic reconstruction effort.[42] Whatever the reason, Europe's overall deficit continued to be acute through both 1948 and 1949, especially that with the United States. The situation improved in 1950, though the Continent still remained in deficit. It is not difficult to add the deficits together to produce a figure of $8.2 billion for that with the United States and a total deficit of $10.6 billion. The latter figure coincides almost exactly with the lower boundaries for the assessment of the value of ERP goods shipped to Europe over the same period.

TABLE 3.8: EUROPE'S BALANCE OF PAYMENTS (BILLION CURRENT $)

	1948 USA	*1948 total*	*1949 USA*	*1949 total*	*1950 USA*	*1950 total*
Exports	4.6	14.4	4.4	13.5	3.6	12.5
Imports	1.3	8.8	1.1	9.4	1.6	9.6
BoT	-3.3	-5.6	-3.3	-4.1	-2.0	-2.9
Invisibles	-0.1	+0.7	+0.1	+0.3	+0.4	+0.4
BoP	-3.4	-4.9	-3.2	-3.8	-1.6	-2.5

Source: UN(ECE) *Economic Survey of Europe in 1950*, 115.

Even someone as sceptical about the quantitative impact as Charles Maier considered that the main contribution came from the easing of the balance-of-payments constraint and the easing of bottlenecks for specific goods but, even then, he judges it more 'like the lubricant in an engine – not the fuel – allowing a machine to run that would otherwise buckle and bind'. Having surmounted the 'crisis' of 1947, he surmised, European growth would have resumed even in the absence of the Marshall Plan, albeit less spectacularly and somewhat more protectionist than it was to be.[43]

Eichengreen and Uzan demonstrate a close relationship between the size of Marshall Aid and the size of the current account deficit that countries were able to run, suggesting that an input equivalent to 1 per cent of GNP allowed an increase in the deficit of 0.9 per cent of GNP. This is not surprising, however, since Marshall Aid allocation was made largely on the basis of the anticipated deficit of each recipient. Using a multivariate regression, encompassing other determinants of current account imbalances, reduced the contribution of a 1 per cent input to 0.12 per cent of GNP. They concede that this analysis makes no allowances for specific bottlenecks, but argue that the potential effects of these were small.[44] Taking a worst-case product (coal) and a worst-case country (Italy – virtually 75 per cent of requirements imported), a separate calculation using an input-output model for the country suggested that if no coal at all had been available through the Marshall Plan (and all sectors had been equally affected), industrial output would have been 6.8 per cent less than it was, transport 7.3 per cent less, but GNP only 3.2 per cent less.[45]

Milward breaks down the imports financed by Marshall Aid into different categories before undertaking two interesting counterfactuals which question the necessity for the Marshall Plan. Before looking at these exercises one has to make a conceptual note. Even if ERP goods are defined in certain categories, it does not mean that the programme was limited to those goods alone. Receiving aid in the form of grain, for example, might allow a country to use the dollars thereby saved for purchasing goods in another category, as for example, machinery or fuel. The results of Milward's exercise are given in Table 3.9.

TABLE 3.9: VALUE AND COMPOSITION OF ERP SHIPMENTS, APRIL 1948-DECEMBER 1951 ($ MILLION)

	Total	*Per cent*
Food, feed, fertilisers	3209.5	32.1
Fuel	1552.4	15.5
Cotton	1397.8	14.0
Other raw materials and semi-manufactures	1883.1	18.8
Tobacco	444.5	4.4
Machinery and vehicles	1428.1	14.3
Other	88.9	
Total	10004.3	100

Source: A.S. Milward, *The Reconstruction of Western Europe, 1945-51*, London, 1984, 101.

Milward observes that the principal category of US aid was food. In 1949, without ERP aid Western Europe could have imported only half the actual quantity from the dollar zone. They would have needed to get the rest from the non-dollar zone (which would have meant raising those imports by 12 per cent). This he considers 'extremely difficult'. Suppose instead, he argues, that national governments had not allowed food consumption to increase and had kept the calorific value of food consumption at the 1947 level (i.e. 20 per cent below the 1949 level), Western Europe would have got away with no food imports from the dollar zone. Of six countries examined (i.e. BLEU, Italy, the UK and Germany) this would have left enough dollars over to maintain capital goods imports from the dollar zone at the 1949 level. This would not have been possible for France and the Netherlands. A second scenario he suggests is that Western Europe restricted their imports of machinery and vehicles to half the value they actually obtained from the dollar zone. This would have meant raising imports from non-dollar areas by 34 per cent. 'This was clearly not possible'. In this case, any shift of demand to European or domestic sources would have entailed an equivalent shift in other ERP goods. Again, France and the Netherlands would have been particularly hard hit.[46]

Kindleberger is not the only commentator to express doubt about whether elasticities of supply and demand in the real-world economy could have produced the results in Milward's counterfactual, or whether the social structures in France and Italy could have survived a holding of food rationing at the levels of 1947 for a further two years.[47] Spagnolo argues that Milward's analysis is overinfluenced by the United Kingdom, which had colonies and commonwealth links sufficiently large to offer alternative sources of supply. He doubts whether other countries possessed the networks to realise alternative sources of imports had that been required. He also suggests that shuffling within different categories of US goods would have been difficult, given Congress' demand that the ECA try to move goods in surplus in the USA and minimise the purchases of goods in short supply – petroleum, farm machinery, metals and meat.[48]

COUNTERPART FUNDS

Counterpart funds were the sums of domestic currency, equivalent to the value of ERP goods received, that member states were to place on a special account which could only be employed in consultation with local ECA officials. By influencing the timing and distribution of these funds, US officials could exert influence on domestic reconstruction efforts, insofar as these were undertaken with government funds. The amounts dispensed, and a broad description of their purpose, are given below.

TABLE 3.10: ECA COUNTERPART FUND APPROVED EXPENDITURE AND DISTRIBUTION, APRIL 1948-JUNE 1952 ($ MILLION)

	Total	*Debt Retirement*	*Production*	*Other*
France	2702.8	171.4	2003.8	527.6
Italy	1042.4	-	823.8	218.6
West Germany	1008.8	-	753.4	255.4
Netherlands	554.6	197.4	209.2	137.4
UK	1762.8	1706.3	2.6	53.9
OEEC Total	8651.3	2541.5	4595.6	1514.2

Source: M. Margairaz, 'Entre Plan Marshall et Plan Monnet' in R. Girault and M. Levy-Leboyer (eds.), *Le Plan Marshall et le Relèvement Économique de l'Europe. Colloque tenu à Bercy les 21, 22, 23 mars 1991* (Paris, 1993) 162-163.

The initial impact of counterpart funds was deflationary. States were forced to defer expenditure of incomes in order to feed the fund until income derived from sale came on stream. Once ERP goods arrived, and their users repaid the sums in full, a countervailing stream of income was received, and the early impact was neutralised. If these funds were subsequently spent, they could be seen as a net augmentation of domestic capital formation. If they were used for debt retirement, they would still add to capital formation to the extent that the partial withdrawal from capital markets that this implied would allow room for private investors (assuming that they utilised the slack). Both scenarios of course assume that states did not use counterpart income to reduce the tax burden. The UK used most of its counterpart funds for debt retirement, and the Netherlands also employed 36 per cent of funds in this way. France, Germany and Italy, however, used most of these funds for investment purposes. Looking at these countries closely *might* allow us to see the impact of American influence in more detail. Before examining the data, however, another caveat must made. There is no way, other than categorisation, of distinguishing a lire spent from counterpart funds and one spent from ordinary receipts. What appears under the heading of counterpart fund expenditure was what the local ECA authorities were prepared to countenance. But if they refused a project, or if governments suspected that they might refuse, there was absolutely nothing to prevent them from going ahead and using other funds (tax receipts or loans). Some of the basic data are given below:

TABLE 3.11: SIGNIFICANCE OF COUNTERPART FUNDS FOR INVESTMENT AND STATE BUDGETS, 1949-1952

		A	B	C	D	E
		Counterpart Funds as % of Gross Investment	*State Share of Gross Investment*	*Counterpart Funds as % of State Investment*	*Counterpart Funds as % of State Budget Receipts*	*Counterpart Funds as % of Fiscal Deficit*
France	1949	25.6	87.2	28.2	17.0	42.4
	1950	14.1	63.7	22.1	8.9	29.8
	1951	9.2	51.1	18.0	6.3	27.5
	1952	10.2	58.1	17.6	6.8	18.5
FRG	1949	2.9	24.0	12.2	2.6*	35.8*
	1950	9.1	30.6	29.8	9.7	48.8
	1951	3.6	25.0	14.2	3.4	32.4
	1952	1.8	22.5	8.2		
Italy	1949	1.8	35.6	5.1	7.9*	21.1*
	1950	5.4	25.0	21.6	17.2	45.8
	1951	10.7	18.3	58.5	12.7	30.1
	1952	9.5	17.3	54.9	6.2	14.8

* The data in these columns are for fiscal years 1949-1950 etc.

Source: C. Spagnolo, *The Marshall Plan and the Stabilization of Western Europe*, PhD thesis, European University Institute, 1998, 268, 270.

Looking first at Column A, it is noticeable that the counterpart funds data reinforces the picture of the *relatively* modest role played by ERP in capital formation that we saw earlier. The most noticeable exception is the large contribution in the case of France in 1949. This is unsurprising since, as we have seen, the size of counterpart funds derives from the size of aid, though there is a difference in the timing of the release. This factor, for example, explains why the contribution in the Italian case comes only in 1951 and 1952, when ERP aid was tailing-off.[49]

Columns B and C need to be read together since they express a relationship between the public and private sectors in the reconstruction effort, and the willingness of local ECA officials to reinforce this relationship. France's investment strategy, led by a state-funded modernisation plan, is well documented in the literature, but it is nevertheless interesting that this strategy was underwritten by counterpart fund spending that consistently boosted state investment expenditures by 25 per cent or more. Both the share of the state in investment and the contribution of counterpart funds are smaller in Germany, but even there the contribution is far from negligible. The data for Italy, where counterpart funds as a share of state investment surged in 1951 and 1952, reflect an interesting insight into leverage the arrangements offered to US officials. Partly to resist US pressure, or more accurately to avoid a parliamentary debate of the potential for American pressure, the Italian government had long resisted using these funds for productive investment, preferring to employ them for debt retirement or to employ them as part of the general budget, for the relief of acute social pressures. At first the ECA authorities acquiesced, but allowed a sizeable transfer to fund investment in (nationalised) railways. In 1949, however, they stepped up pressure for a more forceful investment programme, much of which was concentrated in the poorer south of the country. Whilst such a development was not entirely at odds with government thinking, the effort was significantly accelerated by use of counterpart funds.[50]

The total fiscal contribution of counterpart funds is shown in Columns D and E, which measure the impact on tax receipts and the budget deficit, respectively. The figures show the extent to which taxes would have needed to be raised to achieve the same levels of state expenditure, or the widening of state budget deficits that would have needed to be tolerated in the absence of the counterpart mechanism. In several co-authored articles, Eichengreen has suggested that ECA officials were able to employ their influence over the release of counterpart funds to persuade governments to modify their fiscal policies. Their chosen case is that of France, where they insist that 'French budget deficits were smaller and monetary policies were less inflationary than they would have been otherwise',[51] although they later soften this stance to one where 'if the overall record of conditionality regarding fiscal and monetary policy was mixed, informal pressure for market liberalisation and economic integration was more successful'.[52] Other historians disagree. Esposito[53] and Wall[54] suggest that such conditionality was ineffectual and Milward, while acknowledging that the USA exerted pressure on France, observes that by the end of 1948, the French government had also grown concerned about inflation. In reality, whatever its inflationary stance, US officials nonetheless backed a high (and potentially inflationary) level of investment and allowed the imports required.[55]

SOCIAL PEACE

The discussion of the impact of counterpart funds on potential levels of taxation has recently taken the question into a new and very fruitful area. It takes the debate from one that emphasises the quantitative aspects of the Marshall Plan to one that stresses a more 'institutional' approach. De Long and Eichengreen argue that the main contribution of the Marshall Plan to Europe's economic recovery policy was to facilitate 'the negotiation of a pro-growth 'social contract' that provided the political stability and climate necessary to support the post-war boom'.[56] They describe a continent dominated by class-based political parties, an economy facing acute shortages and a system of government wherein policy-makers were loath to trust the market. It could easily have slipped down Argentina's route of economic stagnation and populist over-regulation. The Marshall Plan helped Europe avoid these traps by restoring financial stability (see Eichengreen and Uzan above) and supplying a critical flow of goods that allowed the restoration of the market. However, the critical factor they isolate in explaining Europe's boom was the consistently high level of investment. For this to occur, labour had to be prepared to defer current claims on resources in favour of economic growth and higher living standards in the future. If labour pressed for immediate compensation, management would have little incentive to reinvest, and if management refrained from reinvesting profits, labour had little incentive to hold back their wage claims. The Marshall Plan supplied a critical difference in resources to dampen the immediate redistributional conflict. This critical margin allowed Europe to shift onto a 'social contract' equilibrium path, and once both parties had assimilated the logic of this superior equilibrium, there was no logic in desisting.[57]

Whilst this argument is speculative, and not fully underscored, it could be developed further. In theory, any input of resources into the system could have produced a critical margin, but it would not necessarily have had an equivalent effect. As we have already seen, resources were being pumped into Western Europe since the war began. This could have allowed an increase in investment, along an existing investment preference curve. Marshall Aid, however, represented a medium-term commitment, a 'structural adjustment program' to keep those resources flowing. Thus what it implies is an upward/outward shift in the entire curve, allowing the achievement of a new and higher equilibrium. This new equilibrium, it could be argued, was reinforced by a new ideology, propagating a future of raised productivity and economic growth.

PRODUCTIVITY

In a path-breaking (and much republished) article published on the 30th anniversary of the Marshall Plan, Charles Maier argued that an essential part of the Marshall Plan was an American vision of resolving distributional crises (and the resultant social conflict) through increased productivity, increased growth and raised living standards. This found its roots in the way Americans had apparently resolved similar social tensions through the New Deal and through the experience of the war effort, which had produced plenty without sacrificing living standards.[58] 'The recurrent ideas all stressed that by enhancing productive efficiency, whether through scientific management, business planning, industrial cooperation or corporatist groupings, American society could transcend the class conflicts that arose from scarcity.'[59] One shared element in these ideas was an abhorrence of monopolies and concentrations of economic power. By 1945 the two themes of productivity and monopoly formed the conceptual axes along which Americans located economic institutions. The combination had the added advantage of seeming to be apolitical.[60] This translated itself into a policy aimed at multilateral exchange and currency stability, on the one hand, and support for new domestic neo-corporatist orders in individual European countries on the other. At first these policies were directed at forming a framework of international institutions, such as the IMF and the ITO, but as the problems of European aid came to a head, they were subsumed into American planning for the ERP. By this time, of course, it had acquired a distinctly anti-communist flavour. Part of this was reflected in a decision to promote non-communist, or 'free', trade unions wherever they existed and creating them where they did not. From then on, they were fully integrated into ERP programmes, particularly into the productivity missions, and fully incorporated into ERP ideology.[61]

Maier concludes that 'In the last analysis, the politics of productivity that emerged as the American organizing ideal for the post-war world depended on superseding class conflict with economic growth.'[62] He then proceeds to make one of those judgements that slam intention and perceived result together and claim success – 'the success of this politics of productivity can be judged by the fact that the 1950s and 1960s turned out to be periods of unparalleled growth and capital formation'.[63] At this point the argument begins to unravel. One instrument to augment productivity was indeed capital formation, but we have already observed that these levels were already high, long before ERP arrived, that this might have fuelled the dollar crisis that precipitated the Marshall Plan, and that by any quantitative standard, the contribution of ERP, whilst useful, was not vital. The other instrument that the US authorities employed was that of productivity missions. These were first introduced into the bilateral ECA agreement with the UK, and later extended to other countries. Funded by counterpart funds, these allowed groups of trade unionists and industrialists to make extended study visits to the USA and to share their experiences once they returned home.[64] However, as one historian observed, the $184 million spent by the USA on technical assistance under the Marshall Plan was insufficient to change entrenched attitudes and to 'create incentives where none were perceived to exist'.[65] A conference on this topic held in 1997 concluded that the productivity missions were a relatively inefficient means for technological transmission and that most economies had other, both national and international, routes towards new organisational techniques and new technologies.[66]

TRADE AND PAYMENTS

there was a last 'institutional' contribution of the Marshall Plan to Western European reconstruction that has not been sufficiently recognised, and that may turn out to be the most important of all, and that lay in the reconstruction of a well-functioning trade and payments mechanism. This took place in two phases.

The first phase is well documented, and we will touch on it only briefly here. The Marshall Plan helped to reintegrate West Germany into the European economy. Indeed there are some historians who see this as the main function of the Plan. By offering it on a Pan-European basis (including Germany) it prepared the grounds for raising and eventually removing the Allied restrictions on the German economy, and by providing generous relief to France, it bought the acquiescence of the French government to these developments.[67] The German economy had provided a crucial motor for continental Europe before the war. Many industries, especially in the smaller European economies, had developed in an almost symbiotic relationship with their German counterparts. The repression of its economy and the trade policy of the Allies (by demanding dollars for most categories of exports, whilst paying local currency for most categories of imports) had virtually transformed it into part of the hard currency area. Notwithstanding the efforts of states to substitute domestic production for German imports, especially in the area of iron and steel production, restoring the German economy to its central position was a fundamental prerequisite for the recovery of Europe as a whole.[68]

The second phase is less well-assimilated into the mainstream literature, and its contribution lay in the restoration of normalised trade and payments throughout Western Europe. The OEEC countries had been stumbling towards a workable system of multilateral clearance of national deficits, but the various arrangements only covered about a quarter of the accumulated national deficits. Almost everywhere commercial transactions required prior approval of national monetary authorities. A similar situation of quantitative import restrictions and state monopoly import authorities covered almost all categories of foreign trade.[69] If the 1930s had seemed bad, the post-war situation was even worse. The data below compare the situation in 1950 with two pre-war years.

TABLE 3.12: REAL VALUES OF INDUSTRIAL OUTPUT AND TRADE IN WESTERN EUROPE, 1950

	Index 1938=100	*Index 1929=100*
Industrial output	125	135
Real value of Intra-European trade	118	93

Source: W. Asbeek Brusse, 'Regional Plans for European Trade' in R.T. Griffiths (ed.), The Economic Development of the EEC (Cheltenham, 1997) 123.

Even compared with 1938, the real level of intra-trade lagged behind the recovery of industrial production, but 1938 was hardly a year to aspire to. It witnessed the spiralling of protection in the wake of the 1937-1938 recession, the intensification of the Nazi trade drive away from Western Europe and the start of nationalistic, autarkic rearmament policies elsewhere. If the height of aspiration was to return to 1938, the American aspiration for a more integrated Europe was in deep trouble. If we take 1929 as the last 'normal' year, then the full extent of the problem becomes immediately apparent. These developments were not lost on the ECA authorities either. In October 1949, against the background of preparing the mid-term report on the ERP for Congress, Paul Hoffmann addressed the assembled OEEC ministers and demanded a greater degree of 'integration'. What he wanted were more dynamic measures to promote the exchange of goods in Europe, and he was willing to commit a substantial sum of $500 million to back any viable schemes.[70]

He was rewarded by two initiatives. In June 1949 the OEEC ministers had approved a scheme for the gradual relaxing of quotas on their mutual trade, but without deadlines and without targets. With American support these plans became much more ambitious. Indeed, American support was necessary since any mutual trade scheme would be in breach of GATT rules which prohibited new preferences, with the exception of customs unions or free trade areas for which strict conditions applied. The OEEC initiative did not meet any of these criteria, and it blatantly implied the maintenance of discrimination against the United States. Thus US support was a critical factor in deciding how to proceed. In November 1949 the OEEC ministers agreed to remove quotas on 50 per cent of the value of imports from member countries by December and, when December came, the target was raised to 60 per cent to take effect once a payments scheme had been agreed (see below), later targeted to October 1950. This target was raised again to 75 per cent, with a minimum of 60 per cent in each of the categories (food, raw materials and manufactures) to take effect by February 1951. Thereafter progress slowed, as Western Europe reeled under a succession of balance-of-payments crises, but in January 1955 the target was again raised, this time to 90 per cent to be achieved by October of that year.

In several respects, the scheme was not perfect. Firstly, members could unilaterally suspend their 'liberalisation' measures in times of balance-of-payments crisis, and Germany, France and the UK were all to do so between 1951 and 1953. Secondly, the targets only referred to 'private trade', thereby excluding imports from state import monopolies, which prevailed in 1949 in agriculture and fuel. On the other hand, reversals aside, the scheme progressed, even between 1951 and 1955 when the targets remained unchanged. This occurred because the base dates upon which the liberalisation targets were calculated were updated, effectively giving the targets more bite, and because the areas covered by state trade were gradually reduced, brought more sectors within the scheme.[71]

Freeing the movement of goods made little sense unless the means for paying for them were also freed. In December 1949 ECA officials prepared a plan for a European Payments Union which would allow the immediate freeing of all commercial transactions within the OEEC, implementing a multilateral clearing of all trade balances and introducing an automatic mutual credit mechanism. The latter worked as follows: each member was allocated a 'quota' (not to be confused with trade quotas) based on its trade volume and deficits and this was divided into five equal steps. If a country slipped into deficit, it paid entirely with its own currency in the first step, 20 per cent in gold or dollars in the second, and so on until the fifth step, when it would pay 80 per cent in gold or dollars. The overall credit received within the quota amounted to 60 per cent. Once the quota had been exhausted, all settlements would be in hard currency. Countries in surplus would also have to make do with soft currency within the first step, and receive 50 per cent hard currency for the rest until the quota had been exceeded, at which point they would be entitled to full settlement in hard currency. Since the scheme operated asymmetrically, there was a potential leakage of hard currency, and this was to be covered by $350 million from the funds reserved by Hoffman in October 1949 (see above). The Payments Union came into operation in June 1950 and survived until 1958. However, in 1954 the credit element in the scheme was considerably reduced to an overall 25 per cent, and for most countries the effect was virtually equivalent to hard currency trade.[72]

One of the effects of these measures was to reverse the situation that had impelled Hoffman to make his speech in October 1949 – namely, that European economic recovery had not been matched by an increase in trade. From now on the growth of international trade exceeded GDP growth by a considerable margin. Of course, there are economic factors that can explain this – European markets were expanding, these were neighbouring countries, their industrial structures were relatively favourable and so on, but the simple fact remains that none of these conditions could exercise any impact if the trade and payments restrictions that prevailed in 1949 were left in place. It is true that the European governments might have moved to eliminate these restrictions themselves, but they would have found it difficult to do so if the USA had refused the relaxation of the GATT rules and suspension of IMF requirements to permit European preferences to emerge, or if it had insisted on reciprocal concessions. As it was, the freeing of trade and payments occurred within the framework constructed for the administration of Marshall Aid, and with the political and financial support of the USA.

This is probably the most lasting 'institutional' impact of the Marshall Plan. By creating a framework of raised expectations, the impact was to stimulate an increase of investment by shifting the investment preference curve, as opposed to an increase along the existing curve. The original schemes were not perfect, but they worked. And, in 1955, they prompted a core group of countries, whose intra-trade was expanding faster than the rest, to start negotiations to cement these mutual trade arrangements into place. Their efforts would emerge in 1957 as the Treaty of Rome, creating the European Economic Community.

POSTSCRIPT

This chapter was published in a volume that I wrote with Victor Sergeev and which was published in Russian. In English the title translates as *Economic Reconstruction: A Comparison of Post-war Europe and Post-Soviet Russia* (Letny Stad, Moscow, 2003). The idea behind the volume was to contrast the impact of the free-market oriented 'Washington consensus' on post-Soviet Russia with the more carefully calibrated schemes offered to Western Europe after World War II.

Not a lot has appeared since then. The sixtieth anniversary was the occasion for an OECD collective volume: E. Sorel and P.C. Padoan (eds.), *The Marshall Plan: Lessons Learned for the 21st Century* (Paris, 2008). An interesting attempt to explore its enduring message is J. Agnew and J. N. Entrikin, *The Marshall Plan Today: Model and Metaphor* (London, 2004). A collection of archive-based histories is found in F. Fauri and P. Tedeschi (eds.), *Novel Outlooks on the Marshall Plan: American Aid and European Re-industrialization* (New York, 2011).

4

The Management of Markets: Business, Governments and Cartels in Post-war Europe[1]

For much of the post-war period, the operation of the free market was seen as too capricious and too unpredictable to be allowed to determine the path and tempo of domestic economic development. The past decade, however, has witnessed a new veneration of the market as the key to growth and prosperity in the world. Free and unencumbered market forces have become the explanation for the boom among the Pacific tigers, the panacea for prosperity among developed countries, the textbook for restructuring former socialist republics and the last hope for the debt-encumbered nations of the Third World. The task of governments is to create conditions for vigorous market competition and to roll back previously imposed impediments and restrictions on factors of production. Unshackled domestic competition and the search for international competitive advantage guarantee the emergence of the robust and dynamic firms of the future. The 'globalisation' of the world economy is a symbol of their success and the 'complex interdependence' and 'globalisation' that accompany their activities transcend attempts at domestic interference.

In this vision, not surprisingly, there is little room for mollycoddled domestic monopolies (natural or contrived). These are credited with dulling the search for innovation and the ability to seize international opportunities. Michael Porter, in his influential study *The Competitive Advantage of Nations*, argues that:

> *It is hard to find examples of true competitive advantage in industries where there are cartels. [...] Cartels dampen or suspend the self-reinforcing process of upgrading that grows out of domestic rivalry. A cartel may maintain profits for a time, but usually it marks the beginning of the end of international success.*[2]

One would not therefore expect cartels to be accompanied by economic growth. This seems to be confirmed by the 1930s, which are generally associated with the high point of cartel activity, and which coincided in Europe with slow rates of economic growth and an even slower expansion in trade. The decade was also characterised by government intervention which, if not actively promoting cartel formation, was at least neutral towards it. The 1950s, by contrast, have been identified with high rates of economic growth and even greater rates of trade expansion. The history of this period has recently been rewritten in terms of the success in removing government-imposed barriers on intra-European trade and payments through the European Payments Union (1950-1958), the OEEC's 'trade liberalisation scheme' for eliminating quotas (1949-1958) and the final elimination of tariffs through the EEC and EFTA (1959-1965).[3] It has also been seen as a period of increasing national legislation to prosecute cartels.

Corwin D. Edwards was one of America's leading cartel experts during the 1930s and the war, and a major participant in the dissolution of German and Japanese cartels and conglomerates by the Occupation Authorities. He wrote three major studies of European cartels in the 1960s. In the last of these, he offers his most extensive interpretation of what happened to cartels after 1945. Insofar as authors consider cartels at all, this has also become the mainstream account. International cartels, he argues, had been 'destroyed or crippled' by the war itself: by members finding themselves on different sides of the conflict, by the disruption of trade and communications and by the seizure of enemy assets. Domestic cartels had seen their functions supplanted by wartime government controls. Once the war had ended, in Germany and Japan the occupation authorities ensured that the reincarnation of cartels was made impossible. Elsewhere, the major firms were preoccupied with problems of reconstruction while national governments continued to control their economies in ways that left little room, or role, for private restrictions. When these controls were relaxed, rather than face renewed competition, firms began to look anew at cartel solutions. At this point, Edwards argues, without determined government action to contain them, the initiatives of these cartels would in all likelihood have been successful. This did not occur, however, because governments had become more aware of the pernicious effects of cartels on their own policies of reducing inflation, freeing trade and increasing productivity. They resolved to take measures to curb cartels and their resolve was strengthened by the official advocacy of, and cultural borrowing from, the United States. Although initially American influence might have been decisive, by the close of the 1950s the movement against cartels had been absorbed into the consensus and had been reflected in ever-strengthened legislation.[4]

Edwards' analysis creates two impressions: firstly, that the post-war years witnessed a continuous and ever-growing determination among governments to oppose cartel practices through legislation and, secondly, that this legislation was actually effective in repressing the re-emergence of the cartel phenomenon. This impression of a determined joint European and American effort to counter cartels has recently been reinforced for the United Kingdom by two separate, archive-based studies. Tony Freyer links initial wartime ideas for cartel control directly to the 1948 Monopolies and Restrictive Practices Act and the 1956 Restrictive Trade Practices Act. He asserts that 'throughout the post-war era' there was a convergence of US and UK anti-trust legislation, and that 'generally, British and American officials consistently condemned cartels'. In particular he describes the 1948 Monopolies Act as part of a 'firm anti-cartel policy'.[5] Leslie Hannah suggests a similar continuity, which he attributes to the 'remarkable' agreement on the need for competition among economists who represented on various committees preparing national British legislation, as on their continuous advocacy of anti-cartel measures against the opposition of industrialists.[6]

There is some disagreement about when and to what extent cartels re-emerged. Sydney Dell, for instance, suggests that the effect of the EEC's removal of internal tariffs upon established national monopolies led to a surge of collaborative and cartelistic producer agreements.[7] Dennis Swann implicitly shares this view when he argues that, in those instances where restrictive agreements did not already exist, 'as tariff barriers went down businessmen might resort to various practices in order to offset the effects of the removal of protection'.[8] Susan Strange, on the other hand, in her influential work *States and Markets*, argues that cartels were 'interrupted by the war and restrained by US anti-trust proceedings' in the 1950s and 1960s, and only 'began again to multiply' in the 1970s, in response to the dislocations following the oil crisis.[9] This article will argue that all these views are misleading. There is no straightforward connection between the early, faltering measures 'against' cartels and the stronger measures that emerged in the mid- to late 1950s. Much of the early European legislation was not in compliance with American pressure but often a deliberate attempt to evade demands for stronger action. Moreover, in those cases that national governments did assume powers, they were employed only with great circumspection if, and when, the existence of cartels was uncovered. The American anti-cartel crusade in Europe was not crowned with success, but became mired in obstruction and equivocation. Cartels did not disappear after the war but became part of the political economy of reconstruction. They often operated not with the disapproval of national governments determined on their extinction, but with their knowledge and, occasionally, support.

We will explore the course of American efforts to thwart the re-emergence of cartels. In particular, we will examine the anti-cartel drive, launched in 1949, that has been virtually ignored in the literature. This produced a policy aimed primarily at legislative reform, and then at employing the legislation vigorously to hunt down and outlaw cartels. We will then follow the fate of American efforts to deal with cartels within a multilateral framework. Various options were tried, including the International Trade Organisation (ITO), the Council of Europe and the General Agreement on Tariffs and Trade (GATT). The only real success in securing appropriate legislation was the Treaty of Paris' establishment of the European Coal and Steel Community (ECSC). Even then, when it came to employing that legislation to dissolve the German coal sales cartel (the major national cartel in the ECSC and the one which had prompted the French to suggest the ECSC in the first place), action was sorely absent.

The American pressure met with even less success in the national arena, where the desired legislation was slow to emerge and usually fell far short of the (American) ideal. The article will examine two national case studies. The first is the Federal Republic of Germany, where the American occupation authorities, for a short time, had a free hand to dismantle cartels. However, once a national German government had been elected, the USA found its leverage insufficient to secure a domestic national effort against cartels. As a second case study, the article examines the United Kingdom and disproves the assertions that have accompanied the recent historiography that the British and Americans had followed one line on cartels, and that Parliament was early in accepting hard anti-cartel legislation. It will also use the archives to follow through the case of the international heavy electrical machinery cartel. The cartel was exposed, and condemned, by the Monopolies Commission, and was condemned by the officials of the Board of Trade, who were responsible for implementing policy, yet was effectively reprieved by the cabinet.

We will conclude by offering an alternative scenario to that provided by Edwards and others for the role of cartels in post-war reconstruction and we will suggest that far from disappearing, cartels emerged to become a widespread and powerful feature of European recovery.

AMERICAN POLICY TOWARDS CARTELS

After an early flirtation with cartels, the New Deal had moved towards a more antagonistic stance. When America had entered into World War II, attention turned to international cartels, especially those involving Germany. In a political philosophy that linked economic liberalism with democracy, it was simple to associate cartels with undemocratic forces and fascism. From there, it was only a small step to identify the international activities of such cartels with an extension of aggression by economic means. And when such cartels embraced American firms, it became easy (with the help of a little back-projection) to see their activities as acts of undeclared war against the United States. President Roosevelt captured these sentiments in 1944, when he warned that:

> *Cartels were utilized by the Nazis as governmental instrumentalities to achieve political ends. The history of the use of the I.G. Farben trust by the Nazis reads like a detective story. Defeat of the Nazi armies will have to be followed by the eradication of these weapons of economic warfare. But more than the elimination of the political activities of German cartels will be required. Cartel practices which restrict the free flow of goods in foreign commerce will have to be curbed.*[10]

After it became obvious that it would prove difficult to graft anti-cartel measures onto the draft charter for the ITO (see below), attention turned towards using Marshall Aid as a leverage to getting appropriate national legislation. Fundamental to the philosophy behind the ERP was the need to encourage economic growth by means of improved productivity; more output per unit of input. This extra output would allow higher rewards for both capital and labour. Improved real wages would, in turn, purchase the loyalty of the working classes for democratic capitalism and insulate them from the twin temptations of fascism and communism.[11] This was inconsistent with the re-emergence of cartels aimed at restricting output in order to artificially boost profits. In the words of Paul Hoffman, the head of the ECA,

> *the ECA is concerned with restrictive business practices because we are convinced that the wide prevalence of such practices in Europe is a major obstacle to lower unit costs, increased productivity, rising standard of living, and to increasingly effective competition of Western Europe in international trade. We must therefore regard these practices as barriers to the attainment of ERP objectives.*[12]

There were more reasons for the ECA's objections to cartels. To begin with, it was feared that if Europeans participated in cartels that included US firms, the marketing arrangements might slacken the European sales efforts in America, and therefore worsen, or at least preserve, the dollar gap.[13] Furthermore, if the

ECA believed their own rhetoric linking cartels to Nazism, they had to face the painful truth that German heavy industry was gravitating towards cartels just at the time that the country was on the verge of regaining its sovereignty, and that no permanent anti-trust measures were yet in place.[14]

These arguments had, by 1949, been supplemented by security concerns. After the first Soviet atomic test, the Truman administration had already decided to demand a higher European defence. It was worried that this would jeopardise the welfare gains already achieved, and this danger would be greater if cartels were allowed to restrict output and increase costs. Moreover, the ECA feared that Communist propaganda against the Marshall Plan would seize on a passive attitude towards cartels as evidence that higher labour productivity meant higher (monopoly) producer profits rather than higher wages.[15] A final argument against cartels was more prosaic. The ECA perceived that US taxpayers would quickly become intolerant of seeing their dollars wasted on inefficient production methods or siphoned off into the pockets of European cartel bosses.[16]

Hoffman had not mentioned the cartel issue directly in his speech to the OEEC Council calling for European 'integration' in 1949, although he had pointed to the necessity of improving competitiveness and productivity. Two months earlier, however, he had berated his staff for being 'too diffident' towards cartels and had demanded a more aggressive stance towards them.[17] Already when the speech was made, ECA officials had prepared a draft programme on restrictive practices. It argued that only 'a revolution in European economic philosophy' would resolve the cartel problem and that this required 'the reformation of economic institutions along competitive instead of restrictive lines'. Without infringing European sovereignty, the ECA's task was to awaken member states to the dangers of cartels and galvanise them into taking action.[18] One month after his integration speech, Hoffman publicised the tougher approach in another speech at Columbia University in New York:

> *Restrictions on trade among the European nations have therefore resulted not only in the elimination of competition between countries in such basic industries as steel, coal, and chemicals, but in the softening of competition within those countries. Furthermore, competition for these industries in the export field has all but been eradicated by the formation of international cartels. [...] In the absence of anti-trust laws, internal competition has been almost non-existent. In the absence of such laws, business managements quite understandably have gotten together, fixed prices, and divided markets.*[19]

In May 1950, Hoffman translated these sentiments into an instruction to all the ECA missions in Europe (A-252). He stressed that the ECA effort was concerned with any restrictive business practice that interfered with economic recovery. Not content with targeting cartels, action extended to 'restrictive attitudes which frequently govern decisions even in the absence of identifiable restrictive arrangements'. In addition to private arrangements, the attack was to embrace legislative and administrative rules encouraging or condoning restrictive practices. Both nationalised industries and public utilities fell within the scope of investigation. The only exceptions recognised were intergovernmental commodity agreements consistent with the ITO and the GATT.[20]

Once a case had been established, 'corrective action' should follow. This started with informal discussion with high officials. If that failed, the ECA should make formal representation to the government. As a last resort, it could threaten to withhold ECA dollars or counterpart funds and guarantees from the offending firms. Moreover, ECA officials were to increase public awareness on the dangers of cartels. The technical assistance provisions of the ERP were to be employed to encourage changes in business culture and the ECA would also attempt to influence changes in national legislation. However, the instruction warned:

> *In all such efforts care should be taken to avoid a doctrinaire attitude, overindulgence in generalized preaching as to the merits of competition or any implication that the US seeks to impose its own economy or legal system on the participating countries.*[21]

Hoffman's instructions partly reflected the disquiet in Congress over the Marshall Plan. The leader of the campaign was the Connecticut senator, William Benton, who in 1951 had introduced an amendment to the Mutual Security Act (the successor to the original act initiating the ERP). The Benton amendment to section 516(2) committed America to encouraging Western Europe in the development of dynamic, competitive economies. Benton suggested that the act be administered in such a way as to 'discourage cartel and monopolistic business practices prevailing in certain countries receiving aid under this act which result in restricting production or increasing prices'.[22] Benton backed up his initiative with a series of highly public and highly publicised meetings and statements. In Paris, he expressed his disappointment at the lack of evidence of growing competitiveness and competition, and at the absence of constructive employer attitudes towards these aims.[23] In London, he voiced his discouragement at the fact that the British seemed unwilling to take the most simple steps to improve productivity and to impose effective anti-trust laws.[24]

These developments impressed upon the ECA the necessity for more serious efforts. Most internal ECA memoranda suggested that the May 1950 instruction was still adequate to the task in hand. The problem lay not in the tactics but in their implementation. Indeed, several mission chiefs had indicated earlier that they were not actively pursuing the programme because they deemed other matters more important.[25] At the end of 1951, the ECA's General Council began a review of the successes of its anti-cartel policy. It was sad reading: the advancement of a contract to an 'outsider' of an international diamond cartel, cooperation with the German occupation authorities in obtaining the dissolution of a Franco-German abrasives cartel and, possibly, the prevention of one or two cartels from coming into existence. The ECA had never used its powers of withholding counterpart funds because of restrictive practices, nor had it ever even threatened to do so. For the rest, therefore, the most it could boast was the success of its educational activities.[26]

AMERICAN EFFORTS TO OBTAIN INTERNATIONAL ACTION AGAINST CARTELS

The American attempt to secure an international understanding on cartels spanned almost a decade and, by the time it had been abandoned, had stretched over several international fora.

The first attempt to obtain an international policy towards cartels was in the context of a joint USA-UK document, *Proposals for Consideration by an International Conference on Trade and Employment* (1945).[27] The Americans intended these negotiations to result in an outright prohibition of all cartels; a policy to be supervised and enforced by the new international body. However, at preliminary talks held in London in October-November 1946, it became clear that they would have to be satisfied with much less. The opposition was led by the representatives of the Benelux countries, who waxed eloquently on the beneficial effects of business collaboration over competition. They argued, successfully, that the mere existence of a cartel should not be the point at issue, but rather whether its activities had negative implications for the world economy. Once it had been decided to define the issue in terms of abuse, further complications arose. If cartels were abusive because of the way they manipulated their monopolistic status, it was logical that monopolies themselves should also be investigated. And if monopolies were included, it followed that the prosecution should also embrace nationalised industries and other public monopolies. This second assumption, however, would limit the freedom of governments to organise their domestic economies as they wished and therefore provoked instant opposition.

The practical problems went further still. If the criteria for prosecution were to be abuse of market power, who should make the complaint? If it were governments, and if they colluded with the cartel, there was a distinct possibility they might not do so. Yet if private enterprise were given this right, there would be no filter to sift out frivolous complaints, and the investigative arm risked being swamped. Once the complaint had been made, who should investigate and judge it, and who should supervise the implementation of a decision? Leaving these tasks to an international organisation might appear the best guarantee of impartiality, but it was equally a recipe for a huge and unwieldy bureaucracy.[28]

Long before the negotiations had been concluded and international action was deemed impossible, the Americans had tried to get a commitment by governments to adopt stronger national legislation. However, instead of an obligation to enact legislation forbidding and preventing cartel abuse, member states only agreed to undertake 'all possible steps' to do so, and only then in accordance with their own legal system and economic organisation.[29] In the end, even this restricted clause represented a pyrrhic victory. In December 1950, the Truman administration acknowledged that it would never get the International Trade Organisation (ITO), agreed in Havana in 1948, through Congress. Although Congressional opposition was not principally directed against cartels, the agreements on this point still perished with the rest. The only part salvaged was the provisional General Agreement on Tariffs and Trade (GATT) which, until 1995, remained the main multilateral framework for world trade discussions.

As it became clear in 1949 that Congress might not endorse the ITO, the Council of Europe suggested preparing a European cartel convention. The British government tried to divert the issue to the GATT, but failed. However, since the draft convention which eventually appeared in 1951 went still further than the obligations accepted within the ITO, they found little difficulty in removing the discussion from the agenda of the Council of Ministers. Meanwhile, in an attempt to make good the failure of the ITO, the US government proposed that the Economic and Social Committee (Ecosoc) of the UN should itself prepare a cartel convention. Again, the UK government tried to bounce the discussions into the GATT. When that again failed, it limited Ecosoc's role to that of an *ad hoc* investigative committee. The existence of this committee was, in turn, employed to keep the question out of the preserve of the OEEC, when the issue was raised there. Thus began a series of procedural manoeuvres that kept the matter off the international agenda until the Americans themselves finally acknowledged defeat. In 1955 they informed the secretary-general of the United Nations that they opposed an international agreement because 'wide differences between national policies, practices and legislation made it improbable that an international body could reach agreement on recommendations or that they would be implemented if it did'.[30] This withdrawal was not simply the result of European opposition. For all its advocacy of stricter legislation, the American government had stumbled on insurmountable resistance at home. As had been the case with the ITO, the government was forced to withdraw cartels from the international arena, because Congress opposed surrendering its powers in order to give wider trade competencies to the GATT, or to any other international organisation.

The singular exception to the catalogue of failure in the international arena was the introduction of anti-cartel measures into the Treaty of Paris, signed in 1951, establishing the European Coal and Steel Community (ECSC). Several circumstances converged to place the Americans in a powerful position to influence the outcome of the negotiations. First, the French government wanted to control the potential activities of German cartels, especially at a time when a glut of steel seemed to be threatening. Moreover, there was a possibility that control over coal sales (that rested either directly with the steel mills or that was united in a coal sales cartel, the Deutschen Kohlen Verkauf, or DKV), could be used to privilege German steel producers over foreign customers.[31] Second, Jean Monnet, the head of the French Planning Commissariat, was increasingly concerned about the constraints that French domestic steel cartels were placing on French reconstruction policy. He was therefore willing to accept that anti-cartel measures intended for Germany apply equally to France. Third, American support for the new organisation would be necessary if it were to achieve the waiver it required for obtaining international recognition within GATT.

The original draft of the ECSC Treaty had not dealt specifically with the problems of concentration and cartelisation, but instead contained a clause committing the Community to recognising any obligations that the Allies might impose on Germany. This was resented by the Germans, and in September their chancellor, Konrad Adenauer, had informed Monnet, who was leading the negotiations, that it was intolerable that Germany be placed under a separate set of constraints in a community supposedly based on equality. Monnet had responded by insisting that the ECSC Treaty, therefore, contain anti-cartel and anti-monopoly clauses of its own. These were to emerge as Articles 65 and 66. The French proposals, which would have effectively banned all forms of market agreement and which left the Community as the sole arbiter over any exemptions (and which imposed strict limits of cross-ownership between individual firms), attracted the unqualified support of the State Department, but were deeply resented by the German and Belgian delegations. The Germans, in particular, were concerned that any agreement they might make with the Allies over the reorganisation of the Ruhr might be overturned in the future by the ECSC. Only when it was agreed to recognise existing structures, as long as they did not impinge on the ECSC's goals, was the logjam over Articles 65 and 66 broken and was the way opened to signing the treaty.[32]

Article 65 prohibited all undertakings and practices that distorted 'normal competition' in prices, sales and market sharing, and empowered the independent High Authority to recognise any exemptions, and refer any breaches in legislation to the ECSC's Court. To the extent that it represented the first 'European' anti-trust legislation, it was a noticeable triumph for an American policy that aimed at a 'reformation of economic institutions'. Whether institutional reform was sufficient to tackle the cartel question was a completely different matter.

Surveying the ECSC's record in 1958, William Diebold, an authoritative early chronicler of its history concluded:

> *Decisions on minor cartels remained minor in their import; the major question of collusive pricing in steel was shunted aside; the scrap cartel was internationalized, legitimized, and on the whole strengthened. [...] [T]he steel export cartel was allowed to function relatively freely.*[33]

A major factor behind the slow progress on cartels was an oversensitivity of the new, supranational High Authority (HA) to the need to keep the goodwill of industrialists, upon whom the success of the Community depended. At a more practical level lay the need to take a decision on the future of the German coal sales cartel that, in 1952, had been subsumed into the Gemeinschaftsorganisation Ruhrkohle (GEORG). GEORG itself was the outcome of the Allies' attempt to force Law 27 on the coal industry in 1950-1951 to prepare it for entry into the ECSC. The Americans and the French had wanted the DKV dismembered into six separate companies, operating under a strictly supervisory central office. After endless German stalling on an agreement, in May 1952 the Allies acted unilaterally and published a new dissolution decree. However, although seeming to comply with the decree, the Germans promptly endowed GEORG with many more powers and responsibilities than the Allies had intended. There was no doubt that GEORG was a sales cartel, acting on behalf of six regional syndicates. It fixed the price of

German coal in times of slack demand distributing orders, and operated a price equalisation scheme among its members. In controlling Ruhr coal, it effectively controlled half the ECSC's coal output. If Article 65 were to mean anything, it had to appear to work first and foremost in this case.

In autumn 1953 the HA had decided to tackle the issue of collusion in the coal market, but without specifying concrete measures its commitment to the task was in doubt. Monnet was convinced that it was better to attempt to limit the power of cartels than to try to remove them altogether, and he was supported in this position by both the French and German members of the HA. He was also afraid that too rapid action against GEORG might prejudice German ratification of the European Defence Community Treaty. By contrast, the Benelux members wanted immediate action and pushed the HA into refusing to recognise the continuation of GEORG as then constituted. This position was immediately undermined by leaving the timetable for reform with the coal industry; it was asked to make proposals, and only then would the HA decide on how and when they were to take effect.[34] Naturally, the Germans were slow in making detailed proposals for the reform in GEORG and even counterattacked by arguing that the ECSC had no business interfering with the daily running of the industry. Moreover, the industry's position was increasingly backed by the government, thereby raising the stakes in the struggle. To avoid a damaging confrontation, the HA in February 1955 produced a compromise solution whereby the six regional organisations were to become more independent of GEORG in certain areas (common pricing, joint selling within the Community, and the pooling of proceeds would cease) but could cooperate in others. The US ambassador to the ECSC reluctantly accepted that this represented the limit of what was attainable at the time. He also observed ruefully that within the HA 'there is no general support for a competitive economy and even less for competition in the coal industry'.[35]

Instead of accepting this reform outright, GEORG only agreed that the proposals should serve as a basis for discussion. It tried to resist the break-up of the cartel into six separate companies and suggested, instead, first two and later three. It also attempted to ensure the continuation of joint sales of larger orders (which it wanted defined as over 20,000 tons, as opposed to the floor of 50,000 preferred by the HA). A new compromise now emerged, whereby the idea of three sales organisations was accepted in return for HA monitoring of joint sales within the Community, and in February 1956 a provisional agreement, for three years, along these lines was reached. Almost immediately, however, it became apparent that the newly independent companies were continuing many of the previous practices of restricting outlets and fixing prices.[36]

As the coal market was deteriorating under the pressure of cheaper petroleum, the HA had been reluctant to enforce greater competition upon the industry. If it had thereby colluded in cartel practices, the Ruhr industry had paid scant regard to even the minimum formalities of HA 'control' over the measures it had adopted. Under these circumstances, the HA in December 1958 decided to recommend the complete abolition of the three sales agencies and the joint agency within eighteen months to two years. These recommendations again fell foul of the German government and they suffered a further setback when they were nullified by the Court for being insufficiently motivated. As Dirk Spierenburg, the Dutch member of the HA in the forefront of the anti-cartel lobby, described this experience recently:

> *The events of 10 years had shown that the industry in the Ruhr had always been able to maintain a monolithic, centralized sales organization, despite the efforts first of the allied authorities and later of the High Authority to introduce reforms. For the time being, German interests had little, if anything, to fear from the High Authority.*[37]

AMERICAN EFFORTS TO OBTAIN NATIONAL ACTION AGAINST CARTELS

There were indeed practical difficulties to implementing multilateral action against cartels. However, such arguments disguised a deeper reluctance to accept surveillance over private business agreements. It is no surprise, therefore, that when American policy turned its attention to action in the national arena, it was equally unsuccessful. We will start this analysis by looking briefly at the efforts to introduce anti-cartel legislation into the two major European powers that were involved in almost all of the major international cartels: Germany and the United Kingdom. The harvest for the ECA was not great, and the immediate record became more damaging still when it came to using this legislation in actually eliminating cartel practices. For reasons of brevity, it is only possible to document the fate of one cartel, and we have chosen the heavy electrical industry because it operated in a sector vital for reconstruction.

In Germany, the American military government started a programme to eliminate cartels, initially in their own economic zone and later, with the UK, in the Bizone. Early in 1947, the two military governments enacted Law 56, which banned all concentrations, cartels and other agreements fostering monopoly or restraining domestic or international trade.[38] Between 1947 and the end of 1948, it was invoked to end over one thousand cartel and restrictive trade practice arrangements. Thereafter, the pace of achievement slowed considerably.[39] With hindsight, most experts agree that it was doomed to become a failure because it embodied potentially conflicting policy aims. Firstly, it reflected the Americans' insistence on deconcentrating and decartelising basic industries, a policy consistent with the undertaking in the Potsdam Agreement to curb Germany's economic potential. As occupation costs soared, and as the Cold War loomed larger, pressure mounted to get German industry back on its feet. Secondly, the American authors of Law 56 expected the prohibition of cartel practices to provide the foundations for a strong and above all *democratic* German economy. As part of this policy, the Germans were entrusted with carrying out sweeping decartelisation measures through *Länder* decartelisation offices. However, in many cases they refused to work as 'Allied accomplices'.[40]

Even after the creation of the Federal Republic in September 1949, the occupation authorities kept reserve powers over decartelisation under Paragraph 2 of the Occupation Statute. The three Western Allies now managed a tripartite Decartelisation and Industrial Deconcentration Group (DIDEG). Between its creation and 1951, DIDEG filed four criminal charges under Law 56, the most spectacular of which concerned the Franco-German abrasives cartel.[41] The prosecution of the abrasives producers, whose product was essential in finishing steels, was ironic. It soon transpired that the cartel owed its existence to a suggestion of the French government, fearful of the industry losing ground once the quotas protecting it had been removed.[42]

Meanwhile, the German government started drafting a trade practices law that, with Allied approval, would supersede the operation of the Occupation Statute. Thus the German government began a hard and prolonged cartel battle that would last more than seven years. The 1951 draft cartelisation law satisfied none of the Allies. The Americans were particularly critical. The general prohibition of trade restraint was too narrow, since it only declared void contracts limiting competition throughout a business sector, almost suggesting that partial agreements were permitted. Moreover, this general prohibition referred only to 'contracts and resolutions', thus hinting that informal, unwritten agreements might be excluded. In addition, the legislation allowed a Federal Cartel Authority (*Bundeskartellamt*), acting under supervision of the Ministry of Economic Affairs, to sanction cartels otherwise considered illegal if these increased the capacity and efficiency of the participating enterprises, or those that protected or promoted trade. In the eyes of the ECA it was not very difficult for 'participants in almost every agreement or conspiracy' to claim that 'the purpose and effect of their conduct is to increase production, to lessen the 'evils of unfair competition', to discourage waste from 'ruinous' competition, and to make business more efficient.'[43] The main task of the Bundeskartellamt, they thought, lay in granting exemptions rather than in enforcing compliance with the law. Nonetheless, the ECA accepted that the whole purpose of the German cartel law, flawed as it was, was 'to preserve competition, even though [...] we recognize that we may have to pay for the preservation of such freedom'.[44] Thus they refrained from demanding too many strict prohibitions, and hoped that the public opinion, informed by public hearings and the publication of official records, might demand more stringent action.[45]

If this compliant attitude was intended to pave the way for a speedy passage of the draft law into official legislation, the Allies were to be deeply disappointed. The draft law initiated a passionate and endless parliamentary debate between those who wanted only cartels that abused their powers to be prohibited and a much smaller and diffuse group of neo-liberals and socialists who favoured an outright prohibition. Initially the former group was in ascendancy and throughout 1953 and 1954 they introduced countless amendments weakening further the already unsatisfactory draft legislation. Its efforts were strongly supported by the German Federation of Industry (BDI) which, in bilateral talks with the government, succeeded in diluting the proposals even more. Dissatisfied with the role of the BDI within the cartel debate, the neo-liberals tabled their own draft bill to Parliament, but this failed to carry the day.[46] It was not until 1957 that the Act Against Restraint of Competition was approved, becoming operative on 1 January 1958.

American efforts to secure effective British legislation began even before the war had ended. They placed the issue on the agenda through Article VII of Agreement of Principles Applying Mutual Aid, signed in February 1942, which required 'the elimination of all forms of discriminatory treatment in international trade, and to the reduction of tariffs and other trade barriers'. This had not initially been intended as an attack on cartels, but in autumn 1943 American negotiators insisted that cartels be included in the discussions.[47] Joint action on international cartels was now seen as an 'indispensable corollary' to action on commercial and commodity policy. Alongside this, US officials demanded cooperation between the two countries in a campaign of 'international trust busting' starting with their own nationals and imposed on Germany by peace treaty. It is fair to say that their British counterparts were completely unprepared. This did not, however, prevent them from reciting what would become the usual litany at such occasions: agreements could promote efficiency, undiscriminating instruments could strike at good and bad alike, blanket prohibitions would be difficult to enforce etc. Nonetheless, it was difficult, having pledged to eliminate trade restrictions, to refuse to examine ways of removing private agreements designed to thwart that goal.[48]

Independently, the Board of Trade had started to examine possible directions for future legislation. Its efforts culminated in an important report that condemned all concentrations of power, whether through ownership or combination. It argued that the wartime experience had equipped the government as never before to adopt a more active role in monitoring the emergence of private cartels and controlling their practices. The report advocated the reform of any legal provisions that favoured the emergence of monopolies, the prohibition of certain 'objectionable practices' and the institution of a permanent commission of inquiry directly responsible to the government.[49] This set of recommendations was clearly in line with the official American position at the time. Yet five years were to pass before the Monopolies Act reached the statute books. It outlawed nothing and instead instituted a (very small) commission to investigate cases referred to it by government on the criterion of 'abuse of public interest', that was itself left undefined. Something had clearly gone wrong.

The most obvious problem facing the government was the existence of a well-orchestrated campaign in favour of cartels as an antidote to powerful destructive forces of unfettered competition. These ideas found a broad response among both employers' associations and trade unions.[50] Disinclined to challenge such sentiments, the government shied away from radical solutions. Even before forwarding recommendations to ministers, Hugh Dalton had withdrawn from any legislative assault against either cartels or specific cartel practices. Instead, the Board of Trade would be given responsibility for referring any cases of possible abuse of the public interest by private industry (i.e. excluding commodities, nationalised industries and services) to a commission of inquiry. On the basis of the outcomes, the Board could recommend appropriate action. These provisions were close to those eventually adopted. Even then, the government was in no hurry to proceed. In spring 1945, ostensibly because of pressure on parliamentary time, the cabinet decided to postpone the presentation of new legislation. Given the fact that national reconstruction necessitated the continuation of some restrictive practices, the president of the Board of Trade 'did not wish to launch a general attack on them or to go too far in seeking power to deal with them'.[51] Thus, it was not until April 1948 that Parliament finally approved the Monopoly (Inquiry Control) Bill, drafted along much the same lines as those agreed in early 1944, and just in time to meet American demands for tougher trust-busting action.

The Americans, though, were not impressed by these activities. In 1949, an initial ECA study concluded that about 1,100 trade associations were involved in marketing arrangements. It identified 78 important products for which prices were rigged, almost always based on the performance of the least efficient producer.[52] Incidentally, Board of Trade officials contested this figure and asserted that they had proof that about half that figure would be more accurate.[53] Nonetheless, the ECA further lambasted the complacency of the British authorities. The Monopolies Commission had started inquiries into building trades, cement and textile machinery, but had taken no action against any of the industries involved. Indeed, it seemed as though the government never intended the Commission to do any serious work. It consisted of twelve people, none of whom had any previous experience with private restrictive practices. Several more knowledgeable candidates had been considered unsafe. The official in the Board of Trade supervising the work had made his career in travel promotion. At that moment the Commission was investigating six cases chosen by the cabinet, cases the ECA considered to be possibly the most innocuous to be found. Those cases alone would take two years to investigate and, until they were completed, it would not look into any others. It did not take much to calculate that, accepting the lower Board of Trade estimate of the number of cartels, it would still take over a century to investigate the lot. Moreover, it appeared as though the Commission was aiming at an amicable settlement, leaving industry to do its own house cleaning.[54]

An exceptionally well-documented cartel was the International Electrical Association (IEA), re-established immediately after the war in London on 5 June 1945. Its operations embraced the entire range of electrical generating machinery (turbines, generators, condensers, switch gear, transformers, rectifiers, rolling mill equipment) and its membership eventually expanded to include the major producers in the UK, Germany, Switzerland, Sweden, France, Italy, Austria, Belgium and Finland. For each type of product, the cartel allocated quotas on global orders to its members. It decided which member should make the winning bid for major orders, and arranged for two other members to make losing bids (the compensation for their efforts being paid by the winner). There were also arrangements for equalising 'profits' among the members, in order to allow for bids to be adjusted to local conditions. Although not all provisions were in operation all of the time, it proved an extremely durable set of arrangements, and it certainly persisted until deep into the 1970s.[55]

Partly in response to complaints from Commonwealth purchasers, the heavy electrical industry was referred to the British Monopolies Commission in 1952.

The report, completed four and a half years later, documented (and condemned as being against public interest) both the prevalence of domestic price fixing, through the British Electrical and Allied Machinery Association (BEAMA) and the involvement of BEAMA in practices of rigged, non-competitive tenders and compensation payments abroad. It was eventually published in February 1957. It is an illuminating case, partly because the cartel was so pervasive in such a strategic industrial sector, and partly because the release of government archives allows us to document how the government backed down in the face of interest group pressure.

The first efforts of BEAMA were directed towards suppressing parts of the report, especially those revealing 'confidential' information about foreign partners or revealing pricing rules that might be beneficial to competitors and embarrassing to the industry.[56] This endeavour failed since the government could hardly cut references to the operation of restrictive agreements when it had been included in the terms of reference. Even less could this be the case since the Commission recommended that they be terminated. Moreover, the government only had power to delete parts of the report's text, and not to make the alterations necessary to hide the fact that it had done so.[57] Once the report had been published, the chairman of BEAMA, Lord Chandos, engaged in an intensive lobbying campaign directed towards getting the president of the Board of Trade, David Eccles, to reject the Monopoly Commission's recommendations. Over one of many dinners, Chandos argued that UK practice of using higher (cartelised) domestic prices to subsidise bids for overseas orders was common practice in both the USA and Germany (and throughout the newly created EEC), and he justified membership of the IEA on the grounds that otherwise the industry would be frozen out of all orders.[58]

These arguments found little response among Board of Trade officials. The domestic cartels, they argued, weakened the incentive to reduce costs, created rigidity in cost structures and the distribution of the market, and were unpopular among overseas buyers. Membership of the IEA was condemned for penalising overseas buyers and for being inconsistent with international agreements. Moreover, it was likely to bring forward the day when markets were captured by American and Japanese outsiders. It also rejected the suggestion that higher (cartelised) foreign prices would do much to finance extra capital by observing that the industry's profits were growing fastest in the (competitive) consumer goods market.[59] Lord Chandos, in meetings with, and letters to, Eccles, reiterated BEAMA's earlier position and then began to offer a deal whereby he would keep the Board informed of all overseas deals and in turn the Board was free to take action whenever it wanted.[60] More meetings followed until at last Eccles demanded that his officials prepare a new draft submission to the cabinet. The criterion from which they should work was 'Which course would earn us more foreign exchange?' Their conclusion, he instructed, was to ignore the Commission's recommendations since 'it would damage British competitive force and export earnings'.[61] This advice Eccles then submitted to the cabinet. At their meeting in September 1956, they endorsed this approach and agreed to make no statement on the participation in foreign cartels whilst referring the domestic arrangements to the newly created Restrictive Practices Court.[62]

ATTEMPTS AT AN ALTERNATIVE HISTORICAL SCENARIO

This article has presented evidence that the American efforts to obtain and enforce anti-cartel legislation in Europe in the first post-war decade were almost entirely unsuccessful. Their efforts were blocked in international negotiations and met with evasion and delay in the national arena. Moreover, the enforcement of the legislation was lackadaisical and weak. This evidence could be repeated for other countries and for other industrial sectors. All of this suggests that European governments had a different analysis of the position of cartels in political economy from that propagated by the United States, and a different attitude from that explored at the start of this article (see above).

Generally, in the 1930s, European governments had not been opposed to cartels. As the early New Deal had been, they were sympathetic to the argument that cartels maintained profits and therefore helped stem the rash of business collapses that had characterised the early years of the Depression. This motivation was reinforced by the introduction of higher tariffs and quotas on national frontiers in an effort to prevent foreign deflationary forces undermining domestic prices, eroding the balance of payments and destroying employment. These controls were intended to keep the home market for home producers, and the effects would obviously be lost if murderous domestic competition were simply replaced by murderous foreign competition. Moreover, where quotas served to create artificial shortages, national trade and producer associations served a useful allocative function. Policy in Europe ranged from neutrality to outright support of cartels, and, under such conditions, the phenomenon flourished.

The factors encouraging a sympathetic attitude towards cartels were reinforced by the exigencies of wartime planning and post-war reconstruction. Firstly, the war effort had centred around national industrial boards that had encouraged the standardisation of products and the diffusion of best techniques. This, together with the later sharing of captured German patents, eroded one of the props of domestic competitive advantage and, therefore, inhibited governments in making subsequent demands for more competition. Secondly, post-war reconstruction elevated government priorities from the *sectoral* protection of the 1930s to *national* reconstruction, whose benefits were for the nation as a whole and not any individual firms within it. Moreover, with domestic priorities directed towards maximising output, for economic and political ends, governments had little time for American concerns of maximising productivity. If marginal firms needed the protection of restrictive arrangements allowing them to add to the national cake, it was a small price to pay. Thirdly, the universal situation of shortages and trade deficits intensified the use of quantitative frontier controls, and therefore the need for means of domestic allocation. This task was often left to national trade associations which, in effect, became the executors of government policies. In addition, when these frontier controls were dismantled from 1949 onwards, there was little official inclination to have the 'gains' of reconstruction wiped out by foreign competition, and so these trade associations were expected, and encouraged, to take care of matters for themselves.

The Americans also made life difficult for themselves by employing arguments that were insensitive to the dominant ideology in different countries and that demonstrated little nuance in the face of the complexities of different coalition governments. Moreover, they failed utterly to unload the ideological baggage from the productivity drive. As one historian recently commented, 'Of all the handicaps which encumbered technical assistance in France, the most crippling was its subordination to Cold War politics.'[63] The danger of American concern over cartels developing into self-justified crusade was pointed out by one ECA official who observed that

> *cartel activities are not unlawful in Europe and cartel members are not criminals. This might change in the future but it is the situation today and we should always keep it in mind. Cartels are, in many cases, condoned, protected and fostered by national governments. Broadly speaking, they are the product of circumstances, or necessity, of normal business habits. There is, of course, a large amount of hypocrisy in the pleas of their defenders who represent them as 'children of necessity' or 'means of rationalizing production'. It would, however, be pure wishful thinking to consider the problem as one of simple ethics or economic doctrine.*[64]

Given the fact that cartels were 'condoned, protected and fostered by national governments', one could question the adequacy of the countervailing measures advocated in Instruction A-252 of May 1950. The addition of one, perhaps two, cartel experts to some of the national ECA missions was scarcely sufficient to do more than scratch the surface of the problem, especially, for example, considering the derision poured on the size of the (larger) staffing of the British Monopolies Commission. Furthermore, if cartels, as suspected, were embedded in the European political economy, it was naive to expect that a cautious, step-by-step approach of informal contact leading to official complaint was likely to produce much more than meaningless sympathetic platitudes. Moreover, the ECA was painfully short of sanctions. The most it could do was (threaten to) withhold dollar aid or other forms of support from the offending firm/government. It only ever considered doing so once, and it is worth pausing to tell the tale because it is illustrative of so much that was happening elsewhere.

After an approach to the Austrian government had already failed to produce action against a list of cartels, the ECA threatened to block the allocation of counterpart funds for the 'obsolete' and 'inefficient' Austrian textile industry, whose high profits had derived from 'exorbitant domestic prices [...] maintained by cartel arrangements and protection from foreign competition'.[65] Because, as had been the intention, the Austrian cabinet responded immediately with a draft anti-cartel bill, it withdrew the threat. However, the triumph was illusory. ECA officials were convinced that it was 'motivated more by a desire to convince the ECA mission of its good intentions [...] than by a genuine interest in attacking the cartel problem'. As if that was not enough, the legislation was so riddled with loopholes that officials considered that 'no legislation would be preferable to the proposed measure'.[66]

The ECA had been out-manoeuvred and knew it, but still could do nothing about it. Austria was a front-line state in the Cold War which depended on US aid for its financial stability and the maintenance of the (very low) living standards of its citizens. Withdrawing assistance to an ally would have undermined overall security objectives in the area, so both sides played the game in full knowledge that it was a sham. Similar considerations prevailed elsewhere. America could not afford to employ economic sanctions against its allies at a time when it was demanding a substantial material sacrifice in the interests of mutual defence. Nor, without surrendering a considerable advantage to the opposition, could the ECA wage economic (or propaganda) warfare against elected national governments. A leading ECA official acknowledged that its financial leverage was excessive for the task in hand:

> *This is because of the overriding importance of these countries to the defence effort of the Atlantic community and their present deplorable financial condition, which we do not intend to make worse by withholding our funds. Therefore, we make only weak and infrequent protests against Benton Amendment violations and do nothing to back up these protests.*[67]

We have argued that European governments in the first post-war decade were tolerant of cartels. Against this background, we have suggested, American international diplomacy and pressure on national governments was doomed to failure. To complete our argument, we would need to demonstrate that cartels did indeed constitute a significant phenomenon in the political economy of European reconstruction. Limitations of space and the current stage reached by our research do not allow us to do this fully in this article. Yet it is sufficient to look back to some of the sectors covered by the great international cartels of the interwar years to confirm an impression that there was more continuity than change between the two periods.

Within the chemical industry, international cartels were re-established over both phosphates and potash, which formed the basis for many chemical fertilisers.[68] Until recently it was thought that free competition in nitrogenous fertilisers prevailed until the formation of a cartel based in Zurich in 1962.[69] The ECA, however, was aware that the cartel was reformed in 1949-50, although we do not exclude the possibility that it may have disintegrated later. American sources confirm the reconstitution of the pre-war cartel in artificial fibres (rayon, nylon etc.) involving the 'Big Four' (Belgium, Switzerland, the UK and the USA) in 1949. By the late 1950s its reach had extended to 76 producers in 17 countries.[70] There was also an extensive European cartel operating by 1953 over pharmaceuticals[71] and the American archives suggest the establishment of patent agreements covering plastics production between the British giant ICI and the Belgian company Solvay. Besides these examples there is evidence of a host of other company-to-company agreements, each tied to a single highly-defined product that provided the major route for 'indirect cartelisation' of the industry.[72]

As had been the case in the 1930s, it is the sector of basic semi-manufactured goods that provides the richest hunting ground for post-war cartels. As rubber was a product characterised by violent terms-of-trade fluctuations, it is no surprise that its synthetic competitor, latex rubber, was also cartelised. By 1949 a major international cartel dominating the world market was already in existence. In 1955, the British Monopolies Commission revealed the existence of a parallel cartel covering pneumatic tyres. The Monopolies Commission also exposed the details of the reconstitution of the non-ferrous metals cartel (covering copper and copper alloys but excluding zinc and nickel) at Lausanne in October 1946, and it remained in business until at least 1964. The American records also suggest the creation of an aluminium cartel between Norwegian and American producers in 1949. The iron and steel industry, dominated on the Continent by the ECSC, was plagued by cartel practices such as parallel pricing within the Community. Moreover, in their dealings with third countries, producers operated in accordance with a separate cartel agreement signed just before the ECSC came into operation.[73] British, Dutch and American sources all confirm the reactivation of cartel agreements in the cement industry in 1949 and their formalisation in Paris the following year. The tenacity of the cartel is confirmed by the fact that it was subject of a European Union prosecution in 1994. Another product employed by the building industry, flat glass, was revealed in the Dutch records to have been the subject of a Benelux cartel in 1949, whilst the Danish records suggests that by the mid-1950s the arrangements had been extended to cover much of Europe and had begun a very durable existence. Paper and pulp were also recartelised by the end of the 1940s, according to American sources, and it was only recently broken up by the EEC anti-cartel officials.

With copper production covered by one cartel and heavy electrical equipment (see above) by another, it should come as no surprise that copper cable was also cartelised. The initial agreement signed in Lausanne in 1947 had been extended by 1950 to embrace eleven European countries.[74] At the consumer end of the electrical industry, the large international electric lamp cartel was not revived. In its place arose a 'network of national cartels, maintained by the major firms' reluctance to invade each others' territory'. International competition in radio and television production was held in check, at least until the 1960s, by the expedient of patent pooling.[75]

It cannot be over-emphasised that this list is far from complete. Yet it demonstrates that the international cartels that had operated in the Great Depression quickly reformed in the post-war period and were able to resume their activities without much interference from European governments. These were the same governments that in 1949 had answered Hoffman's call for closer 'integration' in Europe by adopting policies and targets for the elimination of barriers to trade and payments. These developments have, rightly, drawn the attention of historians of reconstruction and integration alike. However, the history they describe can only be a partial one as long as it ignores the parallel existence of widespread private cartel agreements whose purpose was to prevent the 'creation of a single large market' that was to provide the 'substance' for the integration endeavour.

POSTSCRIPT

this contribution was written together with Wendy Asbeek Brusse and was published in U. Olsson, *Business and European Integration since 1800: Regional, National and International Perspectives* (Göteborg, 1997), 162-188. In the history of European integration, the focus of historians on the erection or removal of trade barriers has usually been on governments. This work tried to show the impact of 'private protectionism' in the process. Moreover, it sought to overturn the assumption that just because there was anti-cartel legislation that anything actually happened, or that, if it did, that the legislation was primarily responsible.

Cartel history is not a burning topic in scientific writings on post-war Europe. An excellent review of US policy towards international cartels after the war is provided by Robert Franklin Maddox, *The War within World War II: The United States and International Cartels* (Westport, 2001). The developments in the UK are reviewed in Helen Mercer, *Constructing a Competitive Order: The Hidden History of British Antitrust Policies* (Cambridge, 2009). Finally, a good overview of EU policy is given by Lee Gowan, *The Antitrust Revolution in Europe: Exploring the European Commission's Cartel Policy* (Cheltenham, 2010). We still have stacks of materials and we might well return to the issue ourselves.

5

Europe's First Constitution: The European Political Community, 1952-1954

There is a tendency among non-historians to force 'practitioners' of the discipline to justify why the study of a particular episode of the past is so important and to articulate the lessons to be learned from the experience. The fate of international constitutions and treaties is particularly prone to demands of this kind. After all, 'constitutional borrowing' has long been a common feature of international law and politics. From the American Constitution to the recent attempts to redefine the former republics of the old Soviet empire, the experience of the past has regularly been drafted to resolve the problems of the present. Historians, however, tend to avoid such exercises. They prefer to downplay the importance of 'significant' documents and to emphasise instead the dynamics that made the arrangements work, or not. They choose to eschew the universality of insight and to accentuate the peculiarities of the circumstances in which they were born. Although, by remaining aloof, historians may preserve disciplinary purity, they forfeit thereby the opportunity to shape current debate. Moreover, the past will be used and abused with or without their participation or cooperation. This article, therefore, will address one such constitution from the past. But it does not aspire to preserve its historical integrity; rather to awaken interest in it in the first place. The fact is that Europe's first constitution has played no role in the most recent discussions on the Community's future. Indeed, from almost the moment of its demise, it was virtually expunged from public memory.

The European Political Community (EPC) was the name given to an attempt by European parliamentarians of the six member states of the European Coal and Steel Community (ECSC) to write a democratic constitution that would govern the affairs of the existing communities (i.e. the ECSC and the newly signed European Defence Community (EDC)) and any future communities that might be agreed. It would also regulate the foreign relations of the member states in the areas covered by these communities and would have powers to develop towards a common market. The EPC, therefore, was a vehicle for carrying considerable ambitions. Yet, until recently, it has been relatively neglected by historians of European integration and has usually been lightly skipped over, or ignored altogether, in the memoirs of the 'Founding Fathers'.

The most immediate explanation is that the entire venture ended in abject failure. However, this was equally true of the EDC and yet that episode has been the object of much early and lavish attention by diplomatic and military historians. The cause of this discrepancy may lie in the fact that the EDC's failure in Autumn 1954 was public and awe-inspiring, with the Eisenhower administration threatening to 'reappraise' its commitment to Europe's defence, with French governments teetering on the edge of oblivion over the treaty and with the French Socialist Party torn asunder in the wake of its rejection. By contrast, the puny offspring, the EPC, pined away at the same time when the experts discussing it simply refrained from reconvening after the summer recess. A second source of the discrepancy may lie in the fact that the EDC dealt with seemingly bigger topics: the German question, Western defence, conflicting assessments of the Cold War. Yet, when it died, it died totally. The problems that had brought it into being were quickly resolved in other frameworks. The passing of the EDC left little more than a dark shadow on the immediate past and few echoes into the future. The EPC, on the other hand, left a far greater stamp on subsequent developments, even though that contribution remained largely unacknowledged, and may yet influence the future.

One obvious example was that the creation of a common market among the six was central to the EPC's economic provisions. It also formed the core of the negotiations started at Messina one year later that culminated with the signature of the Treaty of Rome in March 1957. The fact that the issue of a common market cropped up in different forums is, in itself, little more than a reflection of other underlying forces impelling the idea forward. However, the experience acquired by national economic ministries through these earlier discussions allowed an anticipation, if not an appreciation, of the standpoints adopted later and thus facilitated a fast conclusion. A second example, again from the Treaty of Rome, lay in the unique constitutional position afforded to the European Commission in the decision-making structure. Although ultimate powers of decision were left to the Council of Ministers, they could only vote on policy options prepared and submitted by the Commission which thereby acquired substantial powers in the initiation and manipulation of Community developments. These ideas, again, first found their expression in the draft EPC Treaty and marked a distinct departure from those enshrined in the Treaty of Paris establishing the ECSC. To be strictly accurate, this also reflected current thinking elsewhere. Moreover, more far-reaching solutions for democratic control over the Community were utterly ignored, and remain so to the present day.

The imprint of the EPC on the subsequent development of European integration, both in terms of what was learned and what was missed, are justification enough for re-examining its brief existence in this volume. A second reason was that one of the key people involved in drafting the European Political Community Treaty was Emile Noël. Since 1949 he had been secretary of the General Affairs Committee of the Council of Europe. Because of the organic link that the parliamentarians had hoped to create between the Council and the ECSC, he was asked to act as secretary for the Constitutional Committee of the *ad hoc* Assembly charged with drafting the EPC Treaty. Emile Noël's involvement in the European movement was typical of many of his generation, albeit that few were to become involved for so long and at such a high level. He had completed his studies in physics and mathematics at the École Normale Supérieure in Paris in 1941 and had determined to continue academic work. That, however, was before the Nazis decided to round up the 'class of '22' for compulsory labour service in Germany. Given the alternatives, Noël opted to go underground for some months before returning to Paris as a member of the resistance. The war over, it had been difficult to settle into the previous academic routine and so he was grateful when a friend from resistance days, Georges Rebattet, who had become deputy secretary-general for the European Movement branch in Paris, offered him a job in the organisation. At the time the leader of the French Socialist Party, Guy Mollet, was also looking for someone to work on European questions. Through Rebattet, Noël and Mollet were brought together and he began working with Mollet on an informal basis. When in 1949, Mollet became rapporteur for the important General Affairs Committee for the Consultative Committee of the Council of Europe, he asked, in the best interests of coordination, whether Emile Noël could not act as its secretary. And so Noël came to work in Strasbourg when the EPC project received its green light from the ministers of the Six.

—

It is difficult to pinpoint the EPC's precise origins. To some extent, it can trace its ancestry to the self-same federalist ambitions which had led to the creation of the Council of Europe in 1948-1949. Among its other declarations, the founding meeting, held in The Hague in May 1948:

- Declares that the time has come when the European nations must transfer and merge some portion of their sovereign rights so as to secure common political and economic action for the integration and proper development of their common resources
- Demands the convening, as a matter of real urgency, of a European Assembly chosen by the parliaments of the participating nations, from among their members and others, designed to:
  - Stimulate and give expression to European public opinion
  - Advise upon immediate practical measures designed progressively to bring about the necessary economic and political union of Europe
  - Examine the juridical and constitutional implications arising out of such a Union or Federation and their economic and social consequences
  - Prepare the necessary plans for the above purposes

It went on to specify that membership of the Assembly would only be open to states willing to observe democratic principles and to respect a Charter of Human Rights. The Council of Europe failed to live up to such aspirations, becoming a powerless and increasingly irrelevant debating forum. Instead, the vehicle for constitutional experiment became the supranational communities negotiated by the governments of Germany, Italy and the Benelux countries, the coal and steel community, launched in May 1950, and the defence community, launched in September the same year.

A more proximate antecedent to the EPC, however, lay in the Washington declaration of September 1951 for the formation of a continental European Community as part of a wider Atlantic Community. Back in France, Foreign Minister Robert Schuman elaborated on this by suggesting the creation of a supranational political organ with its own powers. In the course of his exposé he several times mentioned the word 'federalist'. The momentum built up further when, in December 1950 before the Council of Europe, Schuman, Paul van Zeeland, Alcide De Gasperi and Konrad Adenauer set out their visions for a European future. This was immediately rewarded by a Council resolution (Recommendation 21b) for a political authority under parliamentary control with competencies over defence and foreign affairs.

The way in which this potential cry in the wilderness was translated into political reality is a little complicated, but worth tracing because it became part of a set of interlocking arrangements which, even assuming that the original aims ever had a chance, were to be their ultimate undoing. In February 1952 the French Assembly had made clear that a measure of democratic political authority was needed if it were to accept the creation of a European Army.[1] Schuman introduced this demand into the EDC negotiations. This could have ended up as an ECSC-type assembly were it not that De Gasperi was still fighting (and losing) his battle to endow the EDC with greater supranational powers. In order to get Italy to accept a far smaller number of seats in the Assembly than had been originally demanded and to accept unanimous decision-making by the Council of Ministers on the EDC budget (and the decision of when actually to use the army), the ministers introduced a clause whereby the constitutional arrangements were to be temporary. The first task of the new Assembly would be to work out the permanent arrangements (art. 8, para. c, and art. 38). On 30 May 1952, four days after the treaty was signed, the Council of Europe passed Resolution no. 14 calling for the immediate implementation of Article 38 (i.e. to accelerate the process of democratising the EDC) and in July 1952 De Gasperi tabled a motion to that effect at the ministerial conference of the Six in Paris. The ministers did not get round to discussing it on that occasion but when they did so in Luxembourg in September, De Gasperi's motion had been joined by a Dutch amendment: acceleration of the EDC procedure was only acceptable if the Assembly was to be given new specific economic tasks. Both elements were embodied in the so-called 'Luxembourg Resolution'. This allowed for the immediate creation of an '*ad hoc* Assembly', with the same composition as that envisaged for the EDC assembly, charged with the task of drafting new constitutional arrangements.

The EDC Treaty, which was already running into a storm of opposition, was now further burdened with the hopes of the European federalists *and* with Dutch demands for a commercial settlement in Europe. When it collapsed, it buried everything, but the permanent casualty was the European federation. Looking back, there was one good reason for linking federalist ambitions to the EDC Treaty: at least the issue got onto the political agenda. In the light of subsequent developments, there is little reason to believe that this would ever have occurred without the EDC linkage. But even at the time it was recognised as a dangerous strategy – besides the fact that the EDC might fail.

On the one hand it was apparent that any new political organ covering the EDC and the ECSC would mean that each of those treaties in turn would need to be revised. It is true that the French were continually trying to amend the EDC, but so tenuous had been the agreement on the ECSC that the treaty stipulated that it could not be altered for fifty years. With the vehement campaigns in Belgium, France and Germany against the treaty still ringing in their ears, it was unlikely that governments would risk renegotiation and re-ratification. On the other hand, there were those that argued that the EDC and ECSC formed too narrow and too circumscribed a base for further growth towards European federalism. For them, the way out was to add fields of competence in the social and economic areas, but this, in turn, would move the discussion away from its original departure point and its legitimacy. Indeed, it was argued that such an attempt would further undermine whatever lingering consensus might exist on the EDC itself and thus contribute to its premature demise.

—

The *ad hoc* Assembly, under the leadership of the Belgian socialist Paul-Henri Spaak,[2] began its task almost immediately and managed to complete its work, on target, six months later. Although there were a number of plenary meetings, and an especially important one in January 1953, much of the work was conducted in committees and subcommittees. An entire floor of the Hotel d'Orsay in Paris was hired for the purpose, with the dining room sequestered for larger meetings and a bathroom pressed into service as an archive. From almost nothing, an entire secretariat had to be created, including interpreters and translators into the four official languages, rooms and secretarial facilities for the thirty members and fifteen observers who were almost continuously engaged in the work, and rapporteurs for the dozen or so subcommittees that had eventually been formed. For Emile Noël the pressure was on from the start but the tempo increased remorselessly after the January plenary session when it became necessary to translate the recommendations into treaty articles. This, however, was also for him the most interesting phase, when the politicians working in the Constitutional Committee liaised with a group of lawyers who rendered their ideas into draft articles. The politicians met in the day, the lawyers in the evening, sometimes working into the night, and everything would be ready the next morning. Emile worked in both committees. The pace was too much; his health deteriorated and he succumbed to tuberculosis. In the last weeks of the Assembly's work, and during the last plenary session when the completed draft was handed to the ministers, he lay in a hospital bed.

Without going into details of this work, it is worth mentioning that although the Assembly was supposed to have been chosen from among the more pro-integration members of the Council of Europe, the debates were more often than not conducted along national rather than party lines. Those who had expected alliances to form on the basis of political persuasion, or even the genesis of pan-European parties, were sorely disappointed. So too were those who had hoped that the prospect of a new constitution would spark a popular movement in its support. The second point was that although the treaty did move from the narrow terms of Article 38, far enough for the authors to re-title it the European Community (i.e. to drop the word 'political'), it did not stray very far. It was, therefore, more concerned with constitutional form than with staking out a claim to a wide range of new competencies. This was in line with the vision of pragmatists like Emile Noël himself, who felt that although it was necessary to stake out some ground in advance of the intergovernmental frameworks already in existence, new arrangements had to bear in mind the political realities in member states.

The outline of the constitutional form of the new Community was fairly simple:

- Council of Ministers
- Executive Council
- Parliament:
  - Senate
  - Peoples' Chamber
- Social-Economic Council
- Court

Briefly, the Council of Ministers and the Court were familiar constructions from the ECSC. The Social-Economic Council was to represent producer and consumer organisations and have a purely advisory role. Parliament was to be made up of two chambers: a directly elected peoples' chamber (to represent the people of Europe collectively) and a Senate made up of appointees of national parliaments (to represent the people of the states of Europe). There was, of course, a potential overlap between the Senate and the Council of Ministers, who also represent the states of Europe, and it was to become a source of much discussion. The parliament was to appoint the president of the Executive who, in turn, chose the rest of his team. But the Executive Council, as a whole, had to be 'invested' by parliament which also had the right to dismiss it prematurely.

Such, then, was the structure of the new community.[3] Even at the time, however, there were two main grounds for criticism. The first lay in the balance of power within the community. For the first five years virtually all measures had to pass through the sluice of the Council of Ministers which, moreover, would have to vote by unanimity if a measure were to be passed. This gave governments in general (and in the first five years that meant any *one* dissenting government) virtual rights of veto. This might have been a reflection of political reality but it was bitterly resented by, for example, Jean Monnet, who wrote to Spaak complaining that the new system was 'intergovernmental' and not 'supranational' and that it 'would mark the end of the unification of Europe'.

The second criticism lay in the powers to which the new community had laid claim. These can be summarised as follows:

- The right to approve and dismiss the Executive (which would also subsume the High Authority of the ECSC and the staff of the High Commissioner for defence within two years)
- The right to control the budgets of the sectoral communities and any separate budget which might later be set up (it should be noted, however, that these rights extended to the community as a whole; the parliament's rights were far more circumscribed)
- The right of the Council of Ministers to coordinate foreign policy having heard, though not necessarily having listened to, the other organs
- The right of parliament to approve any treaties with third countries (if there is a common army, it is logical to share a common foreign policy, but these clauses were bitterly contested and had been forced through largely by the Italians)
- Finally, the right of the Community to prepare for the progressive creation of a common market

It was this last point which caused concern for the supporters of the Luxembourg resolution and, more particularly, the Benelux countries. Any measures had to have the majority backing of both chambers. The Benelux countries had 35 per cent of the seats in the people's chamber and 26 per cent of the seats in the Senate, so that it was possible that no majority proposal might even emerge. But should one do so, it then had to pass the hurdle of the Council of Ministers voting unanimously for the first five years and by weighted majority thereafter. The Dutch foreign minister, Jan Willem Beyen, had tried and failed to get the ministers of the Six to direct the Assembly to include a common market clause in the treaty itself and he continued to make it clear that the Dutch parliament would not accept the EPC Treaty if it did not have real economic powers.

Spaak, in handing over the draft treaty in Strasbourg in March 1953, began his speech using the same words employed by George Washington when he presented the American Constitution to Congress in 1787. Drawing the direct historical parallel, he suggested that if Europe demonstrated the same audacity and courage, the venture would assuredly be crowned with the same success:

> *It is only ten years ago, that the countries represented here were waging war against one another. Our people were struggling in a horrible fray. We had only one thought, one purpose: to destroy each other as definitively as possible.*

> *In the immensity of our misfortunes, in the ruins that we accumulated, in our weakness and our poverty, in the soaring threat and the reigning anxiety, we suddenly understood, suddenly realized, the mortal danger that our quarrels, our discussions posed to the rules of life which were common to one another, to the age-old heritage that each of us contributed to augment and to beautify.*
>
> *We pulled ourselves together, regained our self-control and without forgetting anything – for it would be heresy – we decided to attempt a great venture which would – if it were to succeed – and it will – allow us to save what we have in common that is most cherished and most beautiful.*
>
> *This treaty proposal is therefore not only a moving message of reconciliation, but also an act of trust in the future. [...]*
>
> *We today have broached a new stage. Let's not break our impulse, let's not reduce our effort. Without wasting time, we must continue our common work.*
>
> *The coolness of Bidault's reply on receiving the treaty was not the only sign that things were going wrong.*

Notwithstanding Spaak's resounding rhetoric and emotive historical parallels, the Assembly's endorsement of its own work had been less than complete. When the treaty was finally put to the vote it was approved by 50 votes in favour and five abstentions. The result, however, was flattering since 83 politicians were entitled to vote! The abstentions included the French socialist bloc, a liberal from Luxembourg and a French Republican who later revealed the true nature of his commitment to the European cause with a statement to the effect that he would only vote for the treaty if Paris were to be the community's capital and French its official language. The bloc of three Gaullist deputies and an Italian liberal were also present at the meeting but refused to vote. The remaining gap in numbers was partly made up of the seven German Social Democrats, who had boycotted the entire proceedings from the start and a Belgian Christian Democrat who had suspended his participation later on. The remaining 22 politicians simply did not bother to turn up. The majority becomes even more tarnished when one takes into account the statement made on behalf of the ten Dutch politicians to the effect that whilst they would vote for the treaty, they reserved the freedom of action to effect changes in both the electoral clauses and the provisions for economic integration when the treaty came up for ratification in the Dutch parliament.

The immediate ministerial reaction also dampened spirits. Although Article 38 of the EDC Treaty had stipulated that the governments would meet to pronounce on the treaty within three months, the ministers decided not to specify *any* date, ostensibly because of the uncertainty over the EDC's ratification. Secondly, members of the Assembly had requested their inclusion in the conference to ensure that it did not wander too far from the letter and spirit of the treaty. This request was flatly rejected although, as a sop, it was agreed to supply the secretariat with the conference documentation.

—

The government conference to discuss the draft EPC Treaty did not meet until September 1953. During the intervening months it was the Germans and the Italians who most consistently pressed for quick action on the draft treaty. For Germany, the situation was more complicated and it is worth pausing to consider it in more detail. The call for German rearmament, made in 1950, was something of a mixed blessing. On the one hand it had strengthened German claims to be readmitted as an equal member of the community of nations but, on the other hand, Adenauer realised that, neither for diplomatic reasons nor for reasons of domestic politics, was it politic for Germany to be seen to be pressing too hard for its own remilitarisation. The draft treaty, and German support for it, could be interpreted as a way of doing something positive for Europe. There was a further reason for something positive in Adenauer's mind and that was a fear that the Americans were cooling in their commitment towards Europe's defence (and, of course, if Europe were invaded, Germany would be the first to go); he felt that the EPC would show that Europe was serious about its own strength and unity and therefore worth defending. It is difficult to say which of these ideas was uppermost in his mind but there are grounds for believing that he wanted a diplomatic coup for domestic electoral reasons. Before the September elections the archive record shows him personally active on EPC matters; after the election, virtually nothing. About De Gasperi's position we know much less – the federalist appeal was far stronger in Italian public opinion than anywhere else in Europe and he too was facing elections, which ousted him as foreign minister. Moreover, the Italian position throughout the subsequent discussions was closest to supporting the treaty as it stood, so it would not be going too far to suggest that they liked the treaty for its own sake.

The German and Italian pressure, however, could not get very far as long as the other governments were unwilling to accept the draft treaty. In fact it was clear that the EPC, far from helping the Defence Community into being, had actually complicated the situation further – both the Gaullists, upon whom the new government relied for support, and the socialists, were opposed to the treaty as it stood. Any move to satisfy one party would only serve to alienate the other even further. Bidault's strategy, therefore, seemed to be designed towards delaying having to place a further treaty before the French Assembly. Of course, the opportunity for doing just this was afforded by the Benelux position – whatever else divided them, they were at least united in the belief that the economic clauses needed to be strengthened before they would even consider accepting the EPC Treaty.

It was in this mixture of enthusiasm and reluctance that events shuffled towards the promised governmental conference to meet in Rome in September 1953. Once there they began with gusto to unravel the draft treaty and to piece it together again more in their own image.

The governments' attack on the draft treaty concentrated on shifting the balance *within* the Community in favour of the nation states. The most transparent way in which they did this was to attack the parliamentarians' concept of the Senate. The draft treaty had attempted to separate the judiciary from the Executive and, at the same time, to balance the supranational and national elements in each. Thus, there would be a directly elected peoples' chamber and a senate composed of members of parliament from national parliaments. It was envisaged too that the members of the Senate would also sit in the Council of Europe, thus creating an organic link between the two. During the September conference the idea gradually emerged that the senate was *too* similar to the peoples' chamber and that the national interest in the legislature could best be protected by having a chamber of national ministers and not national parliamentarians (three or four from each country). The fact that it would then closely resemble the Council of Ministers did not really seem to cause much concern. By the time the Rome Report was produced, this was the official position of France and Germany and was considered acceptable (though not necessarily preferred) by the Benelux countries. The reason for this acceptance by Benelux was because it seemed the only way to obtain parity representation in at least one of the chambers of the legislature. Italy was alone in sticking to the *ad hoc* Assembly's draft treaty, although it was joined later by the Netherlands. The rather too cynical treatment of the parliamentarians' ideas had made it impossible for the Dutch government to maintain its earlier position.

The second main line of attack lay in the appointment of the executive. The draft treaty had envisaged that the parliament would appoint the president who, in turn, would choose his team. The team would then have to be approved by parliament. Now, even after the governments had transformed the senate into a shadow council of ministers, this procedure was still considered too lax; at least by everyone except Italy which, again, stuck loyally to the treaty. By the end of the Rome conference all the others had agreed that the president at least would be appointed by the Council of Ministers. The French wanted that privilege extended to the *entire* Executive whilst the rest were willing to leave that to the president (subject or not to the ministers' guidance) but the composition would then have to be approved by the Council of Ministers. Whether or not parliament's approval was to be required at all was the subject of a deep division of opinion. (The point was that if there were no 'investiture' procedure, the executive could be voted out on a vote of confidence, though even here the system was changed so as to weaken the role of the lower chamber.)

The third main line of attack was on the question of the attributes of the Community. In the first place it was unanimously agreed that there should be *no* discussion or 'coordination' of foreign policy other than that already agreed in the ECSC and EDC treaties (such as very formal questions of association agreements). Secondly, it was almost unanimously agreed that the Council of Ministers could give directives to the Executive on certain matters, whereas in the draft treaty the role of the Council was seen much more as a link between the EPC and national governments. Again, the fact that this blurred the division of powers between legislature and executive appeared of little concern. Thirdly, there was an inconclusive discussion on what exactly was meant by the 'incorporation' of the ECSC and EDC into the new community. The draft treaty had envisaged that there would be *one* executive organ but the drift in the government was towards keeping the separate executives (and thus their means of appointment as specified in the original treaties) intact. The point at which they became a single community was the point at which the separate assemblies would disappear.

That left, then, the final point as to what on earth the new EPC executive was supposed to do. For the French, the answer was absolutely clear. It would do nothing other than to prepare the grounds for a new set of proposals on a common market, proposals which would be the subject of a separate conference and a separate treaty. This was also the drift of Italian thinking which, again, in this matter, came close to the draft treaty which, as we have seen, itself tended to emphasise the 'checks' rather than the 'balances'. The Italian approach was consistent with what was called 'constitutionalism' – it was willing to agree a democratic structure because it was unwilling to concede the new community much by way of power. The other governments, however, were willing to give the community new tasks, which also explains why they were so concerned to strengthen the 'nation state' element within the 'community' structure. But here, too, they were split. The Dutch wanted community management of safeguard clauses and the administration of the compensation fund which would accompany an automatic and autonomous creation of a tariff union. The Belgians and Germans wanted it to administer the creation of that tariff union and the coordination of economic policy which they considered necessary to stop it from falling apart, whilst Luxembourg would consider anything as long as it was exempted.

—

The question of stabilising foreign commercial policy had been taxing the Dutch government since the war. However, rightly or wrongly, it felt specifically disadvantaged by the multilateral approach adopted by the Organisation for European Economic Cooperation (OEEC) in 1950. By concentrating on quota removal, the OEEC left countries free to re-impose tariffs; by allowing freedom within and between broad trade categories, it left countries free to discriminate unevenly; by focusing on private trade, it allowed state trade to escape altogether. In sum, the Dutch felt that they were being forced to expose fledgling industry to competition while their potential agricultural markets remained choked off as before. Moreover, the OEEC's measures could be reversed by national decision in case of balance-of-payments difficulties and when West Germany did so, in late 1950, the impact was felt immediately on the Dutch balance of payments. Under these circumstances, the Dutch delegation launched one scheme after another in various forms and in various gatherings. The idea of a customs union was just one more in a series, designed to bring trade down trade barriers and, once down, to keep them down.

In September 1952, the new Dutch foreign minister Johan-Willem Beyen linked his cabinet's reluctance to support the EDC, and its equal reluctance to accept a complicating layer of democratisation on top, to a demand for a customs union. By the time the details of Dutch thinking were conveyed to the ministers of the Six in December 1952, Beyen had become sceptical about the ability of the EPC arrangements to secure this goal. Thus he demanded that the end date for the achievement of the union was to be fixed in advance and that there be a system of supranationally administered 'safeguard clauses'. A second memorandum, in February 1953, added that the automatic steps for the achievement of the customs union should also be stipulated in the treaty. What was to be known as the Beyen Plan had come into existence.

As with so many of these early European initiatives, the pivotal position was that of the French. Not only was Schuman's replacement by Bidault evidence of a cooling towards supranationality, but the rapid deterioration in the external position of the French economy made them less amenable to contemplating further doses of trade liberalisation. If the EPC had originally been intended to ease the passage of the EDC through the French Assembly, it would certainly not do so if, in such circumstances, it carried the baggage of a customs union with it. In February 1953, at the same meeting as the one in which the Beyen Plan had been tabled, Bidault had questioned whether any economic clauses were needed in the EPC Treaty. Even in the diluted form in which they were to appear, they were considered by the Quai d'Orsay to form an unacceptable infringement upon French sovereignty. The French delegation at the subsequent intergovernmental negotiations was instructed to press for a minimalist construction for the EPC whereby the object was for it to be confined to providing a political structure for the existing communities. Any advice it might have on economic questions was to be the subject of a separate unanimous agreement of the states concerned.

In Germany, the economics ministry was more positive towards the Dutch proposals from the start but tended to stress especially the problem of currency convertibility. Of more immediate concern to Adenauer and the foreign ministry was the need to avoid anything which might complicate the ratification of the EDC Treaty and if that meant an EPC Treaty shorn of any content, so be it. Once the elections had passed, the way was opened for a more serious consideration of the Beyen Plan. These ideas went beyond what the Dutch seemed prepared to consider. Although a start could be made in dismantling European trade barriers, it was felt that the process could not be completed until full convertibility had been achieved. In Erhard's own words:

> *The ordering of [some] areas with the continued disorder in others can never lead to an economically united Europe. A further partial union would mean the definite atomisation of Europe. Accompanying this process, there should be the establishment of a permanent conference of central banks and the gradual transfer of the monetary and fiscal instruments of counter-cyclical policy to a supranational authority.*

The initial Italian reaction was similar to that of Germany and for the same electoral reasons. Italian thinking, however, on the Beyen Plan itself was closer to that of France. The EPC Treaty was interpreted more in the character of a constitution and although the Italians were willing to concede that the treaty's economic powers might require redefinition, they did not consider that there was a place for the kind of technical provisions which the Dutch seemed to envisage. They were totally opposed to any rigid timetable for its implementation and felt that progress should proceed within the limits dictated by the international cycle (viz. acceleration in times of cyclical upswing, freezing in times of recession). They also wanted the fund's scope enlarged to cover investment in backward (Italian) sectors, which would serve to promote the integration process.

The Belgian response was more positive from the start in the sense that they shared the Dutch conviction that the EPC's economic powers were hopelessly inadequate. However, they felt that concentration on a customs union would not, by itself, achieve market integration. Like the Germans, their concern focused on the absence of monetary considerations and other aspects of policy coordination, without which, it was felt, the whole edifice would be characterised by the same bickering as was marring the Benelux. In addition to the customs union, the community should be charged with 'coordinating' a wide range of monetary, fiscal, economic and exchange rate policy. After a transitional period, the Council of Ministers would be able to take decisions binding on member states. A 'Benelux of the Six', as the Beyen Plan was described, was seen as an essentially unstable construction, too vulnerable to being pulled apart by divergent national policies and fatally crippled by the reintroduction of protection as the safeguard mechanisms, envisaged in the Plan, came into operation.

Luxembourg's initial position was to reject the Beyen Plan. Small countries, it argued, had such little sovereignty anyway that they were naturally wary of signing it away to some supranational authority. Nowhere had it been made clear why a customs union was an indispensable condition for creating a European political community. Realising, however, that a small country is ill-placed to deflect larger countries, if they are in agreement, from having their way, the strategy switched to pressing for the inclusion of concrete economic measures in a separate protocol, and to announcing the country's intention of claiming exemption for vital economic interests.

Given the line-up of participating countries, it is unsurprising that the intergovernmental conference spanning two weeks at the end of September and the beginning of October 1953 turned into a fiasco. There was barely enough time for the delegates to set out their conflicting views before they had to turn their hands to producing an agreed report solemnly recording them all. The French position alone, in rejecting any economic role for the EPC, made any agreement impossible. However, the Dutch delegation, tied to the narrow concept of the Beyen Plan, was unable to build any bridges to the Belgian and German delegations, who were not unsympathetic to Dutch goals but who simply did not think that they went far enough. Beyen, for his part, was prepared to compromise on the timescale for the achievement of a customs union, to relax the demands for automatism in the reduction of trade barriers, and to make some concessions in the direction of policy coordination. But he would not bow to the Franco-Italian position of leaving matters entirely in the hands of the EPC institutions or of a separate protocol. Nor was he prepared to offer Dutch concessions until they could be traded off against a movement towards the Dutch position by the rest.

For the French, meanwhile, with the struggle in full swing on the fate of the EDC Treaty, the entire EPC project had become at best an irrelevance and at worst an embarrassment. Although the ministers of the Six had allowed discussions to continue, a Quai d'Orsay report to French embassies abroad made no bones about the fact that the decision had been taken to create the illusion of progress. If the economic talks had any purpose, it was to reveal to the others the considerable difficulties attached to further surrender of sovereignty in the economic field. Their delegation's subsequent position was either to insist that the entire discussion on economic clauses was inappropriate or to pile up difficulties and objections towards what the others were doing. This should have made it easier to obtain a line up of the remainder 'againsts' possible but that too was unlikely. In the first place, Germany's 'European' policy in its widest sense still depended on French cooperation – there was still no European army, still no prospect of German rearmament, no solution to the Saar question, and so forth. Beside these concerns the question of whether or when to set up a common market was of secondary importance. Italy, too, remained far from the Dutch position. Although willing to discuss economic integration, their standpoint was still that it belonged to a separate agreement. That left little more than the possibility of a Benelux front (minus Luxembourg!). When, however, a Belgian delegate raised before his inter-ministerial coordinating committee the possibility of dropping the insistence on policy coordination and throwing support behind the customs union, the foreign ministry quashed such sentiments. Whilst the Dutch position was 'not wrong but insufficient' any shift in Belgium's position 'would be absurd [...] and [we would] cover ourselves with ridicule right in the middle of the conference'.

—

The rest of the story is fairly simple to tell. The report of the Rome conference had already shown that the negotiations were deadlocked. France would not concede that the EPC was to be anything more than a 'coiffeur' for the existing communities and that it might have a 'study group' role on economic questions. This might have been acceptable to Italy but nobody else was prepared to accept the 'democratic' constitution which the Italians envisaged. And France was not going to accept the 'economic integration' foreseen by the rest, which was a condition *sine qua non* for Benelux agreement. More to the point, the French were not really pushing for agreement on the EPC at all: they never once made the point that the introduction of democratic control would make the EDC's acceptance by the French parliament much easier. This is because it would not do so: a further change in the complexion of the French government to include Gaullist sympathisers saw to that. The simplest solution was to carry on talking. Three months of negotiations and a new report, and they were as far apart as ever. More negotiations, now quite openly admitted, on 'non-contentious' points kept the EPC drifting towards the summer of 1954. The EPC had become a structure without a core. In August 1954, the French parliament rejected the EDC Treaty, and the structure vanished as well.

What parallels does this story have for the present? Firstly, the EPC story tells us something about 'linkages': linkages between national problems and international solutions and linkages between different national priorities in an international framework. When negotiations 'succeed', it is easy to point to such linkages as the reason for success without really specifying their exact nature and context. The story of the EPC provided linkages aplenty and all they did was forge a chain which choked the initiative to death. The echoes with the recent past are again striking. The European exchange rate mechanism was an astounding success which created an island of relative currency stability in an uncertain world, especially when compared with the turmoil before its creation in 1979. However, it did not have and still does not have a fully satisfactory adjustment mechanism. Despite this handicap it was conscripted into service as a means of advancing European union. When the next, inevitable crisis arrived it came close to dragging the entire Maastricht edifice with it, and may yet do so. Historians learn early to specify the exact nature of any links *and* the precise context in which they operate if they are to form a convincing historical explanation.

Secondly, the EPC story provides a clear demonstration of the centrality of a coincidence of Franco-German interests in any solution to European questions. A 'European Community' of the kind to which the Benelux countries seemed to aspire never became a central concern of these two countries in this period.

It was decisively rejected by the French and it was viewed with caution by the Bundeskanzleramt, more concerned with appeasing the French and with the symbolic usefulness of any treaty. Erhard's economics ministry seemed to be operating in a grey zone between scepticism and interest. The EPC therefore lacked any real impulse towards giving it real powers and it soon lost its other function of promoting the EDC's ratification. Once that was lost, its fate was sealed.

Thirdly, the EPC story underlines the point that there is no single, logical movement towards European integration. The ECSC may have been a 'first step' towards a supranational Europe but there was no single obvious direction for the second. Did one go for the next sector with an analogous organisational form (as, for example, the EDC or an agricultural community), did one choose general economic integration (as, for example, the Beyen Plan), or did one attempt to create a new institutional structure which would attract popular legitimacy (as the federalists hoped would occur with the EPC)? Moreover, one could question whether the ECSC actually *led* to the EPC at all or whether the parliamentarians' plan did not represent a rejection of a 'technocratic' Europe. And it doesn't matter whether one accepts this or not, but it is clear that the parliamentarians' plan provoked a countermove on the part of the national governments that was ultimately to crush it.

Finally, it forces us to question the criteria for success and failure. In this case, the parliamentarians' vision of Europe was in advance of that held by ministers in national governments at the time. However, they failed adequately either to consider this or to adjust their plans accordingly. When the governments eventually had their say, they immediately wreaked their revenge. For the federalists of the Spinelli school, that, in itself, was the measure of the failure. But pragmatists had already more limited horizons. Mollet had become sceptical of the entire proceedings when their usefulness for EDC ratification had been exhausted. Emile Noël, however, had considered that the ideas in the treaty were essentially good ones and had hoped that what could have been salvaged in the subsequent intergovernmental negotiations would still have represented an advance on current practice. A similar situation had prevailed in the early 1980s when a group of parliamentarians, under Spinelli's chairmanship, had drafted a European Union treaty. The version accepted by the European Parliament in 1984 in the form of the Single European Act was much weaker, but no one doubts that it was a considerable advance on what had gone before. Yet seemingly the EPC had been denied that fate in the autumn of 1954, and in that form, it had.

Its failure had dealt the cause of those who espoused further European integration a severe blow. For the Dutch, however, the one thing that had emerged from the wreckage was that five countries were willing, with greater or lesser degrees of commitment, to accept the creation of a customs union as part of a more wide-ranging integration of their economies. It was a 'certainty' to which Beyen clung throughout the confusion which surrounded the EDC failure and he remained unmoved by various other schemes for 'relaunching' Europe which proliferated in its wake. His faith was shared by no one. Monnet and Spaak were sceptical about tying their ideas for further sectoral integration to a common market idea that had already failed. Yet, without it, there would be no Dutch support for the Benelux memorandum submitted at Messina in spring 1955. A year later, it formed a centre piece of the so-called Spaak Report upon which subsequent negotiations were based. One year further, and surrounded by various escape clauses, it provided the backbone to the Treaty of Rome. And with the common market came many of the institutional arrangements worked out in the Hotel d'Orsay in the winter of 1952-1953.

POSTSCRIPT

This quick survey of the early attempt to form a federal-inspired political community within the framework of the six founding members of the European Coal and Steel Community was published in a festschrift to Emile Noël in S. Martin (ed.), *The Construction of Europe: Essays in Honour of Emile Noël* (Dordrecht, 1994), 19-39. Emile Noël had been secretary-general of the European Commission since its creation and upon his retirement, he became president of the European University Institute, where I had just been appointed to the Chair of Contemporary History and was in charge of the European integration history project. We had first met a few months previously at a conference where he had commented on a history paper by declaring it 'a good scientific paper ... science fiction'. I am not sure if he ever trusted historians. He had an incredible memory, and was always happy to answer questions, if you knew which questions to ask. He left the Institute one year before I did, and I wrote this paper because of the role he played in the events described.

I returned to the topic in a full scale (fully annotated!) book entitled *Europe's First Constitution: The European Political Community, 1952-1954* (London, 2000). For a review of the events in main developments in these years, readers should look in the volume by Gilbert Trausch (ed.), *Die europäische Integration vom Schuman-Plan bis zu den Verträgen von Rom: Pläne und Initiativen, Enttäuschungen und Misserfolge:*

Beiträge des Kolloquiums in Luxemburg, 17-19 Mai 1989/The European Integration from the Schuman-plan to the Treaties of Rome: Projects and Initiatives, Disappointments and Failures: Contributions to the Symposium in Luxembourg, May 17-19, 1989 (Baden-Baden, 1993). For those who want to trace the ideas of federalism further, I can recommend Michael Burgess, *Federalism and the European Union: The Building of Europe, 1950-2000* (London, 2000). Émile Noël's remarkable career has been described in Gerard Bousuat, *Émile Noël, premier secrétaire général de la Commission européenne* (Brussels, 2011).

6

Agricultural Pressure Groups and the Origins of the Common Agricultural Policy[1]

Looking back, there scarcely seems to have been a time when television news broadcasts were not sporadically punctuated by shots of protesting farmers or fishermen. I am sure that we all recall the scenes of Belgian farmers unloading rotting vegetables into the streets, of French fishermen emptying their catch on the floor of market halls, or of town centres blocked by slow-moving convoys of tractors. Particularly poignant were the scenes of the ancient 'parlement de Bretagne' in Rennes engulfed in flames in February 1994 after riots over the price of fish. These are part of the images of farm protest in Europe today.

Equally, there hardly seems to have been a time when these protests, or at least the more usual forms of interest group representation, by agrarian pressure groups do not appear to have been successful. It was not that long ago that the Uruguay Round, an international trade agreement worth many billions of dollars, was held to ransom at the very last moment so that, *inter alia*, the agricultural requirements of a member state of the European Union could be dealt with in a way satisfactory for the national farming lobby. These incidents, and many like them, have originated over the years from a sector of the economy whose contribution to employment and national income is now, in percentage terms, in single digits.

To understand the strength of the agricultural sector in domestic and international politics, it is necessary to go back almost a hundred years.[2] However, most of my focus will be on the post-war developments, leading to the insertion of agricultural clauses into the Treaty of Rome. Already, by that date, the main tendencies were apparent that would leave their mark on the development of a common agricultural policy (CAP) until the early 1980s. Over that period, the

CAP became more than a sectoral policy. In the 1960s it was often credited with being the 'driving force' behind European integration. After the enlargement of the EEC in the 1970s, because of the pattern of UK trade and the way the policy was financed, the CAP became the source of continuous controversy that sometimes threatened to pull the Community apart.

—

Agricultural protectionism was not an invention of the post-war period, far less was it a discovery of the European Economic Community. The origins of modern agricultural protectionism go back more than a hundred years, to the Great Depression of the 1870s and 1880s.[3] The nature of the depression and its fundamental causes have been the subject of considerable debate among economic historians. For agriculture it was characterised by a sharp fall of grain prices in Europe caused by the opening up of temperate farm lands in North America and Australasia, and by a vast improvement of international ocean shipping which slashed the prices of transporting bulk products to Europe. At the time of the outbreak of the crisis, the agricultural pressure groups in Europe were fragmented and lacking much political weight. Yet the slowness of government reactions to the crisis galvanised these loose peasant groups into powerful coalitions that articulated the demands of the agricultural sector for protection.

National governments responded to the fall in prices in two ways: either by granting that protection or by forcing the agricultural sector to adapt. Rather belatedly in France and Germany tariffs were first imposed on grain imports. Because grain is a key product in determining the price structure for the rest of agriculture, a network of protection spread outward from grain into other sectors of dairy and arable farming.[4] For some other countries, however, the fall in grain prices produced a new opportunity. In the United Kingdom, for example, where agriculture employment was down to probably 13-14 per cent of the labour force at the time, the government responded by viewing lower grain prices as a contribution towards reducing the cost of living for the working classes. It would thus allow the majority of the working population to increase their purchasing power, leaving agriculture to adapt as best it could.[5] In Denmark and the Netherlands, where agriculture was already highly developed and oriented towards the export of animal produce, the drop in the price of grain represented a fall in the cost of an important input into the dairy and poultry sector. For those countries, the Great Depression accentuated the already apparent trend of movement from arable to animal farming.[6]

By the mid-1890s the Great Depression had passed and prices were already recovering strongly. Despite more prosperous times, however, the framework of agricultural protectionism was not rolled back. And, after the First World War, it was augmented even further. Again the problem lay in the temperate agrarian countries. It was no longer a question of railways opening up vast new areas of agrarian land; it was the fact that newly discovered techniques of mechanisation were better applied to the large farming units that were possible in Australasia and the Americas. This technology could not be replicated in the fragmented land holdings that typified most of Europe. In addition, because of the war, and the need for shipping across the Atlantic, there was a large surplus of peace-time capacity. This produced a corresponding depression in the freight rates, which further reduced the price of imports from overseas.

Once again, the grain area was uniquely depressed. There were probably no more than one or two favourable years for European grain producers during the entire decade of the 1920s. By 1928, a full eighteen months before the 'real' Great Depression hit the rest of the European economy, the crisis in grain had already started. Grain prices were falling fast, and again the response of governments in increasing the levels of protection was slow. Then, from late 1929 through into 1930, conditions throughout the rest of the European economy deteriorated.[7] As disposable incomes shrank, demand for what were now seen as luxury items (butter, cheese, eggs, milk, meat) especially declined. The prices for meat and dairy products fell dramatically and, from 1931, for the first time, animal production found itself in a serious crisis. By the time governments had reacted to these new demands for protection, the entire agricultural sector had been covered by a web of domestic regulations and frontier controls.

Ironically in countries such as the Netherlands and Denmark, which had previously seen themselves as free traders in agriculture because they were dependent on agricultural exports, the mechanisms of protection were more extensive and more profound than in the rest of Europe. The reason behind this is easy to understand. When the policy objective is simply to isolate the domestic market from cheap imports, the introduction of a tariff (which will increase the price of imports) or a quota (which, through arbitrarily limiting the volume of foreign produce, will restrict supply and therefore raise the price) will be sufficient. For a country with an export surplus, these measures are also necessary, but they are not enough. Usually a central purchasing agency will also be required, to pay the farmers, to sell part of the product at a higher price on the domestic market and to use the 'profits' on these transactions to cover losses on foreign sales. Only by acting as a monopoly could the farmers operate a system of differential pricing.

By the time the downward cycle of the Depression had passed in 1933-1934, almost every sector of agriculture in Europe was subject to government interference. Yet nowhere were these measures particularly successful. There is not a case in Europe where agricultural incomes were restored to the level prevailing in more prosperous times. Nor were governments able to prevent an erosion in differentials with urban incomes. It is against this background that farming communities, which saw themselves falling behind in terms of employment, incomes and social amenities, began to articulate demands for political change. The identity of farming discontent with anti-democratic, usually fascist, parties pledged to undermining or usurping the capitalist system also became a trademark of the 1930s.[8] Thus, by the end of the decade, ideological as well as practical considerations meshed together to justify a framework of agricultural protectionism that was already higher, and more pervasive, than ever before.

—

The Second World War, and its aftermath, served to drive agricultural protection to new peaks and to cement these pre-war systems even more firmly into place. The aims of all post-war agrarian policies can be summed up in one word – self-sufficiency, or as near self-sufficiency as possible. The reasons for this were broadly the same. Firstly, the war had confirmed that the success of agriculture was vital to national survival – vital in the sense of 'necessary for life'. Had it not been for the dramatic reorganisations in European agriculture, the chances of survival for a large sector of the population would have deteriorated.[9] These achievements lifted agriculture from the position it had occupied in the 1930s – a sectoral interest, albeit an important one – to the status where it became a scarcely veiled, and scarcely questioned, truly national interest. I believe that after the war a veritable 'cult of food' came into existence. Anyone who, like me, was a child in the 1950s will remember its main incantation: Do not waste your food.

Secondly, the recovery of agriculture after the war took much longer than did that of industry. Around 1947-1948, European industrial production had already regained its pre-war level and by 1950 it was about 20 per cent ahead of what it had been in 1938. Agriculture, by contrast, lagged behind and it was only in 1950-1951 that European countries regained pre-war levels of output. Since, in the intervening period, the population had increased by about 12 per cent, there was still a long way to go before European agriculture regained its pre-war per-capita levels. In the interval, there was a gap between supply and demand. This, in itself, was nothing new. Western Europe had been an aggregate food importer since the 1870s. So, after the war, policy-makers had to take account of the probability that they would have to import more food than before. The real problem was where to obtain it. The largest single source of disposable exports was in the dollar area. It was to the United States, in particular, that governments had to turn to make up the overall shortfall in domestic output. The situation was aggravated, moreover, by the fact that traditional Eastern European supplies had virtually disappeared and, to complicate matters further, food supplies from Asia had also diminished. The result was a total disruption of the normal pattern of international food trade. A few examples will illustrate this situation. In the 1930s Western Europe had obtained 35 per cent of its wheat imports from the dollar area, in 1948-1950 the figure was 76 per cent. For sugar the relevant figures were 37 per cent and 64 per cent, respectively, and for coarse grains, 10 per cent and 24 per cent. Thus, a situation soon emerged in which food imports from the dollar area represented the single largest source of Europe's dollar deficit.[10]

In the longer term the cure for the dollar deficit lay in producing more food. When the Korean War broke out in 1950, the Americans urged the OEEC (the Organisation for European Economic Cooperation comprising 16 West European states that had come together to distribute Marshall Aid) to make it a priority to increase food production by 25 per cent. This would contribute to European security and contribute to solving the dollar problem. Accepting these targets was, of course, no problem. This was, after all, the very policy that the agricultural lobbies had been urging upon their governments since the end of the war. If the government wanted more food, the agricultural sector was prepared to provide it, as long as governments implemented policies to facilitate that goal. Those policies centred on raising agricultural incomes and therefore raising the incentive to produce more food. If, in the process, agriculture improved its position relative to the rest of the economy, this would be an extra bonus for the agricultural pressure groups. These were not only advocating such policies but were also becoming increasingly integrated in their planning and execution.

It is a false dichotomy in this period to talk of a split between government and agricultural pressure groups. In many cases the agriculture pressure groups were the executive agent of government policy. In West Germany, for example, where there was no agricultural ministry, or national government, until the foundation of the Federal Republic in 1949, the Bauernverband had represented agricultural interests before the Allies. It never lost this comparative advantage in power and experience. In Denmark after the war, the government quickly dismantled the state-sponsored agricultural system and transferred many of the powers directly to the Danish agricultural cooperative societies. When I spoke to Sicco Mansholt, the father of the common agricultural policy, I told him that agriculture in the Netherlands seemed to be run like a family firm. He replied that that was because it was like a family firm. Mansholt was the minister of agriculture; one of his cousins was in charge of the European section of the Agricultural Ministry and the other cousin was the head of the Agricultural Alliance of producer groups in the Netherlands. They didn't disagree very often. These are perhaps extreme examples but similar situations prevailed elsewhere in Europe. In many countries there was almost a revolving door between the agricultural lobby and agricultural ministries as they exchanged personnel and people in key areas. This was often complemented by strong cross-party representation in national parliaments that allowed direct and effective pressure on ministers. Thus post-war Europe was characterised by a situation where agriculture was seen as a national priority, where it performed essential economic functions, where the policies underpinning it benefitted the farmers, and where the farmers' interest groups were strategically placed to articulate and exercise these policies.

There was just one problem: What did European self-sufficiency mean? The term had different meanings for the different actors on the scene. For the Americans it obviously meant that Europe as a whole should become less dependent on the dollar area. But for each European country individually the term meant that each tried to liberate itself from imports. And so European self-sufficiency became nothing more than the sum of various, increasingly autarkic policies that were not only reducing dollar imports but were cutting off imports from other European countries as well. This, in itself, was not a new situation. However, the levels of protection throughout Europe in the years 1945-1950 made the 1930s look like a children's playground by comparison.

—

Partly through European self-interest and partly through American pressure, the OEEC countries took the decision at the end of the 1940s to 'liberalise' European trade. This implied the removal of quotas on mutual trade, on the basis of a series of targets culminating, within a relatively short period of time, in their complete elimination. This should have been the perfect forum for freeing trade in agricultural products, since quotas were particularly prevalent in this sector. Yet the scheme failed for agriculture for a variety of reasons. Firstly, no American government, and no European government for that matter, wished to interfere in the internal affairs of another country, and the OEEC's rules made sure that they did not. Whether a national government chose to have a free market for agricultural or to employ rationing through a central purchasing agency was not a question for decision at a European level. Thus, 'state trade', as it was called, was exempted from the scope of the entire operation. And state trade dominated agriculture. France and the United Kingdom both had large state purchasing monopolies from the start, and West Germany introduced the system in 1950-1951. Secondly, it was argued that tariffs were the preserve of the GATT, and so the OEEC's scheme left the issue aside. In this way it ignored a situation whereby tariffs that had previously been suspended (since quotas had rendered their primary function redundant) were reimposed to compensate for quota removal. Thirdly, and finally, countries could choose what to liberate within three broad categories: raw materials and semi-manufactures, industrial goods and agriculture. The usual strategy for agriculture was to eliminate quotas on non-competing tropical produce, to remove them on grain (where almost all countries had large deficits and anyway usually had been secreted under 'state trade'), to remove them on one or two areas of marginal importance, and to leave most of the remainder firmly intact.

By 1950-1951 it was quite clear that the method by which Europe hoped to achieve freer trade in industry was not going to work for agriculture. Against this background another initiative was born, inspired partly by the failure of the OEEC and partly by the success of the Schuman Plan for a European community for coal and steel (ECSC). The idea for a European agricultural community, known as the 'green pool', originated almost simultaneously in France and the Netherlands, and in 1951 a conference was called of European agriculture ministers to discuss the prospect.[11] The discussions involved all the OEEC states and they lasted from 1951-1952 until the 'green pool' was buried in January 1955. The negotiations revealed the extreme reluctance among virtually all the participants to accept the principle of a supranational authority over agriculture. The Dutch were the strongest protagonists but they were completely isolated in their demands for an effective supranational body. At times the French came close to the Dutch position but always retreated in the face of opposition from elsewhere, more concerned to reach some practical solution for their export surpluses than with the form of that solution. The other countries of the Six (Germany, Belgium, Luxembourg and Italy) that had embraced a supranational body for coal and steel certainly did not want one for agriculture; nor did the United Kingdom. The opposition of the United Kingdom was particularly important. The six ECSC countries together faced the prospect that they would soon form an agricultural surplus area for many products; with the United Kingdom included they would be a deficit area. At the time, therefore, the presence of the United Kingdom was seen as essential for any scheme to work. But it also condemned any scheme to failure because the one thing the United Kingdom did not want to do was sacrifice its Commonwealth preferences for the rather dubious advantages of an unformed European agricultural market.

Unsurprisingly, during the green pool negotiations national delegations tended to favour agricultural schemes on a multilateral basis that would allow them to keep domestic protectionism intact and still allow them to share out any extra markets that might emerge. That, in turn, could only occur if extra-European suppliers were pushed aside to make room for high-priced European surpluses, which, of course, was exactly what worried the United Kingdom. A community of this nature would also serve to legitimise high levels of protection, especially where they were already being questioned. Indeed so bizarre had become the negotiations that agricultural ministers were staking out positions way in advance of what would be backed by their national governments. It was schizophrenic, for example, that the German delegation was pushing for ever higher levels of protection, when national government policy was aimed in the opposite direction. Gradually, the national governments regained control over the conference, which was beginning to run away from them in rather dangerous directions. In 1955 they closed it down and transferred the forum to the OEEC.

Mansholt considered that if there was a common market, agriculture had to be part of it. He is important to our story. Sometimes people do change history, and even if you find the external pressures to 'explain' the same changes, sometimes the 'how' is as important as the 'why'. He had two main reasons to push for the incorporation of agriculture in the more global framework of a common market. Firstly, agriculture itself did not provide sufficient scope for trade-offs that would lower protection. There was little point in trade-offs between one highly protective product and another since it would not succeed in lowering the overall level of protectionism. If, on the other hand, you could trade off agricultural protection for gains in industry or elsewhere, you increased the scope for bargaining. The spectacle of the green pool had also persuaded Mansholt that agricultural ministers should never again be left alone to make international policy. He thought that in a wider community countries would largely be represented by ministers of foreign affairs and economic affairs, and that they would securely tie down their agricultural colleagues. Finally, more than ever, he was sure that agriculture had to be run with a supranational agency, and that it could not be left to a set of *ad hoc* bilateral or multilateral deals.

—

There was never any guarantee that agriculture would have become part of the common market treaty. When the ECSC foreign ministers met in Messina, early in the summer of 1955, it was far from certain that the common market itself would ever have made it beyond the agenda. As they flew into Sicily, the French were not particularly enamoured by the idea of a common market, and the Germans were not inclined to cross the French on this issue. It was probably only the fact that an atomic energy community, which at the time was France's highest priority, was being discussed alongside the common market that kept it alive at all.[12] And once the subsequent intergovernmental conference on the Messina proposals, under the chairmanship of Paul-Henri Spaak, got under way, within the group working on the common market there was no will to tackle the question of agriculture. The topic was not even mentioned until seven weeks into the negotiations, and then only summarily. It was left for the drafters of the 'Spaak Report', who began work at the end of 1955, to sort out for themselves what to do with agriculture. At that time only the Netherlands was pushing for its inclusion. What changed the course of the negotiations was that a new, more European-inclined French government came into power in early 1956. In the delegation reports that have been preserved in the archives, one can see a marked change in direction and tempo of the negotiations for a common market. A common market would come into being, but in a form that could accommodate specific French interests. It would therefore also have to include some arrangements for agriculture.

Many histories stop their interpretations at this point. It is an historical fact that requires no further explanation; there was a 'process of integration', the Treaty of Rome advanced that process and it embraced agriculture. Newly released archives, however, allow us to review the range of options discussed and see the alternative clauses that were never signed, never even negotiated, because they were not acceptable. We can see now why the common agricultural policy was protectionist from the start.[13] It was because five agricultural ministers wanted it that way, and because the sixth had to accept an imperfect solution or risk everything. Within the context of this paper, it is sufficient to demonstrate this simply by reference to the aims of the policy (enshrined in Article 39.1):

> *Art 39.1 The objectives of the common agricultural policy shall be:*
> a) *to increase agricultural productivity by promoting technical progress and by ensuring the rational development of agricultural production and the optimum utilisation of factors of production, in particular labour;*
> b) *thus to ensure a fair standard of living for the agricultural community, in particular by increasing the individual earnings of persons engaged in agriculture;*

c) *to stabilise markets;*
d) *to assure the availability of supplies;*
e) *to ensure that supplies reach consumers at reasonable prices.*

The critical statement is 39.1.b since upon this hangs the meaning one should attach to the rest. The Spaak Report had called for the maintenance of returns at a level sufficient for a 'normally productive' enterprise. At the time, the Germans objected to this and suggested instead that the goal be to augment the living standards of *all* engaged in agriculture. The Italians wanted this formulation further enlarged to include the aim of achieving maximum employment in agriculture. Of course neither the German nor the Italian amendment was compatible with the original version. Guaranteeing returns to the 'normally productive' implied, by definition, the sacrifice of the less-than-normally productive. Equally the aim of security of supply entailed a different degree of commitment in the German-Italian version than in the original draft. The latter was compatible with a degree of imports whilst the former implied an all-out drive for self-sufficiency. The Dutch insisted on the original version. At the same time, they secured French support for an amendment stating that the promotion of agriculture should aim at creating the best technical conditions. This would become 39.1.a.

The Dutch then tried to reinforce the direction of these proposals by suggesting that in raising productivity, governments should attempt to adjust the output structure so that it was more in line with global specialisation. Simultaneously, and on this basis, they introduced the commitment that the provision of needs of the population was to be on the basis of 'reasonable prices'. These ideas received virtually no support at all. Both Luxembourg and Italy opposed any reference to reasonable prices which, they argued, would be carried on the backs of the agricultural population. The French rejected any mention of adjustment to global conditions, which, after all, would imply the sacrifice of much of its grain and sugar production. All these positions were supported by the Germans. The Dutch at this point were forced to retreat. By dropping any reference to global specialisation, they could keep the endorsement of 'reasonable prices' (39.1.e). As a further concession, by inserting the word 'thus' at the start of 39.1.b, the goal of raising living standards became conditional on the increase in productivity levels.

The agricultural clauses in the Treaty of Rome established procedures for a policy rather than its contents. If any of the partners had qualms about this, or about the exact nature of the compromises, they swallowed them because there were significant compensatory achievements elsewhere. The lonely battle for a liberal set of clauses had been lost by the Dutch. Their hope was that indeed the supranational elements in the treaty would raise agriculture above the grasp of protectionist pressure groups and their captive ministers. The battle for realising the CAP had still to be joined. The German pressure, in particular, still hoped to use the procedures in the treaty to perpetuate national protectionism. It is interesting that the real provisions guaranteeing that the CAP would be created were hardly debated at all in the build-up to the treaty.

Although there were very few detailed commitments in the agricultural clauses, both phase one and phase two did stipulate stages to be reached in the preparation of the CAP. Moreover, the treaty also contained Article 8, which specified that there would be no progression from the first stage unless all its objectives had been 'attained in substance'. Should there not be unanimity on the transition to the next stage, the first could be automatically twice prolonged by a year. Even then, if progress to stage two were decided by a majority, any state could demand that the question be referred to an arbitration tribunal whose (unanimous) advice would be binding on all parties. In this way, the treaty made clear that if agriculture would be treated on the same basis as other commodities, it could seriously impede progress on other fronts. Indeed, it might prevent advance beyond the first stage altogether since Article 8 was unclear what would happen if the procedures it contained were exhausted without a positive outcome. It was this linkage, forged outside the agricultural clauses themselves, which ultimately proved the motor behind the CAP's creation. Unfortunately no similar linkages existed to steer its final direction.

Mansholt had no qualms about this. He recognised that if he went for a more concrete treaty at the time of the negotiations, it would become even more protectionist than the version actually agreed. Moreover, he was an institutional federalist who believed that if supranational agencies were given a task, they would do it differently and better than individual governments since they could raise themselves above narrow national sectoral interests. He was wrong, because soon the agricultural ministers were alone together, fixing prices and determining the future rules of the policy.

—

In 1958 Sicco Mansholt became the commissioner in charge of implementing the common agricultural policy (CAP) for the new community. Given that agriculture was not usually associated with lengthy tenure or a high profile,

Mansholt was uniquely experienced for the task of commissioner, having served as his country's agricultural minister uninterruptedly since the end of the Second World War. His own experience had left him with little fear of the agricultural lobby. On the contrary, he considered that it was important to work with the farmers' organisations, if a CAP were to be successful. Whilst weak ministers came and went, the barons of agriculture were both stronger and more permanent. It is significant that the policy was launched, and the outlines of the CAP agreed, with a conference of the various national agricultural associations in Stresa in 1959. Even so, it was far from evident that the policy would ever come into being, and it was helped along its way by several factors that could not have been anticipated when the original clauses had been constructed.[14]

The agricultural clauses had been framed in stages which, if read in a negative way, could be interpreted as saying that if the new arrangements had not been agreed, the status quo (and therefore national protection systems) would continue. Apparent reasons for pessimism could be further induced by the fact that agreement for passage to the second stage required a unanimous vote from the Council of Ministers. However, the treaty also stipulated that the creation of the common market as a whole should be synchronised. Thus, a block on agriculture could hold up progress elsewhere. When the Six, therefore, with West Germany in the foreground, wanted to accelerate the dismantling of their industrial tariffs, the French maintained that the first stage for agriculture had to be agreed at the same time, thereby forcing German concessions. After intense negotiations, in 1962, market unity, Community preference and financial solidarity emerged as the principles of a future CAP. This still left important issues, such as the level of support prices and the financing of the system, to be settled before the CAP could become operative. Meanwhile, a regulation was passed establishing the FEOGA (Fonds Européen d'orientation et de garantie agricole) with provisions extended until mid-1965.[15]

The level of common prices as well as the financing of the CAP proved to be very controversial. The fierce negotiations brought the EEC almost to the brink of collapse. It took until the end of 1964 before German reluctance to accept a target price for grain below their prevailing national level could be overcome and a common price level for cereals could be introduced. Proposals for common financing of the CAP were submitted in March 1965. Since these envisaged augmenting the EEC's institutional powers via increasing the budgetary competencies of the European Parliament and through the introduction of majority voting, France flatly opposed the move. In summer 1965 it withdrew its representation at all EEC meetings and, with this 'empty chair' policy, precipitated a major crisis within the Community. It was resolved in January 1966 with the 'Luxembourg Compromise'. This stipulated that, notwithstanding the Commission's rights of initiative enshrined in the Treaty of Rome, it would consult with governments before adopting any important proposal. More significantly, even on issues normally decided by majority, it stipulated that if a country felt its vital interests at stake, the Commission was bound to continue discussion until unanimous agreement was reached. At the same time the financing of the CAP was resolved with a fixed scale of contributions agreed to run until January 1970.

The CAP was modelled on the system used in the Netherlands, which also mirrored those in operation in the other member states. Interestingly, when it was introduced after the war, it relied on high consumer prices rather than budget transfers in order to escape parliamentary scrutiny at times of fiscal stringency. If one accepts this premise, then the principles of the policy make a great deal of sense up to and including the moment that *occasional* surpluses appear. For much of the time, domestic supplies would satisfy much of the market without threatening the base price whilst imports would take care of the rest. Those imports would be taxed so that they did not undercut the domestic price and the revenues would feed into a central fund. When domestic supplies exceeded the market's capacity, the fund could buy up surplus and cover losses involved in selling them on the world market. There might even be sufficient cash remaining to finance schemes for agricultural improvement. If, however, the surpluses became structural, there would always be an obligation to buy up the excess and, without imports, the system would lack the automatic means to fund the operation. The system was the same when applied to one country or to several, with one exception. In a national system, the deficit country would only pay out the foreign exchange involved in buying at world market prices; in the CAP it had to secure those supplies at the same high price prevailing for domestic supplies. Originally, Mansholt had hoped that this mechanism would encourage finance ministers in the food deficit countries (i.e. Germany) to act as a counterweight to the pressures anticipated from the agricultural lobby for higher intervention prices.

Matters did not turn out quite that simply. The CAP negotiations proved excruciatingly drawn-out and complex, and the agricultural ministers moved back into the more central role they had occupied during the 'green pool'. Moreover, there was little counterweight within the Commission. Agricultural policy was conceived and executed by the Community's supranational arm and the CAP became living proof of its achievements. Before long agriculture was being described as the 'motor' for integration or the 'cornerstone' of the Community. Finally, since the German economy was generating one annual balance-of-payments surplus after another, its finance minister was really in no position to complain about the foreign exchange costs of the CAP. Meanwhile, the threshold for success or failure for the policy was determined by the price levels set. It is doubtful whether lower prices would have made for much higher consumption for many goods, but it would certainly have curbed production. For products already moving into 'overproduction' the prices were already way over those commanded on world markets, although one should remember that the world market is more of a dumping ground for surpluses than the 'invisible hand' beloved of free marketers. Bearing this in mind, the price of wheat and barley in 1967-1968 were 70 and 65 per cent above world prices, and that of butter 300 per cent higher.[16] An American estimate suggested that the total transfers to agriculture (45 per cent from higher consumer prices and the rest from national and FEOGA budgets) was already equivalent to 55 per cent of the value of gross output.[17]

Like the sorcerer's apprentice, Mansholt tried to stop the train of events he had set in motion. In 1968, the Commission published new proposals, dubbed the 'Mansholt Plan', designed to tackle the problem of surpluses (through production quotas and withdrawing land from production) and to accelerate structural change in agriculture (further reducing the labour force but hopefully closing the income gap with other sectors of the economy). The proposals created a storm of protest in agricultural circles and by the time they emerged from the decision-making process, nothing much of the original remained intact.[18]

—

The institutionalisation of the cult of food was too strong for governments to resist. As a result, far from a harmonious development of agriculture in balance with the needs of European societies and consistent with the dictates of the world economy, something very different emerged. Even its expansion to include the largest importer of foodstuffs in the world, the UK, did little to offset its inherent deficiencies. The CAP rapidly evolved into a policy that became so expensive that it throttled the movement and dynamism of the community in any other direction. It was a policy that was so contentious that it absorbed between 70 and 80 per cent of the time of the Council of Ministers in trying to thrash it out and caused the Community to lurch from one crisis to another. It was a policy that did not meet its own goal of supplying food to its population at a reasonable price. It was a policy that did not even leave the rest of the world alone, but one where the dumping of subsidised European products on world markets undermined the efforts being promoted through other sectors of the Treaty of Rome for less developed countries to sustain their development in a healthy direction. It was a policy that has never shaken itself loose from the dead hand of history, that has brought more than one set of international trade negotiations to the brink of collapse, and that still has the capacity for further harm before, and if, it is ever brought under control.

POSTSCRIPT

I love the Common Agricultural Policy. I can rant about it for hours, as my students will be willing to testify. This modest incursion into the field was published in *The European Review*, vol. 3, no. 3, 1995, 233-242. I later returned to the theme in a more up-to-date context in 'Waarom kunnen wij het GLB niet hervormen?' ['Why Can't We Reform the CAP?'] in W. Asbeek Brusse et al. (eds.), *De Toekomst van het Europese Gemeenschappelijk Landbouwbeleid* (Utrecht, 2002), 49-62.

As far as the history of the creation of the CAP is concerned, there have been several detailed and comprehensive publications, including Guido Thiemeyer, *Vom 'Pool Vert' zur Europäischen Witrschaftgemeinschaft. Europäische Integration. Kalter Kreig und die Anfänge der Gemeinsamen Europäischen Agrarpolitik, 1950-1957* (Munich, 1999), and Ann-Christina L. Knudsen, *Farmers on Welfare: The Making of Europe's Common Agricultural Policy* (Ithaca, 2009). The biography of Sicco Mansholt, who was the driving personality behind the creation of the policy, has recently been translated into English by Johan van Merriënboer, *Mansholt: A Biography* (Brussels, 2011).

7

'Thank You, M. Monnet; I'll Take Care of That': Some Counterfactual Reflections on Institutional Creation and the Origins of European Integration

Jean Monnet, in his memoirs, tells how on 28 April 1950 he was about to send the copy of his preliminary scheme for a Franco-German coal and steel community to French Prime Minister Georges Bidault. Before he could, he met Bernard Clappier, a high official in the Foreign Ministry, who, on being shown the document, asked whether he could not take a copy immediately to his boss, Foreign Minister Robert Schuman. Schuman, in turn, raised the issue in cabinet the following Tuesday and secured their approval to proceed. Afterwards Monnet had an uncomfortable interview with Bidault who, feeling bypassed, complained about receiving the letter too late. Monnet was inclined to accept that Bidault had, in fact, read the letter before the meeting but distracted by other matters of state, had failed to act on it. Nonetheless, Monnet writes, this is how it became 'not the Bidault Plan, but the Schuman Plan'.[1]

—

The economic imperatives behind the Schuman Plan have already been amply demonstrated by historians. Yet the ECSC not only produced a common regime over the coal and steel industries of six countries, it aspired to regulating conditions of competition, to the execution of joint crisis management and to the implementation of a joint transport policy (since 60 per cent of rail freight comprised coal and steel produce).

In 1949 the Americans were concerned to raise the limits imposed on German industrial recovery and these aims had been reinforced by the installation of a sovereign federal government in the same year. At the same time, European demand for steel was beginning to slacken and the prospect of millions of tonnes of unused German capacity being reactivated was greeted with some trepidation. Moreover, an added worry for the French lay in the fact that their own steel expansion programme was predicated upon the supposition that they would continue to receive deliveries of Ruhr coal. This assumption was undermined by the possibility that German coal supplies might be diverted to German industry, a prospect made more likely by the existence of a domestic coal cartel and by the traditional ownership of mines by steel concerns.[2] Many of us historians have enjoyed contrasting Robert Schuman's lofty rhetoric in his 9 May radio broadcast announcing his plan for a Franco-German coal and steel pool (the first step in the 'federation of Europe' meaning that 'any war between France and Germany was not merely unthinkable, but materially impossible' etc.) with the more prosaic explanatory memorandum prepared by the then head of the French planning commissariat and architect of the Schuman Plan, Jean Monnet. In this he set out the French national interest in unambiguous terms. Thus, the Schuman Plan could be seen as an attempt to avert a threat to French industrial recovery by controlling German freedom, and if France had to sacrifice direct national control over its own industry to accomplish that aim, so be it.[3]

What would have happened had Schuman not made his dramatic intervention in May 1950? At two levels, the answer is very easy. Firstly, there would have been a new multilateral control board with supervisory powers over Ruhr industry. We know this because that is exactly what the British, French and Americans were gathering to discuss in London on 10 May. It was intended to replace the International Ruhr Authority which had been negotiated when an occupied Germany was in a much weaker diplomatic position and which was itself incapable of keeping a lid on agreed levels of output. The French worry was that the new organisation would be looser and less effective in its operation than its predecessor. Secondly, the Americans would have used Law 27, stuffed down the throats of a reluctant government, to break up the vertical ownership of the mines by the steel industry, to break up the large concentrations of steel mill ownership and to outlaw the coal sales cartel. They would have ensured compliance by threatening to leave remaining occupation controls in existence until it was done. We know this because it is exactly what they did in autumn 1950. Again, the French concern was that these measures might not stick once Germany regained effective sovereignty. And again they had a point, because the coal cartel was never effectively wound up and because, from the mid-1950s, the

German mills again began to merge. Both these developments occurred with the compliance of the 'supranational' High Authority and with scarcely a ripple on the French national consensus.

Why did actions that supposedly threatened the survival of the French state in 1950 cause so little concern a few years later? The answer lies in the fact that the feared recession never materialised. The outbreak of the Korean War and the surge in rearmament restored buoyant conditions to the steel market. This so restored business confidence that by the mid-1950s considerations had turned to the need for larger production units to reap productivity gains necessary to meet American competition.

The only remaining snag in this alternative scenario lay in the French desire to secure adequate coal supplies. One reason why the French had ceased to worry so much about the question of the structure of German ownership lay in the fact that under the ECSC it obtained non-discrimination in prices and, in times of shortage, equality of access to raw materials. What else could have produced those results? Firstly, assuming that the new Ruhr control organisation proved incapable of obtaining compliance, the OEEC was itself moving against discriminatory trading practices such as double pricing. Moreover, during the commodity shortages occasioned by the Korean boom, it also set up a number of product committees to coordinate supplies. West German compliance in these agreements was likely given its weak international position and its need for the political and military umbrella provided by Western Europe and the United States. It was doubly guaranteed by the fact that, because of the 1950-1951 balance-of-payments crisis, Germany was dependent on dollar credits from the European Payments Union. Secondly, these conditions could have been fulfilled by a cartel.

A horizontal producers' cartel would have fixed domestic prices in different markets, would have had regulations to deal with booms and slumps and would have jointly operated on foreign markets. It would not have been much different, in fact, from the functional operation of the High Authority in these areas. Indeed the ECSC sanctioned a producers' cartel of the Six to operate in third markets. With concentrated patterns of ownership and domestic cartels in operation, France and Germany were ideally suited for an international coal and steel cartel. Indeed a steel cartel had existed in the interwar years, albeit with mixed success,[4] and in 1949 there was evidence that businessmen in both countries were trying to renew the links.[5] It is not such a shocking idea. Europe at the time was replete with cartels, both national and international. Indeed, had it not formed one, it would have been almost alone among metals not to have done so since non-ferrous metals and aluminium were all covered by international cartel arrangements.[6] The Americans would have been horrified but they would probably have been unable to do anything about it, in the same way as they failed to break up cartels in other areas.

—

The next major shock that produced a supranational response was the American call, in the wake of the outbreak of the Korean War, for German rearmament. Yet there was no avoiding the strategic logic. Ever since the recording of the first Soviet atomic test in autumn 1949, it had become clear that unilateral nuclear blackmail had only a limited credibility. Even with the calls for a more intensive Western European military build-up, allied strategic planning had to take account of the prospect, in the event of a Soviet attack, that large parts of Europe would be overrun before the advance could be checked and the awesome task of reconquest begun. The only way to mitigate this unwelcome scenario was to put more bodies between the East-West frontier and the Atlantic, and these would preferably be German bodies. If a reindustrialised German economy had been cause for deep disquiet, the prospect of recreating an independent Wehrmacht was regarded by the French with absolute horror.

The French reacted almost instinctively and in short order Monnet's staff produced a supranational framework within which to regulate German rearmament, in the form of the Pleven Plan, for a European Defence Community (EDC). But whereas the Schuman Plan at least subjected *all parties* to the same control, even if German industry may have lost more options through joining, the control mechanisms of the Pleven Plan were more lop-sidedly discriminatory. It is an eloquent statement of Germany's perceived international weakness that its government was willing to go along with the scheme for so long.[7]

Firstly, presumably to stop the Germans getting together and doing some invading on the sly, the maximum size of any national unit was strictly limited. Since this made little military sense the figure was subsequently raised but the principle remained intact. Secondly, although the arrangements for a *European* army were to apply to *all* German troops, France wanted to exempt those parts of its armed forces deemed for colonial use as well as its navy. While solving one problem, this expedient immediately created two others since it would leave Germany as the largest single component within the EDC. Since there was to be communal funding (and some proportionality in the spending in different states) there was a danger of Germany acquiring a large military complex at communal expense. This was effectively resolved by declaring that strategic military equipment should not be produced in strategically vulnerable areas and promptly defining all German territory as constituting such an area. To prevent German military dominance spilling into the political sphere, the scheme envisaged communal political control over the immediate decisions through a directly elected European Assembly. It was at this point that the entire scheme, conceived largely to assuage French public opinion in the first place, began to unravel.

The French parliamentary assembly reflected only the most tenuous 'consensus' at the best of times and was really a sequence of shifting centre-left and centre-right, usually single issue, coalitions. Even the centre was split on the issue.[8] In the EDC context, the left wanted a strengthening of democratic control whereas the Gaullists were determined to strengthen national sovereignty. Concessions towards one wing served to alienate the other only further. Mesmerised by the impasse, successive French governments tried several times to renegotiate the treaty whilst refraining from submitting the result to a parliamentary vote. When Prime Minister Pierre Mendès France eventually did so in autumn 1954, the treaty was rejected.

In virtually complete contrast to the ECSC, which acquired swift adherence of the Benelux states and Italy, the EDC was regarded with considerable caution. Wiebes and Zeeman have recently demonstrated that the Benelux states had been far from convinced of the immediacy of a Russian threat. They had joined NATO largely because of a conviction of the indirect political and economic benefits that could flow from membership, or that could be curtailed had they remained aloof.[9] They were also both noticeably reluctant to expand arms production in the wake of the Korean War. Sceptical of the Soviet threat, they were even less convinced by the argument that a rearmed Germany, with large foreign troop bases on its soil, would constitute a political maverick on the post-war scene.

The Dutch government, especially, saw no need for an EDC. Despite appeals to a 'solidarity of the Six', it joined the initial talks only as an observer. It regarded the military arrangements as slightly absurd and was extremely worried about the impact of a joint military budget for its defence industry. Since the cutting edge of Dutch technology lay in its naval dockyards and the advanced electronics that a modern navy required, it stood to lose out in a land-based arrangement. If it was not careful, the Netherlands could see its role as knitting socks for soldiers and providing their tinned rations.[10] When talk shifted in 1952 to giving the political control organ an enhanced status, its patience snapped. It responded by refusing to accept such a political construction unless it were charged with real economic tasks. This remained the Dutch 'national' position, although it scarcely reflected a consensus.[11] The Dutch demands represented a compromise rather than a consensus and in this way, the EDC construction, and the political community, became further complicated with the task of creating a customs union. This only helped undermine its attraction for the French, experiencing at the time a deep balance-of-payments crisis, still further.

The EDC was designed not to control the German problem but to resolve a question of French political opinion. And that was the reason – the only reason – it failed. Notwithstanding misgivings, the treaty had been ratified by all the others except Italy where the delay was attributable to the length of parliamentary procedures. Moreover, the United States government, which had initially been sceptical about the entire venture, became an enthusiastic advocate and threw its considerable diplomatic pressure[12] behind securing its acceptance. Germany was rearmed and no government fell as a result.

For the purposes of my own argument, the EDC case reinforces the utility of existing multilateral frameworks in the 1950s. German rearmament took place, as agreed in 1955, within the framework of NATO. At the same time, the country was admitted into the Western European Union (WEU), a loose defence pact established in 1948 and embracing, until then, the rest of the Six and the United Kingdom. Finally, as part of the package, the British government pledged itself to maintaining its troops in Germany. Except for France, this was everyone's preferred solution back in 1950-1951 and the only function of the EDC interlude was to provide time for France to recognise that it had no viable alternative.

—

Unlike the ECSC or the EDC, the idea of a common market was not prompted by any specific crisis. It stemmed largely from the concern of two successive Dutch foreign ministers, Dirk Stikker and Beyen, about the inherent unfairness for the Netherlands of the OEEC's trade liberalisation scheme and the potential reversibility of the concessions. The latter had been amply demonstrated by the re-imposition of direct import controls by Germany, the United Kingdom and, finally, France during successive balance-of-payments crises in 1950-1953. The appeal of a customs union in such circumstances lay in the eventual treatment equality of different sectors and, by removing national trade controls from the competence of national governments, in the irreversibility of such measures. It was a defensive arrangement, based on a fear of a return to the 'traditional' trade cycle of the 1930s rather than the forward-looking arrangement of liberal economic theorists. Although the initial Dutch plans were crude, during their exploration in 1953-1954 there grew an appreciation that such measures would need to be accompanied either by a measure of policy cooperation or by a supranational control agency. The introduction of the customs union demands into the EDC had brought the plans within the ambit of the Six, but that did not exclude efforts within other multilateral forums, including the GATT, the Council of Europe and the OEEC, to obtain a greater measure of trade liberalisation by other means.

When the famous 're-launch of European integration' at Messina in May 1955 was being prepared, the position of the Dutch foreign minister Jan-Willem Beyen was that five countries, all except France, had agreed in principle to the creation of a common market and that it was therefore a natural starting point for discussion. Monnet and Belgian foreign minister Paul-Henri Spaak took a diametrically opposing view and argued that since the one country to disagree was France, it was the very point not to start. Without Beyen's stubbornness, and Monnet's wish to have the Dutch involved in a joint memorandum, there would have been no common market on the agenda at Messina. Nor was there any consensus behind it when it was on the agenda: the Germans, expecting the French to reject it, arrived with instructions to do likewise. Nonetheless, the idea managed to survive in the final text of the Messina meeting that set up a hotchpotch of committees to examine various, primarily sectoral schemes of which the most important was an atomic energy community.

It is difficult to say when the French decided seriously to support the idea for a common market. I, personally, favour a date early in 1956 when a new government including the socialists came to power and I base that judgement on a reading of the 'delegation reports' which suggest a rise in the seriousness of the discussions from that point on. Milward adopts the same position even though it seems difficult to speak of a *national* consensus if its implementation depends on the transient confluence of governing parties that characterised the Fourth French Republic.[13] It is difficult to speak of an obvious consensus behind the common market in France. Nor was there one in Germany where, when the UK's free trade area proposals were announced in November 1956, Minister for Economics Ludwig Erhard embarked on a long personal campaign in favour of their acceptance, if necessary in preference to the common market. Even in the Netherlands, Drees persisted in his opinion that in signing the Treaty of Rome, the Dutch had committed themselves to a small protectionist club.

What would have happened if no common market negotiations had opened in 1955? Certainly, the trade boom would not have ended. Trade is driven by many factors and the link between economic growth and trade is not a one-way path. The presence or absence of frontier impediments is only one element in the equation and not necessarily the most important. Insofar as trade barriers did play a role, quantitative restrictions had largely been removed on intra-European trade in industrial goods already through the OEEC's trade liberalisation scheme. In January 1955, the organisation had adopted a target of freeing 90 per cent of 'private trade' from quotas and it is probable that it would have been capable, possibly through a system of gradually increasing imports allowed under the remaining quotas similar to that agreed within the EEC, to remove the remainder.

That leaves the question of tariffs. Assuming that tariffs were important, there are two scenarios for the subsequent development. The first would leave tariffs within the scope of the OEEC. Already in January 1955, the so-called 'low tariff countries' of Scandinavia, the Benelux and Switzerland had made their acceptance of the further removal of quotas conditional upon adoption of measures to deal with tariff disparities. At the time the Belgian minister of foreign commerce was contemplating proposing a free trade area within the OEEC. By mid-1956, the low-tariff club had come up with a scheme for decapping (i.e. with a 25 per cent cut) high tariffs on goods important for intra-European trade. That move was stalled by a UK countermove to establish a committee on how the common market could be accommodated within the OEEC's framework. Without that, and the promise it held that some new proposal would be forthcoming, the pressure for immediate action on tariffs would have been difficult to counter.[14]

The second scenario relies on the development of the American balance of payments and the role of the GATT. The American balance of payments had been in deficit throughout the 1950s but this had been seen as furnishing a welcome opportunity to replenish foreign exchange reserves. Towards the end of the 1950s most European countries had reached saturation point and wanted America to take corrective action. The US deficit in these years fell into two phases: in 1956-1958 the cause of the problem was a sharp collapse in the surplus on the current account; from 1960 onwards it derived from an outflow of private investment. Although the latter has been interpreted partly as a response to the common market's creation (jumping tariff walls etc.), it was equally a response to higher levels of growth and higher interest rates in Western Europe and would have occurred in some measure anyway. The US response was that, whatever the cause, one solution would lie in an improved commercial balance with Europe. In 1958 Under-Secretary of State Douglas Dillon of the United States called for a new round of tariff cuts within the GATT, followed later by the even more successful Kennedy Round. Just as a European solution for payments (the EPU) had been wound up to make way for a multilateral management under the IMF, so the USA might have called for the end of discriminatory trade arrangements aimed against itself and the implementation of a worldwide solution.

—

Milward includes agriculture as one of the three pillars of his post-war consensus, arguing that the widening gap between agrarian and industrial incomes had been a major factor in the 1930s in driving rural voters towards anti-democratic parties.[15] Yet, it is only this assertion, placing agriculture squarely in the middle of his equation of the nation states' survival, that distinguishes his subsequent analysis from a straight 'interest group' approach. The remaining difference is that these strategies were implemented not through the farmers' lobbies themselves but through the agricultural ministries that they had mastered, and often utterly penetrated.[16] It is only this that turned (and presumably still turns) narrow sectoral goals of income maximisation, if necessary through international fora, into the higher level politics of nation state survival. And if the problem was so obvious and so pressing, why was it that it took nearly a decade and a half from the first plans in 1950 to effectuate a supranational policy?

The answer, as Milward correctly observes, is that there was no consensus on whether an international policy was relevant, let alone the form that it should take. The legacy of the so-called 'green pool' negotiations was the realisation of the polarisation of the Six and a reluctance to jeopardise progress in other areas by reopening such a contentious issue. It was only seven weeks into the intergovernmental discussions agreed at Messina that agriculture was first seriously discussed at all, a clear sign of the equivocation of the representatives on this point. Again, as with the common market, it was a change in government in France that produced a swing in attitudes towards a supranational solution for agriculture.[17]

That hammering out the treaty articles was left late reflected less a lack of desire to include agriculture in the package than an awareness that as soon as one moved to fill in the details, the old wounds would reopen. The Dutch were virtually isolated in wanting reasonably low levels of protection and equally isolated in defending policies necessary to accomplish this goal. When, after the Suez debacle, pressure was put on the negotiators to conclude the treaty quickly (before the French government fell and the majority for ratification evaporated), the Dutch were content to leave the provisions of the treaty vague. They realised that had they insisted they would have liked the outcome far less than the risk of all (or nothing) later. This position, in turn, was reinforced by the attitude of Sicco Mansholt, the Dutch minister for agriculture and destined to become the first commissioner in charge of the agricultural portfolio. He had great faith in the EEC's Council of Ministers, which would represent the 'general ministries' of economics, finance etc., controlling their protectionist colleagues in agriculture. He also had great faith in the ability of the Commission to propose sensible solutions. Thus, away from the hothouse of the treaty negotiations, a more competitive regime could be constructed. History would demonstrate how wrong he was.

Again we could ask the question of what would have happened had there been no CAP. In this case it is difficult to envisage any multilateral solution. But did agricultural trade need such a solution anyway? Trade would have continued on the basis of annual or fixed-term contracts in the same way as trade with UK and Germany had done before, and for Denmark was to continue throughout the next decade as well. Milward's argumentation anticipates this line of reasoning and he posits another objection.

He asks whether, under such circumstances, the nation state could afford to maintain the high level of subsidies it did and whether the post-war consensus could survive a more stringent budgetary climate. There are two possible scenarios to answer this question. The first argues that states could have supported higher claims on national budgets. Norway, Sweden and Switzerland, all with highly protectionist regimes and all locked outside the CAP, have done exactly that since the Second World War. The second scenario argues that states could not. This would have shown itself through a taxpayers' or consumers' revolt. A new voting coalition would have appeared in national parliaments. One consensus would have passed and would have been replaced by another. And given all the distortions of the CAP in wasteful output, domestic consumption patterns, international trade structures, growth in underdeveloped countries and the outcomes of successive international trade negotiations, would that have been a bad thing anyway?

—

The purpose of this exposition has been to demonstrate that integrationist solutions were not 'essential' to the survival of the nation state. It goes further and suggests that the second-best solutions were not so demonstrably functionally inferior to the supranational options actually adopted as to posit a history different from that which occurred. But that is the problem with counterfactuals: one is still left explaining the actual ‘factuals’.

Why, if supranational solutions were not functionally necessary, were they nevertheless chosen in the 1950s? The first part of the answer must lie in the acceptance of the fact that they were addressed to the solution of real problems in a ‘fair’ way for the participants; in other words, in a way that defended their national interests. It is surely time to put this beyond doubt. It does not have to be at odds with other lines of explanation.

Jean Monnet recognised as much in his memoirs. It has to be said that Monnet did not write his own memoirs since he had a lousy memory. They were written, like many other histories, on the basis of the paper record left behind. The ‘explanations’ they contain for specific events are therefore more in the nature of ‘rationalisations’ or ‘justifications’. Like the Bible, they reflect a moral (or, in this case, a political) truth rather than a strictly historical one. Anyway, Monnet’s recipe for ‘integration’ was to find a problem requiring a solution and solve it. In doing so, however, it was not the solution of the problem that was important but the way in which it was solved. Monnet believed in the rule of law, in the ability of regimes of decision-making to modify national behavioural patterns, and in the importance of constitutions. These views he shared with his many, legally trained, friends in the United States. It also formed part of the reference sets for the European politicians often occupying positions of power in the 1950s. Thus, as we saw clearly in the case of agriculture, there was a predisposition towards leaving a set of processes in a treaty rather than to tie up every solution. For them, multilateralism alone was not enough.

POSTSCRIPT

This chapter was first published in Dutch in a festschrift for Professor Henk Wesseling, on his retirement from Leiden University. It appeared as ‘“Dank U mijnheer Monnet; Ik zal er voor zorgen.” Enige contrafactuele beschouwingen over het oprichten van organisaties en de oorsprong van de Europese integratie’ in M.P. Bossenbroek, M.E.H.N. Mout and C. Musterd (eds.), *Met de Franse Slag. Opstellen voor H.L. Wesseling* (Leiden, 1998), 107-122.

I have been fascinated by counterfactual history ever since studying the debate on the impact of railways on the US economy in the 19th century when I was an undergraduate. Since then I have found counterfactuals a useful way to pose the question whether a particular event was important or not. The festschrift gave me a chance to experiment in the genre myself. There has been only one attempt, to my knowledge, to do the same kind of thing for the European Union and that was by Barry Eichengreen and Andrea Boltho, 'The Economic Impact of European Integration', CEPR Discussion Paper no. 6820, 2008. For anyone wanting to delve deeper into the genre, I can recommend the classic Robert Cowley (ed.), *The Collected What If?* (New York, 2001), and there is also a volume of essays in Dutch by Tom van der Meer (ed.), *Wat als ... Pim Fortuyn niet was vermoord? Dertien alternatieve geschiedenissen van het Koninkrijk Nederland* (Amsterdam, 2011).

8

The Dynamics of Policy Inertia: The UK's Participation in and Withdrawal from the Spaak Negotiations

Early in June 1955 the six foreign ministers of the European Coal and Steel Community (ECSC) met on the island of Sicily, at Messina. It was the first time that they had come together since the previous summer and the debacle of the European Defence Community (EDC) project. That failure had not only witnessed the death of a series of interlinked supranational projects but it had also threatened to leave a dangerous gap in Europe's defences since the EDC was supposed to provide the framework for a limited West German rearmament. The cause of the failure had lain clearly with France's inability to find a parliamentary majority but part of that, in turn, was attributed to a French fear of being isolated with Germany in a military alliance. French socialist leaders, in particular, had urged that the United Kingdom should commit its troops in Europe as a gesture which would save the EDC and permit German rearmament to go ahead. At the time the UK had refused. Once the EDC Treaty had failed, however, it had not only given a pledge to maintain troops in Europe but also entered a defence pact with 'the Six', the Western European Union, which allowed German rearmament to take place within the framework of NATO. Moreover, in this period, it had further strengthened its links with the Six by signing the first ever association agreement with the ECSC itself. Given these closer ties which had developed between the UK and 'little Europe' since the summer of 1954, it was natural that when the Six decided in Messina to investigate ways of increasing cooperation among themselves in the fields of atomic energy, trade, classical energy and transport they should have invited the UK to become associated with that venture too from the start.

The rest of the story is well known. The UK decided to send representatives to the talks but withdrew them in November 1955 when work on drafting the final report began, and did so in such a way as to make clear that it would reject any scheme offered. A year later, however, it offered to negotiate an industrial free trade area, within the framework of the Organisation for European Economic Cooperation (OEEC), which would embrace the customs union that the Six were planning to create. In December 1958 the talks with the Six collapsed when De Gaulle vetoed any further participation, but the UK pressed ahead to create the European Free Trade Area with a more limited membership. In 1961 the United Kingdom applied to join the European Communities on the basis of full membership, but two further French vetoes later and the inevitable long period of negotiations meant that it was not until 1971 that a treaty realising this aim was agreed. It is this tortuous subsequent history which has led to the spurning of the original opening in November 1955 being seen as some great missed opportunity for which the British were to pay by slower growth, whilst they were locked out, and traumatic adjustment problems once they were eventually let in.

No matter how ironic subsequent events might make the November 1955 decision appear, I would argue that this judgement is basically ahistorical. It would have taken a major overhaul in policy assumptions and parameters to have envisaged British membership of a supranational community way back in 1955. A more meaningful counterfactual analysis could be made, however, if one postulates a situation in which the UK had formulated a strategy aimed at preventing any supranational construction from coming about whilst at the same time trying to find arrangements to accommodate its interest with the Six, even if they attempted to move further in certain areas alone. It is true that such a strategy might not have worked, but it was not even tried. It is against such an alternative, however, that the policy formulation of 1955 can more properly be judged.

In the literature explaining foreign policy and international relations, many early approaches conducted analysis at the level of national governments, as 'acts of nations'. The underlying assumption is that the government attempts to maximise the national interest within a given international context.[1] This model has its adherents for the history of European integration. Stanley Hoffman suggests that the European Community's 'establishment resulted from the conviction that purely national action in a variety of economic domains was no longer satisfactory'[2] and if we extend this line of thinking we would be invited to conclude that the UK did not share this conviction. It is true that there were 'objective' factors which could be used to 'explain' the UK's tepid participation in and eventual withdrawal from the Spaak negotiations. Whether they did so and whether such factors were really so objective rather than widely held mythology, is open to question.

Looking at the economic domain, it could be argued that UK trade was not, and never had been, particularly oriented towards Europe, let alone towards the Six. In 1954 the Commonwealth absorbed over half of UK exports and provided over half of its import requirements. OEEC-Europe took a quarter of UK exports and supplied a fifth of imports but, within this, the shares of the Six were 13 and 11 per cent respectively. Now it is true that the trend of European shares for exports had been upwards since 1950, but it could be argued that this represented a catch-up with the pre-war position and, as far as the Six were concerned, this still left their importance lesser that it had been at the end of the 1930s and still further below the levels at the end of the 1920s[3]. This, therefore, is the picture which policy-makers had before them in 1955, and it was certainly held by the then Commonwealth secretary (and later prime minister) Lord Home.[4] We now know that the upward trend was not some statistical readjustment towards an old equilibrium but rather the reflection of the emergence of one of the fastest-growing markets in the world. Something of this might have filtered into the 1955 consciousness, had the figures been broken down to isolate trade in manufactures, but the background briefs for policy analysis did not reach down so deeply.[5] It might also have emerged had the Federation of British Industry been consulted earlier but they were not brought into the decision-making process until late in the day. After the UK withdrawal, its overseas director, Peter Tennant, had expressed open sympathy with the customs union idea and frank amazement at the UK's decision.[6] When finally consulted about the industrial free trade area proposals at the end of 1956, the reaction of the FBI's membership was overwhelmingly in favour.[7] As a leading industrialist, Sir Edwin Plowden, expressed it, industry needed to open access 'to markets which were dynamic rather than static or even contracting',[8] which is really what 'catching-up' looks like from the board room. Thus the shares-of-trade argument provides one component for an objective explanation – it was a 'reality' but one which was probably imperfectly perceived and certainly wrongly evaluated.

Linked to the trade-shares picture, one needs to consider the question of Commonwealth preferences: the system whereby the UK was a preferential purchaser of primary products from these countries and received, in exchange, privileged access for its own industrial exports. About one fifth of all UK exports 'benefitted' from preferential arrangements to Commonwealth markets, a figure which suggests that it was an important 'reality' in shaping policy attitudes.[9] But that, too, was based on an illusion. If you wanted to assess the effectiveness of the preference system you had to know the products covered, the countries of origin and the areas of destination, and then you had to assess what would happen to UK imports and, more particularly, to UK exports if preferences were removed. The Board of Trade recognised that such figures would be difficult to acquire, but what really made it sceptical about obtaining a solution was that industry would be unlikely to provide assistance because it was so 'strongly attached' to the preference system.[10] What compounded this absurdity was that the Board of Trade felt that this would be the case even if an objective study were to show that exports would perform better without preferences. Then, to make matters worse, it abdicated its own responsibility for even making a serious attempt at assessment and confined itself instead to vacuous analysis based on figures, would you believe, from 1948 which were known to be incomplete and unreliable.[11] British thinking in this area, then, can be characterised as carefully considered irrationality.

The Commonwealth, of course, formed part of the political 'reality' of British policy-makers. In two world wars (one of which, it must be remembered, had only ended ten years before the events we are discussing) the Commonwealth had provided credit, raw materials and men for a united war effort and was still an important factor in Far Eastern defence policy. It further served, after the war, to smooth the decolonisation trauma by substituting the UK's image of Empire with one of leadership of a federation of free and independent nations. It served, in fact, to bolster the selfimage of the UK as a world power. Any surrender of sovereignty to another body, especially a European body, was seen to be somehow in conflict with this overseas direction of UK foreign policy. Indeed, to rationalise and accommodate this fiction, Churchill had coined the image of the UK at the centre of three overlapping circles – the Commonwealth, a special relationship with the United States and an association with Europe.[12] It is not clear, of course, why membership in a European Community should have been at odds with maintaining commonwealth links in 1955 any more so than it was in 1961, but few voices were raised to contradict this impression.[13]

The rejection of sovereignty surrender did not derive simply from Commonwealth relations or geometric world visions, but had strong historic roots of its own. Looking at the postwar period one can really trace its origins back to Bevin's refusal to consider any real powers for the Council of Europe in 1948, but the true touchstone was the events of late 1949. At that time the United States had increased its pressure for some deeper 'integration' in Europe and if, as now appears, they had never really considered that the UK would join, then that part of the message had somehow got lost en route. There was a huge flap in the foreign office as they attempted to find someone 'sane' in the US administration and to marshal their arguments for not being dragged along.[14] These were presented in a speech by the chancellor of the exchequer to the council of the OEEC in November 1949,[15] which was continuously alluded to whenever the principle of supranationality was raised. It was a kind of talisman used to ward off evil spirits like Schuman Plans, Mansholt Plans and Pleven Plans, and, as the 1950s progressed, it had proved its worth. But the issue itself was never reexamined. Nor was there ever any consideration whether it covered a large or small sector of the economy, whether sovereignty surrender was to be substantial or whether by unanimous voting, it would preserve a basically intergovernmental institutional form.

The foregoing paragraphs have listed a number of plausible factors which could be used to demonstrate that the UK withdrawal from the Spaak negotiations was a logical response to the need to maximise national interest within existing international constraints. Trade with Europe was too small to justify the risk to the economic advantages of existing commonwealth relations, especially if it implied acceptance of a reduced world status and the loss of control over (part of) the affairs of the nation state. The fact that it can be demonstrated that such visions may have been flawed does nothing to diminish the sincerity with which such convictions were held. As an explanation it looks convincing and it fits with the observed facts. To make it really convincing, however, one would have to demonstrate how the alternative offered by the Messina invitation was weighed up against such considerations and was found wanting. At this point the explanation would begin to fall apart because this simply did not happen.

There were two ways in which the original invitation to join the Six could have been interpreted. The first would have been to examine it in the light of events since 1950: a group of six countries had been trying to federate Europe in coal and steel, defence, foreign policy and economics; they had been checked in 1954 but, having patched up their difficulties, they were ready to pick up the threads and start again. The UK was to be invited because it was bad form not to do so. In this interpretation it is the creation of a supranational community which is the primary object of the exercise. The second interpretation would focus on the events since 1954: the UK had reattached itself to continental Europe, had helped resolve European/German problems and was considered important to continue to strengthen these links together. In this reading of events it is British participation which is the primary goal, and the exact form of arrangements a secondary consideration.

This second interpretation was not even considered. Instead it was assumed from the start that the Six were about to embark on a new drive towards supranationality. It was perhaps unfortunate that Jean Monnet, the high priest of the federalist movement who had just resigned from his chairmanship of the ECSC to form the Action Committee for the United States of Europe, was the first source of news for the Foreign Office. On 6 May 1955 he informed the British about new integrative initiatives but he expressed the hope that the British would wait 'until something had happened before deciding in which way they would cooperate with it'.[16] It implied that UK participation would be reduced to a spectator role. When, four days later, the Foreign Office received the Beyen/Spaak memorandum calling on the Six to increase cooperation in atomic energy and create a customs union, the opinion of the head of the Mutual Aid Department in charge of coordinating policy was tantamount to rejection since there was little point in preparing a position 'when we are not prepared to take part'.[17] Although the Messina resolution studiously avoided any reference to supranationality and despite reassurances that this had been meant seriously, British scepticism must have been kindled by the appointment of PaulHenri Spaak as chairman of the conference – Spaak, the chief apostle of federalism who had previously chaired the committee which had drafted the European Political Community Treaty and who had earlier resigned his chairmanship of the Council of Europe because it was not doing enough in the cause of European unity. With the Messina initiative being treated as a question of supranationality, the kneejerk response would have been rejection.

However, within the Foreign Office it was felt that the impetus behind the initiative was 'political' and that it would be damaging for the UK to refuse participation outright. The Mutual Aid Committee interdepartmental committee (whose brief covered this area) advised the cabinet to approve constructive though noncommittal participation.[18] This was accepted by the cabinet despite protests from the Chancellor of the Exchequer Rab Butler who felt that simple 'observer' status was all that was called for in light of the fact that the UK had no intention of joining anything.[19] Harold Macmillan, the foreign secretary, favoured a more active role, not to help the Six (or 'the Seven' if the UK were to join) create any new institutions but to keep matters 'in a form in which we could join' (i.e. intergovernmental) and then shunt them to the safer havens of the OEEC.[20]

If this were to be the strategy, and I will argue later that something of the kind might have worked, it meant coming up with an attractive alternative pretty fast,[21] but although some of the actors in the Spaak negotiations seemed to have had the impression that the British were under tight control from Whitehall, their main representative, Russell Bretherton, a top official in the Board of Trade, really had no more that a watching brief. This stressed that there should be no commitment to anything resembling supranationality and suggested that if a customs union was formed by the rest, a low external tariff would be preferable. To help direct the delegation and to assess whether the UK could join any of the initiatives a subcommittee of the Mutual Aid Committee was created.[22] The pace at which it worked did not suggest appreciation of the need for urgency. It was a month and a half before the preliminary report was completed (1 September)[23] and a further month and a half before the final reports were ready (24 October).[24]

There is no room to analyse the reports in detail. They were not based on any contemporary statistical analysis nor had outside bodies been consulted. The industrial sections of the Board of Trade had largely taken a pessimistic line on the negative consequences for them of participation in a common market and the loss of preferences which was likely to follow; so much so that the chairman felt himself obliged to put in writing that they should be treated with a pinch of salt:

> *The general tendency of the Departmental analysis suggests that practically every major sector of United Kingdom industry and agriculture would lose. [...] These conclusions do not seem to be altogether consistent with the size and trend of United Kingdom exports at the present time. [...] We think that the production Departments have tended generally to underestimate the competitive ability of United Kingdom industry, and we consider that the enquiry should be taken as an indication of the broad sectors of the United Kingdom economy likely to contract or expand, rather than those which are likely to be overwhelmed by disaster.*[25]

On the financial side Treasury officials stressed the danger to sterling and the loss of some measure of control of the domestic economy which would ensue from closer interdependence. The whole direction of the arguments was towards rationalising a UK withdrawal. Nonetheless the chairman summed up as follows:

> *First, that we should not on any account encourage the constitution of a European Common market by the six countries, but second, that if they ever succeeded in establishing such a market, regardless of our membership, it is quite likely so far as is possible to judge [...] that in economic terms, we should lose more than we should gain by holding aloof.*[26]

It would be wrong to attribute the negative UK decision to the workings of the committee. The slowness of its work, the bias of the approach and the shallowness of its analysis were not faults inherent in the Whitehall policymaking process, as I will demonstrate later, but were reflections of the fact that there was no decision to take. Even when agreeing to join the negotiations, most of the upper echelons of policymakers had made the mental reserve that once the beast showed its full federalist colours, the British would deal with it in the usual way. It had been standard British practice throughout the 1950s to lead offending initiatives gently by the hand towards a labyrinth of technical subcommittees of some compliant intergovernmental organisation, wave them a fond farewell and hope never to see them again.[27] If, therefore, there was no intention of joining, there was little point in expending too much energy in convincing oneself why one shouldn't join.

This still leaves open the question of why there was no pressure to deflect the Six from their apparently chosen course within the negotiations. In retrospect it might seem strange but the fact is that the top of the foreign office succeeded in convincing itself that the Six would fail! We do not know what information came in from the capitals of the Six (all those files are closed to historians) but we do know which ones reached the policy dossiers – and they virtually all point to sources of division within governments and between them. Among the 'evidence' they piled up was the fact that Benelux ministers launched the initiative to bolster weak political positions at home,[28] a split in the French government on the question of supranationality,[29] the question of French fear of German domination,[30] and French disillusionment with the whole venture.[31] It was a pleasant game and one which the British continued to play virtually up to the signing of the treaty. The result, though, was that the feeling was created that any positive UK contribution might actually 'save' the conference but that left alone, or nudged onwards by a UK withdrawal, it would probably collapse.

This tenor is apparent when the formal round of policy evaluations on the internal reports began. The Mutual Aid Committee meeting on 27 October recommended that the UK should join neither Euratom nor a common market. It recorded the opinion that if the Six went ahead, it would create severe difficulties but 'it was improbable that the six powers would have the necessary tenacity to proceed with this idea'.[32] At the Economic Steering Committee (an interdepartmental committee dealing with economic as opposed to foreign policy issues) on 1 November these decisions were endorsed, although withdrawal should be delayed because it was felt that the French would bring the venture to collapse and 'it would be undesirable for us to appear to be the cause'.[33] The question then passed to the Economic Policy Committee on 11 November where these findings were approved again. This committee was a cabinet committee on which the ministers responsible for questions with an economic content were represented. This time it was Butler who came out with an impressive list of characters who would do the dirty deed – the Americans for fear of a discriminatory trading bloc, the French for fear of everything, and everyone else, except the Germans, for fear of Germany.[34]

Hints from the United States that a withdrawal early rather than late would be appreciated,[35] coupled with concern that news of the decision might leak to the press, accelerated the timetable. On 18 November, ambassadors in the capitals of the Six were instructed to inform the governments concerned of the UK's decision.[36] On 6 December the British went 'public' with a tactless, illtimed speech by Sir Hugh Ellis-Rees at an 'informal' meeting of the OEEC heads of delegation not only announcing the withdrawal but also launching an all-out attack on the efforts of the Six.[37]

The tragedy of course was that the Six did not disintegrate. Otto Clarke from the treasury brooded afterwards that as late as November 1955 'The Foreign Office was insisting that there was not the slightest possibility of the Messina "common market" coming into existence, and that the only troublesome point was whether we should strive to kill it or let it collapse of its own weight.'[38]

For policy analysts who try to view government behaviour as the outcome of a policy process rather than as the rational action of a unitary decisionmaker, this description of the events of 1955 offers a veritable treasure trove of information which would confirm their expectations.[39] The whole complex problem of relations with Western Europe which the Messina invitation implied was never properly examined. Instead, it was seen as a 'foreign policy' issue and the response was predetermined by the subunit, in this case the Mutual Aid Department, responsible. It, in turn, did not conduct a comprehensive search of possible policy options but turned to the nearest course of action, which seemed to resolve the perceived problem. Supranationality was the problem, rejection the solution, and the only remaining questions were when and how that was to be achieved. This represented a safe, tried and tested response and much of the top of the foreign office then concentrated on finding evidence in support of the 'decision'. The subsequent process of policy evaluation seemed more designed to provide fuel for any justification which might have been required at a later date than an effort to re-evaluate the original response or construct an alternative response should the original assumptions prove invalid. Whilst in this particular case the British policymaking process may appear peculiarly myopic and inept, studies ranging from the bombing of Pearl Harbor to the Cuban Missile Crisis suggest that it is far from unique.

It is dangerous to put forward an alternative policy/strategy, since you cannot just unravel the past and put it back together differently. However, in making judgements on historical events there is always some intuitive standard against which the real history is weighed and found wanting and in this case that alternative is that the UK went along with the course which the Six were to follow; the UK should have become the seventh member of the European Communities. I suggested at the beginning of this chapter that such a scenario was highly improbable and I believe that this evaluation is reinforced by the description of the course of events.

The alternative course of events would have meant that from the start policymakers took the Beyen/Spaak memorandum seriously, especially the section calling for the creation of a customs union. This would have meant that contingency planning could have got underway from midMay.[40] If British intelligence had been any good, they would have known that in the course of the European Political Community negotiations in the spring of 1954 five of the countries had accepted the idea of a customs union in principle although there were differences over the steps by which this could be achieved. The odd man out had been France.[41]

If policymakers had considered that there was a distinct probability that a customs union would emerge from the negotiations, they could then have evaluated the likely impact on the British economy. In doing so, they would have set alarm bells ringing throughout the economics ministries. We have already seen that the chairman of the interdepartmental study group had pointed out that such an eventuality would probably prove harmful to longterm British economic interests[42] and this view was shared, almost hysterically, by the president of the Board of Trade, Peter Thorneycroft, when he eventually got round to considering the prospect. In January 1956 he wrote to Antony Eden, the then prime minister, in the following terms:

> *No fine words would disguise the reality of a discriminatory bloc, in the heartland of industrial Europe, promoting its own internal trade at the expense of trade with the other countries of the free world [...] the system of GATT and all we and the Americans have built up would be smashed. [...] The whole basis*

> *of the postwar settlement of our international trade relations would be in the melting pot.*[43]

At about the same time Macmillan, who had been moved from the Foreign Office to the Treasury, was coming to the same conclusion and became convinced that a positive British initiative was necessary to divert the threat.[44] These two ministers were behind the drive in 1956 to formulate an alternative policy and they continuously alluded to the need to come to terms with the threat posed by the Six and to the impermanence of the economic concessions gained from the Commonwealth.[45]

Had all this been considered from the start, work on contingency planning could have begun immediately and with the correct ministerial pressure and support, the results would have flowed much more quickly. The study group eventually set up to explore possible alternatives for a UK initiative in Europe took five weeks from its first meeting[46] to produce a comprehensive draft report, which included all the alternatives eventually incorporated in the final draft.[47] From that list the ministers decided to select the option of an industrial free trade area as the most promising way forward and instructed that all further work be concentrated on working out that approach in more detail.[48] If the same speed and direction had been shown from mid-May 1955, it is not impossible to envisage this phase being completed by the end of June. The process of working out the free trade area plan took one month from start[49] to finish.[50] It is not impossible to envisage Commonwealth consultations being undertaken concurrently and, similarly, informal soundings of the trade unions and the Federation of British Industry. Since there is no reason to assume that there should have been any dramatic shift of opinion between the middle of 1955 and the end of 1956, the results of this exercise would in all probability have been positive.[51] Thus, by the beginning of August the British cabinet could have been ready to have taken a decision on the question. We will come to the possible outcome of that discussion later. Firstly we need to examine whether a free trade area initiative would have worked.

An industrial free trade area had a number of advantages from the British standpoint. In the first place it would not have required a strong supranational element in its structure, although administratively it would be less tidy than a common market (but not necessarily more so than a customs union as the current litany of complaints over customs formalities attests). This would have made it attractive for a larger number of potential participants so that it could be argued that it would have been more unifying than a 'little European' customs union. In preparing their plans, the British had envisaged that Ireland and the

Scandinavian countries would want to join and the experience of 1956-1957 showed that it was possible that Austria, Switzerland and Portugal could have been added to the list.

The exclusion of agriculture might well have proved a problem but the experience of the 'green pool' negotiations, which terminated at the end of 1954, had demonstrated scarcely any support for a common agricultural policy. Even the Six had been split on this point – with Germany, Belgium and Luxembourg firmly opposed, France wavering but preferring a more pragmatic set of deals and Italy less than enthusiastic.[52] As long as something could be done on the agricultural front there was no reason to believe that a British stance on this question would have ruled out the whole scheme. For the UK, the exclusion of agriculture meant that it could maintain its own domestic policy and continue to offer preferences to Commonwealth producers, thus perpetuating the foundations on which it could hope to continue receiving preferences for its industrial exports. Any loss of advantages in this area would be the results of developments already apparent in the 1950s, but not worsened by any initiative in Europe. A loss of industrial preferences had been built into the assumptions of the evaluation of the impact of a customs union undertaken in 1955 and may well have contributed to the pessimistic nature of the conclusions. Without that assumption, a new evaluation was left to look at the possible impact on European trade alone, and the prognosis on this front was favourable.[53]

If the UK had entered the negotiations with a declaration that the government would be willing to consider joining an industrial free trade area, to which other OEEC members could be admitted, but that it would not oppose the Six going further in some areas if they wished, it would have been consistent with the interpretation that the initial invitation had been extended to build further on the UK rapprochement to 'Europe' which had culminated in the forming of the Western European Union. It would have implied an acceptance at face value that the absence of any mention of supranationality in the Messina resolution meant exactly that. The Luxembourg prime minister Joseph Bech had attempted to reassure the British on this very point: '"supranational" was a coin that had endured two years of hard use and was now worn out'[54] and the soulsearching within the French cabinet over how far to go along the supranational road, which the Foreign Office so gleefully and gloatingly recorded once the negotiations were underway[55] suggested that there was little enthusiasm from that quarter either. The Foreign Office must also have been aware of the division in the Dutch cabinet on the issue,[56] despite the foreign minister's bravado when explaining Messina to UK cabinet ministers,[57] and equally of the hostility of

Erhard in the West German cabinet.[58] Moreover, the question of the institutional arrangements had been postponed in the negotiations until the form of the economic arrangements had crystallised,[59] so that the UK could have seized the initiative before the discussion had become 'politicised'. Nor would the omission of agriculture have been an insuperable hurdle since the Six, realising the extent of their own division, pushed that issue into the background as well and when it was eventually to surface at the end of September, Germany, France and Luxembourg held out for some *ad hoc* solution in preference to the integration of agriculture into a common market.[60]

It is not so fantastic, therefore, to envisage a situation whereby an industrial free trade area could have been one of the first things to be agreed (though the sticking point would still have been the French position), especially since not to have done so would have placed upon the Six the odium of forcing the UK out of the negotiations. With the issue of the form of UK association resolved, the Six could have embarked upon the more complicated task of negotiating a common market, though the acceptance of the free trade area would not have made that work any easier. This form of association was, of course, what the UK had wanted when it eventually launched the proposals in November 1957. By then, however, Britain had lost a great deal of its credit by its earlier spoiling tactics and the agreements made among the Six themselves had made any confluences of the two approaches infinitely more complicated.

The real problem with this counterfactual is that it is difficult to see the cabinet in June or July 1955 agreeing to any such approach. The prime minister, Antony Eden, was opposed to the idea. Virtually all the memoirs of those who worked with him placed him firmly in the 'antiEuropean' camp and complain how difficult it was to oppose his authority on such questions. When confronted with the free trade area proposals his preferences were still for strengthening Commonwealth links and 'maintaining the solidarity of English-speaking peoples'.[61] Rab Butler, then chancellor of the exchequer, Eden's deputy and heirapparent, was against the initiative because the increased economic interdependence which such a scheme implied would undermine the country's ability to conduct an independent, full-employment policy – the argument of a national Keynesian.[62] Lord Salisbury, the leader of the party in the House of Lords and kingmaker of the Tory Party, opposed the scheme with the use of the interlocking circles logic. For geopolitical reasons, he did not consider that the UK should enter a European arrangement which did not include either the United States or Canada.[63] Both the Commonwealth[64] and the Colonial Ministers[65] were also found in opposition for reasons which require little guessing. It is difficult to see any 'European' plan getting through a block of that kind, especially when reinforced by a shared assumption that the Six were incapable of achieving anything anyway.

Since all these opinions were voiced as late as autumn 1956 and yet the free trade area was accepted by cabinet in November of that year, the question 'What had changed?' has to be posed. Part of the answer may be in the evidence of support: the idea had received positive support from industry and the acquiescence, at least, of the Commonwealth and trade unions. However, this was probably not the critical factor. Nor was the messianic fervour with which Macmillan and Thorneycroft were pleading their case: both ministers seemed to be turning the issue into a virtual crusade.[66]

The critical factor would seem to have been the Suez Crisis. As it proceeded it was clear that Eden was losing his nerve and when the invasion collapsed in ignominy, his fate as prime minister was sealed. With the country split and party loyalties under strain, it was not the time to provoke a cabinet rift on European policy, especially since news of an impending development had leaked to the press.[67] Butler's star had also been fading fast and Macmillan looked increasingly to be the likely successor; this too may have explained some of the shifts in alignment. It is also possible indeed that the 'new, decisive initiative' was welcomed in its own right as deflecting attention at home from the fairly deplorable mess in which the government found itself and the appeal for a new European venture could serve to mitigate the country's dangerous international isolation. It is even possible that the enthusiasm of Secretary of the US Treasury George M. Humphrey for the scheme which he described as 'the most important single move on the economic front since the Marshall Plan',[68] was not really on the merits of the idea, still less a sign of preparedness to resuscitate the 'special relationship'. Rather it could be interpreted as an attempt to strengthen the hand of a politician whom the United States wanted to be the next prime minister of England.

Historians are wary about the role which should be ascribed to individuals in determining events. In longterm perspectives individuals often either disappear altogether or else they are seen as agents of historical forces outside their own control. At the other extreme, when the focus is sharply reduced there is a tendency almost to trivialise the analysis by ascribing a central role to the individual and their negotiating methods. The history of European integration is no exception to this dichotomy of analysis. However, the preceding paragraphs would suggest that key ministers were personally responsible for the change in the direction of policy in the sense that they galvanised the policy-making process. Policy in this case cannot be explained simply by the suboptimal workings of bureaucratic empires alone since their attitudes and stances are turned around by clear ministerial directives: treasury officials, for example, who had had a decidedly negative attitude under Butler appear in the vanguard for the new initiative under Macmillan. The personal factor also comes into play at the moment of cabinet decision when the accepted hierarchy begins to collapse under the stresses of Suez and provides the environment in which a 'new' policy, strongly identified with an emerging leader, becomes 'acceptable'. By then, however, it was some eighteen months too late.

This chapter has attempted to construct a scenario against which the United Kingdom's decision to withdraw from the Messina initiative can be properly assessed. It argues that the failure lay not so much in it not joining the Six in a new experiment in supranationality but in not recognising the need to formulate an adequate response in the form of arrangements which would have allowed it to maximise its perceived national interests in coexistence with a little European customs union, should one come into being. In the process this analysis has sought to contribute to the discussion on the various approaches to the analysis of international policymaking. It has revealed that whilst all are potentially useful, none is singly capable of encompassing the complexity of historical reality. The new archive-based study of postwar history is still in its infancy but historians are now entering the most richly-documented historical period ever. It will probably be many years before a new consensus interpretation of events will emerge but it would be a waste if, in the meanwhile, research were to be restricted by selfimposed limitations in vision and approach.

POSTSCRIPT

This essay was published in Italian for a festschrift for Enrico Serra who retired soon after I arrived in Florence. It appeared as 'La Dinamica delle Inertia Politica. La partecipazione ed il ritiro del Regno Unito nella confernza Spaak, 19551956' in E. Decleva and A. Magliazza (eds.), *Diplomazia e storia delle relazioni internazionali. Studi in onore di Enrico Serra* (Milan, 1991), 677697. The British archives are useful for allowing an historian fairly easily to trace a policy as it moves up and down through various committees until it reaches the cabinet. This was a stage in my writing when I tried to place my work in more specific political science contexts – such as 'rational policy-making'. I was stunned with what I found. I hope it shows.

Since writing this article, much of the story of the UK's failure to join the EEC in the 1950s has become integrated into the textbook literature. N. Piers Ludlow's book, *Dealing with Britain: The Six and the UK's First Application to the EEC* (Cambridge, 1997), has appeared. The most authoritative coverage is in the official history by Alan Milward, *The Rise and Fall of a National Strategy, 1945-1963*, vol. 1 of *The United Kingdom and the European Community* (London, 2002), 177-264.

9

The European Integration Experience, 1958-1973[1]

The explicitly federal implications of the EEC made it superficially unattractive for the rest of Europe. A variety of political, economic or security reasons confined the supranational course initially to a limited group of countries; albeit a group that comprised more than half of Western Europe's output and foreign trade. Nonetheless the outsiders still constituted a sizeable market of considerable sophistication and one that had shared with the Six the same pan-European movement towards commercial liberalisation and growing interdependence. Among smaller trading economies as Denmark, Sweden and Switzerland in particular there existed the same drive towards a further relaxation of protectionism as had motivated the Benelux countries. This drive was reinforced by the fear of what might happen once the mutual preferences, implied by the formation of the customs union by the Six, began to take effect. The government of the United Kingdom was particularly concerned about the possibility of an economic division of Europe and, at the end of 1956, tried to neutralise the effect of EEC preferences with a proposal for a wider industrial free trade area to be constructed inside the OEEC.

The initiative was launched at a particularly testing moment for the Six since the common market negotiations had still to be concluded and the outcome to be ratified by national parliaments. The Commission of the EEC itself did not begin work until January 1958. If the free trade area offered the non-member states a solution for their dilemmas, for the Six it posed a distinct threat. Distrust of British motives suffused the following negotiations but there were more prosaic reasons why the Six were reluctant to embrace the UK initiative. For example, the French, in the final stages of the common market negotiations, obtained a set of favourable conditions and safeguards that they could not replicate in the free trade area. Moreover, the French, Italians and Dutch had obtained some 'compensation' for opening their industrial markets through the prospect of a common agricultural policy, but agriculture was exempted from the British plan. Finally, those who hoped that the Community institutions would rapidly develop in a federalist direction were worried whether their energies might not be dissipated by the free trade area.

The free trade area negotiations dragged on for nearly two years, before finally being terminated by the French in November 1958. Under De Gaulle, France had decided to embrace the treaty without recourse to the opt-out provisions contained therein. This commitment was worth infinitely more to Adenauer than the dubious prospects of a free trade area and thus the move received German acquiescence if not support. The Commission, especially its first president Walter Hallstein, had never liked the British plan and was generally pleased to see the back of it. Indeed, among the Six by the end of the year, only the Dutch government and the German minister for economics, Ludwig Erhard, could be numbered amongst its supporters. In the face of the opposing coalition there was little they could do.[2]

The failure of the free trade area negotiations left the UK without any coherent strategy towards the Common Market. In the absence of an alternative, the idea of forming a smaller free trade area amongst the 'outer Seven' (Britain, Denmark, Norway, Sweden, Switzerland, Austria and Portugal) rapidly gained ground. With the exception of Austria and Portugal, these were relatively low-tariff countries and also shared a desire to maintain tariff autonomy towards third countries. They therefore preferred the concept of a free trade area to solve Europe's trading problems, rather than the more restrictive principles of a customs union. Formal negotiations started in June 1959 and culminated, in January 1960, in the Stockholm Convention establishing the European Free Trade Association (EFTA).[3]

EFTA's ambitions and its structures were simpler from the start than those adopted by the EEC. It was essentially designed to 'build a bridge' to the EEC, thereby obtaining through bilateral negotiations *en bloc* what the previous multilateral negotiations had failed to deliver. The differences can be summarised as follows:

- The EEC wanted a customs union; EFTA did not.
- The EEC had to build a common external tariff; EFTA did not but required instead a 'certificates of origin' regime.
- The common external tariff meant that the EEC needed a common commercial policy; EFTA did not.

- The EEC wanted to eliminate the cause of trade distortions at source and required the machinery to do so; EFTA instituted a procedure to deal with complaints if and when different national practices were felt to have distorted trade.
- The EEC wanted a common agricultural policy; EFTA excluded agriculture but relied instead on bilateral agreements to expand agrarian trade.

In a way EFTA was almost designed to disappear in the form in which it had been cast. It was only the subsequent failure of the 'bridge building' strategy that forced EFTA to assume an identity of an individual trading organisation in its own right.[4]

—

Even before the establishment of EFTA, the Macmillan government had begun to consider applying for full membership of the European Community. By late 1959 it had become increasingly apparent that the UK would be unable to negotiate a settlement aimed at a parallel removal of barriers within the EEC and EFTA *and between* the two blocs. The 'Hallstein Report' of 1959 which outlined the EEC's foreign policy perspectives left little room for a purely commercial settlement in Europe. Moreover, the United States, faced with a mounting balance-of-payments problem, made clear that it would not accept the discrimination implied by an interim settlement unless it conformed with GATT rules. This meant that any solution ended in a foreseeable time and according to a fixed schedule with the complete abolition of trade barriers. At the time the most that was on offer was a Benelux plan for the mutual exchange of the next scheduled tariff cut.[5]

Throughout 1960 there was a mounting tide of calls for a reappraisal of the UK's relations with the Six from the press, business circles and certain politicians. However, the strongest statement for a drastic change in course came in May 1960 from an interdepartmental committee, headed by Sir Frank Lee. It advanced the view that Britain should abandon attempts to negotiate loose economic agreements with the Six and instead seek full membership of the EEC. The Committee's arguments, based more on political than economic considerations, can be summarised as follows:

- The offer of a purely commercial 'bridge' between the EEC and EFTA would never be acceptable to the Six.
- The UK would decline in relative political significance if it remained outside of the EEC.

- The danger of a European federation would be mitigated if the UK joined while De Gaulle, who was notoriously anti-federalist, was still in power in France.
- Special arrangements for UK problems, such as Commonwealth trade and domestic agriculture, could be negotiated.

Macmillan was in any case predisposed to accept these arguments. Although he had been its victim, he was impressed by the power and influence of France and Germany within the EEC. He saw herein the reinforcement of traditional great power diplomacy within which Britain could easily function, somewhat missing the point that the attraction of the arrangements to both Adenauer and De Gaulle was their exclusivity. Yet it was more than a year later before a formal application was made. This was primarily because of the daunting array of individuals and organisations which had to be persuaded of the desirability of EEC membership (from the party to the parliament, the press and public, not to mention the Commonwealth and EFTA). Macmillan also faced the 'presentational difficulty of explaining why a policy which had been repudiated inflexibly since 1948 had now become both desirable and necessary'.[6]

In July 1960, Macmillan appointed Edward Heath as Lord Privy Seal, with special responsibilities for Europe. His major task over the ensuing year was to appraise the attitude of the Six, and France in particular, to the prospect of British entry. There would be little point in even considering a membership application if the French remained determined to keep Britain out. However, by summer 1961, it was evident that the French would not discuss possible concessions to UK interests prior to a formal commitment to negotiate. Indeed many, including President Kennedy, felt that De Gaulle had no desire whatsoever to share French leadership of the Six with Britain.

This placed the Macmillan government in an extremely difficult position. Speculation in the press and business circles had already anticipated an announcement on Britain and Europe. Thus, rather than make an open commitment to EEC membership, it was decided to open negotiations with the Six to see whether suitable arrangements could be made. It was hoped that this fine distinction would put an end to public uncertainty and keep Britain's options open in Europe. The formal announcement was made in the House of Commons on 31 July 1961.[7]

The three major problem areas for negotiation in Brussels were the Commonwealth, EFTA and British agriculture. In each case, Britain held outstanding commitments which, in the absence of special arrangements, were incompatible with EEC membership. The negotiations that opened October 1961 proceeded extremely slowly due to a mutual unwillingness to offer concessions. It was not until May 1962 that the first specific agreement was reached on Commonwealth industrial goods. By the end of July, arrangements for most Commonwealth countries had virtually been finalised, although these often fell short of Commonwealth demands. However, it was the agricultural issue which later brought the negotiations into deadlock. The British system of guaranteed prices and deficiency payments to farmers was manifestly incompatible with the artificially inflated prices of the Common Agricultural Policy (CAP). Disagreement on the best means to reconcile the two dragged on into December 1962, when the EEC Commission appointed a committee under the direction of Commission vice-president Sicco Mansholt to explore possible solutions.

In the meantime De Gaulle had become increasingly concerned about the political consequences of British membership. Although Macmillan was aware of these views, neither he nor any of the delegations in Brussels anticipated De Gaulle's unilateral statement, at a press conference on 14 January, that Britain was not yet ready for the full commitment of EEC membership and that therefore there was no point in prolonging the negotiations. De Gaulle referred to the deal with the United States on Polaris nuclear weapons as evidence of Britain's 'special links' outside of the Community structure. However, it is clear that this episode was used to mask an underlying fear of a British challenge to French leadership of the Six. The veto came as a monumental blow to British aspirations in continental Europe, and the wider world. It also served to generate considerable ill will and mistrust among the Six, which in turn impaired the prospects of further political initiatives. Finally, it served to repudiate the approaches of other states for membership or association with the EEC.

The applications of Denmark, Norway and Ireland[8] for EEC membership were essentially a reaction to the decision of Macmillan to negotiate with the Six. Denmark was the strongest supporter of this decision, as it provided the opportunity to bring its two largest customers, the United Kingdom and West Germany, together in a single market. The breakdown of the British negotiations was crucial to the Danish position. Although De Gaulle separately offered Prime Minister Otto Jens Krag membership for Denmark alone, an offer that would have been echoed by the other countries if it was not interpreted as overtly cynical, this was turned down after consultations with the British.

Norway was somewhat less enthusiastic in applying for EEC membership. Einar Gerhardsen's government was uneasy about opening Norwegian fisheries and agriculture to foreign competition but the simultaneous application of important trading partners Denmark and Britain led many to the view that Norway could not afford to remain outside. Before any application could be made, the Constitution had to be amended to provide for the transfer of sovereign powers to international organisations. This amendment was passed without difficulty by the Storting in March 1962, followed soon after by the EEC announcement. Only one meeting at ministerial level had taken place when the collapse of the UK application brought the Norwegian case to an equally abrupt end.

Ireland's membership application was perhaps even more closely linked with that of the United Kingdom. Ireland had not taken part in the EEC/EFTA split of the late 1950s, but had special trading arrangements with Britain dating back to when it formed part of the United Kingdom. Edward Heath specifically mentioned Ireland in his opening speech to the EEC governments in October 1961, expressing the hope that their trading relationship would be 'subsumed in the wider arrangements of the enlarged Community'. The EEC Council of Ministers signalled the start of negotiations with Ireland in October 1962 but, as in the case of Norway, substantial negotiations never actually opened.

—

The return of De Gaulle to power in France on 1 June 1958 was decisive for the EEC's development. Given his long antipathy towards the integration efforts of the Six, nobody expected him to look favourably upon the new supranational organisation in Brussels. After all, he viewed France's participation in the ECSC, the EEC and Euratom as humiliating consequences of a regime 'more concerned with pleasing others'. Thus it was with considerable relief that 'Europeanists' saw his early recognition of the Rome treaties. In part, this reflected the support in industrial and especially agrarian circles for the EEC. It also marked an appreciation of the treaty's usefulness, and its safeguards, for the liberalisation of the French economy upon which the regime embarked at the end of 1958. However, it soon became evident that the General had his own concept of 'Europe' which differed markedly from the federalist ideal.

At a press conference in May 1960 De Gaulle launched his proposals to develop political cooperation among the Six. He announced his intention 'to build Western Europe into a political, economic, cultural and human grouping organised for action and self-defence [...] through organised cooperation between states, with the expectation of perhaps growing one day into an imposing confederation.'

The use of the phrase '*une coopération organisée des États*' was particularly significant and reflected a desire to ensure that any future political integration of the Six would not be at the expense of French national sovereignty. De Gaulle gained the support of Adenauer on 29 July at a meeting at Rambouillet. Central to the plan was the establishment of a permanent political secretariat of the Six in Paris, responsible to a Council of the Heads of Government. It would comprise four permanent directorates dealing with foreign policy, defence, economics and cultural affairs. There would also be an assembly of delegates from the national parliaments.[9]

The scheme met strong opposition from federalists such as Walter Hallstein and Paul-Henri Spaak. They feared that the inclusion of defence and economics within the competence of the new organisation would tend to undermine both NATO and the existing Economic Community in Brussels. These problems were discussed by the heads of government of the Six in Bonn in July 1961. The outcome of the meeting was the 'Bonn Declaration', which tried to allay doubts on the plan by including references to political union as a means for 'strengthening the Atlantic Alliance' as well as an affirmation of the intent to 'continue at the same time the work already undertaken in the European Communities'. However, the Declaration had been cleverly drafted to conceal the many points of disagreement, and the illusion of consensus proved to be short lived.

The preparatory work was entrusted to a commission, chaired by the French ambassador to Denmark, Christian Fouchet. Its brief was to submit 'concrete proposals concerning meetings of the Heads of State and the Ministers of Foreign Affairs, as well as all other meetings that might appear desirable'. In November, the French government presented a draft *Traité d'union d'États* which became known as the Fouchet Plan. The Fouchet Plan adhered firmly to De Gaulle's earlier proposals and it represented some backsliding from the text of the Bonn Declaration. Most notably, the draft treaty included the key issues of defence and economics within the scope of the political union, despite the earlier protests by France's partners. Negotiations among the Six on the Fouchet Plan commenced in early 1962, with numerous redrafts of the treaty submitted by the Five. However, as the negotiations progressed, a further point of disagreement emerged among the Six over the issue of British participation in the Fouchet negotiations.

At this time, simultaneous negotiations were being held in Brussels on Britain's application to the EEC. The Dutch, in particular, were adamant that the UK should also be included in discussions on political union. Their foreign minister, Joseph Luns, saw British participation as essential to ensure the primacy of NATO and to keep a check on French ambitions. This lay in stark contrast to the French position: that Britain would have to make a separate membership application to the political community, if and when it came into existence. Throughout the spring of 1962, this divergence of opinion became an ever greater source of antagonism among the Six. Meanwhile, the British themselves had begun to take a more active interest in the Fouchet negotiations, which, after all, coincided closely with Macmillan's preferences for Europe's organisation. In April, at the Council of the Western European Union, Edward Heath made a long statement indicating Britain's desire to participate directly in the discussions. Coming at a crucial stage in the Fouchet negotiations, this announcement had the effect of rallying Belgian support for the Dutch position. Spaak now declared that he would not sign any proposed treaty until after Britain had been admitted to the EEC. The negotiations were then formally 'suspended', and the Fouchet Plan was abandoned.

The failure of the Fouchet Plan represented the first of many political complications to emerge among the Six in the 1960s. Moreover, by stiffening French resistance to British intervention in continental affairs, it had a marked effect on the atmosphere in the Brussels negotiations on British accession. Four weeks after the suspension of the Fouchet discussions, De Gaulle held a press conference in which he defended the Fouchet Plan and delivered one of his most scathing attacks on European federalism. His response to Belgian and Dutch intransigence was to proceed with negotiations on a political treaty with Germany alone. The summer and autumn of 1962 were marked by a number of high-profile meetings and state visits. This process culminated, a mere fortnight after the collapse of the first British membership application, in the signing of the Franco-German Treaty of Friendship and Cooperation. The treaty has also been described as a 'bilateral version of the Fouchet Plan'.

—

Despite these external threats, and perhaps partly even because of them, the early years of the EEC were startlingly successful. In 1958 it had yet to commence operations and had still to recruit its staff. Although in Washington, DC, its president, Walter Hallstein was almost welcomed as a head of state, in the United Kingdom, as the head of the secretariat of Europe's smallest and newest international organisation, he was virtually shown the tradesmen's entrance. Nonetheless, the Commission quickly became a formidable force in European politics. This was partly because it was remarkably well-staffed, especially at its peak. For example, Walter Hallstein had been involved in European affairs since he had led the German delegation in the Schuman Plan negotiations. Sicco Mansholt, an ardent federalist, had served as an agricultural minister (not usually a post renowned for length of political tenure) for over a decade. Hans von der Groeben had already served as his country's representative to the High Authority of the ECSC. Each of these men recruited highly skilled and experienced personal staffs.

Its success, however, was more than a personnel question. At an organisational level, the Commission was quickly able to establish its own priorities and, still more importantly, to implement them. This, in turn, was facilitated by the compactness of the Commission itself as evidenced by the small number of portfolios. Already, when the EEC was merged with the ECSC and Euratom, its focus became blurred and was further diluted by the addition of new commissioners to satisfy new members in 1973. It is also undeniable that political factors played an important part of the explanation. Firstly, the early support of the Americans helped to legitimate of the new organisation. Secondly, foreign policy challenges, which represented an area in which the Rome treaties had given the commission an important role, presented themselves in the form of GATT trade rounds and in preparing the response to UK initiatives. Finally, the favourable economic climate provided new opportunities in the shape of an accelerated creation of the common market and thus created new areas for the Commission to exercise its functions at an early stage.

I once asked a senior official with a lifetime of service in the Commission what was the difference between an intergovernmental organisation, with a large and efficient secretariat, a supranational community, controlled by a Council of Ministers (often voting by unanimity) and a large and efficient Commission. He replied that often there was no discernible difference, especially if there were sources of disunity within the group. However, he argued, if the political or economic constellation were favourable, a supranational community could respond more quickly and effectively to issues which an intergovernmental agency might not be able to respond to at all. He argued that the first Hallstein Commission was fortunate to find itself in such a situation.[10] Small, uncertain and untried, the new Community soon found itself basking in a golden age, and inspiring a whole branch of political science theorising into the bargain.

—

The first step in economic integration of the Six was the building of a customs union for industrial goods. All tariffs and quotas on trade between members were to be reduced gradually to zero and a Common External Tariff (CET) installed. The first 10 per cent tariff cut on intra-EEC trade took place in January 1959, according to schedule, bilateral quotas were multilateralised and extremely restrictive quotas (less than 3 per cent of output) were expanded. At the same time, the benefits of tariff cuts (other than those on tariffs already below the planned CET) were extended unilaterally to other GATT members. This was partly to anticipate criticism in the GATT that the EEC would develop into a closed organisation and partly to cool the row that had erupted after the failure of the free trade area negotiations, and that would have been aggravated had the Six immediately begun tariff discrimination against the rest of Europe.

The next two tariff cuts of 10 per cent each were to take place in July 1960 and December 1961. Hallstein suggested accelerating the schedule, ostensibly to take advantage of the favourable economic climate but also to accentuate the EEC's own identity at a time when there was still an active interest in subsuming its commercial arrangements in a wider European grouping. As a result, in May 1960 the Council of Ministers decided to proceed with the July reduction on schedule but to make the next cut a year early, in December 1960. Similarly, in May 1962, the Council decided that the state of the economy allowed the 10 per cent cut scheduled for July 1963 to be brought forward a year. Due to these accelerations, tariffs between the EC members were dismantled completely by July 1968, two years ahead of schedule.[11]

The creation of a customs union by the Six also implied a common level of tariff protection towards the outside world. This too was completed ahead of time. The first problem was to define the tariff itself. The CET should have been the unweighted average of tariffs in four areas but for a number of products (mostly in the semi-manufactures and petro-chemical sectors) this formula was opposed. Given the lack of time in the Treaty of Rome negotiations these goods had been consigned to List G and left to be decided by January 1962. Because of the need for a complete tariff schedule before entering GATT negotiations, this operation was completed by March 1960 and the outcome, moreover, was far less protectionist than had originally been anticipated.[12] Because the timetable of internal tariff cuts had been accelerated, so too was the re-alignment of national tariffs. In January 1961 and July 1963, the margin between national and projected rates was reduced by 30 per cent each time and the final gap was closed in July 1968.

Although the Commission boasted that the level of the CET was moderate and its incidence considerably lower than the British tariffs, Paxton stresses that 'in practice, the Common external tariff as originally fixed was higher and more restrictive than the average incidence of the 1957 tariffs'. Germany had already in the mid-1950s been concerned that its first post-war tariff had been fixed at too high a level and had already engaged in some unilateral reductions of its own. The Dutch, too, had been alarmed at the upward revision of tariffs on semi-manufactures especially. Neither country was happy with the upward drift in protection that the CET implied. They therefore welcomed the call in 1958 by the American under-secretary of state, Douglas Dillon, for a new multilateral tariff round in the GATT. So too did the Commission. The Treaty of Rome had constituted from four, already large, trading entities a single bloc. Under GATT rules, which worked with negotiations between major suppliers, this enhanced its importance and its international recognition, especially in relations with the United States. Moreover, since the treaty also allocated the Commission a specific role in preparing and negotiating foreign commercial policy, the Dillon Round immediately promised it a prominent role in the national policies of the Six.[13]

The Dillon Round was delayed by the need firstly to construct the CET and then to get it approved by the GATT. Once underway, the Commission suggested a 20 per cent 'linear' reduction in the CET, subject to reciprocal concessions by other countries. This idea floundered on the inability of the USA to react to an offer framed in this way, but it is far from certain whether it would have been endorsed by the six member states anyway. Thus the negotiations proceeded bilaterally on a product-by-product basis. No fewer than 4,400 bilateral deals were made covering trade worth $4.9 billion and resulting in tariff cuts of about 7 per cent. This outcome, however measured, was twice as good as that of the previous 'round' in Geneva in 1956 but was still considered disappointing. However, the Dillon Round did have one important side-effect in that it convinced the Kennedy administration, in framing the 1962 Trade Expansion Act, not only to reopen tariff negotiations but also to empower the USA to negotiate across-the-board tariff cuts.

The Kennedy Round lasted from May 1963 to June 1967. It resulted in the largest tariff cuts in modern history, although the across-the-board method was not employed. The EEC argued that the disparity in US tariffs, compared with those in Europe, would lead to inequitable results should the method be used.

Nonetheless, over 8,000 deals were made with a trade coverage of $40 billion and an average reduction of 35 per cent. Over two-thirds of the cuts, with the steel and chemical sectors especially heavily represented, were reduced by more than half. Textiles, on the other hand, recorded only minor gains. Equally, little progress was made in grains, meats and dairy produce which were rapidly being embraced into the Common Agricultural Policy (CAP) and where the French, especially, were reluctant to make concessions. The need to conclude the CAP, and the 'crisis' that had accompanied this, served to delay progress. More importantly, it prevented the trade-offs that might have made deeper cuts possible elsewhere. Nonetheless, despite the tensions that inevitably accompanied the process of establishing a single position, the Commission emerged from the exercise with its international status considerably enhanced.

—

The Commission also succeeded in making the EEC the focus of international relations with the wide range of African territories that had made up the previous French and, to a lesser extent, Belgian and Dutch empires. These countries were overwhelmingly dependent on the Community markets for both exports and imports, and on the metropolitan countries for much of their capital. Their future had been introduced at a late stage into the Treaty of Rome negotiations as a way of reducing the burden for their upkeep on the French budget in return for France's renunciation of its bilateral preferences (or, more to the point, the multilateralisation of those preferences). Thus the Six would remove tariffs and quotas on imports from these areas in the same way as those on intra-trade. By March 1963 tariffs had been reduced by 50 per cent for manufactured products, 30 per cent for most of the liberalised agricultural products and 35 per cent for the remaining agricultural products. It was unforeseen that these reductions would be strictly reciprocal, but protection retained by the overseas territories had to be applied equally to the Six.[14]

After a five-year period, the association agreements were put on a new basis with Yaounde I, negotiations for which lasted from mid-1961 to July 1963. The negotiations for Yaounde I were difficult insofar as many territories had ambivalent feelings towards their (ex)colonial masters and towards the prospects of neo-colonialism on a European scale. Moreover, the member states' views were far from identical. Whilst France shared with the Commission a desire to renew and extend the association, the Dutch were rather critical. Large Dutch economic interests in Commonwealth Africa led them to demand an agreement that could also accommodate these territories and they linked the outcome of Yaounde I to the question of British accession. Only when the French veto blocked this possibility could real progress be resumed. The principles of the agreement were:

- free trade area, dismantling of tariffs and QRs;
- technical and financial aid;
- payments and capital liberalisation;
- freedom in rights of business establishment and services.

In 1969, after only six months' negotiations, Yaounde II was concluded to govern the relationship for another five years. These talks were much easier since many of the earlier problems had passed. Albeit not without traumas, France and Belgium had accepted post-colonial status. The issue of widening the association had been resolved by the Arusha Convention of July 1968 that put relations with Kenya, Tanzania and Uganda on new footing. Finally, and most tellingly, the agreements had positive effects on the development of the African territories concerned.

The preferences established by the association clauses and by Yaounde I and II have prompted much criticism. Non-associated countries in Africa, Asia and Latin America were opposed to the arrangements. So too were the United States and the United Kingdom. Since the very beginning, the arrangements were condemned as incompatible with the GATT and this discussion remained alive throughout the period. George Ball, then US secretary of state, suggested that it 'tends to result in a poor use of world resources'. Of course this was true, but efficiency in the global allocation of resources had not been the Commission's main objective. Its first General Report defended its association policy in unambiguous terms:

> *it was the duty to promote the economic and social development of the Overseas countries and territories associated with them by letting these countries and territories share in the prosperity, the rise in the standard of living and the increase in production to be expected in the Community.*

—

The trade-off of industrial for agricultural market access had been a key cornerstone in negotiating the EEC. Yet there was so little chance of agreeing on the form of the policy or the level of protection during the negotiations that, unlike the clauses on the customs union, the clauses on the Common Agricultural Policy (CAP) were largely procedural. Erhard, who was anyway opposed to much of the Treaty of Rome, argued that the vagueness of the clauses attested to the fact that they were designed to be forgotten. The key to ensuring that this did not happen lay not in the agricultural paragraphs but in Article 8 that made progress through the three stages towards the customs union contingent upon equivalent progress in agriculture.

The commissioner in charge of agriculture was Sicco Mansholt, who started his work by rallying national agricultural pressure groups behind a European policy. In June 1960 he submitted a first proposal to the Council of Ministers. This foresaw free trade in agricultural products within the Community but with uniform target prices and variable levies on imports. In addition there would be structural policies designed to raise productivity. After intense negotiations, in 1962 market unity, Community preference and financial solidarity emerged as the principles of a future CAP. This still left important issues, such as the level of support prices and the financing of the system, to be settled before the CAP could become operative. Meanwhile a regulation was passed establishing the FEOGA (Fonds Européen d'orientation et de garantie agricole) with provisions extended until mid-1965.[15]

The level of common prices as well as the financing of the CAP proved to be very controversial. The fierce negotiations brought the EEC almost to the brink of collapse. It took until the end of 1964 before German reluctance to accept a target price for grain below their prevailing national level could be overcome and before a common price level for cereals could be introduced. Proposals for common financing of the CAP were submitted in March 1965. Since these envisaged augmenting the EEC's institutional powers, via increasing the budgetary competences of the European Parliament and through the introduction of majority voting, France flatly opposed the move. In summer 1965 it withdrew its representation at all EEC meetings and, with this 'Empty Chair' policy, precipitated a major crisis within the Community. It was resolved in January 1966 with the Luxembourg Compromise – usually described as an 'agreement to disagree'. It stipulated that, notwithstanding the Commission's rights of initiative enshrined in the Treaty of Rome, it would consult with governments before adopting any important proposal. More significantly, even on issues normally decided by majority, it stipulated that if a country felt its vital interests at stake, the Commission was bound to continue discussion until unanimous agreement was reached. At the same time the financing of the CAP was resolved with a fixed scale of contributions agreed to run until January 1970.

The relatively high price levels within the CAP soon led to serious problems. Besides raising the cost of living, the impulse of high guaranteed prices contributed to a rapid growth of agricultural surpluses. By the beginning of the 1970s, the EEC had turned a deficit in wheat and barley into a surplus of 10 per cent above requirements. An equilibrium in butter had been transformed into a surplus of 16 per cent, and a 4 per cent surplus in sugar beets had been bloated to closer to 20 per cent. Mansholt responded in 1967 by calling for more emphasis on structural policies that would allow a reduction in prices but this appeal floundered on violent opposition from agricultural organisations. The Council of Ministers capitulated before this pressure by rejecting any consideration of price cuts and by diluting considerably the proposals for structural policies.[16]

One of the principles of the CAP was that the same price and marketing conditions prevailed throughout the Community. Thus, when the CAP began, unified support prices were expressed in units of account (u/a), a measure of value equivalent to the US dollar. If, however, there were changes in exchange rates between currencies it would require an alteration in producer prices expressed in the national currencies concerned. Thus, when the French franc devalued in 1969 domestic producer prices should have been raised by an equivalent percentage. Similarly, domestic returns for German producers should have been reduced to make allowance for the Deutschmark revaluation. However, governments were reluctant to adjust farm prices in the direction of, and to the degree indicated by, the changes in exchange rates. As a temporary solution therefore they established a system of Monetary Compensation Amounts, i.e. subsidies and levies for imports and exports, to bridge the gaps that had emerged between domestic and 'common' European prices. This *ad hoc* provision was later virtually institutionalised in the introduction of special exchange rates, the so-called 'green' rates, that applied exclusively to agriculture and allowed the agricultural support prices expressed in national currencies to diverge.[17] This procedure increased the costs of the CAP, perpetuated and aggravated distortions in competitive conditions in national markets, returned effective control of agricultural prices to national governments and undermined the entire logic of having a 'common' policy in the first place. Indeed, the divergence in national prices sometimes exceeded those experienced before efforts at price harmonisation began in 1967.

On balance, the major achievement of the first fifteen years of the CAP was the removal of arbitrary quantitative controls that had characterised intra-European trade since the late 1920s and early 1930s. It also erected an external regime that created an EEC preference zone, although this could also have occurred without common policies. Finally, it attempted to implement a single system and level of protection throughout the Community. All these factors generated a sizable increase in intra-European trade. However, all of this was at considerable costs. Nobody in the post-war period questioned whether agriculture should be protected, and all protection is paid for some way. The 'consumer pays' principle chosen for the CAP was in the nature of a regressive tax on food that augmented the cost of living. The effect of this was compounded by the increasingly high price levels that repressed domestic consumption whilst stimulating output. As production swung towards structural surpluses, so the costs of intervention buying and storage increased and ate into the funds intended for structural renewal. The solution of disposing (or dumping) the surpluses on the world market served equally to undermine relations with external trading partners who had already been disconcerted by being squeezed out of EEC markets and who now had to carry the impact that the sporadic sale of large commodity stocks had on the fragile levels of world prices.

—

The removal of tariffs and quotas ahead of their original schedules was, as we have seen above, a milestone in the histories of both the EEC and EFTA. Since EFTA, too, had in 1961 and again in 1963 decided to accelerate its own timetable, within the blocs of the Six and the Seven tariffs had vanished completely by 1969.[18] Yet, as it was understood at the time, the dismantling of tariffs and quotas was a necessary but insufficient condition for ensuring free competition:

- Both organisations allowed the retention of some quotas for cultural and similar reasons.
- Both faced customs formalities for the restitution and re-imposition of indirect taxes (and EFTA also had to contend with certificates of origin).
- Both saw individual administrative and technical obligations assume a more restrictive character.
- Both had to act on situations whereby methods of levying taxes on business, incentives for investment and the granting of subsidies all acted to distort competition.
- Both had still to tackle the problem of cartels and restrictive practices.

The EFTA ducked many of these issues by only investigating complaints made by governments (and there were not many) whereas the Commission was dedicated to eliminating these sources of trade distortion in principle. Yet the EEC only really started to address these problems at the end of the 1960s and made only slow progress. Even discounting new measures of protectionism introduced after the oil crisis, the Commission's own judgement in 1981 is revealing: 'The customs union, the implementation of which is intended to ensure the internal market, is proving to be increasingly inadequate for the achievement of this aim.'

As tariffs and quotas were dismantled, so the impact of non-tariff barriers became more apparent. Some argue that their incidence became more prevalent as business turned to new protective devices to compensate for their loss of traditional forms of protection. However, there have been no historical studies to substantiate, or to deny, this. The Treaty of Rome stressed the need for a general system to protect competition from distortions (art. 3(f)) and developed the fields of policy, the competences of the Commission and Council, and the rules and procedures in Article 85ff. Above all, they declared that agreements between enterprises and dominant market positions capable of distorting trade were incompatible with the Common Market. Furthermore, these articles prohibited dumping and state subsidies (the latter with a long list of exceptions). Lastly, state monopolies (art. 37) should be reshaped, and fiscal as well as legal dispositions should be adjusted. All these provisions remained sketchy and it was the task of the EEC institutions to fill them with life. This formidable task, given the different interests and perceptions in this field, fell to Commissioner Hans von der Groeben. However, this was not the only problem that had to be dealt with. Competition policy was not only ambiguous as a concept, but the possible negative sides of a stringent competition policy were much resented. This was articulated in more positive terms by suggesting that what Europe needed was more, rather than less, concentration in the interests of maximising efficiency.[19]

On the question of state monopolies, the Commission could, after the first stage, recommend measures for reshaping them. It did so in several cases, usually proposing gradual adjustments to increase imports, to eliminate the disparity of margins and to adjust to market conditions. There is insufficient data available to judge the impact of these rulings but in some cases, such as tobacco, it was shown that imports from other member states increased considerably. Yet, given the facts that the Commission tried to work with rather than against member states and that these had often and publically voiced firm opposition, there is general agreement that the policy of the Commission in this field must be judged as rather cautious. Moreover, celebrated successes such as tobacco need to be counterbalanced by equally significant setbacks. For example, the reintroduction of a French petroleum monopoly represented a *de facto* break of the standstill agreement of Article 37 to the effect that no further state monopolies would be introduced.

State subsidies also presented a thorny and difficult problem, the more so since subsidies were poorly and ambiguously defined. Generally subsidies were deemed incompatible with the Common Market since they could distort trade between member countries. Yet industrial or regional policies were seen as necessary adjuncts to a mixed economy – and this implied financial aids. Thus, it was necessary to distinguish between 'adjustment' and 'unfair government aid'. The Commission had the power to scrutinise existing state subsidies. Should they distort trade, it could ask that they be abolished or amended. It could also rule that the subsidy was compatible or necessary. Similarly, new 'other' subsidies could be introduced with a qualified majority vote of the Council.

In early 1959 the Commission had already become active in this field and demanded information on the financial aids in use in the member states. Following this, it indeed had some success in persuading governments to amend and/or end subsidies – as in the case of German synthetic rubber or on the more rapid depreciation allowances for French producers buying French equipment, and similar practices in Italy. Moreover, considerable progress was made in the early 1960s in completing the inventory of existing aids and agreeing on information procedures. Yet, in 1974, Cairncross and Giersch argued that the praxis of state aids was still not transparent. On the whole, some agreement exists that EC policy failed adequately to tackle the problems of state aid. Especially after the Luxembourg Compromise, the Commission's attitude can best be described by the 'pragmatic awareness of the difficulty of successfully challenging determined member governments'. One initial contributory factor was the difficulty with financing subsidies from the EEC's own funds, though this diminished over time. Not surprisingly, the level of government subsidies showed little inclination to decline. What is more, the Community had still failed to define uniform criteria and conditions for judging the admissibility of aids.

The Treaty of Rome empowered the Commission to submit proposals on restrictive business practices and dominant positions which were able to distort competition – i.e. cartels and imperfect competition. It did so in 1960, and in 1962 the Council adopted Regulation 17, called by Swann and McLachlan an 'in some degree obscure, legal document'. It reaffirmed the prohibition on restrictive business practices (art. 85 (1)) and ruled that they could be dissolved as well as subject to a fine. First of all, though, it provided for a notification of such agreements and a procedure to determine the action taken. This succeeded in attracting the notification of more than 35,000 restrictive agreements, most in the hope of securing acceptance and many involving fairly innocuous trading practices. By the end of 1962, however, Commission officials had isolated almost five hundred as constituting serious impediments to international trade.[20] Even so, many of the 'traditional' cartels had not registered at all. After some struggles with the Council, which initially refused to give the Commission regulating powers, a policy emerged via a combination of exemptions, rulings of the ECJ and decisions by the Commission. This policy tried to ban price fixing, market sharing, production quotas, vertical distribution agreements, certain aspects of the exploitation of commercial property rights and collective exclusive dealing. The implementation of this policy, however, remained fraught with difficulties. Obviously, restrictive agreements which the participants felt unlikely to be accepted were rarely notified. The villains of the piece were secret, large, international, horizontal producer agreements where the Commission had problems in securing evidence and prosecuting cases. Progress on this front was halting and sporadic but, since there is still no assessment of the prevalence of cartels in the 1960s, it is difficult to assess the effectiveness of the Community's efforts. A complicating factor lay in the merger boom and the spread of multinationals in these same years. To some extent these new commercial arrangements built on tacit measures of cooperation existing earlier.

The Spaak Report (1956) argued that the advantage of a Common Market 'lies in the fact that it reconciles mass production with the absence of monopoly'. It was assumed – and hoped for – that European enterprises would adapt to the new situation by becoming bigger entities that enjoyed economies of scale and enhanced productivity. Herein lay the route to improved competitiveness with, above all, US firms. Throughout the discussion on the 'technological gap' and the 'American challenge', the size of enterprise was seen as the main reason for their superiority over their European counterparts. On the other hand, the Treaty of Rome hoped to avoid dominant positions – or at least their abuse (cf. art. 86) – and to ensure competition. The European Communities thus had to find some way through the dilemma and define their policy.

Initially the Commission adopted a largely passive stance: in 1963 the question of 'concentration' was handed to a group of experts who produced a first memorandum in 1966. Although this reiterated the need to preserve competition, it laid more stress on the positive aspects of concentration. Its first aim was to reduce impediments to certain forms of merger, perhaps induced by the poor results for cross-frontier mergers within the EEC (only 257 in the period 1961-1969) compared with domestic mergers (1,861) and those involving third countries (1,035). At the same time it demanded powers to control mergers that threatened to acquire a dominant market position. It did not acquire these powers until 1973, and even then only in the form of rights to prior notification.

The intervening years had been marked by complex legal arguments on the way in which the relevant articles were to be applied, arguments that could have been avoided, 'if there had been any real political will amongst the member states for a merger policy'.

—

It is obvious that the dismantling of tariffs by both the EEC and EFTA as well as the EEC's introduction of a CET were going to have some impact on the international pattern of trade. Modern customs union theory expected two effects from the dismantling of tariffs and the introduction of a CET: trade creation, that is a shift from higher-cost producers to other EEC sources whose goods had become cheaper with the dismantling of tariffs; and secondly, trade diversion, that is a shift from lower-cost foreign sources to higher-cost EEC sources that benefited from tariff preferences whilst the external tariff was maintained. In both cases intra-area trade would expand; in one case because of a more optimal use of resources; in the other at the cost of less optimal. Much empirical research has been done to determine the balance of advantage.[21]

Trade within the blocs rose considerably. That of the EEC increased from $7,53billion to $49,8 billion between 1958 and 1971, and of EFTA in the same period from $2,80 billion to $11,19 billion. In both cases trade between bloc members grew faster than their trade with the rest of the world. EEC exports to EEC countries rose from 32.1 per cent to 49.4 per cent in these years while the percentage share for EFTA exports to EFTA countries rose less dramatically from 17.5 per cent to 24.3 per cent. Before trying to apportion the balance of advantage, one has to consider that increased intra-bloc dependence is not exclusively a function of the manipulation of commercial conditions. In a period when the growth centre of world trade lay in the exchange of increasingly sophisticated manufactured goods, it would be unsurprising to see developed economies in close geographical proximity doing particularly well. Equally, performance within groups may be determined by differential growth rates. EFTA, which includes the relatively sluggish UK economy, may appear less 'successful' than the EEC, with the rapidly expanding German economy at its core. Illustrative of this effect is the fact that EEC exports to EFTA fell from 21.1 per cent to 16.6 per cent whilst the share of EFTA exports to EEC countries rose from 22.8 per cent to 25.4 per cent despite maintaining tariffs or deflecting agricultural trade.

Singling out an EEC-effect is not easy and various attempts have been much discussed in the literature. The so-called ex-post models cover a period in which the EEC was operative and try to uncover what the world would have been like if the EEC had not existed. To estimate trade in such cases one has to rely on some *ceteribus paribus* assumptions and thus the findings are always problematic. This and other aspects led to the warning by Sellekaerts

> *that all estimates of trade creation and trade diversion by the EEC are so much affected by ceteribus paribus assumptions, by the choice of benchmark year (or years), by the method to compute income elasticities, changes in relative shares and by structural changes not attributable to the EEC but which occurred during the pre- and post-integration periods (such as the trade liberalization among industrial countries and autonomous changes in relative prices), that the magnitude of no single estimate should be taken too seriously.*

Notwithstanding this destructive comment, it has to be admitted that, despite the different methodologies employed, most studies suggest that trade creation outweighed trade diversion, and thus a net gain was achieved. Furthermore, Davenport has stressed the fact that 'the divergence in estimates is relatively limited, with the majority clustered in a range going from $7.5 billion to $11.5 billion for trade creation and from $0.5 billion to $1 billion for trade diversion'. Very few estimates break this 'gain' down into individual national components. Two studies that do this come to broadly similar conclusions. The Benelux countries benefited least since they already had the lowest tariffs and because the mutual Benelux preferences had to be diluted in the common market (a case of trade erosion). There is a noticeable gap between these countries and the other three. Despite having the next lowest tariffs, Germany benefited the most, reflecting both its export structure and its ability to make inroads into the markets of partner states. France and Italy followed close behind.[22]

Some authors contend that these calculations underestimate the impact of trading blocs. They stress that increases in market size and the impact of certainties in (irreversibly) reduced frontier barriers to trade induced a favourable investment climate and economies of scale, at least in sectors engaged in trade. Indeed, in the Italian case, the difference between a hyper-efficient export sector and a more backward domestic sector led to the economy being analysed in terms of 'economic dualism', even before the full impact of the EEC was felt.

—

The growing commercial interdependence, especially among the EC states, prompted concern over whether or not to tie their currencies closer together. The implications of the move to convertibility in 1958 quickly became apparent as the US balance-of-payments deficit remained acute. In the 1950s, this had been the main source for replenishing reserves. By the early 1960s, however, central banks in the EEC member states held about all the dollars they wanted. Still, the inflow of dollars continued unabated, attracted by the investment opportunities offered by the rapidly expanding EC economies or seeking a quick return by exploiting the relatively high interest rates on offer in Europe. Some of these funds were exchanged for US gold, some remained in the vaults of European central banks, and some were held by the private banking system. The latter formed the basis for the so-called Eurodollar market and provided a growing wash of international liquidity highly responsive to changes in, or rumours of changes in, market conditions. International speculation in foreign currencies became a daily fact of life. In such circumstances the desire for some pre-emptive, collective defence mechanism assumed a higher place in the aspirations of the Six.[23]

Unfortunately, in the words of Tsoukalis, the Treaty of Rome provided 'very little, if any, guidance with respect to monetary policy'. This was hardly surprising since conventional wisdom at the time was still anticipating the implementation of the multilateral arrangements enshrined in the Bretton Woods agreements and not their imminent demise. Thus, although expectations were high, the treaty's provisions for monetary integration or cooperation (arts. 104ff.) were rather pale and dim. They stipulated the liberalisation of payments on both current and capital accounts. Within a framework of *overall* equilibrium in the balance of payments, member states were enjoined to pursue policies directed at high employment and stable prices. To accomplish this, it was seen as necessary – and apparently sufficient – that there should be a loose coordination of economic policy and the creation of an advisory monetary committee to observe, report and comment on current problems. Although exchange rate policy fell within its purview, it remained a national prerogative. Should countries face difficulties, the Community could offer financial assistance in addition to making recommendations, but no fund for this end was created.

The first decade of the EC's existence was marked by various proposals but by few achievements. It was characterised by almost uninterrupted balance-of-payments surpluses for the EEC members and a parallel decline in the position of both reserve currencies: the dollar and sterling. After the devaluations of the French franc in 1958, the payments situation within the Community attained some equilibrium. The small 5 per cent revaluations by the Deutschmark and the guilder in 1961 stemmed largely from the size of their respective surpluses with non-members. The only internal EEC crisis was the Italian deficit in 1963-

1964 and this was resolved by non-Community credits and without recourse to changes in exchange rates. Several initiatives for institutional change and closer monetary integration came from the European Parliament and the Commission.[24] Suggestions for closer consultations and the creation of a separate committee of central bankers were accepted in 1961 and 1964, respectively. More radical proposals that were not rejected outright, however, found little positive reception among the member states. This was partly because monetary reform was seen as an issue that required the involvement of the USA and the UK and partly because the ever-open question of British membership in the Community made several members reluctant to press ahead with more drastic schemes.

Nonetheless the increasing outflow of dollars and the need for a common line by the 'surplus' countries (and this included all the EEC states) kept the issue of regional monetary reform on the agenda. In 1964 the French finance minister Giscard d'Estaing proposed the creation of a new reserve unit to eliminate the dollar and to serve the needs of intra-European trade. This was killed by the point-blank refusal of the USA to contemplate the arrangements, the reluctance of some EC partners and a policy conflict within the French government. Jacques Rueff, the architect of the French reform programme of 1958, favoured an attack on the dollar within the 'rules' of the international system rather than through changing them. Since the dollar was convertible into gold, France decided in 1965 simply to do just that; a decision that provoked d'Estaing's resignation. Although the underlying concern behind this decision was shared by member states, there was considerable disquiet about the tactics and a considerable difference too in the susceptibility of different states to American diplomatic pressure. On this last point, Germany was particularly sensitive to US concerns since the country depended upon American troop presence for its security.

A further impetus towards a Community attitude towards monetary problems came from the decision in 1964 to adopt a common 'unit of account' for determining national prices. This implied that domestic prices would need to adjust proportionately to any future change in exchange rates. Although such adjustments were considered unlikely, the Commission wanted mechanisms to reduce the chances further still. At this point it faced opposition on the grounds that tying one part of the monetary equation made no sense without tightening other components. This line of argument had been voiced by German delegations at various international gatherings for over a decade. They demanded economic policy coordination as a prerequisite for monetary union.

The essential underlying assumption that international parities were somehow immutable was punctured by the crises of 1967-1968. Sterling devalued in November 1967, and a two-tier gold market was introduced in March 1968. As speculation built up against the franc, France introduced exchange controls in spring 1968. Germany was a safe haven for these funds, but the government denied that an overvalued Deutschmark was the cause of the problem. Instead, in autumn 1968, it imposed extra taxes on exports and took fiscal measures to encourage imports. The pressure for a realignment of exchange rates could not be avoided, but it was a symptom of the depth of the conflict that when the decision was made, the action was not coordinated. France, unilaterally, devalued by 11.1 per cent in September 1969. German honour thus satisfied, the Deutschmark was allowed to float in September 1969 and was formally revalued by 9.3 per cent the following month.

All these events produced a surge of interest in regional solutions. The Commission tabled two memoranda in the course of 1968 and in February 1969 the so-called Barre Report was submitted. Although they differed in emphasis and tactics, they agreed on the need for a new reserve unit, on improving policy coordination and on establishing a mutual aid system. These suggestions struck a chord with the Council of Ministers which also 'recognized the need for fuller alignment of economic policies in the community and for an examination of the scope for intensifying monetary cooperation'. Even so there was no immediate follow-up. Meanwhile the need for some initiative was underlined by the situation created by the 1969 currency realignment. Since neither France nor Germany had wanted national farm prices to change in line with the new exchange rates, rather than allow the CAP to collapse, the Commission had to produce a system of 'green' exchange rates to preserve the fiction of common price levels. Moreover the stubborn refusal of the Bundesbank to revalue, despite massive pressure, gave cause for concern.

It was some relief when, prompted by Chancellor Brandt of Germany, the Hague summit of December 1969 endorsed the aim of 'Economic and Monetary Union (EMU)' and set up the Werner Group. Although Brand's proposal seemed a major departure from the usual German line of insisting on the primacy of prior policy coordination, the Werner Group very soon found itself embroiled in old conflicts. Two schools of thought prevailed: the 'monetarist', which saw fixed exchange rates as a means to force policy coordination, and the 'economist', represented by Germany and the Netherlands, which saw the maintenance of fixed parities as impossible without convergent economic policies. The Werner Report, submitted in October 1970, adopted a compromise position. Within ten years, it called for the realisation of complete and irreversible convertibility, closely aligned exchange rates, the full liberalisation of capital movements and the creation of a common central bank system. To achieve these ends it called for a narrowing of the margins of fluctuation (from 1.5 per cent either side of par) and a better organisation of policy cooperation, especially in the area of foreign monetary policy. It took until March 1971 before the measures were approved. Although the French endorsed the monetarist approach, they wanted to avoid at all costs any discussion on the political and institutional aspects of EMU. But it was exactly a commitment on these aspects that Germany and the Netherlands saw as the price for their concessions. As a result, the resolution approving the goal of EMU left the questions of the transfer of power and institutional reform undecided.

Thus nothing was in place when the Bretton Woods system experienced its next, and ultimately terminal, crisis. In 1970 the USA, still experiencing mounting balance-of-payments deficits, had eased its monetary policy and consequently speculative funds flowed back to Europe, and to Germany in particular. German Bundesbank thinking now moved quickly in the direction of a Deutschmark revaluation as a means to reduce the attraction for foreign funds, but there was still the question of how to reconcile this with maintaining parities within the EEC. In spring 1971, the German finance minister, Karl Schiller, apparently against the majority feeling within the Bundesbank, proposed a joint float of all EEC currencies against the dollar. This was resisted by those countries that did not want their currencies dragged upwards in the slipstream of the Deutschmark and so something 'reminiscent of the Luxembourg "agreement to disagree" from 1966' was decided. The Deutschmark and the guilder were allowed to float, while other countries introduced capital controls. The decision by President Nixon to suspend dollar convertibility in August 1971 only reinforced the divide. Italy now joined Germany and the Netherlands in advocating flexibility of exchange rates, while France, Belgium and Luxembourg preferred a system of exchange controls. Action was further delayed by a general agreement that the key to a global currency realignment lay in a dollar devaluation and not in a revaluation of other currencies. Thus another four months elapsed before the Smithsonian Agreement agreed to a change of most EEC rates against the dollar of between 7.5 and 16.9 per cent.

The Smithsonian Agreement also allowed currencies to float by 2.25 per cent on either side of the new central rates. This implied that EEC currencies could diverge by as much as 9 per cent before triggering intervention to stabilise the exchange rate. This prospect produced a compromise whereby European currencies would maintain a tighter rein on their rates with each other whilst moving jointly against the dollar: the so-called 'snake in the tunnel'. The system was also briefly joined by the aspirant members. However, there was still no mechanism to produce convergent policies, nor were convergent policies adopted. Soon the new rates appeared as unrealistic as the old ones they had replaced. In June 1972 sterling left the snake and floated downwards. Ireland and Denmark, heavily reliant on the UK market, immediately followed suit, although Denmark rejoined after four months. These mutations notwithstanding, the 'success' of the system prompted new moves, agreed in October 1972, to reinforce the EMU although, significantly, no agreement was reached on the second step towards attaining the ultimate goal. Meanwhile divergent policies continued to exact their toll. Attempts to get the UK to rejoin the float in January 1973, when it joined the EEC, were rebuffed by a government that did not want to sacrifice recovery for exchange rate equilibrium. The following month, the Italian lire was forced out of the system. The fact that Sweden joined was little consolation. However, the final blow to the system, and to the chimera of economic and monetary union by 1980, was the fate of the French franc. In January 1974 it too was left to float. By this stage, in the words of Tsoukalis, a group comprising Germany, the Benelux and Scandinavia had to be understood as 'little more than a Deutschmark-zone'.

—

The Luxembourg Compromise of 1966 had allowed the Council, and thus the EC, to resume its work by postponing the introduction of majority decision-making and allowing the persistence of national veto rights. For many observers, who had looked for further progress towards supranationality and who had contributed to a body of neo-functionalist literature to rationalise their aspirations, the Community appeared interesting but no longer exciting. Moreover, the issue of UK membership again strained relations among member states. The second British application in May 1967, which was followed by applications from Norway, Ireland, Denmark and Sweden, was aborted again by a negative French vote in December 1967. It was clear that on this particular question France was immune to the feelings of its European partners. They tried to maintain pressure by using the WEU for initiatives to extend cooperation to the political as well as monetary field. This 'rebellion' could only be prevented by an intervention by De Gaulle who used the so-called 'Soames Affair' (whereby the British had leaked details of confidential conversations with the general that had suggested a revival of a free trade area, though one including agriculture) to produce an 'empty chair' here as well. This contributed to a further deterioration in the mood. If the Community was ever to be enlarged to embrace the UK, something in France itself would have to change.

In fact French attitudes shifted surprisingly fast. It is possible that there were objective factors behind the change. For example, new concern about German economic power emerged, especially as France's balance of payments weakened. The refusal of Germany to revalue during the monetary crisis of 1968 reinforced fear for the balance of power within the Community. This may have produced a feeling that the UK could serve as a countervailing force. Secondly, the Warsaw Pact's invasion of Czechoslovakia had led De Gaulle to repair relations with the USA. It has been argued that this made it senseless to persist in seeing the UK as an Anglo-Saxon 'Trojan horse' in the Community. Although both of these arguments are plausible, until evidence is provided to the contrary, it seems most likely that the contemporary opinion attributing greatest importance to the shift in power from De Gaulle to Pompidou was closest to the truth. Although the government was still 'Gaullist', it contained four ministers who were members of Monnet's Action Committee for a United States of Europe. Whatever the cause, in July 1969 Maurice Schumann announced that France was willing to countenance some European *rélance*. Proposals linking the completion, strengthening and enlargement of EC would be forthcoming at the Hague summit in December.[25]

The Commission quickly entered the Hague summit into its heliography by calling it a 'turning point in its history'.[26] It would be churlish to deny that much was accomplished, although different countries laid different emphasis on different parts of the package. France was most interested in completion of the Community, namely the financing of the CAP. The others were primarily committed to enlargement. Altogether the decisions taken in The Hague represented an ambitious programme for future development. It was agreed to find a 'definitive financial arrangement for the CAP by end of 1969'. By July 1970, the ministers requested a report to deal with possible development in the field of political unification. By December 1970, the ministers wanted a report on Economic and Monetary Union (EMU). Last but not least, it was agreed to open negotiations with candidate countries.

Immediately after the conference, a start was made in implementing the agenda. Between 19 and 22 December agreement was reached on the financing of the CAP and on the financial resources of the EEC. The latter involved allocating the Community all receipts from levies and from customs duties as well as national contributions to cover any deficits and their gradual replacement by receipts calculated on the basis of assessment of the harmonised VAT. Furthermore, committees were installed to work out the requested reports. In July 1970 the Davignon Report on political unification was published and in October the Werner Report on Economic and Monetary Union. The fate of the EMU has been dealt with in the previous section. The cornerstone of Davignon's recommendations was a procedure of foreign policy coordination, described as 'European Political Cooperation (EPC)', which rested upon regular meetings of foreign ministers and high officials. Its first achievement was to produce a concerted position during the Conference on Security and Cooperation in Europe that resulted in the famous Helsinki Accord in 1975.

The main achievement of the Hague summit, however, was to open the enlargement negotiations. Within the UK, studies attempted to balance a calculable economic 'loss' (attributable entirely to the structure and funding of the CAP and the structure and direction of UK foreign trade) against a potential economic gain (as the economy benefited from the static and dynamic effects of the customs union). Most managed to come to a favourable result. Nonetheless, the negotiations did result in the adoption of new policy areas, noticeably the creation of a regional fund, from which the UK was likely to emerge as a net beneficiary in an effort to redress at least part of the transfer problem. These measures, however, stopped short of any automatic redistributive mechanism. No such problems arose with Denmark or Ireland, which were expected to emerge as net beneficiaries from the system.

The membership negotiations were successfully concluded, following a top-level meeting between Heath and Pompidou the previous month, in June 1971. Running parallel and concluded in the subsequent months were negotiations for a series of industrial free trade agreements with the remaining EFTA states. Thus, in a way, January 1973 represented not only the moment of the first Community enlargement but the closing of a passage of history that had begun in 1958 with the failure of efforts to secure industrial free trade in Western Europe. The moment was marked by an optimism scarcely dented by the nagging differences on monetary policy. However, 1973 was also the year in which the inflationary boom of 1971-1973 was savagely punctured. An immediate casualty was the prospect for economic and monetary union. Although it was not immediately apparent, other treasured assumptions that had marked the 1950s and 1960s were destined to be discarded – economic growth, full employment, the efficacy of Keynesian economic management and technological leadership, to name but a few. It was in these conditions that the Community had to absorb its three new members.

POSTSCRIPT

Just as with the first contribution in this volume, this first appeared as a chapter in Keith Middlemas, *Orchestrating Europe: The Informal Politics of the European Union, 1973-95* (London, 1995). At the time, the archives covering most of the matters discussed were still closed to historical research. Evidently, a great deal has since been published and I will limit myself to those areas where new literature has reached such a critical mass as to shift our knowledge. The first step for historians must be to the multi-country (and multi-language) collective volumes produced by the European Union Liaison Committee of Historians:

- Anne Deighton and Alan Milward (eds.), *Widening, Deepening and Acceleration: The European Economic Community, 1957-1963* (Baden-Baden, 1999).
- Wilfried Loth (ed.), *Crises and Compromises: The European Project, 1963-1969* (Baden-Baden, 2001).
- Jan van der Harst (ed.), *Beyond the Customs Union: The European Community's Quest for Deepening, Widening and Completion, 1969-1975* (Brussels, 2007).
- Antonio Varsori (ed.), *Inside the European Community: Actors and Policies in the European Integration from the Rome Treaties to the Creation of the "Snake" (1958-1972)* (Baden-Baden, 2005).
- Marie-Thérèse Bitsch and Gérard Bossuat (eds.), *L'Europe Unie et l'Afrique. De l'idée d'Eurafrique à la convention de Lomé I* (Baden-Baden, 2005).

The question of Britain's troubled relationship with the EEC has also received wide attention. The fruits of a twin set of conferences in Cambridge and Florence were published in a book I edited with Stuart Ward, *Courting the Common Market: The First Attempt to Enlarge the EC, 1961-63* (London, 1996), and in George Wilkes (ed.), *Britain's Failure to Enter the European Community, 1961-63: The Enlargement Negotiations and Crises in European, Atlantic and Commonwealth Relations* (London, 1997). The whole period has now been authoritatively covered by Stephen Wall, *The Official History of Britain and the European Community, Volume II: From Rejection to Referendum, 1963-1975* (London, 2013).

The single figure dominating EEC history in these years was undoubtedly General Charles de Gaulle. A surprising amount of debate was thrown up by the publication of a two-part article by Andrew Moravcsik: 'De Gaulle between Grain and Grandeur: The Economic Origins of French EC Policy, 1958-1970' *Journal of Cold War Studies*, 2. 2, 2000 and 2. 3, 2000. Heated reactions to the first instalment appeared in the same volume as the second, together with a rejoinder by Moravcsik himself. Robert H. Lieshout, Mathieu L.L. Segers and Anna M. van der Vleuten, 'De Gaulle, Moravcsik, and *The Choice for Europe*: Soft Sources,

Weak Evidence', *Journal of Cold War Studies*, 6. 4 (2004), 89-139, poured salt on the wounds and the debate, which seems ready to reawaken with the appearance of Christian Nuenlist, Anna Locher and Garret Martin (eds.), *Globalizing De Gaulle: International Perspectives on French Foreign Policies, 1958–1969* (Lanham, 2011).

I have discussed some additions to the CAP literature in the bibliography to Chapter Six, but two additional contributions are worth mentioning here, namely N. Piers Ludlow, 'The Making of the CAP: Towards a Historical Analysis of the EU's First Major Policy', *Contemporary European History*, 14. 3 (2005), 347-371, and Katje Seidel, 'Taking Farmers off Welfare: The EEC Commission's Memorandum "Agriculture 1980" of 1968', *Journal of European Integration History*, 16. 2 (2010), 237-255.

Finally, this is perhaps also the moment to draw attention to the rich collection of articles in Michael Gehler (ed.), *Vom gemeinsamen Markt zur europäischen Unionsbildung. 50 Jahre Römische Verträge, 1957-2007* (Vienna, 2009).

10

'An Act of Creative Leadership': The End of the OEEC and the Birth of the OECD[1]

Writing to his superior on New Year's Eve, 1958, the deputy secretary-general of the OEEC 'Flint' Cahan reflected:

> *The year which has now ended has been a momentous one for the Organisation. I am fully confident that 1959 will present even greater opportunities for achievement. After such a resounding demonstration of the importance of the OEEC as that which we have just had, [...] I can no longer doubt that our troubles over the Free Trade Area will shortly be resolved.*[2]

Even a cursory look at the OEEC's record would have led an observer to the conclusion that it had been one of considerable attainment. The introduction, in December 1958, of non-resident convertibility represented the fulfilment of a goal set over a decade earlier. This permitted the dissolution of the discriminatory, soft, automatic credit regime of the European Payments Union and the belated operation of the Bretton Woods agreement. Simultaneously, however, the OEEC lost one of its main functions, which had been management of the European payments system. The other major achievement of December 1958 was the decision by France to abolish quotas on 90 per cent of its private trade. France had been in breach of the Liberalisation Code for several years and the announcement meant that, under the auspices of the OEEC, all the major trading nations in Europe virtually abolished quotas on their mutual trade. This success, however, also raised questions about the future of the trade liberalisation scheme, the other major prop of the organisation's activities. Should the OEEC respond by concentrating on the total elimination of quotas on intra-European trade and, if not, what else should it be doing?

In December 1958 one could argue that the intra-European trade and payments schemes, introduced initially to solve the dollar deficit, had been too successful. Quota discrimination against the USA was still widespread at a time when the outflow of dollars was becoming a source of deep concern for the American administration.[3] If the European payments position no longer justified regional discrimination, if intra-European trade discrimination ceased to be a part of the solution and became part of the problem of international disequilibria, and if international forums in the shape of the IMF and the GATT already existed for dealing with these issues, was it not time to contemplate a change in the OEEC's character?

All the above considerations have been used to explain the transition of the OEEC, with Canadian and American association, to the Organisation for Economic Cooperation and Development (OECD), with Canadian and American membership. They all appear, for example, in the 'Group of Four' report on the future of the OEEC, published in April 1960.[4] Thus one could argue that the OEEC's very success had put it out of business. Unfortunately the historical record reveals a story that is neither so tidy nor so kind. At the end of 1958, officials in the OEEC had little time for self-satisfied contemplation. Instead, they were embroiled in a crisis that divided its membership and that sapped the organisation itself of its leadership and sense of direction.

—

The crisis that gripped the OEEC in its final days originated in questions that had been smouldering for several years, questions that lay at the core of the operation of the Liberalisation Code. Nonetheless there was no reason to anticipate that they would so come to dominate the agenda; far less that they would signal the beginning of the end of the organisation.

The tariff issue had never really been properly tackled by the organisation. In 1954-1955 the Benelux countries had been considering the creation of a free trade area (FTA) within the OEEC as a means of linking the process of quota removal irrevocably to the elimination of tariffs. Since this never even reached the agenda, in January 1955, the so-called 'Low Tariff Club' signalled their dissatisfaction with developments by making their acceptance of a new 90 per cent liberalisation target conditional upon progress on the tariff front. In eighteen months time they demanded a review of progress, with the possibility of reversing the relaxation of their quota regimes if nothing had been done. It is probable, too, that this rebuff kept the customs union issue on the political agenda in the Netherlands and provides a direct explanation for why it re-emerged in a Benelux memorandum to the six foreign ministers of the European Coal and Steel Community when they met in Messina in June 1955.[5] At that meeting the Six agreed to initiate an investigation into the issues addressed by the Benelux memorandum and extended an invitation to the UK to join them.

The UK, caught unprepared by the invitation, considered trying to steer the initiative to the OEEC where it could use the chairmanship to stall progress.[6] This strategy, and a loose preference expressed for an FTA, both failed to deflect the Six from continuing their discussions on a common market. By this stage, remarkable though it may seem in retrospect, policy-makers had convinced themselves that the venture would collapse. Unwilling to be seen as responsible for its failure, the UK, in November 1955, announced its withdrawal.[7] Since the assumption that the common market negotiations would fail proved to be manifestly misplaced, ministers were soon confronted with the need to formulate a policy that would cope with the prospect of 'the reality of a discriminatory bloc, in the heart of industrial Europe, promoting its own internal trade at the expense of trade with the other countries in the free world'.[8] By May 1956, ministers had reduced the range of options to one, which would neutralise the dangers of the customs union and might prove sufficiently attractive to the Six: that of a pan-European FTA.[9] The scheme, announced officially in November 1956, was limited to industrial goods only in an effort to preserve Commonwealth preferences and UK (and others') protectionist agricultural policies.[10] By this time, the fate of the FTA had become inextricably entangled with the OEEC.

In July 1956, the OEEC Council was due to deliberate the renewal of the liberalisation scheme and the 90 per cent target. The 'Low Tariff Club' had come armed with a proposal for automatic tariff cuts of 25 per cent on commodities whose trade was primarily intra-European, with the benefits extended to other GATT members. The British cabinet wanted to reject this but was understandably concerned that this step would risk the re-imposition of quota restrictions, a paralysis of the OEEC and the loss of all credibility when its FTA scheme was eventually announced. The ideal solution would have been to trump the low-tariff scheme with the FTA as a more attractive and radical option but the plan was not ready, let alone approved. Thus, the solution was to resort to the tried and trusted method of referral to an OEEC working party: this one to study 'cooperation' between the Six and the rest of the OEEC. Fortunately the OEEC's secretary-general, René Sergent, was willing to front the manoeuvre.[11] The transparency of the ploy was obvious to all and left a bitter aftertaste. The Six saw it as a UK attempt to 'sideline Messina and smother it' and the proponents of the European commodities scheme were incensed that their proposal was not discussed. This second sentiment was shared by the Americans who had hoped to benefit from the non-discriminatory elements in the scheme and 'reproach us bitterly for shelving it'.[12]

It was in this atmosphere of suspicion, disappointment and recrimination that Working Party No. 17, chaired by Baron Snoy d'Oppuers, was born. The working party moved smartly to discussing, particularly, what rules would be needed by an FTA and how these would differ from the requirements of a common market. It also spent much time listening to the difficulties that any such arrangements would cause Europe's less developed countries (LDCs). The excellent final report, published in January 1957, listed an impressive range of technical difficulties,[13] difficulties that could be exploited to kill the proposal if the political climate were not right. Moreover, although the UK plan need not have been presented in the OEEC, the creation of Working Party No. 17 and the nature of its deliberations made it difficult to do otherwise. Besides, since the UK held the chair, the OEEC offered the advantage of shaping the agenda and controlling the discussions. The fate of the OEEC thus became linked to the outcome of the FTA negotiations.

—

There is no room here to describe the often tedious negotiations on the FTA or to analyse the reasons for their eventual failure. It is important simply to note that by early 1958, the discussions were veering sharply away from a pure, ideal-type FTA. French counterproposals, for example, wanted restrictive entry rules for certain sectors, a share in UK preferences in Commonwealth markets and separate decisions for each step in moving towards the FTA.[14] Until this point the Eisenhower administration had supported the creation of the EEC, despite potential commercial disadvantages, because its creation had advanced its political goals in Europe. It made a clear distinction between the positive appraisal of the EEC and the more neutral tolerance of the FTA, which threatened to spread discrimination against the USA on a wider geographical scale and which also lacked the same political content.[15] Nonetheless, as the chasm began to grow between the UK and the Six, the State Department urged US ambassadors to use their good offices to avoid a complete breakdown.[16] This brought a response from Paris and Luxembourg asking whether the effort was worth expending on something that bore little resemblance to the GATT interpretation of an FTA which was likely to embody 'significant restrictive and preferential aspects' directed against US commerce.[17] These developments occurred against the backdrop of a sharp fall in the size of the American trade surplus and a correspondingly sharp deterioration in the overall deficit on the balance of payments. The balance on civilian goods and services had fallen from a 1957 peak of $8.6 billion, to $5.3 and $2.9 billion in the following two years. During this period, net military sales and government grants alone stayed within a range of $5.5 billion. Other capital movements experienced only a small decrease, thus leaving an overall increase in the balance-of-payments deficit from $0.4 billion in 1957 to $4.5 billion in 1959.[18] What had previously been regarded with haughty equanimity or disdain now became the subject of a more prosaic reassessment. Although the basic State Department position remained unchanged, it now warned against stopgap solutions inconsistent with the GATT and against any solutions that would endanger implementation of the Treaty of Rome.[19]

In the event, the threat to the Treaty of Rome came first not from the FTA, but from the collapse of the Fourth Republic and the coming to power of De Gaulle, who had always been a fervent opponent of supranationality. Although he immediately dispelled any ideas that France might abrogate the treaty, there still remained the possibility that France might approach the first tariff cuts, scheduled for January 1959, by employing all the exemption clauses it contained. On the other hand, if the French wanted to liberalise the domestic economy and expose it to competition, the Treaty of Rome, with its safeguard clauses and provisions for harmonising certain social legislation, offered a controlled environment for doing so. As the French finance minister Antoine Pinay told Reginald Maudling, who was chairing the OEEC's negotiating committees, France had no intention of jeopardising the painful process of economic restructuring by 'premature indulgence' in the FTA.[20] In an attempt to circumvent the danger that France might not assume its full EEC obligations, both Germany and the EEC Commission threw their weight behind French efforts to shape the FTA to its own liking. Thus the Six supported French demands for special studies of paper and pulp, aluminium, chemicals, and automobiles and autoparts, to determine what extra restrictions they would require for their inclusion in the FTA. In a letter to Macmillan, Maudling branded this initiative as an attempt to ensure that 'when the Free Trade Area comes into being, there is no freedom and very little trade'.[21] Nonetheless, in September 1958, the OEEC agreed to undertake these studies.

The US undersecretary of state Douglas Dillon's call in the GATT in September 1958 for a new round of tariff negotiations afforded the occasion for another French diversionary tactic. This was seized upon by the head of the economic section in the Quai d'Orsay, Olivier Wormser, to suggest the possibly that the OEEC states should agree their bargaining positions in advance to prevent the erosion of preference margins agreed in the FTA or to prevent new trade distortions emerging. It took little fantasy to realise that, if it came about, this extra preliminary negotiation would render GATT procedures virtually unworkable.[22]

If the FTA was turning into a bizarre travesty, there was little doubt that the lead was being taken by France. It was also France that now appeared willing to derail, at the outset, the US initiative to improve its trading position through a new GATT round. Wormser bluntly informed US embassy officials that France 'was not ready to be led down [the] path of trade liberalisation via FTA and GATT'.[23] At the end of October, the French ambassador Hervé Alphand had a meeting with Dillon. It was to mark the beginning of a period of close cooperation between both governments at the end of which there would be no pan-European FTA and no OEEC. The archive record of that encounter is cryptic but, with a little imagination, it is clear what went on. Things, Alphand probably conceded, were indeed a mess and France appeared to deserve the blame. But everything was caused by the FTA, which France had never wanted from the beginning. As long as the threat of the FTA remained, the liberalisation of the French economy was in danger, the GATT round was in danger and France's participation in the EEC was in danger. What, he asked, did the Americans really want: the EEC or the FTA? Dillon replied that the USA had always preferred the EEC above the FTA, from which Alphand deduced that he would acquiesce in any decision to terminate the former if it would preserve the latter.[24]

On 7 November, immediately after a ministerial meeting of the Maudling Committee, Jacques Soustelle, the French minister of information, announced that France saw no point in continuing negotiations along the present lines. Although the statement was open to different interpretations, a letter from De Gaulle to Macmillan the same day put the issue beyond any doubt.[25] Also the same day, Dillon was asked at a press conference for a statement on events. In a reply that emphasised American interests in wide tariff cuts and a liberal EEC tariff regime, he uttered not one word of regret or blame about the demise of the FTA.[26]

With the FTA dead, the OEEC member states faced the likelihood that on 1 January, when the EEC put into operation their first mutual tariff cuts and extensions of quotas, the organisation would be faced with renewed, institutionalised discrimination within its ranks. In truth, the indignation surrounding this prospect was somewhat contrived since customs unions, by their nature, favour their membership, but are nonetheless permitted by the GATT. Besides, the initial 10 per cent tariff cut was unlikely to have an immediate impact on the pattern of trade. However, in the standoff that the FTA negotiations had become, the 'discrimination' had come to acquire a symbolic importance. Thus, on both sides of the divide, policy-makers tried to find ways to mend the breach. One obvious solution would be to extend the EEC concessions to other OEEC member states, as a 'first instalment' on the FTA. This, too, had occurred to French policy-makers but they were dissuaded by the Americans from making any such suggestion. John Tuthill, the US commercial attaché in Paris, informed Wormser that the USA would not accept a preferential discriminatory proposal aimed against itself, 'which contained only the negative political merit of avoiding a clash within Western Europe'. The following day, the US ambassador to the EEC virtually sat at the shoulder of French officials until they got things right: the tariff concessions would not be offered to the OEEC members but to the GATT as a whole, as a demonstration of the Community's commitment to a liberal world commercial order.[27] The USA was beginning to use its privileged relationship with the Six, and with the French in particular, as a vehicle for realising its own commercial global strategy aimed at reducing tariff and non-tariff barriers against US exports. Aside from the EEC, this view had no room for further discrimination in Europe.

At the next OEEC Council meeting, in December 1958, the Six offered to share their tariff cut on a GATT basis, without demanding reciprocity.[28] On the other hand, they wanted to deal with the opening of quotas bilaterally. It was this point that caused controversy since, under the OEEC Liberalisation Code, a country that had not fulfilled its 90 per cent obligation was not allowed to discriminate against other members. At that precise moment, France was still in breach of the code. In an ill-judged statement which exceeded his brief, the president of the Board of Trade, David Eccles, threatened France with reprisals should it undertake new quota discrimination. French foreign minister Couve de Murville leapt to his feet and exclaimed that he had not the slightest intention of continuing negotiations under threat and withdrew his support for the EEC's compromise on this point.[29] Huddled consultations in corridors and side rooms failed to budge the French and the Council meeting ended in disarray. The OEEC Council did not meet again at the ministerial level for over a year.[30] For American observers the European squabble on sharing out French quota concessions in the interests of non-discrimination must have appeared somewhat obscene: virtually every member state present still maintained differential quota discrimination against the United States.[31]

—

In the months that followed, two groups worked towards a solution. The seven 'non-Six' members in the Maudling negotiations agreed in March 1959 to explore the possibilities of forming an FTA amongst themselves. The move had a certain commercial logic of its own but was conceived primarily to facilitate an eventual reconciliation with the Six based on a wider FTA.[32] The six EEC states had meanwhile instructed the Commission with the task of preparing a common position. There were two lines of thought. One lay in trying to salvage the FTA by incorporating some positions dear to the French; a sector approach to resolve the problem of tariff disparities and to move forward by stages requiring new decisions along the way. The alternative lay in a worldwide solution which would have no European dimension other than consultations on specific projects. This second approach was favoured by the French, who were heartily sick of the FTA; by the German government, still paying the 'price' for full French participation in the EEC; by the commissioners such as Hallstein and Rey, who saw this as the best way to reinforce a separate identity for the Community,[33] and by the Americans, who could hardly have done better if they had written the script themselves.[34]

The first Commission proposals were never published nor were they accepted by the ministers of the Six. Instead, a further committee was established which limped slowly towards a second memorandum. Dubbed the 'Hallstein Report', this eventually appeared in September. It pledged the EEC to a path of commercial liberalism and underscored the global approach of the earlier version. Several months earlier, however, the Seven had started their own FTA negotiations in Sweden that would end in the creation of the European Free Trade Association (EFTA). These developments, in their turn, raised the problem of how to reconcile the two groups. Among the ideas being aired was a mutual extension by the Six and the Seven of the next round of tariff cuts.

The State Department received sharply conflicting advice from its ambassadors. The messages from Brussels and Paris had little time for the Seven, let alone any eventual bridge between them and the Six. They condemned the efforts of the Seven as the outcome of a typically selfish attitude which took no account of the progress towards political unity in Europe or the commercial interests of the United States. To support the EFTA endangered the onwards-looking policy of the EEC and risked creating the impression that it would go to any lengths to avoid a split in Europe. On the other hand, London warned of the heavy political costs involved in opposing the Seven and counselled against 'destroying hope' of a solution between the two groups.[35] Faced with this advice, the State Department modified its position and aired the change when European ministers were in

Washington for the annual IMF and World Bank meetings. As Dillon informed Minister for Economics Ludwig Erhard of Germany, the USA would support the Seven if the arrangement was consistent with the GATT. Its 'real concern', however, was a 'discriminatory arrangement' between the Six and the Seven 'to the detriment of the rest of the world and particularly the United States [...] if such a discriminatory arrangement came into being, the United States would oppose it in the GATT'.[36] This already represented a considerable departure from the position of a year earlier, but the French wanted more: the unequivocal endorsement of the Six and an end to any talk of pan-European FTAs. The problem was that it was still far from certain that the EEC, and France, would develop in a liberal direction. Dillon told Pinay of his worries about French protectionism and suggested that an authoritative statement of French policy on the course the EEC should follow would help dispel US suspicions. Alphand followed up this contact by asking for some help in controlling the British.[37] From the archive record there is no explicit evidence of a deal. However, if there was one, the USA was good to its word. On 13 October, the US ambassador to the EEC was instructed to convey broad US support for the Hallstein proposals.[38] A few days later, Dillon asked for a meeting with Sir Roger Makins who, because of the UK elections, was deputising for his minister. He warned him bluntly that whilst the US Congress had accepted the EEC because of its political function in promoting Franco-German rapprochement, the administration anticipated a much rougher ride for any new regional blocs without a similar political content.[39]

All these manoeuvres had three effects. Firstly, the Six immediately suspended any further consideration of Dutch schemes for mutual tariff cuts by the EEC and EFTA. Secondly, Macmillan called a restricted ministerial meeting to examine UK policy towards Europe and, immediately afterwards, established a committee of officials to prepare a new policy. Finally, it raised a question mark over the future of the OEEC. It had already lost its functions on monetary matters when the EPU had been abolished. The UK especially had hoped to use it to cope with the tariff and quota discriminations stemming from the existence of the EEC. The French were equally adamant that it should do nothing of the kind. But, if it were not now to reconcile divergent commercial policies, what was it to do?

—

To appreciate the next stage of the OEEC's history, it is necessary to consider developments within another international body: the North Atlantic Treaty Organisation (NATO). At its third annual meeting in November 1957, the NATO Parliamentary Congress had called for member states to take measures to enhance their economic collaboration. The motion had been the basis for several pious declarations of intent but precious little else. However, by the beginning of 1959, there were reasons, perhaps, to take the resolution a little more seriously. In the first place, the Soviet 'economic offensive' in the Third World had caught the organisation off-balance for both a material and a propaganda response. Secondly, the French threats to withdraw their Mediterranean fleet from NATO command, following a US abstention on a United Nations vote on the Algerian question, disrupted NATO's unity and sense of purpose throughout the year. Simply put, NATO was in need of a diplomatic coup of some kind.

In March 1959, Hubert Humphrey tabled a motion to the US Senate that, building on earlier NATO Congress Resolution, had invited the Senate to enjoin all democratic states to examine new ways to foster 'more effective and democratic unity in advancing their economic and political affairs, their joint defence and the aims of world peace and individual freedom'. The proposal called for the convening of an Atlantic Congress and, secondly, for a committee of leading citizens to be charged with the task of preparing recommendations.[40] Although the draftees had taken account of Herter's sensibilities, expressed before he replaced the dying John Foster Dulles as secretary of state,[41] the State Department had considerable doubts about complicating the 'democratisation' of NATO (i.e. the Parliamentary Conference and now the Congress) with yet another layer of bureaucracy.[42] Despite misgivings, the so-called Atlantic Congress was opened by Queen Elizabeth II in Westminster Hall in June 1959.[43] It was confronted with a petition, signed by 157 internationally known figures, which emphasised the growing importance of the 'economic front' in the Cold War, and proposed the transformation of the OEEC into an 'organisation for Atlantic economic cooperation' in which the United States and Canada would participate as full members.[44] Cahan, who had addressed the Congress, saw little sense in the idea; as associate members the USA and Canada already had many rights without the hassle of having to pay, or the more onerous obligation of getting legislative approval for membership. He felt that nothing would come of it but suggested that the organisation should nonetheless make some contingency plans.[45] A preliminary State Department evaluation also cast doubt on whether the Congress would make any lasting impact on events. Compared with the Council of Europe in 1949, whose success the Congress had been hoping to emulate, the preparatory work had been inadequate, the level of representation patchy, the quality of the debate imprecise and the follow-up mechanism totally lacking.[46]

The idea of constructing an Atlantic organisation out of the OEEC rather than within NATO began to gather strength after the Congress. For example, in an interview, Jean Monnet called for a partnership between industrial Europe and the United States to coordinate aid to underdeveloped countries.[47] In August, the US delegation to the EEC reported that 'top Commission circles' felt that the OEEC had finished its task of liberalising post-war Europe. Since they were unwilling to give it the role of creating a 17-country FTA, they suggested transforming it into a body that included the USA and Canada and that could discuss 'Free World problems'.[48] The idea was nudged more firmly into the limelight by the French. Alphand and Wormser approached Dillon to sound out American thinking on 'some broader problems of the free world'. In particular, they suggested that the UK, the EEC and the USA could usefully collaborate in two areas: the coordination of responses to business cycles, and policy to deal with the needs of the less developed countries. The proposal, they suggested, was useful in its own right but it could also serve 'to divert the British from their narrower preoccupation with European trade problems'.[49] The US ambassador to NATO, Randolph Burgess, added another consideration. Pointing to the OEEC's proven record against protectionism and the reserve of pan-European spirit, he urged its revitalisation to forge a front against Soviet economic expansionism. 'There is no other organisation in sight to do it better. The destruction or substantial impairment of OEEC [...] would amount [...] to handing the Soviets a tremendous victory on a silver platter.'[50] A final consideration, of course, was that sitting together with the Europeans would allow the Americans to keep a tighter grip on any future European attempts at trade discrimination against the United States.

The growing head of steam behind a reorganisation and redefinition of the OEEC did not dispatch the NATO claim. In November, the secretary-general of NATO, Paul-Henri Spaak, asked Herter for 'quick and spectacular' action to solve NATO's economic problems both within the alliance and in its assistance towards less developed countries. Without wanting to increase the US economic contribution, he nevertheless called for its imagination and leadership. The State Department's position, however, was that NATO was not the appropriate body for dealing with the aid issue since its close identification with the aid effort might embarrass friendly governments.[51] The Department of the Treasury and Department of Defense were also concerned that linking defence and foreign aid might allow Europeans to try to shift the balance within the total towards increased aid and lower defence. Accepting these arguments, however,

> *would leave us with no concrete and immediate initiative for the NATO Ministerial Meeting [the summit meeting scheduled for mid-December] and we would be reduced to continued exhortations for Europeans to do more without*

> *any further impetus to crystallize the situation and generate pressures on Europeans as a group.*[52]

The 5th NATO Parliamentary Conference in Washington, DC, on 16-20 November recommended better coordination within the OEEC but deliberately held aloof from choosing between a transformation of the OEEC, with US and Canadian membership, and the creation of a new NATO Economic Council.[53]

At the end of November, Herter decided the issue. In a memorandum to Eisenhower he advocated reform of the OEEC and American membership. The new body would mobilise the resources of industrialised countries to assist the LDCs and would redirect emerging trade rivalries in Europe into 'constructive channels'. He concluded, 'This action would symbolise our determination to work with Western Europe on the basis of full partnership in attacking the major problems of development and trade. It would constitute an act of creative leadership in a recently deteriorating situation.' The Americans were particularly concerned to 'provide for some form of participation by Japan' in the new organisation, preferably as a full member. However, despite the composition of the organisation, it was underlined that US commitments would not go beyond acceptance of basic objectives and agreement to discuss and provide information.[54]

The task of securing European support for the initiative fell to Dillon. After obtaining British acquiescence,[55] if only because it was felt that American involvement might temper the nihilistic predisposition of the French to 'kill the OEEC altogether',[56] Dillon travelled to Paris where the proposal was developed further and adapted to French sensitivities. On the evening of 11 December, Dillon and Tuthill met with Wormser to examine the possibility of future discussions in Europe on the Six/Seven issue and the US balance-of-payments problem.[57] Wormser immediately dismissed the OEEC as the appropriate forum for such discussions and initially rejected a suggestion that, when the ministers assembled in Paris, they should also have informal talks, outside the scope of the main OEEC meeting. However, following conversations between Dillon and Monnet and discussions between Monnet and Couve de Murville, the so-called 'Dillon Proposal' was agreed, based on new French instructions which had 'come down from above'. Nobody, least of all Sergent and Cahan, doubted 'the importance of the influence still wielded behind the scenes by M. Monnet'.[58] The proposal called for the formation of a 'New Group' to meet before the OEEC ministerial meeting, to discuss the future of European economic cooperation and the possibility of strengthening trans-Atlantic links. To demonstrate the group's independence, it would meet at the Hotel Majestic rather than at the OEEC secretariat.

With agreement secure, Dillon now favoured using the December summit meeting between Eisenhower, Macmillan, De Gaulle and Adenauer to make the announcement rather than leaving it for Eisenhower's State of the Union address to Congress the following month. But first he had to overcome last minute Treasury opposition to ceding any responsibilities on aid to the revamped OEEC, or to any new NATO body for that matter. Dillon dismissed Treasury objections as derived from a narrow, parochial interpretation of departmental competencies. To limit the summit declaration to trade would be beneath the dignity of the world leaders and would ignore Eisenhower's commitment to the aid issue. Besides, he observed astutely, 'I feel certain that the President would prefer a broad and comprehensive approach to world economic problems which is entirely in keeping his character and interests. Other heads of government will also prefer this type of approach.'[59] The next day he addressed the president directly, suggesting that

> *the Western summit meeting offers a great opportunity to demonstrate convincingly the determination of the leaders of the Free World to patch up the European trade quarrel and to move ahead with measures to mobilise and coordinate assistance from the industrialised countries to the less developed areas.*[60]

After the foreign ministers had ironed out the remaining problems,[61] it was left to the four leaders of the free world to glaze their otherwise 'initiativeless' meeting with the formal announcement.[62]

—

Throughout 1959, the OEEC's headquarters in Paris was not a happy place. The deep divisions in the membership in the wake of the December 1958 Council meeting were also reflected within the organisation's hierarchy. Sergent and Cahan had both gradually become disenchanted with the French delaying tactics[63] and the facade of an impartial secretariat had become more difficult to maintain. This had cost Sergent the support of many top officials in France.[64] Moreover, Cahan had been in favour of even more assertive action, and Sergent was either unable, or disinclined, to restrain him, especially in the aftermath of the FTA's collapse. Cahan, therefore, made a succession of unauthorised and partisan speeches in Strasbourg, Dublin and Ankara. He capped this in

August 1959 by circulating a pamphlet entitled *A House Divided*. This criticised the disarray after the failure of the FTA and, in particular, expressed regret that the organisation was not headed by someone of greater stature.[65] This was the last straw, and the bureau, four heads of delegation who supervised the daily running of the organisation,[66] suggested that he leave the organisation. Indeed, voices were raised in favour of sacking the entire top of the organisation, and were only dissuaded from doing so by the consideration that the time was not ripe for a 'ministerial crisis'. That did not mean that they were prepared to tolerate maladministration and Sergent was summoned and told to take a tougher line.[67] The malaise at the top had spread throughout the organisation. Section heads ran their departments like fiefdoms, with little regard for the overall direction of the organisation's policies. Senior posts were left unfilled because appointment committees became battle grounds for personal prestige. Staff, who would not normally have looked for other jobs, now began to consider them seriously, especially after speculation on the OEEC's future had become rife in the aftermath of the NATO Parliamentary Council meeting in mid-November. When, in January 1960, the head of the trade section, Marc Ouin, left for a senior post with Renault, it sent shock waves through the organisation.[68] The final blow to morale was yet to come. When the Hotel Majestic meeting started on the evening of 12 January 1960, the OEEC was completely excluded. Sergent was furious and described his position as 'highly embarrassing'. He claimed that he had acted in the best interests of the organisation but had been treated with a complete lack of consideration. He could not understand why he had not been invited to a meeting that concerned the future of the organisation of which he was secretary-general. He was particularly bitter towards Wormser, and also towards Dillon, 'who of course would fall over backwards to do anything the French wanted'.[69]

The discussions in the Hotel Majestic were marked by the clear division of the Six and the Seven into opposing camps. Both groups of countries had taken the opportunity to meet separately beforehand to prepare their collective positions. The UK representative, Paul Gore-Booth, noted sardonically that 'the importation into diplomacy of the parliamentary tradition of a Government and an Opposition will not really be very satisfactory'. Moreover, the Americans and the French made little effort to conceal their special relationship. Ignoring the protocol of seating arrangements in alphabetical order, the US delegation sat snugly next to the French: 'an apparently trivial but not unimportant fact'.[70]

Despite such underlying tensions, there was no opposition to the proposed reorganisation of the OEEC, with most parties adopting a 'wait and see' approach.

The outcome of the meeting was a resolution establishing a 'Group of Four on Economic Organisation' (G4). This had reflected the ideas already formulated a year earlier by Jean Monnet who, despairing of 17 countries deciding anything, had advocated the formation of a small executive economic committee within the OEEC.[71] In November 1959 his *Action Committee for the United States of Europe* had called for a round table of the EC Commission, the UK, the USA and one other OEEC country to discuss common problems, to elaborate common policies for aid to LDCs and to coordinate policies for balanced economic expansion. According to American sources, these proposals had earlier been cleared with Couve de Murville.[72] Now, with the exception that there was a member from an EC state rather than from the Commission, the G4 represented the adoption of the formula. It consisted of Gore-Booth, Burgess, a high French official from the Quai d'Orsay, Bernard Clappier, and the governor of the Bank of Greece, Xenophon Zolotas. Their task was to examine the various problems and possibilities for a rejuvenated OEEC and to prepare a draft convention.

The freezing out of OEEC official influence continued when G4 started work not at the Château de la Muette, but in offices provided by the French government at the Centre des Conférences Internationales in Paris. The OEEC member states, the heads of international organisations and the heads of some OEEC departments were invited to express their views on the most appropriate arrangements for reorganisation.

The Americans were the first to outline their position, arguing that the current front in the Cold War had changed from defence to economics. 'In this situation the members of the OEEC must look onwards and combine their own growth and stability with policies aimed at achieving the same results in the outside world.' Burgess emphasised the priority of aid in the new organisation, and the importance of including the Japanese.[73] By contrast, the British were more cautious about going too far in the aid field, and preferred an 'Atlanticist' concept for the new organisation which would restrict membership to North America and Europe.[74]

However, the two most difficult areas of contention within the group were firstly the question of the trade competence of the new organisation, and secondly the degree to which it would be a continuation of the old. On the issue of trade, it became clear from the outset that the United States and France would have nothing to do with the existing Code of Liberalisation, and they were extremely reluctant to concede any competence in the field of trade at all.[75] This was met by the argument that the overwhelming majority of OEEC members who had expressed their views to the group preferred to maintain the code in some way.[76] The task of reconciling these diverging views was given to Clappier who had 'an exceedingly difficult time wrestling on the one hand with his colleagues and on the other with his conscience'. Ultimately a compromise draft was prepared, which argued that the old Liberalisation Code must go, but left open the possibility of a replacement. Equally, trade competencies were not explicitly excluded and could be added to the new organisation's tasks if the members so decided. It was not quite what the British had wanted but was considered a vast improvement on Wormser's views.[77]

The problem of the transition period to the new organisation caused further divisions along much the same lines. The French and Americans were anxious to present the future organisation as a wholly new one. They therefore argued that all OEEC decisions and resolutions should lapse, and the new organisation be reconstituted to include only those acts which were unanimously agreed to. This way, a single veto could be used to block any undesirable aspect of the OEEC. On the other hand, most of the European members stressed their desire for the continuity of the legal personality of the organisation, and argued that all OEEC acts should be preserved unless they were subsequently altered by the new organisation. Under this interpretation, the power of veto could be used to block any change in the OEEC. The French view was forcefully conveyed to the group by Wormser, who stressed that the OEEC, like all international organisations, was an instrument of government without independent existence. 'If on an objective, dispassionate appraisal, it was found to have completed its job, it should be altered, suppressed or replaced without sentiment.' Without the responsibility for the EPU and with a regional trade approach disfavoured by the GATT, 'only the debris of OEEC was left'.[78] A compromise solution was reached in which it was agreed that the legal personality of the organisation should be preserved, but that all acts of the OEEC would be subject to a unanimous vote before carrying over to the new organisation. This in effect meant the lapsing of all OEEC decisions, and the scales were 'thus weighted in favour of those who desire a clean sweep'. However, Gore-Booth felt that this concession was 'part of the price of getting United States, Canadian and French membership at all'.[79]

These compromise solutions, together with a draft convention, were incorporated into the final report of the G4, handed down on 7 April 1960. The report recommended the reorganisation of the OEEC to include the United States and Canada, and to be renamed the 'Organisation for Economic Cooperation and Development' (OECD). In drafting the report, the USA came out strongly for enhancing the role of the secretary-general and making him chairman of the Council. This was partly because they were impressed with what Spaak had achieved for NATO and partly from a philosophy of hiring a good man and letting him get on with the job. Whilst Gore-Booth could see the logic in this, he held the UK line, supported by Zolotas, in insisting on the preservation of the Executive Council. The primary function of the new organisation would be the coordination of aid for underdeveloped countries, but it would also involve a measure of economic policy consultation, and cooperation on trade matters.

Among the EFTA countries, the report received a hostile reaction from the Norwegian finance minister, Arne Skaug, who treated the British ambassador to 'a tirade' about the G4 report. He could not understand why Paul Gore-Booth had 'let us all down' by following the American and French line and agreeing to such a thoroughly unsatisfactory set of proposals.[80] He was angered by the suggestion that all OEEC decisions and regulations should lapse, and by the ambiguity on trade competence. These complaints were echoed by the Swedes, who expressed themselves to be fully sympathetic with Norwegian views.[81] Even greater furore greeted the report in Switzerland, with the appearance of a long and highly critical article in the *Neue Zürcher Zeitung* on 29 April, which was said to closely reproduce the views of the foreign trade minister, Hans Schaffner. From the start, the Swiss had been suspicious of the US initiative. There was some resentment at what was regarded as a 'diktat' by the larger powers, but the main opposition arose from the suspicion that the Americans, together with the French, wished to shelve the Six/Seven problem and establish the EEC as the dominant European organisation. The Swiss felt that France did not want a European regional association, nor a healing of the rift between the Six and the other OEEC countries. This was also felt to be the policy of the United States, which was primarily concerned with its balance-of-payments problem and therefore did not wish to see Europe united on trade questions – hence the relatively weak emphasis on trade questions in the G4 report. They felt that the report's recommendations would lead to the 'emasculation' of 'the only organisation in Western Europe effective in economic affairs as the price of US membership, and as the result of French and US policies'.[82]

In the United Kingdom, the response was, on the whole, quite favourable. Sir Hugh Ellis-Rees saw the report as a success, especially 'considering that the Americans embarked on the exercise with very little understanding of what the OEEC represented and that the French outlook was tainted with nihilism'.[83] Of course, there were objectionable elements, some of which were articulated by the EFTA partners:

We could perform a broad reversal of policy, but that if we did so, we would consolidate the opposition to our views and be left with scarcely a friend in the process. The OEEC cannot go on as it is; if we reject the present initiative we shall have destroyed the only, if imperfect, symbol of free European economic cooperation and unity which now exists.[84]

—

During these proceedings, the atmosphere in the Château de la Muette had become ever gloomier. In happier days, Cahan had considered an overhaul of the secretariat one of the more important tasks since its methods, dating almost unchanged from 1949, were 'quite unsuited' to the current work. He had looked forward to a small team guiding the reorganisation.[85] Instead, the OEEC's operations came under the less-relaxed scrutiny of the G4 hearings. The technical committees received short shrift from nearly all the national delegations and a thorough clean-out appeared an almost universal solution. Of the major committees, the work of the Steering Board of Trade received the most plaudits and pleas for its continuation in some form. This, of course, was opposed by the French, who were still worried that it would allow the reopening of the FTA question. The EPU had already been wound up and its remaining tasks subsumed by the European Monetary Arrangement, an unobjectionable setup to which no one objected. The European Productivity Agency, however, came in for a great deal of criticism. It appeared as a bunch of technocrats following their own policies whatever the aims of the organisation.[86]

None of this helped to improve morale and the British embassy described the headquarters, which was preparing for the farewell party for Ellis-Rees, as being in a 'state of chaos'. Sergent and Cahan were extremely unhappy about the impotence to which the OEEC had been reduced and the bleak future that appeared to await it. When it came to the printing of the report, Clappier had been under strict instructions to avoid any mention of the OEEC on the cover. The OEEC had only been allowed to print the report because they could do it faster than any other printer in Paris – and they had subsequently been told by an official at the Quai d'Orsay: 'Now you have been reduced to a printing establishment. That is the right role for you.' Within a month of publication of the report, some eight or nine counsellors or directors had resigned, and the organisation had no real work to do.[87]

The growing malaise within the organisation brought greater urgency to the need for a quick changeover period from OEEC to OECD. The Americans took the lead in this, proposing the early date of 6 May for a meeting of officials from member countries to discuss the G4 report. However, this seemingly procedural matter also brought out differences among the member countries, with the Swiss, Swedes, Germans and Italians all protesting that this date gave inadequate time for proper evaluation. The British were well aware of the need for rapid action, but were reluctant to meet American requests to pressure the Swedes and Swiss. In the words of a US State Department representative in London, 'the air was not exactly humming with cooperation'.[88]

The meeting was therefore postponed until 24 May. Much as the Americans had feared, this extra time also provided the opportunity for further objections, which began to cut across Six/Seven loyalties. The Germans expressed their concern over the weak trade clauses. They felt that the OECD should do much the same as the OEEC in trade matters, and that certainly the Code of Liberalisation should be retained. They also shared Norwegian and Swiss fears about the lapsing of all OEEC decisions and regulations. If the signatories of the OECD convention had little idea of what they were agreeing to, they would be buying a 'pig in a poke'.[89] Similar concerns were also voiced by the Dutch who felt that this 'loophole' would probably be used by members of the new organisation to get out of their OEEC liberalisation and other obligations.[90] However, by far the most significant development was the appearance of an 'Alternative Draft Convention', put forward by the Swiss. Their draft envisaged that decisions and agreements of the OEEC would remain in force unless otherwise decided by the Council. Moreover, it included a specific reference to the objective of 'liberalising trade and payments and establishing as free and wide a market as possible'. The Swiss desire to settle the Six/Seven dispute in the new organisation was reflected in a further amendment, which provided that the respective heads of both the EEC and EFTA should be represented in the new organisation.[91] The marked divergence between Swiss views on the one hand, and French and American objectives on the other, appeared to guarantee a heated contest at the meeting on the report.

The tone of the May meeting, however, was set by a conciliatory British statement welcoming the G4 report as a basis of further progress, and suggesting that elements of the Swiss draft might usefully be incorporated. They were anxious to avoid a situation whereby a hard line by the Swiss, Swedes and Norwegians would discourage eventual American participation.[92] They therefore called for restraint on the review of OEEC acts, so that the identity of the organisation could be preserved as fully as possible. Later in the day, the Swiss formally presented their alternative convention and emphasised that the acts of the OEEC should be maintained. On this point they received strong support from the Swedes, Belgians, Dutch, Norwegians, Portuguese, Spanish, Austrians and Italians. In addition, they proposed that a special committee should be established within the new organisation to discuss the Six/Seven problem.[93] Some heat was taken out of the discussions by an American intervention that made clear that they were not opposed to a continuation of the OEEC's work on trade but only to the discriminatory, regional character of previous measures. This took much of the wind from the French argument that the elimination of jurisdiction over trade had been to assuage American sensibilities. The British played an intermediary role, seeking to 'strike a balance between supporting reasonable demands of EFTA partners, and securing a compromise to earn the gratitude of the Americans'. The final resolution was a UK-brokered compromise. It created a working party to draw up a draft convention based on the G4 report, the Swiss proposals and the matters raised at the meeting. It would also establish a criteria and a procedure for deciding which acts of the OEEC would be carried over to the new organisation. A further ministerial meeting would, hopefully, endorse the results and approve the designation of a new secretary-general.[94]

On 22-23 July, a ministerial meeting was held in Paris to initial the draft convention. Much had been achieved by the working party in the intervening weeks, especially in the dispute over preservation of OEEC acts. It had reached sufficient agreement on 'fundamental' OEEC acts to allow the Swiss and others to sign the convention without fear of a radical transformation. The ministerial meeting was therefore able to achieve a substantial settlement of most of the difficult points. The critical issue remained the trade competence of the OECD. Initially, the French had continued to block the trade issue, and insisted that they would accept what the US government could accept, 'no more and no less'. They were clearly embarrassed when the Americans were prepared to go as far as accepting a separate 'trade' paragraph in Article 1 of the Convention but bravely agreed 'for the sake of European agreement'. Finally, the conference appointed the former Danish finance minister Thorkil Kristensen as secretary-general-designate of the OECD, and secretary-general of the OEEC during its final phase. Under his direction continuity during the transformation would be achieved.[95]

—

The final draft convention establishing the Organisation for Economic Cooperation and Development was signed on 14 December 1960. The OECD went on to establish itself publicly for the quality of its economic analysis and, less well-known, for providing a forum for the discrete discussion of economic problems. That, however, cannot detract from the fact that its birth was neither easy nor uncomplicated. 'Lessons' from history are hard to draw, especially for a development so embedded in the specificities of the past as was the origin of the OECD. We began the article with a quotation from Flint Cahan's New Year's Eve letter looking forward to 1959. It is perhaps appropriate to end with an extract from his reflections for 1960:

> *Nobody has yet succeeded in convincing me that all we do now is good and useful. Much of it is a hang-over from our past, and we all know that countries and organisations who cannot escape from their pasts are doomed, one day, to die. This is the inevitable fate of human beings, but it need not be the fate of organisations, provided they are sufficiently adept at adapting themselves to changed circumstances.*[96]

POSTSCRIPT

Little has been written about the Organisation for European Economic Cooperation, although it was responsible for most the intergovernmental efforts to remove trade barriers in Europe in the 1950s, and much else besides. Although I believe that archives are best left where they are created, as Head of the History Department at the time, I was responsible for negotiating the transfer of the OECD archives to Florence. In this context, we held a celebratory conference and this was part of the resulting publication. This article appeared in R.T. Griffiths (ed.), *Explorations in OEEC History* (Paris, 1997).

To be honest, I had not expected the history to turn out as it did. As far as there is an 'official' account, one organisation just morphs into another and I expected this to be much the same – a sweet triumph to close a chapter in the history of a much undervalued institution. That was not the case, and I found myself drawn into a history that was infinitely more complex. The OECD Council was a little hesitant about publishing the essay, since all publications have to be unanimously approved and some of the details in the chapter did not reflect well on some of the member states, or on the organisation itself. Still, giving credit where credit is due, they not only released it for publication, but published it under their own label as well. The story of the birth of the OECD has not been returned to since, and little has been written about the history of the OEEC in this period, either. For an introduction to the work of the OECD itself, see Rianne Mahon and Stephen McBride (eds.), *The OECD and Transnational Governance* (Vancouver US, 2008).

11

The United Kingdom and the Free Trade Area: A Post Mortem

When the negotiations that were eventually to result in the Rome Treaties began in early summer of 1955, there were not six countries represented but seven. Also present was a delegation from the United Kingdom. Partly because of an antipathy towards federalist ventures and partly reflecting the lack of orientation of the UK's trade towards Europe, in November 1955, the British cabinet decided against joining the Common Market. Since, at the time, the Foreign Office was cultivating the view that the most likely outcome of the talks was failure, the cabinet ignored the warning that should the Six succeed, Britain's position outside the group could be painful. Therefore, when the Common Market negotiations singularly failed to collapse, the need for an alternative strategy began to penetrate some sections of the government.[1]

The driving force behind the new approach was Peter Thorneycroft, president of the Board of Trade. He was firmly supported by Harold Macmillan, who had recently been transferred from the Foreign Office to the Treasury. Their concern was to channel the effort of the Six in directions that could contain British interests. As Thorneycroft warned the prime minister in January 1956: 'No fine words would disguise the reality of a discriminatory bloc, in the heart of industrial Europe, promoting its own internal trade at the expense of trade with other countries in the free world.'[2]

A restricted meeting of ministers decided in May 1956 to focus the study for an alternative policy on the possibility of creating a partial free trade area in Europe.[3] Properly conceived, it seemed big enough to be attractive to Europeans, whilst leaving open the possibility for keeping privileged access to Commonwealth imports.[4] At the end of July the plan was ready for consideration by cabinet. It would apply to all OEEC countries, but only to industrial products. By excluding agriculture, policy-makers hoped to be able to keep preferences on most goods bought from the Commonwealth (and thus the reciprocal preferences enjoyed by UK manufacturing exports) and to keep tariff protection for British horticulture. Largely because European trade gains no longer had to be set against Commonwealth losses, the balance of official reaction was more positive than it had been on the Messina initiative.[5] However, it was not until November, after consultations with the Commonwealth and the Federation of British Industries, that the cabinet finally approved the scheme.[6] A week later it passed through Parliament without a vote. Closing the debate, Thorneycroft expressed the challenge in the following terms:

> *Here, in Europe, we have the cultural centre of the free world. We should not leave it balkanised, divided and weak, but growing closer together, stronger, more compact and linked through us with a great Commonwealth and Empire. Here is a chance of achieving something which matches the scale of present events.*

Instead of launching a great crusade, the formal announcement of the UK's free trade area initiative marked the start of two years' frustrating and increasingly acrimonious negotiations. In February 1957 the plan was presented to the OEEC Council, which decided to create three working parties (to investigate industrial trade, agriculture and the problem of Europe's less developed economies) under Thorneycroft's chairmanship. These duly submitted their reports just before the summer and in October the OEEC authorised the start of formal intergovernmental negotiations under the chairmanship of the UK paymaster-general, Reginald Maudling.

British policy was directed at securing an agreement before 1 January 1959 when the first mutual tariff cuts within the EEC would take effect. Although allowed under GATT rules, this would mark the start of tariff discrimination against non-members. Nonetheless, events moved at an excruciatingly slow pace. Early on the French made clear their reluctance to accept the British proposals but took their time presenting their own. Once they arrived, they went first to the Six who were attempting to coordinate their approach throughout the conference. And then, in April/May, with still no concrete counterproposal on the table, everything was delayed as France tottered on the brink of civil war. For France the crisis was resolved by the accession to power of General De Gaulle, but this did little to speed up progress on the FTA. When the considered reactions of the Six finally appeared in September 1958, their contents were unacceptable.

Time was running out, the sides were still poles apart and there was little evidence of a genuine willingness to compromise. This painful situation was abruptly terminated in November 1958 when the French minister of information announced the impossibility of continuing any longer along the lines wanted by the British. The same day, De Gaulle in a private letter to Macmillan, repeated the message. Conservative politicians and the press boiled with righteous indignation and hurled angry recriminations across the Channel but to no avail; the pan-European free trade area was dead.

The story of these negotiations have been told and analysed in several contemporaneous histories,[7] in subsequent political memoirs,[8] and in two interesting 'eyewitness' collections.[9] Each of these has its drawbacks: the contemporary analysts, however assiduous, are short of 'insider' information; the politicians' memoirs, however objective, are invariably shaped by subsequent selectivity of memory. What, we ask ourselves, did they really think at the time? Just occasionally, we get an answer.

In 1959 a number of British civil servants and a junior minister exchanged notes, in the form of a post mortem on the events spanning these two years. The initiative was taken by Sir Frank Figgures, a leading Treasury civil servant destined to become the first chairman of EFTA. It was adopted and further coordinated by Otto Clarke, also from the Treasury, who chaired the interdepartmental committee that coordinated UK policy planning throughout the negotiations. Among the other participants was Dennis Wright, the senior Foreign Office official directing policy on the subject; John Coulson, Reginald Maudling's senior assistant and Figgures' successor as chairman of EFTA; Paul Gore-Booth, a junior Foreign Office minister who steered UK policy towards France through the aftermath of the November 1958 veto; and Russell Bretherton, the senior Board of Trade official involved in the negotiations and the man who had led the UK delegation at the 'Messina' talks in 1955. Their analysis and the archival record of UK policy-making in this period form the basis of this article. Before starting, however, it is interesting to note that they never once questioned whether a free trade area was a sound or an appropriate policy in its own right. Instead, they preferred an organisational paradigm for the analysis of foreign policy problems.

—

The first error that Figgures identified was that 'We assumed we were wanted'. Whilst conceding that most governments wanted closer UK involvement with the Continent, he considered that as early as 1949 influential federalists 'had hesitation about us being full members, lest we hold up the march to federation'. This tendency had only been strengthened by the vacillation on troop commitment during the European Defence Community debacle of 1953-1954. Clarke, at least, recognised that there might be some reality behind the 'Europeans'' view. The UK, he suggested, underestimated the political value the Six attached to the EEC; the stress on economics was therefore bound to slow things down.[10]

There is a remarkable disingenuity about this analysis, with its pathetic plea that the genuine motives had been misunderstood. It totally ignores the ways in which British tactics contributed to poisoning the atmosphere. The UK withdrawal from the Common Market negotiations was a case in point. Instead of a polite recognition of differences in aspirations, Ellis-Rees (head of the OEEC delegation) openly denounced the actions of the Six as divisive to the cause of European solidarity.[11] Similarly, Macmillan's request, that the Six delay their own work on the customs union so that provisions common to it and the FTA could be drafted together, was seen as an attempt to sabotage the Rome Treaties.[12] This could be interpreted as an unfortunate misinterpretation, were it not for the fact that British policy was indeed to derail progress on the Rome Treaties and hold it hostage.

After the failure to delay the conclusion of the Treaty of Rome, officials in Whitehall considered re-establishing the link with the FTA by trying to delay the EEC's ratification in one or more member states. Alternatively, they kept open the option of encouraging opposition within the GATT against the waiver that the EEC required. The problem with this tactic was that it could also work in reverse. The French, especially, refused to begin work on an FTA until the Treaty of Rome was 'safe'.[13] They argued that they could scarcely accept a less attractive deal within the OEEC than they had already secured in the Treaty of Rome.[14] However, if the French refused to start serious bargaining, then the rest of the Six could not start either, since the Treaty of Rome bound them to a common commercial policy. Then, nothing would happen. And for the first three or four months 'nothing' is precisely what occurred. In the end the British decided to abandon this tactic. Approaches were made to France and West Germany to obtain 'binding commitments of support' for the FTA once national parliaments had approved the Treaty of Rome.[15] In effect, this meant that from then on the British colluded with the Six in emptying the preliminary discussions of any meaningful content.

It was not as though the bad atmosphere generated by these manoeuvrings was quickly dispelled. For example, three weeks after bludgeoning the French to provide statements of good faith, the president of the Board of Trade, David Eccles, addressed an audience of Commonwealth and Empire businessmen. Twice in a lifetime, he reminded them, they had joined wars to oppose the formation of 'a hostile bloc across the channel'. Now, although not military or hostile in intent, 'six countries in Europe have signed a treaty to do exactly what, for hundreds of years, we have always said we could not see with the safety of our own country'.[16] Equally, in June 1958, immediately after his accession to power, Macmillan virtually threatened De Gaulle with the withdrawal of UK troops from Europe if the FTA failed.[17]

A second policy error identified was that 'almost insensibly, and without considering the consequences, we became committed to negotiating a 17-country Free Trade Area'. Figgures thought that the UK should have approached the Six directly in autumn 1956. The only other person to address this issue, Wright, mentioned that the OEEC link also increased the apprehension of Europeans who, like Marjolin, had already abandoned it as a vehicle for greater unity.[18] The consequence was that the UK became saddled with the organisation's requirements for unanimity and therefore, with having to secure the acquiescence of Greece, Iceland, Ireland and Turkey, which were unlikely to join the FTA anyway.

In retrospect there is no reason to disagree with the opinion that the OEEC proved an inappropriate forum. However, it is difficult to see an early bilateral approach being made since the UK's first preference was for the common market to collapse and the second was to get it into a framework where it could be contained. The OEEC, with 17-country unanimity rules, was the perfect vehicle for the second option. Indeed, when Ellis-Rees suggested that the initial UK response to the Messina invitation should be to steer it into the OEEC, he slavered at the prospect of adding to the impressive list of initiatives he had already smothered there.[19] The move was so transparent that the Six wasted little time in even considering it and, theoretically, the UK's options were still open. They closed irrevocably a year later.

Since the OEEC had started its scheme for removing import quotas on intra-European trade, the smaller European countries had complained bitterly that it was inherently unfair since abnormally high tariffs could neutralise its impact. The UK had continuously denied this. As a result of the subsequent discontent, the decision in 1955 to move from 75 to 90 per cent quota removal had been made provisionally for 18 months, conditional upon appropriate action being taken on tariffs. The intervening months had passed without anything happening so that, by July 1956, the UK faced the prospect of losing trade concessions if nothing were done. The Benelux countries, Scandinavia and Switzerland arrived at the OEEC meeting with a new tariff-reduction scheme.[20] The British cabinet wanted to reject this too, even though it realised that 'there may well be complete deadlock' and that this 'might leave the Messina group as a focus of further activity in Europe'.[21] The solution was sought in the tried-and-tested method of yet another study group. The costs of this victory were high. The Six felt that the British were trying to 'sideline Messina and smother it' and the sponsors of the new plan were incensed that it would not even be discussed.[22] Nonetheless, in June 1956 the OEEC-created Working Party No. 17 to study future relations between the Six and the rest of Europe. It was here that the free trade option was initially discussed. Although its creation had been designed to solve a completely different problem, politically the linkage was then established. It was impossible thereafter to propose the FTA plan elsewhere, far less to discuss it bilaterally with the Six – always assuming that they were prepared to listen.

As chairman of the OEEC at the time of the FTA launch, the UK also exercised the option of chairing the negotiations. Figgures admitted that this had provided great advantages but it had also created the impression that the FTA was largely a UK interest. Although another chairman would have led to greater embarrassment for the UK position, it might also have built up more pressure on the French. Coulson, anxious to defend his minister, thought that the UK decision to chair was understandable since it attempted to force the pace at a time that country's bargaining position was considered to be at its strongest. Once progress had been registered, he contended, Maudling would have handed over the chair and concentrated on his function as a negotiator. Gore-Booth could not see the fuss. Had things gone better, having Maudling in the chair would have been no worse than Spaak being in the chair in the final stages of the EEC negotiations.[23] It is difficult to refute the argument that chairing negotiations in which one is a major protagonist is going to create the illusion of partiality. Yet historical explanations focusing on negotiating methods always seem to end with a collation of successful method and successful outcome. There was no lack of advice of how to improve matters: a neutral OEEC chairman, the creation of more small specialist committees, a stronger role for the Commission in coordinating the policy of the Six. However, it is hard to avoid Gore-Booth's conclusion that had the parties not been allowed to drift so far apart, the chairmanship issue would have made no difference.

While one line of criticism lay in the function of the chairmanship, another questioned the way it was fulfilled. This took two forms. Gore-Booth, for example, thought that if someone was in the chair, he should have 'lived on the job' rather more. In order to mute the personal criticism implicit in the remark, he asked whether this was compatible with the task of a cabinet minister.[24] If this line of attack was valid, it was only when applied to Thorneycroft, who chaired the Conference while holding the office of chancellor of the exchequer in its study group phase between February and July 1957. It was true that he was not an ever-present driving force in these months and that unfavourable parallels were drawn with Spaak; not least by Spaak himself.[25] This analysis ignores the curious circumstances surrounding the start of the FTA's career: the need for a second study round, the stalling of the Six and, after May, the collusion of the UK in this tactic. What difference, under these circumstances, could a minister's vigilance have achieved? Like the growing pile of paper, Thorneycroft's more visible presence would only have represented the illusion of progress.

A more serious charge was that of a lack of political leadership. The cabinet seemed content to shove the project onto the portfolio of a couple of ministers and forget about it; parliament was not really mobilised to add political weight. As a result there was no 'large and vocal political interest to over-ride sectional opposition' and observers drew their own conclusion on British commitment to the project.[26]

The explanation lay in the considerable reserve within the cabinet towards the FTA. The then prime minister, Anthony Eden, stated that he would have preferred a Commonwealth initiative. He warned that the Conservative Party would not take happily to abandoning 'traditional policies based on maintaining the solidarity of the English speaking peoples in favour of closer union with European nations'.[27] Rab Butler, who became Macmillan's home secretary, feared that the FTA would inhibit the government's ability to pursue full employment policies, would damage industry and would weaken sterling. He, too, warned that a poor treatment of agriculture would damage the Conservative vote in the Shires.[28] Lord Home, first commonwealth secretary and later lord president, yearned for a 'return to our old Conservative Policy goal of United Kingdom producer first, Commonwealth producer second, and foreigner last'.[29] The colonial secretary felt that colonial development plans would be destroyed as their products were ousted from British markets by European competition.[30] Finally, James Stuart, of the Scottish Office, voiced what was probably really behind these attitudes:

> *Any idea that we were departing from these principles [the unity of the English-speaking peoples] in favour of a mixed collection of Europeans, who have not all been our friends in the past, would have disastrous repercussions within and beyond the Party.*[31]

Notwithstanding the almost messianic fervour with which Macmillan and Thorneycroft supported the scheme, cabinet and party support for the FTA was decidedly thin. In fact, it probably only secured acceptance because the party needed some new initiative to deflect attention from the Suez fiasco, and because its main proponent looked increasingly likely to become the next prime minister. Having steered it through cabinet and parliament once, Macmillan was obviously reluctant to risk attracting too much attention to such an obviously divisive issue. But this meant that the public crusade began and ended in the House of Commons in November 1956.

This squeamishness before domestic interest groups was also reflected in the FTA proposals themselves. In particular, the omission of agriculture was universally recognised as a mistake; the only question was how large. Opinion ranged from 'a major error' (Figgures) to 'an irretrievable blunder' (Gore-Booth). Still, as Figgures suggested, the error appeared unavoidable because without Commonwealth agreement it would have been politically impossible to secure domestic acceptance in the first place. Probably worse, in his eyes, was the continuous reassurances about agriculture to the Commonwealth and to domestic interests. Clarke saw these pledges as reducing negotiating room until the position became frozen into 'complete immobility'. The overall result was to antagonise not only opponents but also the friends that the UK needed (the Netherlands, Denmark) as well as the peripherals that had to be kept out of the way.[32]

The exclusion of agriculture from the FTA had been designed partly to pacify the domestic agricultural lobby. It also served to maintain Commonwealth preferential access to UK markets, upon which reciprocal British industrial preferences depended. Both were thoroughly British interests. Yet for agricultural exporters on the Continent this appeared like wanting to have one's cake and eat it: to gain access to their industrial markets without purchasing their foodstuffs in return. Although the riposte, that arrangements within the EEC did not envisage agricultural free trade either, was inherently correct, it did not diminish the resentment still felt in the Netherlands, France and Italy. However, it was in Scandinavia, where the British had hoped to find a real basis of support for the FTA, that the price for agricultural exclusion was exacted. Although Denmark was the most deeply affected, it was Norway that effectively derailed any hopes for an early start to negotiations. When the OEEC met in February 1957 to decide which course to take, Norway declared that its participation was dependent upon the creation of a study group rather than a fully fledged negotiating committee.

The UK position was resented on two grounds. Firstly, by trying to push agriculture almost completely off the agenda, the British were seemingly indifferent to the possibility that others might want to reach some understanding among themselves. In particular, they deprived the Danes of the possibility of using the industry-agriculture link as a means of leverage to advance an agreement with the Six. Secondly, whereas there was some understanding (though not much) of the UK's Commonwealth argument, there was none at all for its commitment to domestic protectionism. In May 1957 officials were 'considering quite advanced changes of policy on the agricultural front'. This changed with the decision to collude with the Six in suspending serious negotiation until the ratification of the Rome Treaties removed the immediate necessity: 'we no longer feel under compulsion to go fast or to make concessions to others to go fast'.[33] During the summer the cabinet did modify their stance. In the first instance this was to take the form of allowing the rest of the OEEC to conclude an agricultural agreement from which the British themselves would seek exemptions. If they failed, so much the better. Neither the suggestion to offer a freeze on future levels of protection nor the option of offering specific product concessions was implemented. There was a recognition that something would eventually need to be done, but:

> *We have borne constantly in mind that the further we move at the October meeting the less we have to play with in actual negotiation later on and the further we shall ultimately be pushed. We must clearly move in this matter, but we must not move one step further at this meeting than is absolutely necessary in order to start off serious negotiation.*[34]

Whereas, in the summer the French had suggested that all they wanted was some reassurance that they could keep their share of the UK market plus 'a little *douceur* on individual products',[35] the British intransigence led to a hardening of attitudes. For example, it so annoyed the Scandinavian countries that they issued a joint note endorsing the Danish standpoint on agriculture; a standpoint which they had never previously shown the slightest inclination of applying to themselves.

All in all it was a pretty gutless performance from a government that had seethed as the French failed to curb the activities of the French employers association, the Patronat. Yet it would be unfair to pretend that the FTA failed on the point of agriculture – the position of the Six was too ambiguous for that to happen. However, it afforded an easy position from which opponents could attack.

The inflexibility or 'woodenness' in UK policy-making, as exhibited in the treatment of agriculture, was identified by Figgures as an independent factor explaining the demise of the FTA. Another example cited was the reaction to the Carli Plan (see below) which Gore-Booth interpreted as evidence of insufficient sensitivity to the 'vulnerabilities, vanities and susceptibilities' of difficult negotiating partners. All this puzzled Clarke, who had coordinated the interdepartmental effort. He thought that the Whitehall machine had 'never operated more efficiently', dealing rapidly with issues of great complexity, and still the UK always seemed tactically outmanoeuvred by the French. He placed part of the blame on the few negotiating margins left by politicians but, equally, he recognised that the machine 'will inevitably argue to convince itself and not the Europeans: it is sensitive to Departments' fears and not to the Europeans". Bretherton distanced himself from too glowing an appraisal of the Whitehall machine, recalling the 'deliberate obstruction' of the Commonwealth and Colonial offices. He went on, 'But, apart from that, what impressed me [...] was the enormous proportion of our energies which had to go into the management of departmental differences and difficulties.'[36]

The image of redrafts of redrafts as arguments were refined and redefined must stay with a researcher that ploughs through the swathes of documents in the European Integration Subcommittee of the Economic Steering Committee. That was the forum for the first rounds of policy coordination before policy documents were passed up and down the policy chain. It is easy to believe, but difficult to document, that this could lead to a false sense of perfectionism.

It is interesting that, in this connection, the Carli Plan was cited by two of the correspondents. The so-called origin question was one of the superficial causes of the failure of the Maudling negotiations. At its core were the practical difficulties involved in aligning the trading system of the Common Market with that of the FTA. French negotiators especially made a meal of the fact that, unless other measures were taken, the removal of tariffs on intra-area trade would lead to serious distortions, because countries enjoying access to cheaper (lower-taxed) inputs would receive an artificial advantage in selling the endproducts. They argued that the system could not work unless the external tariffs of the member states were closely aligned, if not identical. In March 1958 the Italian minister for foreign trade, Guido Carli, suggested a compromise plan for a regime of tariff bands and compensatory duties charged on articles made up of inputs carrying lower tariffs. Carli described his proposals as 'window dressing' and a 'facade'[37] which had 'great potentialities for hoodwinking Italian and French public opinion'. French approaches appeared to confirm this. Foreign Minister Maurice Faure had accepted it because it was something he could use as a political platform and a senior French official suggested that 'whether there were more exceptions to the rule than the rule itself was of no consequence'.[38]

The British position had always been that this problem could be adequately tackled by a combination of rules of content and certificates of origin. The reaction to the Carli Plan was to secure the plan's referral to a study group where, away from the spotlight of the negotiations, they proceeded to produce a report exposing the manifold inconsistencies and weaknesses.[39] The Six themselves did not abandon the plan altogether. They argued that for certain products rules of origin would need to be particularly restrictive if something like the Carli arrangement was not considered. As the Six were preparing their reply, Maudling urged UK ministers to relax the British negotiating position. The original British standpoint (complete freedom of trade within the area, complete freedom on tariffs and commercial policy outside) 'would clearly have immense advantages for the United Kingdom. [...] [T]his is one of the reasons why it is very hard to achieve our objective in the negotiations.' Possible modifications included accepting some tariff harmonisation or a combination of liberal origin rules and some compensatory taxes (but under the control of the FTA institutions) or agreeing to tariff harmonisation for one or two product groups.[40] These suggestions were blocked by the argument that they represented a radical departure from what had been agreed with the Commonwealth. Once any concession had been made on the external tariff, there was no telling where matters would stop. Despite Maudling's appeal to the effect that resolving the origin issue would do much for the negotiations' chances of success, ministers insisted on prior discussions both with the Commonwealth and with the Federation of British Industry.[41] Maudling persisted. Most countries (except France and Italy) acknowledged the correctness of the UK's arguments but they were willing to countenance some tariff harmonisation if it would clinch an agreement. If only the UK would move, he argued, it would provide the test whether the French really wanted an agreement.[42] This missive was never considered by the prime ministerial committee to whom it was addressed. By September 1958, when the cabinet eventually made a gesture at least to study possible sectoral difficulties, the moment for seizing the initiative had long passed.[43] Figgures later suggested 'that we committed a major error [...] on the crucial, and almost the only crucial, question of origin, when we failed to take advantage of the gap which the Carli proposals were intended to open'.[44]

Throughout the analysis in the previous paragraphs, it is apparent that France continuously reappears as the main protagonist. It is no surprise, therefore, that most of those engaged in the post mortem isolated French opposition as a major factor in explaining the failure of the FTA. They disagreed, however, on the nature and timing of the problem. Figgures branded French Anglophobia as 'the most powerful single force working against us' and he speculated whether its roots lay in the EDC debacle or in the Suez and Tunisia fiascos. Clarke, on the other hand, considered that the French factor only really became decisive when De Gaulle came to power. Wright also saw mid-1958 as crucial not so much because of De Gaulle but because the deteriorating economic situation would have forced the same reticence to conclude an FTA agreement on UK terms on any Fourth Republic government. Yet, he conceded, tactically they 'left us miles behind'. Coulson observed that the French had never made a secret of the fact that the Treaty of Rome had been accepted only with the greatest difficulty and that the problems with the FTA would be worse. He saw the French constitutional crisis as giving France a legitimate cause to stall and this was supported by the Six. Gore-Booth thought this simplistic. He thought Wormser had done everything to keep matters alive until something turned up, though, because it made the final breakdown more acrimonious than necessary, it had probably been a mistake. And that is the only mention that French policy had ever been anything other than incredibly clever.[45]

British officials were mesmerised by the French: always weak, always wrong, always unreasonable and always able to get their way. They watched in awe as UK allies within the Six such as Ludwig Erhard, Ernst van der Beugel and Baron Snoy et d'Oppuers counted for nothing when it came to the crunch. They were transfixed as France stitched together a coalition with Germany, Italy and the EEC Commission that only seemed to strengthen once De Gaulle took power; a coalition that not only swept all before it within the Six but also ultimately vanquished British hopes. How this occurred will be analysed in the next chapter.

—

As the FTA was dying, a solidarity arose among the seven 'non-Six' countries; a term, incidentally, which reflected the little else that was thought to keep them together. In the aftermath of the French veto they met regularly to coordinate their response to the further initiatives of the Six. Meanwhile, ideas of actually forming some sort of bloc among themselves, that had circulated since early 1958, began to gain more substance. At a meeting in Oslo, in February 1959, two officials from Sweden and Norway were authorised to explore the basis for an agreement. By May their work had advanced sufficiently for the Swedish government to issue invitations for the opening of intergovernmental talks to begin to begin the following month. These in turn led to the Stockholm Convention, signed in January 1960, establishing the European Free Trade Association.[46] Clarke considered this the ultimate vindication of the learning capacity of the Whitehall machine:

> *Our performance since the end of 1958 has in my view shown a considerable improvement. The rapid decision to seek a European Free Trade Association of the Seven; the acceptance that there was an agricultural price to be paid – and ultimately a fisheries price too; the rapid negotiation of the EFTA Convention; the avoidance of alienating the Six during these proceedings – these have been considerable successes. [...] This suggested that we are learning from experience. In terms of history, however, this is the next chapter.*[47]

In terms of history, this judgement would seem premature. There is little indication in an almost unbroken record of UK policy failures, culminating most recently in a decade of fumbling over the Exchange Rate Mechanism and political mismanagement of the Maastricht Treaty, that the British establishment and British politicians have learnt much over the intervening thirty-five years.

POSTSCRIPT

It is not often that a group of officials involved in events leave a record of their reflections immediately after the events themselves. This collection in the archives was a real find, and it was interesting both for what they said, and for what they omitted. It was presented as a paper in a conference that took place on the northern coast of Denmark, where one day merged into the next, scarcely passing through something called 'night', while relaxing with friends as much as colleagues – a group of historians who had gotten to know each other through the European University Institute in Florence. This essay, with others from the conference, was published in T.B. Olesen (ed.), *Interdependence versus Integration: Denmark, Scandinavia and Western Europe, 1949-1960* (Odense, 1995).

EFTA is another of those European organisations that does not receive the attention it deserves. Little has been added since this chapter was published.

The most authoritative UK coverage is in the official history by Alan Milward, *The Rise and Fall of a National Strategy, 1945-1963*, vol. 1 of *The United Kingdom and the European Community* (London 2002), 264-309. Other archive-based studies of these events are Wolfram Kaiser, *Using Europe, Abusing the Europeans: Britain and European Integration, 1945-1963* (London, 1996), 88-203, and Jacqueline Tratt, *The MacMillan Government and Europe* (London, 1996), and finally, the various chapters in Richard Griffiths and Stuart Ward (eds.), *Courting the Common Market: The First Attempt to Enlarge the EC, 1961-63* (London, 1996). I also wrote a background chapter: 'The Origins of EFTA' in K. Bryn and G. Einarsson (eds.), *EFTA 1960-2010: Elements of 50 Years of European History* (Geneva, 2010).

12

'Two Souls, One Thought'? The EEC, the USA and the Management of the International Monetary System[1]

In February 1961, Kennedy's new secretary of the treasury, Douglas Dillon, tried to calm the fears of the European Economic Community (EEC) over the American balance of payments, by suggesting that Europe and the United States represented 'two souls, one thought'.[2] The significance of this encounter lies less in the nature of the reassurance than in the fact that the exchange had taken place at all. Three or four years previously it would have been unthinkable that the fledgling Community, so carefully nurtured by US policy, would have lectured its patron in this way. The facade of American pre-eminence in trade, payments and military security would have precluded such presumption. Even though, with hindsight, the weakness in the dollar's position should have been apparent, its slide took most observers by surprise. Having laboured for a decade and a half under the cloud of a 'dollar shortage', the European economies were confronted, within a surprisingly short period after the restoration of convertibility in December 1958, with the phenomenon of a 'dollar glut'.

The haemorrhaging of dollars from the United States had started in 1958 with a sharp deterioration in the current account surplus, which had worsened the following year and which had not been offset by any corresponding contraction on the capital account. However, the last year of the Eisenhower administration had witnessed a considerable improvement and the Kennedy administration had inherited a current account balance as healthy as that in any of the post-Korean War years (with the exception of the peak of 1957). The problem now lay in a renewed surge in capital outlays. Although government expenditures had continued to expand (a reduction in net military expenditures being more than offset by increased outlays in civilian programs), the cause of the problem became private capital expenditures, both short- and long-term. These had already reached $3.5 billion in 1960. They rose further to $3.8 billion in 1961, and fell back to $3.2 billion the following year before surging to $4.2 billion in 1963. The deficit on regular transactions, the key variable in all subsequent discussions in the three years of the Kennedy administration, was $3.4 billion, $3.6 billion and $3.4 billion, respectively.[3] This fact alone, however, cannot explain why there was such intense cooperation with continental Europe in these years.

This was because continental Europe was seen as an increasingly important component in the deficit. Again the problem lay not in the current account balance, which actually improved modestly over these years, but in the growth of private capital movements. These increased annually from $305 million in 1960 to $748 million, $906 million and $2 billion in the years 1961-1963. As a result, whereas in 1960 Europe had contributed 29 per cent to the overall deficit on regular transactions, by 1963 the figure had grown to 86 per cent. However, Europe was more than being part of the problem. The last three years of the Eisenhower administration had seen US gold reserves fall by slightly over $5 billion. The Kennedy administration was determined not to tolerate gold outflows on such a scale but, unless it succeeded in cutting the deficit, it had to persuade its commercial partners to accept some other means of payment. Europe, therefore, was also an increasingly important part of the solution.

By way of explanation, the EEC coordinated its policy in a Monetary Committee (henceforth EC-MC) of high officials that met on almost a monthly basis. At a higher level, every three months, the finance ministers of the EEC and the Central Bank presidents would also meet to coordinate their responses to international developments. In March 1961 the Organisation for Economic Cooperation and Development (OECD) decided to constitute Working Party No. 3 (WP3) to examine monetary policy. Its membership comprised representatives of the EEC as well as Canada, Sweden, Switzerland, the UK and the USA. Its chairman, Emile van Lennep, also chaired the ECMC and many of the EEC delegates to WP3 also sat on the EC-MC. A final forum within which EEC views could be represented was in the 'Group of Ten' (G10) countries that in December 1961 signed the General Agreement to Borrow. They included the EEC countries (minus Luxembourg), Canada, Japan, Sweden, the UK and the USA. Once again, the EEC delegation was drawn from the same tight circle of high officials from finance ministries and central banks.

The elections and the early months of the Kennedy administration were accompanied by extremely unsettled international money markets. This prompted the EC-MC to discuss the dollar's problems and come up with three immediate options for restoring confidence:

1. The USA could draw on its IMF holdings to the full 75 per cent permitted, implying a loan of $600 million.
2. The USA could raise US interest rates or, in coordination, reduce those in Europe.
3. The USA could give a gold guarantee on European Central Banks' holdings of dollars (an option favoured by the French).

In the longer term, none of the Europeans expected the USA to eliminate the current account deficit fully since the political fabric could not withstand the ferocious deflationary policy this implied. So attention turned to curbing the outflow of US private foreign investment (for example, by phasing out the fiscal incentives dating from Marshall Aid times) and by restricting foreign access to the New York money markets. Europe could also help, although the EC-MC ruled out any inflationary impulse to demand, and thus also to US imports, for the reverse of the reasons that it had rejected US deflation. Instead, European states could recycle some of the dollars gained from American capital export for early debt repayment rather than converting them into gold. Another variant lay in increased development aid, although the Dutch objected to using aid to compensate incidental changes in the balance of payments.[4] Finally, the EEC could help reduce the outflow of foreign investment by lowering the common external tariff, since the prospect of the Common Market had been a factor in accelerating the flow in the first place.[5]

The administration had its first chance of explaining its policy to the Europeans at a meeting of the Bank of International Settlements in January 1961. It expected to inherit a deficit substantially less than that of 1959. The balance of payments in 1960 (excluding military expenditure) would show a turnaround of $3.5 billion and the Federal Reserve wanted a further improvement of $2 billion in 1961. Partly because of this change, it differed in its analysis from the EEC:

- It foresaw considerable problems in drawing on the IMF.
- It considered that the anticipated improvements in the balance of payments rendered any change in domestic monetary policy unnecessary.
- It made clear that any European request for gold guarantees would be refused.

Moreover, the administration was wary of restrictions on capital movements since, in contrast to European opinion, it feared that this would further undermine confidence in the currency. However, any early repayment of debts would be welcome.[6]

This was not well received by the EEC finance ministers and bank presidents. The French Central Bank president, Wilfrid Baumgartner, saw little evidence that the administration was prepared to enact the change of course necessary to correct matters. Nonetheless, it was in nobody's interest to alter the price of gold. Although he considered it the debtor's task to solve its problems, the USA was entitled to a degree of international solidarity. France had done its bit by early debt repayment, estimated at $1.6 billion, by an accelerated removal of quota discrimination and by its support for an early unilateral tariff reduction. Similar measures were announced by the other ministers present but none thought them sufficient to resolve the problem.[7] Thus, although few were as strident as the French, all agreed that, in the absence of appropriate policies in the USA itself, further European credits (in the IMF or elsewhere) should be under revised terms and conditions. Despite the informal, non-binding character of the meeting it decided to inform the new administration of the consensus achieved, underlining the necessity for a rise in US interest rates, the need to restrict capital exports and the fact that the EEC countries would support a USA drawing on the IMF. The task of drafting the letter was left to the Dutch finance minister and host of the meeting Jelle Zijlstra.[8] This was the letter we referred to in the opening paragraph of this article.

The turmoil of foreign exchange markets, with flows of currency out of both the dollar and sterling and into the stronger continental European currencies, continued through the early months of 1961. The year also witnessed a spate of confidence-building measures, including:

- The adoption of Article VIII of the IMF (February 1961)
- The revaluation of the Deutschmark and Dutch guilder and the conclusion of the swap agreements (March 1961)
- The conclusion of the General Agreement to Borrow (December 1961)

In February 1961 the EEC countries accepted their full obligations in the IMF. Although a degree of convertibility had been restored in December 1958, the Europeans still sheltered under the transitional regime of Article XIV of the IMF charter. This had permitted earlier discrimination and would allow the re-imposition of similar measures in the future. By moving to Article VIII, they would accept more restrictions on interference with trade and payments. Moreover, the step was irreversible: the only remaining recourse to discrimination lay in Article VII (the Scarce Currency clause) that has still to be invoked. The implications of the switch for confidence in the system, and therefore in the dollar, were unmistakable. Ironically, the move could have been made much earlier but was delayed by an EEC decision to take action jointly which tied progress to that of the slowest member. Firstly, it was delayed by the French who required extra time to prepare their overseas territories for the move.[9] Then, when the French wanted to accelerate, more cautious ministers preferred to defer any decision until the outcome of the elections was known.[10] Only a German threat to make a unilateral announcement propelled the ministers towards a decision[11] and an offer to the British to make the announcement jointly.[12] In February 1961, almost a year after the IMF had first suggested the step to the German government, the move to Article VIII was made. In one step, the Kennedy administration received a guarantee that there would be no new lop-sided currency discrimination aimed against the USA. The adoption of Article VIII also served as notification that, in the eyes of the IMF, they were now all equals.

A mirror of the flight from the dollar was the accumulation of short-term funds in the Deutschmark. Since the end of 1959, the German authorities had been trying to quash domestic inflationary pressures by a tight monetary policy but had seen this undermined by the expansion of the monetary base caused by the inflow of foreign credit. A currency realignment had been a topic of debate for several months and the announcement on 5 March of a 5 per cent revaluation of the Deutschmark (and the guilder) was not unexpected. The surprise lay in the timidity of the move. The EC-MC had few illusions that the modest revaluation would eliminate the structural imbalance between Germany and the rest of the world. At the most the payments surplus might fall from 5 billion DM in 1960 to 3.5 billion DM in 1961. By revaluing, however, the Germans appeared to consider that they had done their bit – it was up to the deficit countries to do the rest.[13] The modesty of the revaluation, and the expectation that the further adjustment might follow, led to the most chaotic week in the currency market since convertibility as foreign funds poured into Germany and Switzerland. Since the revaluation, 700 to 800 million DM had been added to German reserves. The German finance minister laid part of the blame with the US authorities whom had welcomed the revaluation as a 'first step' towards redressing international imbalances. Both the Dutch and the Germans were insistent that no more realignment was to follow. The EEC finance ministers agreed a joint statement reaffirming their commitment to fixed exchange rates.[14]

In advice to Kennedy, the Council of Economic Advisors (CEA) suggested that there was now general agreement that the currency speculation was less a reflection on the American economy than an inherent weakness in the international system. It wanted a mechanism that, 'in a regular and predictable way' compensated for outflows of short-term private capital by reverse flows of official capital. 'There is no reason to permit every whim of private speculators to move gold from country to country.'[15] This is exactly what Europe's central bankers accomplished, in Basel in mid-March, when they negotiated the first swap agreement whereby they would hold each others' currencies (in this case, mainly sterling) for three months (renewable) on condition that it then be replaced 'at the same exchange rate as the original transfer'. They also agreed to 'recycle' inflows of 'hot money' by depositing a corresponding sum in the account of the central bank from which it had fled.[16]

The increasing movement of 'hot money' which had characterised the early 1960s and the fact that it could be directed against 'key currencies' in the international monetary system had raised two related points: whether the funds resources *in total* were sufficient to allow it to help countries in balance-of-payments problems as a result of such currency shifts, and whether it was not in need specifically of currencies *other than* dollars and sterling. The IMF's solution, first raised in February 1961, was the possibility of itself issuing medium-term, interest-bearing debentures.[17] The initial European reaction to this idea was frosty. The EC-MC thought that if the IMF needed scarce currency, it would do better to sell some of its gold than to resort to the expensive and cumbersome recourse of borrowing. But if it had to borrow, the loans would obviously need to come from the surplus countries and, in that case, the EC-MC felt that there should at least be some consultations with the countries involved. The French were particularly reluctant to lend directly to the IMF, whilst the Bundesbank, by contrast, considered such (guaranteed and interest bearing) investment an attractive proposition.[18] However, the Germans supported the general position that any new borrowing facilities should be accompanied by a new mechanism for consulting the creditor countries in their use.[19]

Privately the French foreign minister, Maurice Couve de Murville, told Walter Heller, the head of the CEA, that he could not see why he should bail out the UK, especially since it had not resolved the structural maladjustments of its economy. He also suggested that although De Gaulle did not interest himself very much in economic problems, he considered the IMF 'an alien and objectionable organization'.[20] Baumgartner later told Dillon straight that France feared that if the IMF received additional resources, it would lose its will or ability to impose restraints on the policy of debtor countries. Moreover, the disposition of additional resources would be decided by a weighted vote of the entire IMF membership, often compliant to US influence.[21] Dillon disregarded these signals and instructed the US director at the IMF to push 'energetically' for $3 billion in convertible currencies other than the dollar and sterling. The USA would then put in $2 billion and the UK $1 billion. It was recognised that since there was no visible shortage of dollars or sterling, these last amounts would be 'nominal' undertakings, but they were seen as essential to maintain US leadership in the IMF.[22]

By the time the EEC ministers next met in July 1961, the positions of the Benelux states and the French were extremely close:

- They questioned whether the IMF's reserves were indeed inadequate, given the relatively limited use made of them.
- If, however, resources were to be increased, they favoured loans to an increase in quotas since a general quota increase would automatically increase the size of debtors' drawing rights.
- Therefore, they preferred arrangements whereby IMF resources were supplemented for specific ends and approval was specifically obtained from the lenders in each case.

The Italian finance minister, Paolo Taviani, was slightly less dogmatic but he did want IMF use of its new resources to be subject to review of the creditors. The German Central Bank president, Otmar Emminger, on the other hand, recognised a need to strengthen IMF reserves and questioned the structural uncertainty built into the French and Benelux arrangements. He was anxious that when a crisis arose, the fund be in a position to react quickly. Although he shared the idea that creditors had rights to be consulted, he suggested that this could be satisfied by giving the Europeans a majority voice in advising on the use of credits without right of veto. Baumgartner, however, wanted to know who would judge whether conditions justified the use of the credits. As Max Holtrop, the Dutch Central Bank president, pointed out, it was impossible to cover all future eventualities in a satisfactory formula. The question was referred back to the EC-MC for further discussion.[23]

Informed of these discussions, Dillon, in a note to individual ministers, applauded the fact that 'agreement' had been reached to increase the IMF's resources, thereby ignoring the evident reluctance and mistrust inherent in the discussion over how to achieve this. He suggested that the matter be concluded by further negotiations in the IMF executive board. He did, however, express doubts whether a borrowing agreement which left the decision to lend in the hands of the creditors would do much to increase confidence in the fund. Instead he offered an arrangement whereby there were 'firm commitments by each participating country to lend to the fund up to a stated amount of its own currency' on the basis of 'operating safeguards' on their use.[24]

On whatever else it disagreed, the EC-MC united in opposition to certain standpoints adopted by Dillon. It rejected the notion that there was any general shortage of IMF resources. At the most, it recognised the need for supplementary funds for special circumstances such as runs on the key currencies. Nor did it want the negotiations to go to the executive board where countries which were not likely to be called upon to do any extra lending would participate in the decision. Moreover, the presence there of underdeveloped countries might push matters towards the end result of an overall increase in quotas (which would extend their own borrowing rights, however modestly).

The main sticking point remained the nature of controls over the additional resources which, it was now agreed, would only be for special cases and would take the form of a general loan agreement amongst the most important industrial countries. Germany and Italy were prepared to accept an *a priori* commitment to partake in any loan operation, albeit to a maximum sum and under certain safeguards, since a simple statement of good-will would be insufficient to restore confidence in the fund. Besides, they doubted whether the USA would participate without a definite European commitment. Among the conditions to be fulfilled were that the IMF would concentrate its borrowing on 'real' surplus countries and that the additional resources would not be used for inflationary financing. In this respect the creditors expected to be consulted on the question whether the 'exceptional circumstances' truly justified the loan. France and Belgium were less willing to accept commitments. They did not want the fund itself to decide when a loan was needed nor the amount in question. The most they would accept was a declaration of intent that, should conditions warrant it, they would be willing to sign a credit agreement. The Dutch took a middle course; namely, that accepting a commitment did not mean that no conditions could be attached. Thus, the group could itself decide if circumstances justified a loan, where the sums were to be raised, how much was to be borrowed and for how long.[25]

All of this had been vehemently opposed by Per Jacobsson, president of the IMF, because it threatened to undermine irreparably the fund's authority. He insisted that the borrowing authority had to lie with the fund, though he was willing to leave some control over the decision whether to lend to the lenders themselves. He had originally wanted each country to commit itself to lend to the IMF sums within a predetermined range. The distribution of the currency basket would be determined by as yet unspecified rules of the IMF.[26] His fears of the creation of a special group within the IMF were substantially dissipated when there was no objection to this procedure from the less developed countries. Moreover, he was convinced of the firmness of the European position.[27]

This agreement left the sums involved as the only unsettled question. Thus, in December the EEC finance ministers found themselves examining a possible commitment of $6 to $6.5 billion. The USA favoured the upper limit, distributed as follows in the first column of Table 12.1.

TABLE 12.1: DISTRIBUTION OF NEW BORROWING FACILITIES EXTENDED BY THE IMF (BILLION DOLLARS)

	US-favoured Upper Limit	*Final Outcome*
USA	$2,0	$2,0
Germany	$1,1	$1,0
UK	$1,0	$1,0
France	$0,5	$0,55
Italy	$0,5	$0,55
Benelux	$0,4	$0,35
Canada, Japan, Sweden	$1,0	$0,55
Total	$6,5	$6,0

The final outcome (in the second column) suggests that, after the total had been pruned back, the EEC countries had acquiesced fairly painlessly. Italy had judged its original assessment too high because of its international debts but, as the Belgians pointed out, if IMF quotas were first recalculated to reflect the shifts in world trade it would have been higher still. The Dutch objected to their assessment because they feared the prospects of seeing no less than 40 per cent of their reserves being tied up in the IMF (when they anyway covered only 5 months' imports) and this probably contributed to the reduction made in their case. All countries, however, only agreed these sums after insisting on the right to revoke the loans in the event that they find themselves under speculative pressure.[28]

The decision on the General Agreement to Borrow was announced at a meeting of NATO finance ministers on 13 December. In March 1963 Switzerland, not a member of the IMF, joined the GAB with a contribution of $200 million. The role of the GAB in this period was more symbolic than real. It was not until the end of 1964 that it was first used, and then to support sterling.[29]

Under-Secretary of the Treasury Robert Roosa described the piecemeal reforms as part of an integrated coherent plan, which could only be realised through confidence and through confidential negotiations. Thus, it had only been made public in snippets, creating the impression that it represented only 'a patchwork improvisation of minor devices'.[30] Nonetheless, he commented later, 'These are an impressive array of innovations; the intricate details of what has been arranged in each of these areas would already make a record of formidable size.'[31]

The US balance of payments had meanwhile been discussed in OECD WP3. In October 1961, before the meeting, Roosa had written to the chairman, Van Lennep, to obtain his cooperation in steering the discussion towards reinforcing certain US policy directions:

- He did not want the USA to abandon its growth policies for the balance of payments; indeed, growth was a prerequisite for attaining long-term payments equilibrium.
- He wanted support for the government's work in discouraging excessive price increases and in keeping wage increases in line with productivity – if the Europeans could specifically mention the need for restraint in the steel sector, so much the better.
- WP3 could stress the need to increase manufacturing investment and to reform the tax structure to facilitate that goal.
- There should be a mention of the link between the US deficit, its military expenditure, *inter alia* for defending Western Europe, and the European surpluses.
- Any help in gaining access to foreign markets would be welcome since it would contribute to relieving protectionist pressures at home.

On the other hand, the USA would oppose any suggestions for restrictions on capital flows, any proposals for untying development aid, and any advice to increase long-term interest rates, since it would repress economic growth.[32]

As far as the balance of payments was concerned, WP3 recommended the investigation of further reductions in protection, whilst the USA continued to encourage an export drive and to provide the necessary credit facilities. Van Lennep argued also for the importance of the competitive position and (surprise, surprise) received a description of the lengths to which the government was willing to go to limit cost increases. Not everyone, however, was willing to endorse the symmetry between the US deficit, military expenditure and the European surplus although they welcomed attempts to reduce the foreign exchange cost of military outlays. There were also questions raised about the fact that almost two-thirds of $3.5 billion of development aid was tied to purchases in the USA. Roosa replied that the choice had been between tying aid or drastically reducing it. When the balance of payments improved, some untying could take place. As for direct investment, the government was determined to remove the fiscal stimulus to foreign investment.

Even if the balance of payments recovered by 1963, it still implied, especially with the economy now recovering, tolerating considerable deficits in the coming two years. The Swiss, French and Italians all questioned the impact of this on confidence in the dollar and asked how the deficits would be funded. Certainly it was feared that renewed gold sales would lead to renewed speculation. Some also mentioned that the problems would be eased if there was a change in the relative interest rates between the USA and Europe. Roosa replied that interest rate policy could not be solely dependent on external considerations and that any tightening of monetary policy could choke off growth. On the other hand, European countries could relax measures that discouraged capital export, whether to the USA or to third countries. Similarly, he reminded the Europeans that they had outstanding loans to the USA.[33]

The discussion in WP3 was concluded in December and a so-called 'Van Lennep letter' sent to the US delegation. The most important points were:

- The central concern must be ensuring a sufficiently large current account surplus in order to cover international transactions. This should happen as soon as possible and although 1963 seemed a suitable target, improvement should already be visible in 1962.[34] The current account surplus should be in the order of $6 to $6.5 billion. To achieve this, whilst maintaining a growth-oriented strategy, placed high demands on US policy.
- Prices and wages should be held down to maintain the increase in competitiveness that was already becoming apparent. (The Labor Management Board and steel industry were specifically mentioned.)
- Productivity should be increased and, to that end, investment should be encouraged whilst ensuring that the means were also available.[35] The elimination of fiscal loopholes should also contribute to reducing foreign direct investment.
- Exports should be encouraged by domestic US policy and also by the removal of trade barriers.

Whilst, thus far, the letter was close to what Roosa had wished, interestingly there was no mention of the impact of defence expenditures on the balance of payments. Moreover there was a veiled hint that interest rate policy needed adjustment.[36] Should, as a result of the recovery, short-term interest rates rise, this development should not be resisted and, if external circumstances required it, should even be encouraged since the impact on long-term rates need not be immediate.[37]

Before the review, Dillon had become increasingly worried about the outflow of short-term funds from the United States. He was inclined to attribute much of the blame to tensions surrounding Berlin, but acknowledged that part of the problem lay in interest rate differentials between Europe and the USA and was determined not to relax short-term domestic rates.[38] Although the Europeans now seemed to urge a tightening of monetary policy, neither Roosa nor Dillon considered this immediately necessary. Roosa was still convinced that domestic economic growth would eventually mop up excess liquidity.[39] On the other hand, the chairman of the Federal Reserve Board, William McChesney Martin, wanted an early hike in interest rates as a pre-emptive strike against a run on the dollar that could come at any moment. At a meeting with Kennedy, he was opposed by both Dillon and James Tobin from the CEA, who argued that a small rise would be ineffective and a large one too damaging for domestic recovery.[40] In March 1962, Dillon outlined his own approach to solving the balance-of-payments problem in light of the sharp deterioration in the basic balance (the balance on regular transactions minus short-term capital movements). He considered that the USA needed a turn-about of $2.5 billion, to be achieved by 1964. This would come as follows:

- $1 billion from military ($600 million from offset)
- $500 million from long-term capital flows (about half as a result of changes in foreign tax treatment)
- $300 million from putting a ceiling on the dollar component of foreign aid
- $700 million from an improvement in commercial surplus, mainly exports[41]

This strategy, laudable though it was, meant tackling the balance-of-payments problem on a piecemeal basis. It did not recognise that a possible imbalance between domestic supply and demand conditions might spill over into the foreign sector.

A year later, in December 1962, WP3 returned to examine US monetary policy. The latest prognosis was that, since the current account surplus would increase from $2.2 billion in 1962 to $2.8 billion in 1963, the deficit in the basic balance would fall from $1.3 billion to $500 million. That still left it, for 1963, a long way short of the basic equilibrium promised twelve months earlier. In addition net short-term capital outflow was estimated at $1.5 billion for 1962 and was likely to persist in 1963. These developments underlay European concern. Only the other deficit countries, Canada and the UK, refrained from criticism. Among the rest there was a strong feeling that, since fiscal policy was directed towards stimulating growth (with a package of tax cuts), monetary policy, more than previously, should be directed towards the elimination of the deficit. The Europeans did not think that a tighter monetary policy would endanger the expansionary fiscal measures adopted by the administration, but thought it would have a positive impact on both long- and short-term capital export. They saw no reason why the USA should not cover its budget deficit on the capital market. The US opinion was exactly the opposite: growth would be weakened and there would be no significant impact on capital movement. Whilst most European commentators were willing to see monetary stringency run parallel with the effect of the fiscal measures (i.e. the growth in the budget deficit), the Benelux and Swiss position was that the external situation brooked no delay.[42]

The question then arose of how the total deficit, estimated for 1963 at between $1.25 billion and $1.75 million even after discounting an early debt repayment of $500 million ($660 million in 1962), would be funded. The Americans expected gold sales of $900 million (the same as 1961 and 1962) and hoped to borrow the rest. Individual European countries would be approached to test their readiness to accept Roosa (medium-term, exchange rate guaranteed) bonds. Both Van Lennep and Emminger, supported by the Swiss, were forceful in condemning this strategy as a way of shirking responsibility for taking adequate corrective measures to restore equilibrium. If the budget deficit were financed on the capital market, it would mop up excess liquidity and have a salutary impact on capital export.[43]

Nonetheless, working on the assumption that the uncovered deficit for 1963 *and* 1964 would be $2 billion each year, the EC-MC considered that half could be funded by gold sales. But that was about the limit without coming dangerously close to the ceiling of reserves dictated by the necessity to cover the domestic note issue. The remainder could be covered by prepayment of debt and by loans. Already the USA had placed Roosa bonds worth $129 million with Switzerland and $200 million each with Germany and Italy. On top of this, it had negotiated $1.1 billion in swap agreements. The French representative, however, still considered that the USA should use the normal IMF channels, and thus submit to IMF discipline.[44]

In April 1963, Roosa returned to WP3 with a less optimistic prognosis. The US deficit was estimated at $3.5 billion in 1962 and $3 billion for 1963. He blamed the lack of improvement on the fact that US recovery was sucking in imports but quoted wage restraint policies, an active export policy, and a reduction in the foreign exchange costs of official overseas expenditure as evidence of the administration's determination to rectify matters. None of this, however, did much to increase the confidence of the Europeans: the failure of earlier promises to materialise muted any natural tendency towards optimism that may have existed. Roosa suggested that the deficit could be covered by $750 million early debt repayment, $1 billion gold sales, $500 million accumulated foreign exchange by Canada and Japan and $750 million in Roosa bonds. Van Lennep's position that there had to be some control over US policy now received more support than it had done previously. Yet, when asked about this and a possible role for WP3, Roosa replied that the US position had almost become a fixed agenda point for WP3 already![45]

The patience of Valéry Giscard d'Estaing, France's finance minister, was almost exhausted. The US deficit was deteriorating with no end in sight. Some means, therefore, had to be found to make American policy more sensitive to external factors. As long as Roosa bonds were being used to fund the deficits, central banks were ill-placed to demand conditions. The other ministers of the Six concurred. Their participation in the Roosa bond operation had been to tide the USA over an immediate 'gold crisis' and none entertained any illusion that they were helping even a medium-term solution.[46] Yet, in July 1963, Roosa told WP3 that in addition to $536 million already funded in this way, he hoped to place a further $350 million by the end of the year: $150 million more than the prognosis three months earlier.[47]

All the time, USA options for funding the deficit were becoming more circumscribed. In addition to the Roosa bond operation, the IMF had been buying up dollars. In 1962 alone, it had augmented its stock by $1.2 billion. Further operations in 1963 had taken it to the level of 75 per cent of the US quota. Thus, in September 1963, the USA was forced to request a 'stand-by' credit of $500 million: still within its gold tranche and still far from the day when the full rigour of IMF controls might come into force, but slowly moving towards that moment. All this, however, still begged the question of what would happen when, and if, the world's major reserve currency was forced to the status previously reserved for a handful of developing countries. It was to postpone, or preferably to avoid, this moment that the US authorities pressed for review of the international monetary system. Equally, the European anxiety about the US deficit and the feeling of impotence in their ability to influence, however slightly, the direction of US monetary policy spilled over into this debate.

Before this point of joint talks on the future of the international monetary system had been reached, a debate on institutional reform had been gathering momentum within the Kennedy administration, since the middle of 1961. Advocates for the primacy of economic growth in administration policy, such as recently-appointed ambassador to India John Kenneth Galbraith, and Heller had never been convinced that manipulation of short and long term does not retard economic growth. Early on, Galbraith decried such an approach as 'mystic claptrap'.[48] Heller was nervous that the drain of dollars would turn into a speculative run and derail policies for domestic expansion. In September 1961 he began to advocate measures to boost confidence in the dollar, the cornerstone of which would be to give a gold guarantee on dollars held in official reserves, 'a guarantee by the United States that our official creditors will not lose by a possible devaluation'.[49] Three months later he returned to the theme. Although economic growth would ultimately solve the problem, for the intervening 18 to 24 months the USA would have to bridge the deficit. He urged that this could only be done in collaboration with Europe through negotiating a pre-payment of the $7.5 billion long-term debt owed by Europe, through coordinating policies with Europe to reduce the impact of short-term capital movement, through borrowing from the IMF, and through a gold guarantee. He informed the president, 'Many people will be ready to tell you the disadvantages of these techniques, but the techniques will work, and their disadvantages are as nothing compared to the costs of alternative measures which would hold down the domestic economy.'[50] In May 1962 he returned again to the theme. The dollar overhang would continue to plague the US economy long after the basic balance was achieved. He was sceptical whether balance could be attained without, in the interval, a run on gold or the adoption of measures that would seriously damage the economy. The core of the problem, in his analysis, lay in the US's international banking function and it was time to spread the burden. He said: 'It is both technically feasible and politically possible to reform the international monetary system so the USA can escape from the trap we are now in, while at the same time our creditors receive assets they will be happier to hold than unguaranteed dollars'.[51] By this stage Carl Kaysen, a member of the White House staff, and Kermit Gordon, the budget director, had added their voices to the chorus. Whilst '[f] ew would advocate gold guarantee as a complete solution to the gold problem; many would argue it forms an important part of the solution'.[52]

By August 1962 an overall package of measures, in the form of an 'interim international monetary arrangement' to be agreed by the G10 (plus Switzerland) had been completed. All members would agree to freeze any conversion of official dollar reserves for two years. To fund the US deficit in the intervening period, the administration would:

- negotiate a drawing right of $5 billion with the IMF (for two years instead of the usual one year);
- acquire a further $1.7 billion (in addition to existing holdings of $800 million) through swap agree;
- engage in substantial forward arrangements, possibly saving up to $1.5 billion;
- conduct gold sales up to $1 billion (possibly in such a way as to produce a convergence in dollar-to-gold ratios in official reserves).

During the two years in which the arrangements were in place, negotiations on longer-term reform could take place. The whole idea would be to get more credit from Western Europe than might otherwise be the case (and far in excess of probable requirements) and, by mobilising such defences, deter speculative attacks. At the same time, the USA would get breathing space to put its external account in order.[53] Heller considered that international monetary reform should seek to defend all currencies against speculative attacks, to internationalise the burden of being a reserve currency and to provide for a means of orderly increments of world liquidity.[54]

Roosa wasted little time in dismissing these proposals. He pointed out that the administration had already been engaged in constructing an impressive array of multilateral defence measures that were already proving their worth in coping with the existing situation and that were at least as capable as any of the panaceas on offer of meeting the future requirements of the world economy.[55] He considered the Interim Arrangements as politically naive in thinking that any country would sign away automatic credits on the scale envisaged without demanding conditions in advance. And if, as one would expect, those conditions sought to place limits on domestic monetary and fiscal policy, the whole exercise would be self-defeating. Moreover, he saw no role for any 'synthetic currency device' that could not be better fulfilled by 'a single national currency, supported by the economic resources of the world's most powerful economy'.[56] Dillon fully concurred with this assessment, adding for good measure that the abandonment of free convertibility would shake the system to its core in the same way as the German standstill announcement of 1931 or the dollar devaluation of 1933 had done. He agreed that the existing arrangements left plenty of still-untapped potential for raising support for the dollar without recourse to the alternatives offered by the Interim Arrangements.[57] Martin was equally aghast:

> *The proposed plan for a standstill monetary agreement, if accepted, would hit world financial markets as a declaration of US insolvency and a submission to receivers to salvage the most they could out of the mess to which past US policies had led. It is incredulous to expect from it any resurgence of confidence in the present international monetary arrangements. Quite the contrary!*[58]

The Treasury and the Fed opinions carried the day and the Interim Arrangements were never endorsed by the administration. Instead it was agreed to make confidential approaches to European governments to encourage more compliant and responsible behaviour on their parts. But there was to be no hint of reciprocal concessions and certainly no hint of a gold guarantee.[59] Unfortunately, these efforts required the active cooperation of the French and the climate within which this was possible was destroyed by the refusal later in the year to sell nuclear and missile technology to France. Already in October 1962 negotiations on offsetting military expenditure in France had ground to a halt[60] and three months later Dillon was preparing a balance of the potential mutual damage should tension with France spill over into an assault on the dollar.[61]

As, through the early months of 1963, the dollar's position again deteriorated, the discussion within the administration flared up once more. Walt Rostow of the White House staff came out in favour of a twin strategy of repealing the requirement backing domestic currency by gold, thereby releasing billions for the defence of the dollar, and of negotiating substantial ten-year borrowings from the Europeans to mop up the outstanding dollar overhang. Tobin (now a former member of the CEA but obviously still within the policy-making circuit) also wanted a campaign of regular long-term borrowing, possibly at the rate of $1 billion a year from the Europeans over a period of five to ten years. Not surprisingly, Dillon's reaction was distinctly cool. He did not think that there would be a congressional majority for removing gold backing and the very fact that the issue was under discussion would undermine confidence. Secondly, he was unimpressed with the idea that the USA could consolidate 'our present liquid liability into ten-year loans and then promptly create new short-term liabilities to take their place'. Not only would Europeans never accept it, but the dollar could never, after such arrangements, regain its position as a world currency. Clearly irritated by the continual sniping at his policies, he offered the following criticism of the 'philosophy' behind the proposal:

> *This philosophy is the natural reaction of those who find their preferred policies threatened by balance-of-payments difficulties. It is only natural that they search for ways to make this very real problem go away without interfering with their own projects be they extra low interest rates in the US or the maintenance of large US forces in Europe. However, such individuals are asking the impossible. The sine qua non of all international monetary dealings, under whatever system may be imagined, is that no country can consistently run a large balance-of-payments deficit.*[62]

Tobin also suggested that the administration should reconsider its attachment to the dollar's gold parity of $35 an ounce. It was not worth defending the parity if the price were draconian domestic deflation. In the event of an agreement that the payments problem had become intractable, and before a run on gold forced the issue, the administration should devalue the dollar: 'Neither God nor the Constitution set the value of the dollar in gold or other currencies, and the world would not end if it were changed.'[63] The attack on the devaluation option came ironically from within the 'economic growth' camp in no less a person than Galbraith. He too was utterly fed up with the drift in policy occasioned by a combination of inadequate measures and overoptimistic forecasts. His solution lay in slashing troop levels in Europe, suspending long-term capital outflows to Europe, breaking off the Kennedy Round (whose results would probably not favour the USA anyway) and raising tariffs against European goods, and implementing a much tighter policy of tied aid. 'Strong surgical action may do less damage to military, trade, aid, and other important things, including our domestic political situation, than the continuing erosion of half-hearted measures that are not really corrective.' However, he ruled out a devaluation because he felt that any US action would immediately be nullified by similar moves by the major trading partners.[64] Tobin reacted violently to Galbraith's suggestions. He was not advocating immediate devaluation, although its threat might make the Europeans more willing to consider the type of long-term loan scheme he favoured. But if devaluation were necessary, it would be preferable to recreating 'the world of Hjalmar Schacht just to maintain the shadow of convertibility without substance'.[65] The devaluation issue was discussed in Cabinet in September 1963 and it was shelved. Reflecting on that meeting afterwards, Tobin commented: 'The unspoken premise, or perhaps the spoken but unargued premise, [...] is that such suspension would be a catastrophe of the first order, like the end of the world or a nuclear attack.' He condemned the concern of Dillon and Roosa with the dollar's value without counting the cost:

> *Their standing with their constituents and their place in financial history depend on getting through this difficult period without devaluation and without suspension of gold sales. [...] The priorities of financiers are understandable. Why Ken Galbraith should share them is puzzling.*

He still felt that if the time ever came to implement the Galbraith proposals, it would be preferable to sever the gold-dollar link instead.[66]

The path favoured by Dillon and Roosa had, from the beginning, been to construct and strengthen multilateral arrangements to support the international monetary system and to bolster the US position within it. This had resulted in 1961 especially in an impressive array of institutional reforms and it was their hope to repeat the success. The context for this new initiative was a reawakening of the 'liquidity debate', occasioned by a concern about whether the growth in the value of international trade was seriously outstripping the growth of money to fund it. The IMF's annual report for 1962 (prepared in December 1962) scarcely mentioned the issue at all but in spring 1963 the fund commissioned an internal staff memorandum on the question. The IMF staff report located a potential 'problem' since in 1960-1963 the stock of money (gold and dollars and sterling, convertible into gold) had risen annually by 3 per cent whilst the volume of trade had expanded by no less than 8 per cent. The lack of international liquidity could choke off the expansion of world trade and increase the system's vulnerability to speculative shocks. Ironically, the outflow of dollars was double-edged in its effects. If it continued unchecked, it would undermine confidence in its continued convertibility and render it dysfunctional as an international monetary unit. If it were curtailed, it would reduce further the growth in the stock of international money. In June 1963, under conditions of top secrecy, Roosa therefore proposed that the G10 should examine the problem of international liquidity. This resulted, in September 1963, in the appointment by the G10 ministers of a group of deputies to undertake a 'thorough examination of the outlook for the functioning of the international monetary system and of its probable future need for liquidity'.[67]

The G10 review of the liquidity situation locked into an already existing debate on the nature and functioning of the system. It was not initiated because of that debate, nor even because of an immediate accentuation of the circumstances underlying it. It stemmed from attempts to control the supply of key currencies (and therefore the domestic policies of those countries) and, equally, attempts to avoid such control. That political struggle was articulated using the vocabulary and concepts supplied by the earlier, and concurrent, debate amongst economists.

Roosa argued heavily in support of the status quo. A reserve currency had to fulfil certain requirements (large commercial use, a metropolitan centre which offers facilities for investing funds, and a wide and free foreign exchange centre) and the dollar did so. All that was necessary for it to continue to do so was to develop further mutual relations within the G10 and for members to increase holdings of each others' currencies. The French response, that articulated the concerns of most of the surplus countries, was that these were necessary, but insufficient, conditions. A currency could not be made a key currency by decree but by the willingness to accumulate it as reserves, and this depended on confidence that it would not be devalued, or placed under restriction, in the future. And as long as domestic policies deviated from those deemed necessary for the maintenance of international monetary objectives this confidence would be undermined. If, because of domestic constraints, the USA was unwilling to assume its international obligations, then it might be time to consider the creation of a new reserve asset. The US position was that this moment was some way off:

> *Only if the reserve currency is held for fear that conversion into gold (or another asset) would put it under too much strain, does it begin to lose the nature of a reserve asset and take on the nature of a credit instrument, for supporting the reserve currency itself.*

Roosa also argued that there were other ways of prolonging the attraction of the existing reserve currencies. These included a further development of mutual credit mechanisms that had already served the USA so well. The British also favoured an increase in IMF resources through borrowing or through quota increases. The French, by contrast, demanded an exchange rate guarantee on all official holdings of dollars and sterling (along the lines of the conditions attached to the Roosa bonds). Failing that, however, the French favoured a radical reform of the system that would confine the use of the dollar and sterling as reserve currencies to regional currency blocs. The rest of the world, and that meant largely continental Western Europe, would create a new reserve currency with a common control mechanism to guarantee against the creation of unconditional liquidity (as had happened with the existing reserve currency authorities).[68]

Reporting back to the president on 14 November, Dillon attempted to put a positive gloss on developments. Although

> *several Europeans, and particularly the French, questioned some of the qualitative aspects of the present system as arbitrary, inflationary, discriminatory, and not sufficiently reciprocal, nonetheless [...] a good*

> *beginning has been made since all concerned were prepared to discuss the basic problems of the functioning of the international monetary system in detail and with complete frankness.*[69]

Galbraith was less sanguine. He continued to urge the imposition of capital controls:

> *Such firmness is a small political price to pay for the economic gains at home and the political gains abroad that a stronger balance of payments provides. It represents also a considerable moral gain over the ass-kissing of the French central bankers and the Swiss private bankers that is otherwise required.*[70]

A week later the president was dead. The reform of the monetary system initiated under his administration resulted most immediately, in 1966, in an agreement for an overall increase in IMF quotas which strengthened the fund's ability to lend assistance in times of crisis. The debate on the liquidity problem was eventually resolved by the creation of Special Drawing Rights (SDRs) within the framework of the IMF. Although erring on the side of caution, the reform did provide a means of augmenting international liquidity. Unfortunately, by the time it was agreed, few would argue that scarce liquidity was an even remote problem. Because of the failure to construct a system to discipline American policy and because of the continuous American deficit, the world economy was awash with liquidity. Meanwhile, the French-led attempts to replace the dollar with a new European reserve asset had been abandoned in 1965, once it was realised that it would be impossible to negotiate. Instead France embarked on a campaign to displace dollars from its own international transactions and reserves by immediately changing any dollars reaching the central bank into gold. This lasted until the strikes and inflationary pay settlements that accompanied the 'events' of 1968 provoked a wave of speculation against the franc and eventually forced its devaluation.

The period spanned by the Kennedy administration marked a watershed in European-American relations as the dollar outflow outran the absorption capacity and turned into the 'dollar glut'. It was in these years that the US payments position first became a 'problem' for the rest of the international system and, indeed, it has remained so ever since. The debate, then, over the blame retains a certain awesome familiarity with that of today. Real factors, linked to competitiveness, protectionism and growth, vied with monetary variables, dependent upon fiscal policy and real interest rates. Policy errors were attributed variously to the surplus or to the deficit economy, depending upon the perspective of the commentator. Thus, more than disagreements over security policy that hinged primarily and exclusively on relations with France, the US payments position drove the first major wedge between the EEC and North America. These three years, therefore, are worthy of closer scrutiny because they straddle a turning point in American international relations.

They also mark an interesting transformation in the quality and the context of the debate on the problem. The period opened concern over how to manage and ameliorate the US payments position, i.e. how to fund the deficit until it could be brought under control. There was a definite willingness to pull together to resolve the problem: 'two souls, one thought'. However, their priorities were different. The US authorities were anxious to fund their deficit in ways that would absolve their policies from outside controls, even or especially those of their own creation, the IMF. So recourse was made increasingly to Roosa bonds, which guaranteed *incremental* borrowing against devaluation, as a means of finance. In this period, when the USA was squirming with a seemingly intractable problem, the authorities also encouraged institutional experiment. The General Agreement to Borrow was part of this solution (although even that contained too many constraints) and so was the initiation of the liquidity debate. Ironically, as the financing problem diminished towards the end of 1963 and into 1964, so the US authorities shrank from radical solutions and reverted to more conservative, and now less threatening, ways of obtaining credit within the IMF. Within Europe, however, the opposite development was taking place. If the USA had sought institutional reform as a means to avoid discipline, so the surplus EEC states increasingly saw therein the means to impose constraints. US economic power, and temporary external economic improvement, enabled it to duck the issue. Yet the essential problem remained unresolved: how to create a system in which the supply and distribution of international liquidity did not depend on the vagaries of the domestic economic policy of the major world economy. It is still with us today.

POSTSCRIPT

This paper had its origins in a glittering conference in Florence that we organised with the Kennedy Library. Almost all of the surviving top officials from the Kennedy White House were present alongside former European ministers and EEC commissioners. We split eyewitness sessions with historians' papers and dined in some of the best restaurants in the city. And, of course, I was there, so, in a way, I should leave a little eyewitness testimony of my own.

Among the eyewitnesses were two members of the Kennedy administration, Ted Sorensen and Arthur Schlesinger Jr, who had written key accounts soon after Kennedy's assassination, and who were in some ways 'keepers' of the history, and there was clearly a little rivalry between them. Sorensen had been a speech writer and was responsible for some of the striking highlights in Kennedy's speeches. Schlesinger tried to burn the torch for a longer-term perspective – a thirty-year cycle of American politics, from which Bill Clinton would be the beneficiary in the forthcoming elections.

Having talked indefatigably for three days one would be forgiven for thinking that, come the final banquet, the participants would have been exhausted (I was), but nothing was further from the case. So, in between the courses, we had a 'spontaneous' round of final speeches during which Schlesinger took the occasion to expand on this thirty-year cycle of American politics. A couple of courses later and it was Sorensen's turn. Somewhat abbreviated, it went something like this:

> *We were flying in India, Arthur and I, and our plane strayed into Russian territory and was forced down. There was a show trial and we were both condemned to death as spies. On the appointed day we were brought out before the firing squad and the officer in charge came up to Arthur and said, 'Mr. Schlesinger, I am sorry it has come to this, but we are a civilised people and so I must grant you a final wish.' 'Well,' said Arthur, 'I would like some time to tell you about my theory of the thirty-year cycle of American politics.' 'Very good,' replied the officer, and then he turned to me. 'And Mr. Sorensen, may I ask you what your last wish might be?' I thought for only a moment and said, 'Shoot me first.'*

There was one person at the banquet who did not appear to find that funny.

Despite the fact that the IMF has started to open its archives, the history of monetary policy in this period is still rather quiet. A recent overview has been written by Michael D. Bordo, Owen F. Humpage and Anna J. Schwartz, 'U.S. Intervention during the Bretton Woods Era, 1962-1973', NBER Working Paper no. 16946 (2011). A UK policy perspective is afforded by Glen O'Hara, *Governing Post-war Britain: The Paradoxes of Progress, 1951-1973* (London, 2012), 53-72. French attitudes are reviewed in C.S. Chivvis, 'Charles de Gaulle, Jacques Rueff and French International Monetary Policy under Bretton Woods', *Journal of Contemporary History*, 41, 4 (2006), 701-720. Finally, a fascinating description of how security and financial policy became intertwined in Germany is to be found in Hubert Zimmermann, *Money and Security: Troops, Monetary Policy and West Germany's Relations with the United States and Britain, 1950-1971* (Washington, DC, 2002).

13

A Dismal Decade? European Integration in the 1970s

The European integration process is often presented in the literature as a 'stop-go-cycle', with spurts of rapid progress alternating with periods of stagnation. The first years of the European Community were marked by many significant advances. Internally, the Commission successfully completed the customs union, created a common agricultural policy and commenced the construction and operation of its own competition policy. Externally, it concluded preferential trading arrangements with former overseas territories, completed a round of trade negotiations within the GATT (the Kennedy Round) and twice engaged in complex enlargement negotiations. The increasingly close cooperation among the member states themselves, and between them and the Commission, led many to speculate that a 'United States of Europe' lay within reach in the not-too-distant future. When, in 1969-1970, the EC began a third attempt at enlargement and committed itself to achieving monetary union within the foreseeable future, it seemed as though a new period of acceleration was about to start. However, despite the successful enlargement (and some would say because of it) progress soon appeared to have stalled and the period from the 1970s to the mid-1980s is often depicted in the literature as the era of 'eurosclerosis' – a hardening of the arteries that could ultimately prove fatal. Suddenly member states appeared hesitant, almost unwilling, to take further steps to deepen the integration process. More importantly, they took measures to restrict rather than advance supranational decision-making within the Community.

THE COURT AND INTEGRATION

This lack of euro-enthusiasm, however, did not stop the Community expanding in areas that had been initially unforeseen. In particular the European Court of Justice kept developing at a staggering pace. This led to the paradoxical situation in which political analysts spoke of the EC in terms of eurosclerosis and stagnation, while jurists were increasingly comparing the European Community to a nascent federal state. It was the Harvard-based jurist, Joseph Weiler, who first brought these simultaneous developments of stagnation in supranational decision-making and progress in judicial supranationalism to the fore. Even more significantly, Weiler postulated a direct causal relationship between the two phenomena; he contended that the stagnation of European integration on the political front was the *result* of progress in the judicial field.

Weiler based his argument on two concepts that he drew from Albert Hirschman's classic study on organisational decay: voice and exit.[1] The concept of *exit* describes the mechanism of organisational abandonment in the face of unsatisfactory performance. Applied to the European Community it refers to the possibilities for member states to default on the implementation of European decisions. The concept of *voice* describes the mechanism of intra-organisational correction and recuperation. In this context, voice is the influence of member states on the political decision-making in the Community. To Weiler, the increasingly active role of the European Court signified the end of – or at least a sharp decrease in – the possibilities of exit. The hardening of community norms into binding law meant that member states could no longer evade their obligations. The closure of exit increased the importance of voice: since it became more difficult to avoid the consequences of European decision-making, the member states were increasingly cautious during the decision-making process, and more determined to regain control over it.

Weiler developed his argument on the relationship between political and judicial developments even further. Crucially, he suggested: 'It would be wrong to consider the relationship in exclusively unidirectional terms. Instead, the relationship has been bi-directional and even circular.'[2] The simultaneous processes of political eurosclerosis and progress in judicial supranationalism had to be seen as antidotes to each other producing, in a two-way process, a certain balance by a cyclical interaction of the judicial-normative process with the political-decisional one.[3] In other words, while political eurosclerosis was the result of member state concerns over the increasing influence of the European Court of Justice, the increased activity of the Court was, in its turn, the result of stagnation on the political front! For historians, the question, then, remains: how plausible is this argument?

European Community law had indeed experienced a dazzling development since the signing of the Treaty of Rome. Initially, enforcement of Community law, like any international law, depended entirely on action by the national legislatures of the member states of the Community. Halfway through the 1960s, any citizen of a member country could ask a national court to invalidate domestic laws found to be in conflict with directly applicable provisions of the Treaty of Rome. A decade later, any citizen could do the same with any national law found to conflict with self-executing provisions of the European Community Council of Ministers.[4] It is also clear that the increasing importance of the European Court was not anticipated by its political makers. Indeed, the political choice had been to create a European Court of Justice that was relatively weak. Potentially more effective models of legal systems had been tabled during the negotiations, and it would have been possible to make the Court's rulings enforceable from the start. The growing authority, then, of the European Court was due to its own jurisprudence, not the result of political (re)considerations within the member states. It is also telling that, while all national courts accepted the supremacy of European Community law, to this day no national judiciary has accepted the reasoning offered by the European Court as the legal basis of Community supremacy.[5]

This, however, does not mean that concerns over the activities of the European Court of Justice were the direct cause of the political stagnation that set in during the 1970s. Weiler himself provides no clear hallmarks or legal cases that could be considered sufficiently important to spur political counteraction among the member states. On the contrary, the story of the growing importance of the European Court of Justice could easily be seen as one of a slow evolution over time. At one point Weiler himself ascribes the success of the Court at least partly to the fact that its activities went largely unnoticed by the interpretative political communities in Europe.[6] How, then, could it have raised sufficient concern within the member states as to cause more than a decade of political stagnation?

Weiler's argument is suggestive but not easily verifiable. However, historians looking at the 1970s do not have to tackle these arguments within the framework set by Weiler himself. There are explanations for the supposed phenomenon of eurosclerosis that are both more plausible and more proximate. Among these one could indicate the disintegration of the international monetary system in the early 1970s, the oil crisis of 1973 and the resulting 'stagflation', and the intensifying British obstructionism within the EC as successive governments sought to resolve the so-called 'budgetary problem'. These factors alone would be sufficient to explain the historical evidence, with or without the added impact of an increasingly authoritative and active European Court.

Moreover, one could also question whether terms such as stagnation or eurosclerosis really capture the historical dynamics. Historical determinism does not begin and end at the decision-making moment. Almost all historical events are 'caused' by factors operating over a longer timespan. Thus, the simple fact that nothing very much seemed to have been decided in these years should not be taken to read as nothing much happened. Indeed, one could argue that the developments of the 1970s prepared the way for the renewed 'dynamism' visible under the Delors presidency in the 1980s.

THE HAGUE SUMMIT

The late sixties and early seventies started with a new sense of optimism about the future of the Community. The completion of the customs union in July 1968, eighteen months ahead of schedule, and the initial successes of the Common Agricultural Policy (CAP) seemed to confirm the dynamism of the Common Market. More important still was the sudden prospect of progress on the political front, made possible by the resignation of French president Charles de Gaulle in April 1968 and his succession by the more pro-European, and less Anglo-phobic, Georges Pompidou. Now, it seemed, the Community could finally decide upon some issues that had lain dormant since the Empty Chair Crisis of 1965.

Although it was clearly not his main priority, Pompidou lifted the long-standing French veto on British entry. The French government was now prepared to accept British membership in the European Community but only in exchange for a permanent solution to the budgetary question, and only after the architecture of the CAP had been cemented into place. The French made it clear that an arrangement for the financing of the Community budget had to be made before British entry was effected. It was no accident, therefore, that enlargement came *after* completion and deepening. The summit was intended to launch the Community firmly on a path of future development that could not be blocked or diverted once enlargement had occurred.

The Hague Summit resulted in a call for completion, deepening and enlargement of the Community. It has been seen as evidence of a renewed surge towards a federal European state. 'Completion' meant, first and foremost, finding an arrangement that would provide the Community with its own financial resources. It also involved the introduction of direct elections for the European Parliament and an expansion of its budgetary powers. The goal of 'deepening' went much further. Deepening meant, 'moving forward the goal of a common market' by introducing Community policies over a wide range of new areas. Before the summit only agriculture resembled anything approaching a common policy. Now, the heads of government called for a common policy in the areas of monetary union, foreign policy, fisheries and regional development. The Commission, however, was not completely satisfied. The issue of institutional reform had not been endorsed, and the very success of the heads of government, and the marginalisation of the Commission itself during the two days of the summit, threatened to shift the balance within the Community in the future towards the nation state.[7]

The Six were more successful in attaining the aim of completion than they were in their attempts to deepen the integration process. By April 1970, negotiations among the Six had resulted in a permanent arrangement for the Community budget. Whereas previously the budget had been financed by direct contributions from the member states, which were renegotiated annually, the Community would now receive its own resources. These would comprise the receipts from the import levies on agricultural products and all other customs duties, as well as a small proportion, not to exceed 1 per cent, of national revenues from value-added tax. Moreover, the European Parliament would get an opportunity to amend the budget, but could only increase its overall amount within certain narrow limits.

The budgetary question was settled before enlargement negotiations were opened on June 1970. Four countries had applied for Community membership: the United Kingdom, Ireland, Denmark and Norway – with the latter withdrawing its application after the negative outcome of a referendum held in September 1972. Applicants were not consulted on the budgetary issues and the Hague Summit decided that applicant states were expected to adopt the *acquis* and to endorse the political aims of the founding treaties. The entire question demonstrated once more the speed with which the Community could act if all member states shared the same sense of urgency.

The more ambitious aim of deepening the European Community proved harder to realise. Of course, the task of 'deepening' the European Community carried far wider implications than did that of 'completing' the existing Community institutions, which made deepening politically more sensitive and harder to agree upon. Indeed, one could question whether some of the goals set by the heads of government at the Hague Summit had not been too ambitious. For example, the aim of creating a common monetary policy envisaged the establishment of an economic and monetary union by 1980. Equally, the aim of extending cooperation in the political field to foreign policy soon raised the problem of finding an issue of foreign policy upon which the member states could actually adopt a common position. However, it was not only the nature of the deepening aims that made them harder to undertake. Two additional problems, which reinforced each other, complicated the deepening efforts. One was the changed international setting in which the European Community had to operate in the 1970s. The other was the impact of enlargement. The three remaining application countries formally joined the EC in January 1973 and almost immediately the Community was confronted with the issue of the 'British budgetary question'.

BRITISH MEMBERSHIP

The British had always had a complicated relationship with continental Europe. The first application, in August 1961, had been abruptly terminated in January 1963. The second application, in May 1967, had been even shorter lived. Both had ended with a French veto. If the original decisions to apply for membership had been hesitant, and divisive, the manner of their rebuff had ensured that the membership issue remained controversial. Even so, the economic dynamism of the Common Market compared to the irregular progress of the stop-go British economy, and the Six's increasing importance as a market for industrial exports, had convinced most politicians, albeit reluctantly, of the need to enter the Community. Public opinion remained far behind. A Gallup poll in April 1970 had shown 59 per cent of the electorate disapproved the government application for membership, and only 19 per cent in favour. Although this changed to a majority of support a year later, unlike Ireland, Denmark, Norway and even France, the United Kingdom did not have a referendum on joining the Community.[8]

After a six-day debate, the longest since the war, the House of Commons approved the terms of UK membership in October 1971. The parliamentary vote to accept the terms of entry had only passed because sixty-nine Labour MPs voted with the Conservative government and twenty others abstained. They outweighed the thirty-nine Conservatives who voted against and the two who abstained.[9] Opposition leader Harold Wilson had declared himself against membership 'on these terms' – although he supported British membership in principle.

Besides the supranational features of the European Community, the main concern of the British had been the implications of the workings of the Common Agricultural Policy (CAP). The British had realised that there would be several 'costs' involved in membership of the Community. Since these derived mainly from the mechanisms of the CAP and the role of agricultural levies in the EC budget, British concerns over Europe in the following two decades focused mainly on Europe's agricultural policy. On first sight, it might seem strange that an agricultural policy lay at the heart of the British concerns over Europe yet it accounted for about three-quarters of the Community budget at the time of British entry and would remain so for a long time to come. Unfortunately for Britain, the way the CAP worked seemed to operate against British interests, with one exception; British farmers soon learned to love it.

Britain had a small but efficient farm sector and, as a result, imported nearly half its food – far more than any other Community member. British farm policy left prices to be determined by world markets, some seasonal import quotas notwithstanding, and compensated its farming community through direct income support. This way, British consumers could profit from low international market prices. To allow British farmers to make a living by selling at these prices, British policy consisted of deficiency payments, sometimes tied to production quotas. The CAP was far less suited for the British situation. A system that supported farm income by guaranteeing minimum prices of agricultural products simply did not make sense in a country that was dependent on cheap agricultural prices. However, since Community preferences lay at the heart of the policy, it was anticipated that the direction of imports would turn in favour of higher priced Community suppliers. This would have an impact on both the balance of payments and the level of inflation and, because of the way the EC budget was financed, it would have a negative impact on the government's budget as well. But all this was known *before* membership.

Because of the fundamental differences in the European and British farm policies, it was possible to predict the impact of the CAP from the outset. Firstly, the British would become net contributors to the budget. As they imported more agricultural products from outside the EC, they would make a relatively large contribution to the budget. However, since expenditure depended on the size of the sector (and increasingly on the size of the surpluses), they could expect relatively little in return. Secondly, the CAP would have a negative effect on the balance of payments. It shifted agricultural imports from the world market to the more costly suppliers from the EC. Thirdly, the CAP would increase inflation. Consumers would no longer be able to buy food at world prices, but had to pay the higher EC price. Finally, the CAP would interfere with Commonwealth preferences. This last problem was seen more as a political 'cost', however, and would become less important as the Commonwealth declined in importance for Britain.

The British government had made some estimates of the costs of Community membership. A 1970 White Paper estimated, in paragraph 28, an increase in food prices of 18 to 26 per cent, which would contribute to a 4 to 5 per cent rise in the cost of living. On the effects of membership on the overall balance of payments and on the budgetary contribution, the white paper was less clear. The problem here was mainly that 'in the crucial area of our financial contribution to the fund, there is just not sufficient basis, in advance of negotiations, for making reliable assumptions either about its cost or our share of it'.[10] The government did allege that the net cost to the balance of payments would be more than the 1967 estimate of 175 to 250 million pounds annually, because of the devaluation of sterling and the increasing costs of the CAP.[11] It is possible that the government was anxious not to get drawn into too precise a public definition of its position before negotiations started. This can be seen from the fact that the white paper does not distinguish clearly between transitional and definitive budgetary arrangements.[12] The conclusion of the government on one point, however, was clear. The overall costs of membership would not be large, and they would be outweighed by the boost in exports that would follow freer access to rapidly expanding EC markets. Thus, on the eve of membership, the overall economic benefits had therefore seemed obvious. Moreover, having apparently shaken off the balance-of-payments difficulties that had plagued it throughout the 1960s and seen the current account move into surplus, the strength of the British economy added to the optimism on the economic effects of Community membership.

This picture changed quite dramatically, however, in the second half of 1973. The year 1973 marked the start of British membership of the European Community. It was also the year of the oil crisis. The rise in international commodity prices had broken the rhythm of post-war economic expansion and introduced a period of crises in which nearly all countries suffered from inflation, balance-of-payments deficits and slower economic growth. Every member of the European Community experienced these problems, but none more than the United Kingdom, which, in mid-1972 had launched a 'dash for growth' fuelled by deficit spending. The timing could hardly have been worse. The balance of payments plunged to a record deficit in 1974 and inflation soared higher than anywhere else in the Community, reaching 28 per cent in 1974 and over 30 per cent the following year. The economy experienced an unpleasant 'hard landing' with GNP falling 2.5 per cent in 1974, unemployment climbing inexorably upwards and the budget lurching into deficit. The original estimates of the costs of membership had anticipated a negative impact on inflation, the balance of payments and inflation, but with all these variables moving out of control, these 'costs' were no longer viewed with the same equanimity. Moreover, with the rest of Europe also in recession there were no longer any dynamic European markets for British industry to expand into. With the balance of payments steadily deteriorating, it was the budgetary costs of EC membership that required immediate attention.

THE BUDGET

before opening official negotiations in June 1970, there had been an agreement that any problems of adjustment would be solved by transitional measures, not by changes in existing rules. An exception to this had been the budgetary arrangements. At the time, the leader of Britain's delegation had argued that the existing budgetary arrangements 'give rise to a problem of balance in sharing financial burdens' and that new decisions taken after 1969 had aggravated the problem. He warned that, unless a fair and sound solution was found, 'the burden on the United Kingdom could not be sustained and no British government could contemplate joining'.[13]

It was not clear, however, what the British could do to ensure a 'fair' solution. It had been no accident that some of the most effective Community decision-making before 1970 had been spurred by the anticipation of British membership. With applicant countries having to conform to the *acquis* and political aims of the treaties, the Six could impose their recently negotiated system on the new members. The only concession that the British obtained was an agreement on a five-year transition period during which they would not have to carry the full weight of budgetary contributions.

The situation changed with the fall of the Conservative government of Edward Heath in 1974 and the coming to power of a Labour government under Harold Wilson. The Labour Party had rejected the membership terms in 1973 and, as opposition leader, Wilson branded the terms an 'intolerable and disproportionate burden on every family in the land and, equally, on Britain's balance of payments'.[14] There is little doubt that, had he been prime minister, Wilson would have accepted the same terms as Edward Heath had negotiated but pressures within the Labour Party had forced him to take a more eurosceptic stance.[15] As a result, Labour had fought the elections with a commitment to renegotiate the Treaty of Accession and to hold a referendum on the result.

Some of Labour's demands had clearly been designed for the growing eurosceptic group within the party and had no significance whatsoever for the negotiations. The Labour manifesto had promised to retain a zero VAT rate on basic items, but EC rules did not obstruct this; neither did the EC prevent Britain from protecting its balance of payments by limiting capital movements within Europe.[16] However, the four main demands that were accepted by the Council of Ministers as the basis of renegotiation were genuine: lower agricultural prices, better access for third world (and Commonwealth) countries to the Community markets; recognition of the UK regional problem; and, most importantly, a new financial arrangement or refund for the budget contribution.

The renegotiations started in April 1974 and were completed almost a year later in March 1975. The outcome was a promise to review agriculture and trade policies, the negotiation of the Lomé Convention, the creation of a regional fund (the last two were not directly linked to the renegotiation although the British government took credit for them in its 1975 white paper), and the introduction of a corrective budgetary mechanism designed to resolve the problem of the excessive British budgetary contribution. At first sight, these accomplishments seemed impressive and the government celebrated the outcome as a big victory for Britain in Europe. However, it was forced to allow cabinet members who objected to campaign against the outcome in the referendum. In the event, it mattered little. The 'yes' campaign was far better funded than the 'no' and the outcome was a comfortable majority of 67 per cent in favour of continued UK membership in the European Community.

It soon transpired, however, that the renegotiation had not met the most important British concern over Europe. The costs of the CAP continued to skyrocket, and the British budgetary contribution followed in its wake. The correction mechanism, seriously flawed, could do nothing to solve this problem and, in fact, was never triggered into operation.[17] The idea behind the budgetary correction mechanism was that countries qualified for a rebate when they met all three of the following criteria: they were net contributors to the budget, they had a rate of economic growth that was not more than 120 per cent of the Community average and they experienced a balance-of-payments deficit. The rebate would then be calculated as the gap between the countries' percentage contribution to the budget and its percentage share of Community gross national product. The problem, however, was not so much that Britain paid too much into the EC, but that it received too little in return (see Table 13.1).

TABLE 13.1: FINANCIAL COSTS AND BENEFITS OF EEC MEMBERSHIP

	% share in Community GDP in 1977 at current PPP	*Gross contribution in 1980 as % of share*	*Gross receipts in 1980 as % of total*
Belgium/Luxembourg	4.3	6.1	11.9
Denmark	2.3	2.4	4.4
France	23.3	20.0	20.0
Germany	28.1	30.1	23.5
Ireland	0.8	0.9	3.8
Italy	15.7	11.5	16.8
Netherlands	5.8	8.4	10.5
UK	19.8	20.5	8.7

Source: W. Godley, 'The United Kingdom and the Community Budget' in W. Wallace (ed.), *Britain in Europe* (London, 1980), 74-75.

In terms of its gross national product, and in comparison with the overall patterns of payments by the member states, the British contribution was not excessively out of line. When the gross contribution is compared with gross receipts though, the picture is completely different. Of the other countries, only Germany was in a similar position, though the discrepancy was not as great as it was for the UK. Table 13.1 relates solely to the sums of money that were paid into and received out of the Community budget. Although these accurately represent the results of the Community system of budgetary transfers, they do not represent the whole transfer system between member countries. From the British viewpoint, the situation becomes even worse if we take into account not only the 'budget costs' of the CAP, but also the 'food costs'.

Before EC membership, the British had paid for its food at world market prices and was liable to pay that in foreign exchange. If there was an import levy, the receipts flowed into the British exchequer. As an EC member, the UK was obliged to pay its domestic producers the (higher) Community price. If it imported from outside the EC, it charged a levy to bring the import price to the EC level, but instead of flowing to the British Treasury, the receipts were transferred to the EC budget, and showed up as part of Table 13.1. However, if the UK imported from within the EC, it paid foreign producers the EC price, and was liable to pay that in foreign exchange as well. This part of the CAP's operation fell completely outside the budget calculations. However, because of the structure of UK trade, it weighed particularly heavily on the British calculations of the costs of membership. It also weighed heavily on Germany, but Germany's balance-of-payments situation in the 1970s was far rosier than was that of the UK. The major beneficiaries were France and the Netherlands, both of whom were large exporters of agricultural products to the other members of the European Community. The effects of these 'excess food costs' are shown in Table 13.2.

TABLE 13.2: NET NATIONAL RECEIPTS ESTIMATED FOR 1980 (£ MILLIONS)

	Net Budgetary Receipt	*Excess Food Costs*	*Total Net Cash Receipt*
BLEU	557	-60	497
Denmark	188	244	432
France	-48	528	480
Germany	-724	-358	-1082
Ireland	289	173	462
Italy	491	-515	-24
Netherlands	193	694	887
UK	-1203	-127	-1330

Source: W. Godley, 'The United Kingdom and the Community Budget' in W. Wallace (ed.), *Britain in Europe* (London, 1980), 76.

The United Kingdom of course did have a point when it called the workings of the CAP unfair. It is interesting to note that two of the three losers from the CAP belonged to the poorest nations of Europe. Both the United Kingdom and Italy had a *per capita* income that lay far below the Community average; both lost from the CAP. On the other hand, three of the four beneficiaries of the CAP had an average *per capita* income that was significantly above the Community average. Of the 'poor' countries, only Ireland profited from the CAP. Instead of achieving an improvement in the relative position of farm income – and even that was questionable – the CAP resulted in transfers between individuals and between member states that in many respects were inequitable. Budgetary squabbles aside, this situation called for some kind of 'relief' for the poorer countries. They received this in the form of a European regional policy.

REGIONAL POLICY

One of the deepening aims of the Hague Summit had been the creation of a regional policy, which would reduce economic imbalances within the Community. After the CAP, regional policy would become the next serious community policy. It would, however, take quite some while to even approach the CAP in size and importance.

The preamble to the Treaty of Rome had already established that member states were 'anxious to strengthen the unity of their economies and to ensure their harmonious development by reducing the differences existing between the various regions and the backwardness of the less favoured regions'.[18] To effect this aim, the European Investment Bank (EIB) had been created. The EIB raised resources largely by borrowing on national and international capital markets, and made out loans either directly to individual investment projects or guaranteed loans made by other financial institutions. The main logic behind the creation of the EIB was a fear that regional problems might destabilise the Community and undermine its long-term political goals. One effect of removing intra-Community tariff barriers, for example, would be increased competition for traditional industries in many relatively weak regions. It was possible that such regions might not be able to resist this competition and that, faced with these prospects, future governments could become reluctant to implement Community policies.[19]

The idea that the European Community itself should be an active participant in regional policy first surfaced in 1969. There were two reasons for this. The first was the goal to create an economic and monetary union (EMU) by 1980, which, because it would make it impossible for national governments to increase their competitive edge in international markets by means of currency devaluations, could increase the disadvantages of backward regions. The EMU, therefore, could have far-reaching regional implications, which had to be offset by the creation of a regional policy.[20] The second reason for its sudden rise in importance was Britain's dissatisfaction with the EC budget and the hope that expenditure on backward regions, with which the UK was relatively well-endowed, would increase its share of EC expenditure, especially if regional policy became an important expenditure item. As one of the poorer members of the Community, Britain could expect large direct transfers through a regional fund.[21] The goal of the British was therefore for a regional policy to overtake the CAP as the most important Community policy.[22]

The question of establishing a regional fund became a major issue during the enlargement negotiations. Not only Britain, but also Ireland and Italy pressed for the creation of a regional fund. Because of its economic size, and because it lacked many poor regions of its own, Germany would become the major contributor to this fund and thus the fund's creation depended upon Germany's agreement.[23] The Germans finally gave their consent at the Paris Summit of October 1972 when it was decided to create a European Regional Development Fund (ERDF). Now, all

Britain had to do was to make sure that this ERDF would be as large as possible. It was then, however, that lightning struck.

The second half of 1973 was dominated by the first oil crisis. The ensuing economic crisis increased Britain's concern over its budgetary contribution to the EC and dashed British hopes of establishing a regional policy sufficiently generous to resolve the budgetary problem. The stumbling block was formed by a renewed German antipathy towards the fund. Germany had reacted to the oil crisis by implementing a forceful deflationary policy entailing deep budget cuts and was therefore reluctant to endorse an expansionist regional programme at a European level. Moreover, since the prospects of establishing economic and monetary union by 1980, or at all (see below), were receding fast, part of the rationale for the fund also disappeared. Perhaps the most important reason of all was German irritation with Britain's 'nationalistic' oil policy. When the oil crisis broke out, both the British and the French turned to bilateral deals with oil-producing Arab states. They argued that no Community norms had been broken as energy policy lay outside the Community system, but this rush for national security played badly in Germany and the government became reluctant to look for compromises in other areas.

Between July 1973 and November 1974 individual governments and the European Commission proposed no less than fourteen different funding arrangements. Only the threat by Italy and Ireland to withdraw from the December 1974 summit, if agreement were not immediately forthcoming, averted a deadlock. The result was the creation of a regional fund on an experimental three-year basis, which was later prolonged for a second three-year period.

The ERDF was not a success, either in alleviating the budget problem or in contributing to the reduction of regional income discrepancies. In the first place, the sums involved were relatively small. The ERDF never claimed more than 8 per cent of the EC budget, less than 0.08 per cent of EC GDP. As long as the ERDF was a temporary arrangement, it was difficult to establish a claim to a larger share of the Community budget. Moreover, the EC had a legal obligation to fund the CAP, whatever the cost, and this was a period in which the costs of buying and stockpiling surpluses began to soar out of control. Secondly, and this was important for regional development, what was instituted was a common fund, not a common policy. The existing development map of each member state defined the areas qualifying for funds and, as long as they were used for development purposes, everything was OK. Later even this minimum requirement was abandoned, and the UK Treasury openly used the fund as a budgetary transfer.

The British budgetary problem would dominate relations between Britain and the Continent for quite some time to come. During the 1979 elections, the Labour and Conservative Parties both took highly aggressive stances towards the EC, which Margaret Thatcher was able to translate directly into government policy, with a vengeance. The demands for equitable treatment came to dominate EC decision-making until the issue was eventually resolved at the Fontainebleau Summit in 1984.[24]

THE BREAKUP OF THE MONETARY SYSTEM

Of all the 'deepening' plans made at the Hague Summit, the goal to establish an EMU by 1980 was by far the most ambitious. The creation of an EMU would change the face of the EC dramatically, since it would transfer to the supranational level the control and implementation of a core instrument of state power. Indeed, the supranationalism involved in the EMU was certainly far more than De Gaulle would ever have been willing to accept. It is interesting to note, then, what brought this sudden interest in EMU to the fore.

Many contemporary observers suggested that, just as the customs union and the CAP had been the main driving force of integration in the 1960s, so would EMU be in the 1970s. If successful, this would have been true, but the comparison did not end there. EMU was also seen as crucial to the survival of both the customs union and the CAP. The background to this was the increasing foreign exchange speculation in the late 1960s and, more specifically, the resulting Franco-German exchange crisis of 1968-1969. If exchange rates fluctuated, it would be difficult to maintain the CAP's system of uniform intervention prices throughout the Community and keep trade open. The short-term response, later to become almost institutionalised, was to introduce a cumbersome system of 'green currencies', effectively a system of subsidies and rebates on trade in agricultural products. The danger to the customs union took the form of higher transaction costs generated by exchange rate uncertainties. In the event, these fears were exaggerated since, over time, forward trading developed and reduced these costs considerably. Thus one major factor in promoting EMU became the need to 'save' the agricultural policy. What this implied was a significant interference in a major area of domestic economic policy-making to alleviate a problem in a policy that had scarcely yet taken shape. Yet, the argument fitted the goals and strategy of some 'Europeanists' of turning a problem into an opportunity for further integration.

In short, EMU was not only promoted as the new driving force towards further integration but as an instrument crucial to the survival of the Community as a whole. It is no wonder, then, that, as monetary cooperation began to unravel and the goal of EMU to recede, many commentators regarded the Community as being in an acute state of crisis. This view was rather exaggerated. Firstly, although not achieving EMU by 1980, the Community did succeed in creating a regional currency bloc by 1978. This European Monetary System (EMS) perhaps better answered Europe's needs at the time than a complete EMU could have done. Secondly, one could question whether, or at least for how long, the ultimate goal of EMU remained a serious aim of the Community. Tsoukalis[25] has suggested that the convergence of interests following the Franco-German crisis of 1968-1969 was quickly dissipated. At the Hague Summit in December 1970 the French government had already made clear that it no longer accepted the desirability of a complete monetary union.

Most explanations of the failure of the early EMU plans start with the disagreement between 'monetarists' and 'economists' over the strategy to be adopted during the transitional period before the EMU's creation. This involved a discussion over whether fiscal and monetary policy should converge before beginning to 'lock' exchange rates (economists) or whether to move early with exchange rate convergence in order to force states to adopt appropriate policies (monetarists). More important for the fate of the EMU, however, was an inconsistency between the goal of the European currency bloc and its relationship with the international system of Bretton Woods. On the one hand, the decision to achieve EMU was motivated by concern over the growing instability of the international monetary system. On the other hand, the steps taken towards EMU took Bretton Woods and fixed exchange rates against the dollar for granted. In other words, the EMU depended on the system to which it was a response. The inconsistency was there from the start. The 1970 Werner Report proposed achieving complete EMU in three stages. Stage one, beginning in 1971 and lasting three years, would achieve a 'concentration' of national macroeconomic policies with a goal of narrowing exchange rate fluctuations among member countries. Stage two would create a European Monetary Cooperation Fund, which would evolve into a European central bank managing a common currency in the final stage by 1980. Unfortunately, unlike the Delors Plan of 1990, there were no specific policy targets or criteria. In the event, international developments, however, forced the member states to postpone the implementation of the first stage.

In August 1971 the Bretton Woods system collapsed. European policy concentrated on saving the international monetary system, while at the same time reinforcing regional currency stability. In response to the decision, at the Smithsonian Conference of December 1971, by the Group of Ten major industrial countries to increase the margins against the dollar from 1.5 to 4.5 (allowing a total swing of 9 per cent), the EC decided in March 1972 to restrict the margin of fluctuation of their cross-rates to 4.5 per cent. Together the European currencies moved as a 'snake' (range 4.5 per cent) within the 'tunnel' (9 per cent) against other currencies. The system came therefore to be known as the 'snake in the tunnel'.

Unfortunately although the Smithsonian Agreement had set more realistic exchange rates, it had done nothing to remove the underlying causes of exchange rate diversity. The US budget deficit continued to pump dollars into the system and this, together with the acceleration in raw material prices, fuelled inflation. As countries responded differently to these challenges, so confidence in the future viability of the new exchange rates evaporated and the system finally collapsed in March 1973. The oil crisis, at the end of the year, killed off any lingering hopes that it could be revived. By that stage, the UK, Ireland and Italy had already decided to give priority to domestic policy aims and had abandoned the snake. France followed suit in January 1974, though it rejoined briefly (for nine months) eighteen months later. What remained of the snake was a small core made up by Germany, the Benelux and Denmark, with Austria, Switzerland, Sweden and Norway as associate members.[26] Obviously it was Germany that orchestrated the arrangement, and not the 'European Monetary Cooperation Fund' envisaged by the Werner Report. Despite these developments, the goal of EMU was never officially revoked. Whilst denying its feasibility in the medium-term future, member states kept paying it lip service. One example was the United Kingdom's affirmation of its commitment to EMU, immediately after floating the pound in June 1972.[27] However, as the 1970s progressed, it became increasingly clear that the Community could not even agree on the establishment of the next option: a regional scheme of fixed, but adjustable parities (the so-called 'floating peg' system). Indeed, all attempts at reform were doomed as long as the member states disagreed on how to react to the economic turmoil that was dubbed 'stagflation'.

The reaction to the economic crisis of the 1970s varied from state to state. Faced simultaneously with the problems of high inflation and low economic growth, the German authorities gave preference to the maintenance of price stability. The Bundesbank adopted a restrictive monetary policy and was prepared to accept the consequence of this: an economic recession.[28] Other countries aimed instead at the maintenance of high growth levels but had to bear the inflationary consequences of this decision. As shown in Figure 13.1, whereas at the beginning of the 1970s France, Germany, Italy and the United Kingdom had comparable inflation levels, by the mid-1970s, these had diverged considerably.

FIGURE 13.1: INFLATION IN MAIN EC COUNTRIES, 1971-1976 (%)

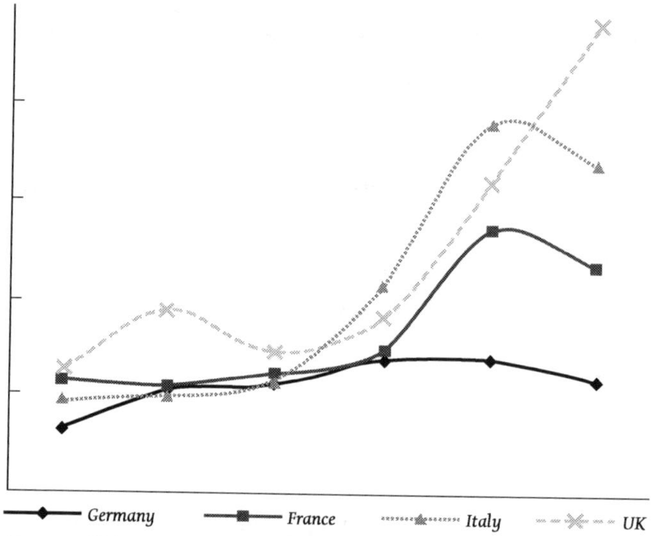

Source: IMF 1982, 203, 197, 263 and 463.

With differences of this magnitude, any attempts to re-establish monetary cooperation on a Community basis were doomed from the start. When it was launched in 1969, on the back of a decade of economic convergence and international monetary stability, European monetary cooperation had seemed straightforward. A decade later, this was no longer the case. Yet the conviction grew that it was necessary to do something.

Towards the end of the 1970s, it became increasingly clear that German macro-economic management had been more successful than that of the other main European countries. The German export sector experienced a renewed boom, and both inflation and unemployment were among the lowest in the OECD-area. By contrast, the other main European countries had witnessed a sharp erosion of their competitiveness, and experienced both higher inflation and higher unemployment. In 1977 France, the United Kingdom and Italy all cautiously implemented stabilisation programs directed primarily against inflation. The *Modell Deutschland* [The German Model] served as their main example.[29]

It is not an accident, then, that European monetary cooperation was suddenly 'in the air' again, and again concern over the dollar served to trigger a new European monetary initiative. The Germans, especially, were concerned over a renewed slide of the dollar that had started in the second half of 1977. A new scheme was launched at a meeting of the heads of government in March 1978, and was presented as a Franco-German initiative. This time, the EC was more cautious than it had been a decade earlier. The aim of EMU was replaced by a 'zone of monetary stability' in which the European countries could operate. This proved to be hard enough, as it was difficult to agree on an arrangement that answered to the varying needs of all Community members. At the start of negotiations, the inflation rates within the Community still varied by as much ten percentage points. The French, especially, had emphasised that the new scheme had to be sufficiently different from the existing snake, calling it an '*animal de la préhistoire monétaire européene*'[30] and they were worried that once more the new arrangements would be dominated by Germany.

The Community members agreed on the establishment of a European Monetary System (EMS) that would start formally in March 1979. To accommodate French concerns, a parallel European Currency Unit (ECU) was created. This basket currency, comprising specific weightings for each currency in the ECU, would be used to calculate the margins of fluctuation within the system. However, the essence of the intervention system would remain the same as in the snake. It would therefore not take long for the system to become known as another 'German mark zone', just as the earlier snake had been.[31] To accommodate members with initially high inflation rates, large intervention bands of 12 per cent were envisaged, instead of the 4.5 per cent agreed upon by the other participants. Even so, the UK government, emerging from the strike-ridden 'winter of discontent' and facing elections, eschewed membership.

The EC had little success with the timing of its monetary schemes. Just as the first one had almost been derailed by the first oil crisis, so the launch of the EMS coincided with the second. As wave upon wave of speculation buffeted the European currencies, only regular crisis meetings and periodic realignments preserved the fiction that there was anything like a stable system. By March 1983, the Deutschmark had appreciated by a little over 15 per cent against the ECU, whilst the French franc had slumped by 11.15 per cent and the Italian lire by 14.25 per cent. Although this caused some satisfaction among detractors of the scheme, and no little concern among those trying to make it work, there was little else to be done. As long as inflation rates continued to diverge or, more to the point, the different government priorities and policies that lay behind them, there was no realistic alternative. However, a structure was in place, and pressures were growing that would form a new consensus among members on macro-economic policy options.

SLOWER GROWTH

Many of the problems confronting the members of the EC and affecting their propensity, and ability, to cooperate, can be traced directly to the economic slowdown of the 1970s. The immediate aftermath of the oil crisis, the years 1974-1975, had been a shock for the Community. For most countries, for the first time in the post-war period, output actually contracted, and quite sharply too. The Keynesian analysis suggested that the oil producers had removed a chunk of demand from the economy, and that governments should step in to plug the gap. However, the recession was accompanied not only by rising unemployment on a scale not previously experienced in the post-war years, but also by very strong inflationary pressures.[32] The phenomenon of 'stagflation' had arrived, and with it 'the crisis of economics'.

The inherited wisdom from Keynesian economics was that when the economy threatened to slow down, and unemployment rose, governments should increase their expenditure in order to make up the shortfall in demand. It was assumed that the downturn would relieve any inflationary pressures in the economy and that the inflationary impact would be negligible, or at least containable. On the other hand, if countries faced inflationary pressures and, with fixed exchange rates the rule, a subsequent deterioration in the balance of payments, a sharp dose of monetary and fiscal deflationary medicine was required. The arrival of stagflation presented governments simultaneously with the challenges of recession and inflation, whereby solving the one problem would merely aggravate the other. Governments were now faced with policy choices they had not earlier confronted and the felicitous coincidence when one policy instrument, depending on the direction in which it was used, could solve all problems, no longer existed.

The crisis of economics, however, went one level deeper. Critics now levied charges that Keynesian demand management had never worked properly. In the first instance, the time-consuming process of planning, approving and executing changes in expenditure had meant that, instead of being countercyclical in their impact as intended, demand management tended to be pro-cyclical. Secondly, critics suggested that government expenditure had a greater impact on inflation than had been assumed, and was relatively ineffective in raising demand. What these critics argued about was the use of monetary policy as the tool. The problem with monetarism, the Keynesians argued, was that Monetraiams worked no better than Keynesianism, and that changes in the money supply were ineffective in promoting growth. Nonetheless, by the end of the 1970s, most countries adopted some form of control over monetary aggregates, together with fiscal policies designed to stabilise or lower public sector deficits.[33] However, as governments tried to use monetary instruments, it transpired that money, as a variable, was neither easy to define nor to use. But what really plunged economics into a crisis, was the fact that monetarism offered no way out of the policy dilemmas posed by the coincidence of low growth and high inflation.

It was at this point that another element entered the debate. If oil dependence had been the cause of the recession, Japan should have been on its knees. Although Japanese super-growth belonged to the past, Japan had recovered strongly from the oil shock and was expanding faster than European economies. Moreover, in Asia, the 'tiger' economies of Korea, Taiwan and Singapore were also surging ahead. Slowly, European policy-makers began to see the problem neither as one of choice between policy instruments (Keynesian or monetarist), one of choice between conflicting goals (inflation or growth), nor even as a question of economic management, but rather one of an adaptation to structural change. At this juncture in the policy debate, a group that had previously been considered at the right of the spectrum began to enter the debate: the so-called supply-siders, whose most famous exponent was Chicago economist Milton Friedman. Supply-side economics suggested that the undermining of the market, by government, lay at the heart of Europe's problems. By neglecting the long-term growth in economic capability and competitiveness, conventional demand management had weakened the microeconomic base in return for small temporary gains in the level of employment.[34] Governments made choices that consumers would not necessarily make for themselves and charged for their services in ways that did not reflect their true costs. Moreover, governments themselves were monopoly suppliers of many services, with a generous 'banker of last resort' to underwrite any losses. Government spending had increased substantially over the past decades. By the mid-1980s, government outlays averaged over 50 per cent of GDP as against 32 per cent in 1960. More significant was the change in its composition. By the late 1970s European governments were spending more on transfer payments to individuals than on purchases of goods and services.[35] Finally, even in areas where the government was not a supplier, it was a regulator, restricting and distorting market incentives with swathes of social and environmental legislation. Not surprisingly, given its antagonism to government spending as a regulator, supply-siders found ready allies among monetarist economists and policy-makers. Monetary caution, combined with deregulation and privatisation, began to assume an ever more central role in the policies of EC member states. Germany had been a late convert to Keynesianism and was an early, and ultimately successful, proponent of monetary constraint. The Keynesian experiments in Italy and the UK in the early 1970s were wrecked on the rocks of IMF relief schemes and in the UK, the Conservative victory in 1979 was to usher in the Thatcherite revolution.

The second oil shock of 1979 marked the final break with conventional post-war policy thinking. Recessionary impulses would normally have signalled a move towards expansionary policies, but a host of unresolved problems stemming from earlier shocks – for example inflation, budgetary deficits and wage pressures – ensured that governments could no longer afford to contemplate accommodating external shocks as they had done previously. The main exception remained France. The election of the socialist François Mitterrand to power in France in 1981 led to the last great Keynesian experiment in Europe. A mixture of expansionist policy and social reform, engineered by the finance minister, Jacques Delors, would light the way to a different future. Two years later, battered by currency speculation, a depreciating currency and a deteriorating balance of payments, the experiment was abandoned and the French, too, committed themselves to the primacy of low inflation and fiscal prudence.

CONCLUSION

From the mid-1970s onwards, contemporary observers almost universally used terms such as 'eurosclerosis' and 'europessimism' to describe the state of the European Community. By 1980 some academics warned of the disintegration of the European Community and even leading members of EC institutions openly spoke of the dismal affair Europe was in. At the twenty-fifth anniversary of the Treaty of Rome in 1982, the president of the European Parliament compared the Community to a 'feeble cardiac patient whose condition is so poor that he cannot even be disturbed by a birthday party'.[36]

At the start of the chapter, we contested whether this picture was true by suggesting that throughout the 1970s, integration continued, but less through the taking of bold new decisions at a Council of Ministers level as through the inexorable extension of European law. However, we rejected a specific link between those two phenomena. Governments did not become hesitant to make decisions because they realised that these would indeed be binding. If governments did become more restrained, it was more likely the consequence of the fact that having replaced 'Gaullism' in France, the EC found it quickly replaced with a British variant, which would eventually reach its apogee as Thatcherism. At the heart of this new obstructionism lay the workings of the budget and the CAP, or rather their impact in an economic environment where the key variables of budget, inflation and the balance of payments, were deteriorating fast.

We also suggested that the apparent absence of important decision-taking moments should not be taken to imply that 'nothing' was happening, or even that what was happening was moving the EC in the wrong direction. The EC persisted with some initiatives despite an unfavourable environment whilst shifting national preferences in other areas might have hindered short-term decision-making but opened perspectives for more dramatic moves in the future. Instead of seeing the ambitious slate of initiatives realised or launched under the Delors presidency as an outcome of favourable developments in the 1980s, it might be worth tracing the ancestry of some to their roots in the 1970s.

First among the achievements of the 1970s, the aims of enlargement, agreed at the Hague Summit, had been realised. It was true that, in the case of the UK, this was not without difficulty but both Denmark and Ireland slipped, without too many difficulties, into the EU system. One could postulate that, had it not been for the oil crisis, the UK might have created fewer problems but, the difficulties notwithstanding, the second enlargement did not deter the EC from further rounds of enlargement, embracing Greece in 1981 and Spain and Portugal five years later. Secondly, the continuous hammering on the need for reform of the CAP, by the British, and increasing reluctance by the Germans to keep underwriting its costs, did lead in 1984 to the first moves to restrain agricultural expenditures. The milk quotas introduced at Fontainebleau (at the same Council that resolved the UK budget question) seemed a timid step at the time but paved the way for more ambitious moves culminating in the MacSharry reforms of May 1992 that allowed the EC to conclude the Uruguay Trade Round in the GATT. Thirdly, the reform of the CAP, in its turn, made room for expenditure increases in other directions, and the direction chosen was that of structural reform (mostly on a regional basis). The ERDF, born under such inauspicious circumstances and initially so cynically deployed, had served to point out the new direction. Under the guides of 'structural funds', introduced in 1986, it was to grow to account for over 20 per cent of the budget by 1990 and closer to 35 per cent a decade later.

The events of the 1970s were to presage two further moves of possibly even greater significance. We will take these in chronological order. In 1986, the member states signed the Single European Act (SEA), a major revision of the Treaty of Rome that underpinned the 1992 single market programme. The European countries might not have been able to agree on the SEA without the lessons learned over the previous decade. One area of special concern had been Europe's competitive position in the high technology field. By the 1980s it had become clear that the Community was suffering from a loss of competitiveness on world markets. The policy of national champions had led to a considerable fragmentation of markets at a time when research and development costs were escalating and product life was shortening. It was increasingly apparent that firms even as large as Philips and Siemens could no longer afford to develop the next generation of products on their own; their markets were just too small to rationalise start-up costs.[37] In 1981 the Commission urged the Council of Ministers to develop a framework for intensive collaboration in the field of research and development, which emerged in the mid-1980s in the form of EUREKA and ESPRIT. However such initiatives were deemed insufficient to regain competitiveness. Thus the Commission suggested a complete removal of barriers within the Community in order to generate greater efficiency through competition and scale economies. With Europe's governments already beginning to target domestic market impediments, they were ready for a European initiative and willing to accept a suspension of unanimity in decision-making to realise it. This commitment to 'completing' the common market required the long gestation period and the paradigm shift of the 1970s.

In 1992 the Treaty of Maastricht, or the European Union Treaty, made the largest leap forward in European integration since the Treaty of Rome. Central to its aims was the creation of an economic and monetary union, with the introduction of a single currency, a single monetary authority and a single monetary policy. This would have been impossible to contemplate had the EC countries in the 1970s not persisted with their experiments in closer exchange-rate management. It would have been easy, after the obvious failure of the Werner Plan, to have accepted the fact that the regime of floating currencies was the most appropriate, on both a global and a regional level. It would have been easy, as the newly constructed EMS seemingly limped from crisis to crisis, to have bowed before the inevitability of market forces and to have acknowledged the frailty of institutional constructions to avert them. Yet, having weathered three years of almost continuous battering, in 1983 the EMS emerged into calmer waters and it oversaw a long period of exchange-rate stability among its members; long enough to adopt monetary policy as a major plank on the agenda of deepening the Community when the occasion arose.

POSTSCRIPT

This essay was written only a few years ago and appeared in Desmond Dinan, (ed.), *Origins and Evolution of the European Union* (Oxford, 2006), 169-190. Not much time has elapsed since this was written and little extra has been published. The second volume of the UK official history moves into the start of this period and gives an inclination of the UK budget problems which were to bedevil these years. See Stephen Wall, *The Official History of Britain and the European Community, Volume II: From Rejection to Referendum, 1963-1975* (London, 2013). Again, I would like to draw attention to the rich collection of articles in Michael Gehler (ed.), *Vom gemeinsamen Markt zur europäischen Unionsbildung. 50 Jahre Römische Verträge, 1957-2007* (Vienna, 2009).

14

EFTA and European Integration, 1973-1994: Vindication or Marginalisation?

I first became interested in EFTA when I started teaching undergraduates contemporary European history in Manchester in 1972. In a survey course on European post-war economic development, at that time, I devoted one lecture to EFTA and one lecture to the European Community (EC), just to keep some balance. Later, as I became increasingly involved in researching the EC's history, I became ever more aware that 'European integration' no longer referred to increasing cooperation and interdependence within Europe, but had become a term that had almost entirely been taken over by the European Union (EU). The problem with this definition is that there is a tendency, when dealing with the EU, only to look at other, non-member, countries when they actually take the decision to join it, and that the only history of these other countries, therefore, that is worth studying is their pre-history to accession. For the rest, they simply do not exist. Greece, Spain and Portugal pop up on the scene only because their revolutions allow them to be considered for European Community (EC) membership. Then Austria, Sweden and Finland crop up, all of a sudden, towards the end of the Cold War – no concern, however, about their thirty or forty year history that gets expunged at the same time. To be honest, on reflection, I feel that EFTA is also partly responsible for selling itself too short, and that it contributes to its own invisibility and its own non-history. One unfortunate consequence is that the political scientists, who see 'European integration' as synonymous with the history of the EU and its current performance, lose many opportunities for comparative research.

Throughout the world now there are many attempts by groups of countries to integrate their economies – for example, ASEAN and APEC and various other experiments in Asia, Mercosur in Latin America and SADEC in South Africa, to name but a few. In the available literature, almost all of the publicists and propagandists for these experiments genuflect before the altar of the European Union. The EU is often represented as the inspiration for what they are trying to do and, not infrequently, it is even portrayed as the model for what they are trying to achieve. Whereas even a cursory glance at the current situations of these countries, and the current level of development of the EU would suggest that there is such an enormous mismatch that it would be something approaching a miracle if these countries would look like the EU within the lifetime of the negotiators. There are many other lessons of integration and many other models of international cooperation that are not the EU – the European Space Agency and CERN on ways of technical cooperation, the OECD as a model of economic cooperation and EFTA as a model of for experimenting in achieving regional free trade. Now, this is important because I see the period covered in this chapter – 1973-1994 – as one in which the goals enunciated at the time of EFTA's creation were actually achieved.

If one looks back at the negotiations for the a wider European free trade area that preceded the creation of EFTA, and the meal that everybody made of the impossibility of creating a free trade area if it was not going to look like the EEC, and if one then looks at this period of history, one can see who was right and who was wrong. EFTA demonstrated that not only could a relatively small group of countries create industrial free trade without supranational organisations, but also that industrial free trade could be created between the EFTA countries and the EC without recourse to supranationality, or the surrender of sovereignty on the part of the EFTA states. It also proved that industrial free trade could exist and be operated perfectly simply with rules of origin and that far-reaching measures of tariff harmonisation were unnecessary. It demonstrated that one could deal with technical barriers to trade by a mutual recognition of standards and testing procedures and not through the very cumbersome process of product harmonisation, a phase that the EC was going through at the time. Finally, although limitations of space mean that we cannot deal with it here, EFTA pioneered an innovative and successful development aid scheme.[1]

EFTA is a successful model of integration, within its own self-imposed, limited definitions, adopted at the time. And it is those limited definitions to which many of these integration experiments around the world are aspiring today. There are lessons in EFTA's history still to be learned; if people look at the right history. But if you do not tell that history, those lessons can never be found, let alone learned.

In this chapter, I am going to plough the usual historical furrows. I will look very briefly at the moves towards European industrial free trade in the early

1970s and put them in their historical context. This is important because these developments coincide with the oil crisis and stagflation that engulfed Europe at the same time. I will then move onto the 'Luxembourg Process' and the brief but unhappy era of the European economic space, before cantering through to the creation of the European Economic Area (EEA) and the various defections and associations which also occurred at the same time.

EFTA, THE EC AND THE BILATERAL FREE TRADE AGREEMENTS

Table 14.1 shows the situation on the eve of the bilateral free trade agreements. For both EFTA and the EC, intra-trade (i.e. trade within the bloc) represented the most important export outlet – more so for the EC than it was for EFTA. Even so, for the EC, EFTA as a bloc was the destination for 17.4 per cent of totals exports; not a bad proportion.

TABLE 14.1: DESTINATION OF EXPORTS, 1971 (% OF TOTAL EXPORTS)

	EFTA(9)	*EC(6)*
EFTA(9)	28.0	17.4
EC(6)	25.4	49.3
USA	9.3	7.7
Rest of world	37.3	25.6
	EFTA(7)	*EC(9)*
EFTA(7)	19.0	12.1
EC(9)	48.8	50.7
USA	7.0	8.4
Rest of world	25.3	28.7

Source: Calculated from United Nations, *International Trade Statistics*, various.

That situation changes with the shift of membership. The defection of Britain and Denmark to the EEC radically alters the relative importance of each grouping, one for the other. Far from being of primary importance, the share of intra-EFTA trade in the exports of member states drops by almost one-third, and is virtually eclipsed by their dependence on the markets of the enlarged EEC, whose share in EFTA exports almost doubles. The fact that the changing affiliation of two states (one actually – the UK) had such a far-reaching impact reflects the lopsided nature of EFTA's original composition, which was dominated by one large economy. Reduced in size, the new EFTA constellation represented a far more homogeneous grouping which may have made decision-making more even and more easy. That might have been some consolation but the effect is difficult to measure. More importantly, for the EEC, enlargement diminished the importance of EFTA as a market quite considerably. The decision of Britain and Denmark to leave EFTA and join the EEC, therefore, altered the economic balance of power in Europe and therefore, also, the mutual perceptions between both blocs. And that shift in power and interest certainly had an effect on the developments described in this chapter. What is very interesting in this context is that the EFTA countries, throughout twenty or so years of the *EFTA Bulletin*, kept insisting that, despite all, they remained more important to the EEC as a market than did the United States. This may have been true, but it was most likely not always perceived quite as strongly on the other side of the negotiating table.

When the UK joined the EEC, it also made good on a promise made way back in the early 1960s, with the first membership application, that it would use the opportunity to facilitate the conclusion of free trade agreements between the EFTA members and the EEC. This so-called 'oath of the musketeers' – all for one and one for all – was not taken too seriously at the time since no one really believed that the UK would relinquish the opportunity for membership if the free trade agreements were to prove unobtainable. However, in the event, the EEC announced that it was willing to conclude bilateral industrial free trade agreements with each of the remaining EFTA member states, rather than with EFTA as a bloc. Although, in theory, this could have resulted in a confusing layering of overlapping preferences, rights and obligations, in practice the EEC negotiated the same agreement with each. Industrial free trade was not created immediately. For most of the industrial products the target date was mid-1977. For ferro-alloys, silicon-carbide, zinc, magnesium and rayon-wool the target was January 1980 and for timber and paper it was January 1984. Interestingly these were the self-same products that the French were so insecure about back in 1958, during the wider free trade area negotiations.

The staggering of the introduction of industrial free trade was over a time span of twelve years, and this had serious implications for several of the member states, none more so than Norway. The products selected for an extended transition period represented 34 per cent of Norway's exports to the EEC6. By way of a side-payment, Norway secured a reduction on the tariffs imposed on frozen fish fillets from 15 per cent to 3 per cent and cuts in other fish products.[2] Another major deviation from the standard bilateral agreement was that made with Portugal. Much poorer than most Western European states, Portugal had already secured a privileged schedule of tariff reductions within EFTA, and that privileged schedule was carried over into the agreement with the EEC.[3] Finland had its tariff scheduled delayed by one year because its agreement came in a year later than the rest.[4] And finally, there was the case of Iceland. Iceland had joined EFTA only in 1970 and had been given ten years to remove its tariffs on intra-EFTA trade, whilst benefitting immediately from duty free access to EFTA markets. A similar extension had been agreed with the EC but, just as was the case with Norway, the EC had also granted tariff concession of Icelandic fish exports. However, it was exactly at this moment in time that Iceland had decided to extend its fishing limits from 12 to 50 miles in September 1972 and then again to 200 miles in November 1975. The 'cod wars', as they were called, delayed the entire application of the agreement to Iceland as the objections of EEC members, first the UK and then Germany, were resolved. Only in 1976 was the issue settled, and the delayed schedule for tariff reduction came into force.[5]

By the middle of 1977 the stage had been reached where free trade within Western Europe had been achieved in most product categories. There was reason for celebration, reflection and setting the course for the future. Against this background, the EFTA heads of government met in Vienna in May 1977 and, at the conclusion of their meeting, issued a ten-point declaration. The fourth point was the most interesting. The declaration began by reaffirming EFTA's importance in world trade and committing members to cooperating in international economic forums. It then celebrated the creation of a market of sixteen countries and 300 million inhabitants, before moving on to commit members to strengthening cooperation within EFTA. The fourth point covered the development of trade and economic cooperation with the EEC. This was to be achieved by

> *increased exchange of information and closer consultations on economic questions and, where appropriate, coordinated efforts in order to secure free trade and to improve the general economic environment. Possibilities and methods should therefore be explored of enlarging cooperation in fields such as the 'stimulation of a stable economic growth, the fight against unemployment and inflation, the promotion of monetary stability and the concordant elaboration of legal norms in sectors of common interest.*[6]

There was every reason why, in 1977, the EFTA heads of government should call for some measure of policy cooperation between the EFTA states and the EC. The problem was that they were calling for something that they could not even achieve among themselves. The oil crisis was experienced differently in the different member states and had left them at different stages of the economic cycle. Norway and Austria were still on respectable growth trajectories whereas

Iceland and Finland were teetering on the verge of recession. Unemployment in Portugal was over 16 per cent of the labour force while the comparable figure in Switzerland was 0.5 per cent. This uneven development reflected their different economic structures, but also their different policy priorities. These factors alone would have made coordination amongst themselves extremely difficult, but matters were further complicated by the fact that the EFTA convention, enshrining as it did the principle of national sovereignty, had made no provision for enforcing such cooperation,

What was becoming obvious, as stagflation bit into the European economies, was that a 'new protectionism' was emerging, and with it, a whole new set of issues which had been almost irrelevant in the growth period of the 1960s, when an unemployment rate of above 2 per cent was seen as a 'crisis' and when average growth rates of around 5 per cent per annum were the norm. As Europe moved into the 1970s, inflation remained stubbornly high and average growth rates were halved. Against this backdrop, new forms of protection took root; forms that had nothing to do with frontier barriers to trade such as tariffs and quotas.

National subsidies became an increasingly important way of shielding industries from foreign competition. One calculation has suggested that in Western Europe they absorbed between 3 and 5 per cent of GDP.[7] The automobile and shipbuilding industries were the most visible beneficiaries of this new shift in policy. EFTA states, too, turned to subsidies in an effort to maintain both output and employment.[8] Barter trade became increasingly common as considerations of price became subservient to the need to avoid foreign exchange losses. In the wake of the collapse of the Bretton Woods system, currency manipulation, known as 'dirty floating', was employed to keep currencies permanently undervalued and thereby maintain export competiveness. Japan was the most notable target of such accusations. It was also the main object of voluntary export restraints, a form of quantitative restriction on exports accepted by the exporter, where they were imposed mainly on Japanese exports of telecommunication equipment and automobiles.[9] Anti-dumping measures began to be used (whether correctly or spuriously is difficult to ascertain) to impose countervailing duties on competitive imports.[10] Finally, a whole host of technical regulations were increasingly used as non-tariff barriers. Noticeably, technical regulation was an area where EFTA has been rather more alert than the EU countries.

Meanwhile, there had also been two important shifts in economic structures in most European economies. Firstly, government had become an increasingly important source of demand and government procurements were equivalent to 10 per cent of GDP. Most governments placed orders with national suppliers, arguing that national taxes should benefit national producers, but the effect was to shield an important part of the economy from international competition. A second shift was that during the post-war boom, services had become increasingly important so that, by the 1970s, services were by far the largest sector of the economies of most European states. If one defines services as everything that is consumed other than goods, then they contribute slightly over 62 per cent of Western Europe's gross domestic product. At the most 10 per cent entered international trade (certain transport, banking and insurance services).[11] It was time for a shift in the agenda.

By 1984, the ambition of a wider free trade area in Western Europe had finally been realised. Before moving to the next stage in this history, it is worth pausing to examine Table 14.2, which shows the development of trade over the period 1972-1983. The first thing to notice is the shift of exports from both EFTA and the EC towards the rest of the world: a development in response to the shifts in the terms of trade and in patterns of demand that accompanied the two oil crises. Given this trend, the relative importance of exports between EFTA and the EC looks remarkably stable. EFTA's exports to the EC had grown, but that was a trend that was already visible from the 1950s onwards. But trade is not just a question of tariff barriers; it is also a question of distance, culture and relative economic size. Given the propensity of the large EC economies to trade with each other, EFTA's performance in these years is more remarkable than it seems at first sight – the impact of tariff reductions counteracting the 'natural' tendency for interdependency among the EC members to increase.[12]

TABLE 14.2: DIRECTION OF EFTA AND EEC EXPORTS, 1972 AND 1983 (%)

	EFTA 1972	*EFTA 1983*
EFTA	19.0	13.9
EEC	48.8	52.0
USA	7.0	6.6
Rest of world	25.3	27.2
	EEC 1972	*EEC 1983*
EFTA	12.2	10.6
EEC	53.0	52.4
USA	8.2	7.8
Rest of world	26	29.2

Source: Calculated from United Nations, *International Trade Statistics*, various.

THE LUXEMBOURG PROCESS

The achievement of industrial free trade in 1984 was marked by a joint EEC-EFTA ministerial meeting in Luxembourg in April of that year. Much had been achieved but, as we have seen already above, the agenda had quite clearly altered and this, then, required a new set of initiatives. After the meeting, the ministers declared that they 'were convinced of the importance of further actions to consolidate and strengthen cooperation with the aim of creating a dynamic European economic space for their countries'.[13] It was certainly a change in rhetoric. Whereas before, we had been talking about industrial free trade, the challenge had shifted now to a dynamic European economic space. The only problem was to determine what exactly that meant.

For the EEC it rapidly became the Single European Act, aimed at creating 'Fortress Europe' or simply completing the Treaty of Rome, depending upon where one sat in the debate. The act aimed at four freedoms: free trade in goods, free trade in services, the free movement of capital and the free movement of labour. In total there were 280 decisions to be taken, and to ease the process the member states had renounced their use of vetoes. Decisions on the Single European Act were to be taken by qualified majority voting and the whole process had to be rounded off by December 1992. That was dynamic economic space seen from the standpoint of the EEC.

What happened with the dynamic economic space in EFTA looked rather different. In the same period, a total of nine EFTA-EC agreements were concluded. It is not quite a symmetrical harvest. That is not to say that the agreements were unimportant. Three of the agreements concerned border agreements. Firstly, a single administrative document (with the acronym SAD) was introduced and served to eliminate the between 35 and 40 separate documents, in as many as 360 copies, needed to conduct an operation of international trade in Western Europe. The new document saved an estimated 2 to 5 per cent of the cost of an international transaction.[14] Secondly, the origin rules were changed which, because of the EEC's original insistence on a rather more complex set of rules than those prevailing within EFTA,[15] had for long been a bone of contention between the two blocs. Since their introduction, industrial tariffs had been considerably reduced and, with them, also the danger of trade deflection. These rules were now simplified, saving an estimated 3 per cent of the costs of international transactions, costs that were often higher than the tariff differentials for which they were supposed to compensate.[16] The third of these dealt with the removal of some remaining export controls. Of the remaining agreements, three dealt with early notifications and exchange of technological information on national standards, but explicitly with no policy implications. The dynamic economic space was quite clearly a rather different area depending on which side of the EFTA-EC line you happened to be standing.

There were various reasons why the Luxembourg Process failed. Firstly, the form of cooperation was weak to start with, with no binding targets and no standard mechanisms. One observer described it as a 'weak kind of functionalist co-operation' and condemned it for being 'both costly and ineffective'.[17] Secondly, in order to adopt a common position towards the EC, EFTA was often forced to take common positions in areas that were not even covered in the Stockholm convention. Even then, the agenda was not determined by their mutual interests in intra-EFTA trade, but by issues advanced by the EC. Thirdly, the EC and EFTA quite clearly had different priorities. The EEC's priority was the Single European Act. Bilateral negotiations with EFTA came quite clearly in second place whereas for EFTA agreement with the EC was of the highest priority. Fourthly, not only were the priorities asymmetric but so were the diplomatic resources. Often EFTA negotiators would go ready to a meeting to discuss some issue and find the EC unready. And then, at a date unknown to anyone, the EC would arrive with an extremely strong delegation and demand an answer by the end of the day. Overall, however, regardless of the initial weakness, it is clear that the movement toward a dynamic economic European space was simply overwhelmed by events, which were dictated very largely by the overriding priorities of the EC. One commentator observed, 'EFTA countries faced both the risks of marginalisation, that is, to be excluded from the integration momentum, and satellisation, that is, to have to adjust their own regimes after EC Directives and regulations that have been adopted.'[18]

The Luxembourg Process was going nowhere fast and the realisation was beginning to dawn that EFTA was losing out. Paul Krugman suggested that, through the SEA, the EC would gain unique access to scale economies unavailable to EFTA resulting in either a loss of export markets or a loss of profitability (and investment incentives) if EFTA states tried to preserve their markets by reducing prices.[19] One recent study offers some empirical confirmation of these suspicions. It suggests that, whereas previously EFTA's trade with the EC had kept pace with the increasing intensity of intra-trade within the EC, from 1986 onwards it began to lag behind. It is never easy to isolate a single cause for structural changes in trade flows, especially when the standard has been generated by an econometric model. However, if the reasons for the earlier favourable development were found to lie in the preferential trade treatment afforded to EFTA states through the bilateral agreements, so their exclusion from the market-deepening effects of the Single European Act may provide (part of) the explanation for the weakening of relative trade intensities.[20]

THE EEA AGREEMENT

By mid-1988 the perception of EFTA that it was being sidelined in its dealings with the EC had begun to harden. On the other hand, so too had EC suspicions that EFTA was only interested in cherry-picking issues that suited itself. Towards the end of the year, Commission officials tested whether the EFTA countries really wanted a deeper relationship with the EC and, more particularly, whether they were willing to accept the full obligations that such a relationship would entail. Following positive assurances that this was indeed the case, in January 1989, before the European Parliament in Strasbourg, Jacques Delors invited the EFTA countries 'to look for a new, more structured partnership with common decision-making and administrative institutions to make our activities more effective and to highlight the political dimension of our cooperation in the economic, social, financial and cultural spheres'.[21] Here at last was a recognition that EFTA had to operate outside of the Stockholm convention and move deliberately but hopefully in a more structured way into a dialogue and cooperation with EU partners. Two months later the EFTA ministers responded by accepting the offer for

> *negotiations [that] would lead to the fullest possible realisation of free movement of goods, services, capital and persons, with the aim of creating a dynamic and homogeneous European Economic Space. To this end we are ready to explore various options and ways and means to strengthen the institutional links between the EFTA states and the EC.*[22]

The name was altered later to European Economic Area.

Talks started almost immediately and stretched over eighteen months. Some points stayed unresolved for months and occasionally it seemed as though the process might stall altogether. I will refrain from a chronological account and concentrate instead on the main issues.[23] Before doing that, it is worth making one observation about the negotiations. From the start, the positions were uneven – EFTA needed the EC more than the EC needed EFTA.[24] It was made even more uneven by the development of EC membership applications, especially in the final stages. Already in July 1989, Austria decided to apply for EC membership and Sweden did so too in July 1991. Thus, for an important part of the negotiations, several EFTA states were negotiating an agreement which they did not expect (for long) to apply to themselves. It did not exactly strengthen their negotiating position.

The EFTA states initially pushed for a regime of mutual recognition of national legislation as the basis for cooperation between the two blocs but that position soon became untenable and it was agreed that the *acquis communautaire* (the entire legal basis of EC law that had been developed over the previous thirty years) should form the basis of any EEA agreement. The immediate question then focused on the question of how much of the *acquis* members would have to accept (or, turned around, what derogations could be obtained and for how long would they be valid). This was eventually resolved in the EC's favour and EFTA agreed to accept the entire *acquis* – present and future. The EFTA countries gained access to the single market for the movement of goods, persons, capital and services. In addition, it was decided that there would be close cooperation on so-called *horizontal* and *flanking* policies. Horizontal policies are those that have an impact on the competitive position on the four freedoms: social policy, consumer protection, company law and environmental legislation. Flanking policies involve cooperation in specific projects such as in education and research, in the audio-visual sector and in civic protection.

The next question, then, was how much influence EFTA states would have on future decision-making. Initially, the EFTA states favoured a parallel track structure, with either party taking initiatives and, with mutual consultations and even representation on each other's committees, moving towards an EEA consensus at a full meeting of all nineteen partners. Initially the EC leant towards a solution along these lines, whilst rejecting EFTA participation in its own decision-making processes. Thus there would be an EEA Council and an EEA Court (but with an EFTA Surveillance Authority to monitor enforcement, responsible to the Court).

Finally there was a set of side-issues to be resolved. These included a demand that the EFTA states contribute to a Cohesion Fund to support the development of poorer EC member states and, later, a demand for improved market access to EFTA markets for Spanish agricultural exports. There was also a demand by the EC for access to Icelandic and Norwegian fishing waters in return for improved access for fish and a counterclaim by Norway and Iceland for a permanent derogation of EC regulations on investments in the fishing industry. Finally, Austria and Switzerland concluded bilateral deals with the EC on the subject of

Alpine road transit. With this, the agreement was all but ready, were it not for one last obstacle.

Into the EEA negotiations resurfaced an issue that had bedevilled the wider free trade area negotiations back in the late 1950s – namely that the Treaty of Rome had established supranational decision-making procedures for the EC member states, which could not easily be reconciled with sharing powers, on a different basis, with non-members. If the EFTA states were to have a role in final decision-making, it would override the powers afforded to the EC Commission, Council and Assembly. Early in 1991, the EC Court of Justice (ECJ) had articulated these concerns but it was not until the summer that the Commission had formally asked the Court for an opinion. Not surprisingly, when it reported back in December 1991, it reaffirmed the primacy of EC law and procedures over EC member states. In effect, there would be no joint EC-EEA Court deciding on the application of EEA legislation and the ECJ would be the sole arbiter of the compatibility of EEA legislation with EC law. This was a striking blow to the remaining autonomy of the non-EC members of the EEA, but it met with little open opposition. It is interesting, however, that it was in this period that Norway, Switzerland and Finland joined Austria and Sweden in applying for EC membership – seen from this perspective, the new arrangements would eventually only apply to Iceland and Lichtenstein. When the appropriate changes had been made, the EEA Agreement was signed in Oporto in May 1992.

The drama was still not over since the agreement still needed to be ratified by all the nineteen signatories. In Switzerland, the Federal Assembly had overwhelming endorsed the EEA Agreement before submitting it to the populace in a referendum. It had also committed SFr 6 million in a campaign to inform the voters on the agreement's provisions and benefits, but these efforts were to no avail. The opponents drew a picture an unrestrained influx of foreign labour (once the five-year derogation period had lapsed) and the loss of democracy in shaping or in approving EC law. On an extremely high (78.7 per cent) turnout the Swiss electorate rejected the agreement by the narrow margin of 50.3 per cent. More tellingly, however, 29 of the 36 cantons also voted against the agreement, killing any chance of the EEA obtaining the double majority required. The country was split along linguistic lines. All six French-speaking cantons and the German-speaking canton of Basel voted heavily in favour of the agreement; all the German-speaking cantons, except Basel, and all the Italian-speaking cantons voted against.[25] The result was to delay the implementation of the EEA until January 1994 while the necessary revisions to deal with the absence of Switzerland were decided.

Following the application of Switzerland and Norway to join the EU in May and November 1992 respectively, the unlikely scenario of a two-member EFTA (combined population around 300,000) managing a lopsided arrangement with a seventeen-member European Union (population around 300 million) pursuing additional new goals of economic and monetary union and joint foreign policy and defence, never materialised. Following the referendum defeat, the Swiss government withdrew its membership application in December 1992, though it still remained formally outside the EEA. In this latter respect it was probably more important that Norway also abandoned its quest for EU membership following its rejection in a referendum in November 1994. Switzerland has observer status with the EFTA delegation in EEA matters and applies most of the decisions taken to itself. In this way it also maintains access to the EU single market, although it is not guaranteed such access.

As one EFTA scenario disappeared, another emerged, if only briefly. The end of the Cold War in 1989 witnessed the emergence of newly democratic transition economies in place of the communist, centrally planned economies of East-Central Europe. EFTA was quick to respond, negotiating series of cooperation agreements (mostly with free trade provisions envisaged for the future) with the Baltic states, Poland, Czech and Slovak republics, Slovenia, Romania and so on. This was a time of flux and uncertainty, with much discussion over how they would arrange their foreign economic relations – local customs unions and soft currency regimes passed the revue, as did membership in EFTA. This last scenario was not such a strange idea. EFTA could provide a waiting room for an eventual EU membership (which was the ultimate ideal of all the states). The gradual removal of trade barriers was a good place to start the transition and, as EFTA's experience had shown, it placed fewer institutional demands on members than would the EU. Once this stage had been reached, economies transformed and competitive and institutional capacities enhanced, the new democracies could request EEA membership. What is interesting in this respect is that in contrast to bilateral free trade agreements negotiated in the early 70s, EFTA countries together, by virtue of their EFTA membership, had a right to EEA membership and its benefits. And then, once they had fully absorbed and implemented the *acquis*, there would be little economic or institutional reason to deny them full EU membership, should they still desire it.[26]

Among those arguing along these lines was myself. I had a nice title: 'European Algebra: Resolve EEC+EFTA=EEA (+/-n)' and had started airing the paper in the conference circuit. It was never published and the clue to the question 'why not?' lies in the last sentence: 'And soon there is going to be a meeting of the EU ministers in Copenhagen.' In June 1993 in Copenhagen, Jacques Delors opened up the prospect of the EU membership for the Eastern Europe and Baltic states and offered substantial economic aid and institutional support to achieve this. The EFTA option evaporated at the same time.

In 1989 EFTA had lessons to learn, but in this case they were not needed. I consider the offer made by the Copenhagen summit to be one of the most important in post-war European history. Unfortunately this is part of the EU history and not part of EFTA's history. So too, was the further political future of Austria, Sweden and Finland. EFTA's lessons are not universal – its ambitions were limited and its institutions simple – and they may not be appropriate to resolving the difficulties and dilemmas inherent in managing complex interdependence among highly sophisticated, highly developed market economies. But the world is not made up of mirror images of ourselves and there are many experiments in the world today that could benefit from a model for limited (transitionary) ambitions and simple institutions, and lessons too in the spirit of open cooperation and friendship that helped make it all work.

POSTSCRIPT

This essay was written for a conference celebrating the 50th anniversary of EFTA's creation, held in May 2010. It appeared in the conference volume edited by Kåre Bryn and Guðmundur Einarsson (eds.), *EFTA 1960-2010: Elements of 50 Years of European History* (Reykjavik, 2010). The conference was informative and the atmosphere relaxed. The dinner accompanied by reminiscences, storytelling and much laughter. I was told once that the EFTA ministerial meetings and those of the EEC often took place at the same time and that the EFTA ministers would derive some considerable satisfaction, at the meal and the dance that followed in the evening, over the fact that their EEC colleagues were still locked in grim negotiations that were destined to drag on until the early hours of the following morning. This is just a reflection. Historians tend to be fixated by archives and hotly anticipate their opening after thirty years. But paper, once made available, stays available for a long time. The same cannot be said for eyewitnesses. To be highly placed and involved in the policy process, most eyewitnesses have to be at least in their mid-thirties at the time. It is likely that the majority of them, therefore, are in their sixties (or older) when the archives are released. The window for collaboration between historians and eyewitnesses is small – so we should either release archives earlier (and they are needed if collaboration is to be successful) or we need to give more thought to encouraging collaborative conferences ... and here the organisations themselves could be more proactive. The rewards will far outweigh the costs.

15

The Concentric Circles of the European Union's Trade Regime, 1989 to the Present

INTRODUCTION

The European Union[1] is undoubtedly the most successful regional trade agreement created in the post-war period. It is often cited as the inspiration for other regional trade experiments, I suspect usually by people at a loss for better openings for their speeches or articles. It has also attracted the adherence of neighbouring countries to the extent that its membership has grown from the original six countries in 1951 or 1957 (depending on the starting point chosen) to twenty-seven today and, in the process, has become the world's largest trading bloc. As such, it has been an attractive potential partner for countries seeking to intensify bilateral trading relations through preferential trade agreements.

This chapter examines the development of the EU's external trade policy since the end of the Cold War in 1989. One can view the various stages in the hierarchy of this trade policy as a series of concentric circles which starts with enlargement, the inclusion into the European Community itself and the full incorporation into its internal trade regime. The steps to full membership of the European Union have recently been preceded by a period of association, which confers limited free trade status (usually excluding agriculture) and which is accompanied by the financial and technical assistance to prepare countries for the institutional and legal demands of membership. This has also included demands for norm changes and the adoption of democratic structures. Association has not only been employed for candidate countries, but also for European countries that have opted not to apply for full membership. Although it is not explicitly stated, an eventual application for membership on their part would obviously be considered sympathetically. More recently, the EU has started using trade agreements with countries which it has no intention of admitting. This has been the case of its relation with former colonies and overseas territories which had been the beneficiaries of preferential trading for over thirty years but which, because of WTO rules, had to be converted to reciprocal free trade agreements, known as Partnership Agreements. Similarly, in an effort to stabilise the situation on its borders, the EU has started to construct a ring of free trade agreements, first among the Mediterranean countries and, later, it extended the strategy to cover neighbouring countries among the former states of the Soviet Union. For Russia itself, this group treatment proved unsatisfactory and a separate arrangement had to be conceived. Thus far, the EU's activities have been conceived largely within its range of political and/or geographical influence – i.e. they were either longstanding client states or were geographically close. Recently, however, the EU has embarked upon a new round of initiatives of bilateral regional trade agreements directed further afield both towards individual countries and towards other regional trade groupings, such as ASEAN. What countries remain fall mostly within the scope of traditional MFN arrangements under the WTO.

The Concentric Circles of the EU's Trade Regime

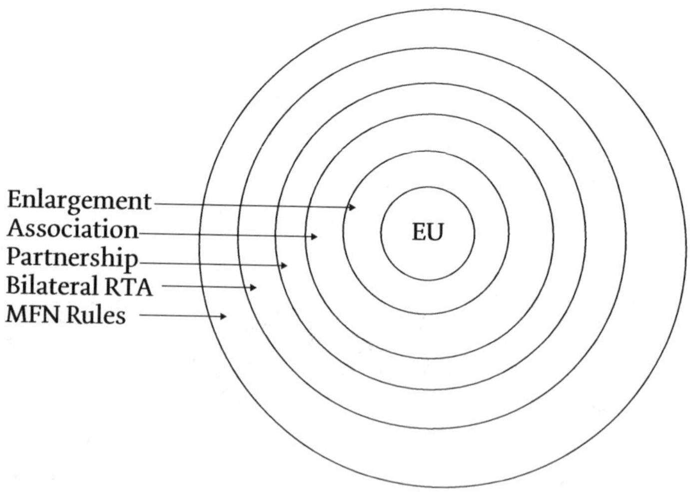

The EU's efforts at establishing regional trade agreements are indeed remarkable. They represent a sustained effort over nearly twenty years that has contributed to a more than doubling of its own membership and to reaching agreements with, or opening negotiations with, over half the countries in the world. Perhaps even more remarkable is that

> *the Union is not only a formidable power in trade. It is also becoming a power through trade, using access to its huge market as a bargaining chip to obtain changes in the domestic policies of its trading partners, from labour standards to human rights, and more generally to shape new patterns of global governance.*[2]

There are many interpretations offered for this development. On the more positive side it is viewed as an employment of 'soft power' to project into foreign policy Europe's own norms and values.[3] Other observers emphasise the use of soft power to compensate for Europe's lack of military power, or at least its reluctance to employ it.[4] Some argue that the introduction of a reform agenda into regional trade agreements reflects an inability to realise its agenda at a global level.[5] Still others see, behind the facade, a neo-colonialist effort to impose Western standards of civilization upon third-world countries.[6] And, finally, some see it as a reflexive use of a policy instrument employed successfully in one context to other situations where it might not be so appropriate.[7] Whilst the EU's efforts to link trade access to political and institutional reform certainly succeeded when the ultimate prize was membership of the EU itself,[8] one could question whether the recipe would prove successful in the absence of such powerful leverage.

THE EC AT THE TIME OF THE FALL OF THE BERLIN WALL

At the time of the fall of the Berlin Wall in 1989, the European Community as it was known then comprised twelve separate states, all united within a customs union but each still with its own currency. At the time, the member states were working on a programme of legislation that would create a single internal market with freedom not only for the movement of goods, but also for services, labour and capital. The twelve states of the EC had a population of 248 million and accounted for 20.1 per cent of world GDP (measured at PPP). The total foreign trade of the member states was responsible for 36.7 per cent of world total, though much of that was between the member states themselves. If the latter is excluded from the totals, the external trade of the European Community amounted to a less impressive but still significant 14.6 per cent of the world total.[9] It is true that, for 1989, this exclusion is not particularly relevant for comparative purposes, but one could make a case for present-day comparisons when by far the largest part of the EU economy is in an economic and monetary union, and indeed the WTO does exactly that. After all, trade between the individual states of the USA is not counted in foreign trade calculations. Thus for comparative purposes, I have offered the same adjustment here.

In 1989 there were only twenty-five active Regional Trade Agreements in the world and the European Community was responsible for over half of them – two were its own founding treaties; six were accession treaties with Denmark, Ireland and the UK, Greece, Portugal and Spain; six were free trade agreements concluded with the individual member states of the European Free Trade Association, and one was a trade preference agreement with a group of former colonies known as the Africa-Caribbean-Pacific (ACP) countries.[10]

The separate industrial free trade arrangements with the seven EFTA states were signed at the time of the European Community's enlargement in 1973. This enlargement had included two former EFTA states – Denmark and the UK. If nothing were done, the adoption of the common external tariff, required by their membership of the European Community, threatened to impose new trade barriers where they had once been abolished. By way of response, the European Community negotiated separate industrial free trade agreements with each of the EFTA states, eliminating most trade barriers within four years and the remainder after a transition period of twelve.[11] At this time, the members of the reduced EFTA together represented 1.5 per cent of world GDP and but a much more significant 6.0 per cent of world trade.[12]

The other major RTA in existence was the Lomé Convention, a lopsided preferential trade agreement between the EEC and the ACP countries. There were a mixture of motives involved in this engagement – initial optimism that they would provide growing markets (an illusion long since lost), an effort to perpetuate political influence in former colonies and to bind their support for European policies and an effort to promote economic development in areas with which officials were already familiar. Among the ACP countries are many that ranked, and still rank, among the poorest and most desperate in the world. There had been several such agreements since 1975 and Lomé IV was signed in December 1989. The geographical scope of the agreements had expanded between the two dates with the number of ACP signatories climbing from 46 to 69.[13] The trade concessions contained in the first three agreements probably had little impact of trade flows between the ACP and the EEC – in agricultural goods it did little more than cement traditional neo-colonial trade patterns into place whilst the impact on trade in manufactured goods was inhibited by the non-competitiveness of ACP exports. Moreover ACP preferences had been undermined by the rapid expansion of the General System of Preferences for LDCs, introduced by the EU in the early 1970s. The number of beneficiaries and the depth of trade coverage of these GSP concessions had both increased. Moreover, after 1980 they had also included traditional ACP agricultural exports such as tea, coffee, cacao and palm oil.[14] Like its predecessors, Lomé IV had been anchored on the non-reciprocal trading access offered by the EEC to its poorer partners, coupled with a range of social and economic goals liable for technical and financial assistance. The trade instrument underpinning the agreement involved tariff-free access to EEC markets for most industrial goods and privileged access (vis-à-vis third party suppliers) for other goods – mostly non-competitive agricultural exports.

ENLARGEMENT: GERMAN DEMOCRATIC REPUBLIC

The first enlargement occurred almost via the back door. In June 1990 an economic, monetary and social union was formed between West Germany (founding member of the EU) and the German Democratic Republic. For almost forty years, East Germany had been one of the most conservative Communist countries in the Eastern bloc, but also one of the more advanced. As a part of West Germany, the former GDR was automatically absorbed into the European Community. At the time, the GDR represented only 0.34 per cent of world GDP. As far as West Germany was concerned, the absorption of East Germany would increase the German population by some 23 per cent (from 64 million to 79 million) but would augment its GDP by only 7 per cent. Its GDP was equivalent to only 1.5 per cent of that of the EC 12.[15] The impact, however, was more devastating than most commentators, before the event, would have anticipated.

Since the union was achieved by establishing exchange rate parity between the two former currencies, the impact was to render much of the East German economy hopelessly uncompetitive and to contribute to a spiralling burden on West Germany to prop up the economy. The rising interest rates in Germany itself (deemed necessary to control the inflationary impact of reunification) produced a sharp slowdown in the German economy which persisted for the rest of the decade, and which initially spilled over onto Germany's trading partners. It also triggered a wave of emigration from the East to the West in search of a more prosperous existence.[16] In Brussels, the lesson was obvious: if absorbing one (small and more developed) Communist state could cause such disruption to the largest and one of the richest West European economies, what would be the effect of extending membership to other states of the former Soviet bloc?[17] The attitude of the West towards Eastern enlargement was already cautious, and the German experience only made it more so.

ENLARGEMENT: AUSTRIA, FINLAND AND SWEDEN

Meanwhile the deepening of the EC into a single market by 1992 was threatening to confront the EFTA group with new discriminations, especially in finance and services that had not been covered by the free trade agreements of the early 1970s. Many of the EFTA states had remained outside the mainstream of European integration on the grounds that membership in the European Community would impinge on their definition of sovereignty. As the Warsaw Pact crumbled and as the Soviet Union itself began to wobble, this consideration appeared less compelling than before. Scarcely had this '1992' landmark been passed than the EEC, with the Treaty of Maastricht, set itself new targets for deepening its integration – expanding its range of competencies into foreign and security policy and justices and home affairs and setting itself the goal of attaining economic and monetary union, including the adoption of a common currency. It signalled the magnitude of these changes by renaming itself a European *Union* rather than a *Community*. As a result of these changes, the EFTA countries began to reassess their options.

Austria had already applied for membership in 1989 and it was now followed in short order by Sweden, Finland, Switzerland and Norway – Switzerland and Norway would eventually withdraw. Negotiations for membership began in February 1993 and, given the close existing ties and the relative prosperity of the candidates, they were rapidly concluded. In 1995 the three countries became full members of the European Union.[18] All three countries had prosperous, developed European economies. Although all three were relatively medium states in terms of population (totalling almost 20 million) at the time of enlargement, they represented 1.2 per cent of world GDP and an even more impressive 3.4 per cent of world trade (measured by exports).[19]

EASTERN EUROPEAN ENLARGEMENT

The fall of Communism had brought a wave of public sympathy towards the former victims of the Cold War – the countries of Eastern Europe and the Baltic. There was also a realisation that their transformations from state-controlled, command economies to free market economies and the reorientation of their trade patterns from their trade partners in Comecon to their former markets in the West could not be accomplished without considerable assistance. And, if any more compelling argument for generosity were necessary, it was provided by the bloody spectacle of the collapse of Yugoslavia into civil war and ethnic cleansing.

However, there was difference between assistance and EU membership, and the experience with East Germany made for increased caution among many of the existing EU member states. On the other hand, for the Eastern European countries themselves, there was a compelling rationale for speed, namely that only integration into Western institutions – NATO and the EU – would provide a guarantee against the perceived danger of being drawn back in to the Russian orbit. The European Community initially responded with a three-pronged strategy. This involved inaugurating a programme of technical and financial assistance (the PHARE programme), stimulating the creation of regional trade agreements among the former Comecon countries themselves and initiating the first steps towards bilateral trade agreements. Although the Eastern bloc countries were more concerned with deflecting exports towards hard currency markets in the West, the efforts at encouraging regional agreements were rewarded in 1992 by the creation of the Central European Free Trade Agreement (CEFTA) with the Czech Republic, Slovakia, Hungary (with Poland joining in 1996) and in 1994 by the Baltic Free Trade Agreement.

The process of creating bilateral free trade links between each of the former Communist countries and the EU was somewhat more complicated (involving negotiating the agreements and ratifying each one individually in the member states). To speed up the process the European Commission implemented 'interim agreements', which were within its own field of competence. The first of these agreements were signed in March 1992 with Hungary, Poland, the Czech Republic and Slovakia. All agreements had in common a target for the total elimination of industrial trade barriers by 2002.[20]

The depth of the recession that had hit the former Communist states in the early stages of their readjustments prompted a reassessment of EU policy towards them. The European Council meeting in Copenhagen in June 1993 offered them full membership in the Union on condition that they fulfil certain conditions, known since then as the 'Copenhagen criteria'. The criteria could be summed up as a respect for democracy and human rights, possessing a competitive market economy capable of coping with the competitive pressures of a single market and an ability to implement the entire body of legislation accumulated by the European Union since its inception, known as the *acquis communautaire*.[21]

The criteria posed no small hurdle to membership and, for a time, it appeared that enlargement would take place in stages, as and when countries were ready. Negotiations were opened first in 1997 with the Czech Republic, Estonia, Hungary, Poland and Slovenia and only two years later with the rest. However with German pressure for quick Polish membership (and Poland's reform effort was slower than some of the others) and Scandinavian resistance to de-coupling the Baltic states it was decided in 2001 to admit ten countries together as one group. In May 2004 the most ambitious enlargement in the European Union's history was a fact.[22]

It is worth noting that membership did not mean that the countries had fulfilled the Copenhagen criteria but that the European Commission said that they had and that the heads of government were willing to go along with this. The consequences of this primacy of *real politik* and of the cavalier disregard for the truth came to roost rather sooner than most observers anticipated. Twelve months later, in two referenda, French and Dutch voters rejected the draft constitutional treaty determining the future direction of EU competencies and the rules for the EU's future governance. A feeling that the EU was moving too fast was a common feature in the 'no' votes in both countries.[23]

By this time, negotiations with Bulgaria and Romania were too far advanced to defer their membership. They too were deemed to have met the criteria and they were admitted to the European Union in January 2007. However, as a gesture towards public disquiet, the EU decided to continue monitoring both countries even after accession.[24] The two recent expansions have brought twelve countries into the European Union, which will complicate an already difficult, and often obtuse, decision-making process. Moreover, all of the accession states have been poorer and more agrarian than the existing members, which has increased the need for structural support for their economic development. The twelve new member states together accounted for 2.0 per cent of the world's population but only 1.5 per cent of world GDP. Together, however, they were responsible for 3.3 per cent of world trade.

ASSOCIATION: TURKEY

The feeling among the European populace that the EU was moving too fast, alluded to above, had its most immediate impact on the environment surrounding an eventual Turkish membership. In the wake of the referendum many European politicians sought to assuage the fears of the population either by opposing Turkish membership outright or by promising to put the question to referenda when the time came. Turkey's level of per capita GDP was about the same level as that of Romania and Bulgaria as was the relative size of its agricultural sector. Moreover, when it came down to its performance on the major governance indicators, there was precious little separating the three. However, there were several important differences between Turkey and the other new members. First, Turkey's population was considerably larger which meant not only that the financial burden of membership would be higher than for the rest (though well within the capacity to pay!) but also that Turkey would also play a large individual role in the EU's decision-making. A second factor was that, since the 1960s, Turks had been recruited to work in Western Europe, particularly into Germany and the Netherlands. The large reserve of un- or underemployed labour in the countryside, combined with the existence of a large resident population in the West, would create the basis for a renewed immigration flow if and when barriers to labour mobility would be eliminated, as they would eventually have to be in the event of Turkish membership. Finally, and this gave these other two factors an extra twist, Turkey's population was predominantly Muslim. Even though Turkey has been a secular state ever since the creation of the Republic in 1923, the association with Islam, and the association of Islam with terrorism, sat uneasily in the minds of xenophobic citizens throughout the European Union.[24]

Turkey has been associated with the EC since signing the Ankara Agreement in 1963. Although the commitment itself was vague, it was there and it shaped much of Turkish expectations towards the EC. In 1972 a supplementary protocol was agreed, setting out a timetable for a customs union but two successive oil crises robbed it of most of its momentum and a military coup in 1980 killed off whatever momentum was left. In 1987, a new democratic government formally applied for membership but the EC was preoccupied with completing the single market programme. Turkish membership would complicate not only this achievement but also threaten other initiatives aimed at deepening the Community and turning it into a true Union. The EU, therefore, delayed its response until 1995 and offered not membership but the completion of the customs union (exempting agriculture).[26] To sweeten the pill, the EU also offered financial assistance but coupled this to a demand to open a dialogue on democracy and human rights. The offer mimicked the situation of the Eastern European candidates, but without a guarantee of eventual membership. The offer, however, provoked irritations on both sides, especially when relations with Greece and the 'Cyprus question' were added to the equation.

In 1999, the EU changed its position by officially making Turkey a candidate country and including it in its pre-accession programs. Negotiations began in 2005 and have continued ever since. These have been complicated by the slowness of Turkish reforms, by problems over Cyprus and human rights and by the growing fear of 'Muslim fundamentalism' in Europe since the Madrid and London bombings.[27] Even if the negotiations were successful, enlargement demands a unanimous decision by member states, and several have already declared their intention of putting the Turkish membership question to a referendum – the outcome of which may well be negative.

Should Turkey ever join the European Union, it will be – with 70.4 million citizens – the second largest country in the EU in terms of population and, given the demographic dynamics of the country, would become the largest state within the foreseeable future. Turkey's population is a shade under 1 per cent for 1 per cent of world GDP. However, Turkish exports represent only 0.7 per cent of world trade.

ASSOCIATION: OTHER CANDIDATE STATES

In 2004 the EU returned to the problem posed by the successor states of the Yugoslav Republic by granting Croatia candidate status and negotiations for membership have already commenced. At the end of 2005 the Former Yugoslav Republic of Macedonia was also recognised as a candidate for membership, but it is still awaiting the start of membership talks. The remaining republics (Bosnia-Herzegovina, Montenegro and Serbia) and Albania have all been recognised as potential candidates.[28]

ASSOCIATION: THE EFTA STATES

In the academic literature on the European Union, the relationship with the EFTA states is one of the least visible – though this is not the case among the remaining EFTA members. The incorporation of three EFTA states in 1995 proceeded painlessly on both sides and provoked scarcely a ripple in the literature. For the remaining EFTA states, however, the relationship with the EC remained critical, especially from the mid-1980s when progress towards a single market threatened to introduce a new set of discriminations in finance and services on top of the 'new protectionism' that had emerged in the wake of the oil crises.[29] The EC responded initially by promising the creation of a 'dynamic European Economic Space' without, however, giving the concept much content. The result was deeply unsatisfactory. Often the EFTA states were forced to adopt coordinated positions of issues beyond their mandate and yet they had no guarantee in the resulting dialogue with the EU that they could influence the results. Not surprisingly, the harvest of agreements produced under the new arrangements was derisory.

In 1989 the EC announced a new initiative. It offered to create a European Economic Area whereby the benefits and obligations of the Single European Act would be extended to the EFTA states, *en bloc* and as a right. At the same time, it contemplated a greater degree of common decision-making. Although this last aspect was subsequently severely modified by the European Court which argued, successfully, for the supremacy of EC decision-making, the EEA came into force in January 1994.[30] Because the agreement was (narrowly) rejected by the Swiss in a referendum, it now applies only to Norway, Iceland and Lichtenstein; Switzerland remains associated with the EU through the earlier, bilateral free trade agreement. All four remaining EFTA states are advanced European economies. Together they represent 0.75 per cent of world GDP and 2.4 per cent of world trade.

ECONOMIC PARTNERSHIP AGREEMENTS: THE ACP COUNTRIES

As we have seen above, since the 1970s inception the EU has concluded preferential trade and aid agreements with a group of African/Caribbean/Pacific countries that comprised former colonies, overseas territories or otherwise dependencies of the EC member states. However, the transformation of the GATT into the WTO in January 1995 implied a change in the rules governing such arrangements and this necessitated the renegotiation of these agreements in order to ensure their full compliance with the non-discriminatory Most-Favoured Nation principle.[31]

In June 2000 APC countries and the EU concluded the Cotonou Agreement which envisaged the conclusion of Economic Partnership Agreements, compatible with WTO rules, by the end of 2007. The underlying idea was that these agreements would contain a commitment to complete the transition to fully reciprocal free trade within twelve years. The partnership agreements, however, were supposed to move beyond free trade by enhancing trade-in services and cooperation on finance and investment. The EU also stated that it would encourage measures to deepen regional integration among the ACP countries themselves and it gave this effect by negotiating the agreements in the regional groupings, and not with the states individually:

- (West Africa) ECOWAS plus Mauritania
- (Central Africa) CEMAC plus São Tomé and Príncipe
- (East and South Africa) COMESA
- (Caribbean) CARIFORUM
- (South Africa) SADEC
- ACP Pacific

The prospect of forcing countries, with often different interests, into adopting uniform positions has greatly complicated the negotiations with the EU and has often placed existing regional agreements under strain. The situation was made even worse by the offer to allow the poorest ACP countries to hang on to their previous preferences under the EU's general system of preferences (non-reciprocal preferences granted to *any* country meeting certain criteria) or under the 'everything but arms' initiative (which is open to only 49 countries worldwide). These would impose more restrictions of access to EU markets but impose no reciprocal obligations. The effect of this two-track (or three-track) option could have the effect of creating new divisions within these existing regional trade blocs.[32]

The negotiations have been hard-going. The main problem is that the ACP countries will have to remove tariffs on over 90 per cent of their imports from the European Union. Moreover, they will have to do this at the same time as they lose their own privileged position in EU markets to competing (poor and underdeveloped) countries that had been outside the Lomé agreements. Doubts prevail about the probable (limited) impact of access to EU markets, especially given the increase in competition from other primary producers and newly emerging industrial powers.[33] The EU has tried to sweeten the pill by offering to remove all of its own tariffs and quotas on ACP imports from the start of the agreements (aside from transition periods for sugar and rice until 2009) and to help compensate for loss of government revenues resulting from the removal of tariffs in ACP countries.[34] These concessions, however, leave unaddressed the main concerns of the ACP countries, namely the effects on both employment and the balance of payments, which no not share the same faith as the West in the positive, transforming effects of competition and the free market. At the time of writing it was still not clear how many of the six negotiating groups would reach an agreement before the end of the year. On the eve of the December 2007 deadline, at the EU-Africa Summit, it seemed as though the initiative might be derailed when the head of the African Union declared that the continent was not ready for such far-reaching liberalisation. Nonetheless, at the time of writing (mid-December 2007), fifteen African countries had already signed interim agreements – the most vociferous exceptions being South Africa, Namibia and Senegal. In the process, divisions within African trading blocs, such as SACU (South Africa Customs Union; part of SADC), are threatening their future – a result that runs counter to EU efforts over the past decades to encourage such regional trading groups.

Although ultimate success of the Partnership Agreements is still in doubt, there is no doubting the scale of the ambition. The European Union is dealing with over seventy countries with a population of nearly 730 million (12 per cent of the world total). On the other hand, one way or the other, the economic impact on the EU will be slight. The ACP counties represent unsophisticated, low-income and slow-growing markets. Together they account for 2.7 per cent of world GDP and only 2.1 per cent of world trade. The latter figure is lower than the 'rump' states of a truncated EFTA. Over half of the GDP and trade totals are accounted for by two countries – Nigeria and South Africa – and presumably, if it were ever deemed expedient, the EU could deal bilaterally with both. On the other hand, the EU could revise its entire strategy and shift the focus from trade to development, though what it would need to do then is no easy question.

ECONOMIC PARTNERSHIP AGREEMENTS: EUROMED AND EUROPEAN NEIGHBOURHOOD POLICIES

In November 1995, at a Euro-Mediterranean Conference in Barcelona, the EU launched a process aimed at creating a zone of stability along its Southern Mediterranean border and, presumably more in hope than in expectation, with the Middle East. The countries initially involved were Algeria, Cyprus, Egypt, Jordan, Israel, Lebanon, Malta, Morocco, Palestine, Syria, Tunisia and Turkey. As we have already seen, Cyprus and Malta have since joined the European Union and Turkey is a candidate country for membership, with an industrial customs union with the EU.

The EuroMed initiative conformed to a template that should by now be becoming familiar to the reader of this chapter. In return for market access and financial support, the partner countries were encouraged to undertake legislative reform (in order to participate in the single market), to advance their society towards democracy and respect for human rights and to commence regional integration. By 2010 there should have been created a European-Mediterranean Free Trade Area. This policy combination was apparently working in Eastern Europe, but it is doubtful whether it was appropriate collectively to this particular group of countries. Eastern European countries were in the process of rejecting an old order, they had clearly defined economic and security interests in Western Europe and they legitimised their past (and their present) in terms of a shared European heritage. Precious little of this existed in the case of the EuroMed countries – they were not caught in a process of political and social change, they had no economic or security interests in Europe and their identity was often formed as an antithesis towards European norms and values. Moreover, although not as disadvantaged as most ACP countries, the region was characterised by relatively high levels of protection and uncompetitive production structures. Couple these considerations to the fact that the European action plans lacked operational detail and any clear structure of incentives and conditionalities, and it is not surprising progress is slow.[35] The one tangible result was the Agadir Agreement, signed in February 2004, for a free trade area to be completed within two years embracing Egypt, Jordan, Morocco and Tunisia. At the time of writing, it had still not be ratified by all signatories.

Undeterred, the EU refined the strategy and relaunched it in May 2004 under the guise of the European Neighbourhood Policy. The date coincided with the Eastern enlargement of the EU which created a new reality not just for the EU but also for the former Soviet states that had hereby acquired a new border relationship. The new proposal encompassed the remaining EuroMed countries (i.e. minus Cyprus and Malta, which had joined the EU, and Turkey, which had become a candidate for membership) and added to it Libya and the former Soviet republics of Belarus, Moldova, Russia, and the Ukraine (with recommendation to extend the arrangements to include Armenia, Azerbaijan and Georgia). The policy offered, in the medium term, the prospect of the creation of free trade areas (and the extension of existing ones into the field of agricultural trade) and, in the longer term, provisional upon legislative reform, progressive participation in the European single market.

The policy was cloaked in such positive terms as the need to create 'a ring of friends' or to create a 'zone of prosperity', but the move was essentially defensive. Both to the south and to the east the policy was intended to enhance domestic political, social and economic stability in neighbouring regions, since the impact of any instability would quickly spill over onto EU territory either in the form of a flood of refugees or a rise in terrorism. At the same time, the new policy spelled out a simple message – these countries were *outside* the EU and the situation was intended to stay that way. In the case of Eastern Europe, one could argue that the countries would have introduced reforms anyway but the fact remains that the prospect of EU membership provided a powerful incentive to change and, equally important, channelled the direction of that change. Without the incentive, one wonders whether the states concerned will readily undertake the difficult transformation process with the dislocation that it would entail. Moreover, the attraction of market access is reduced by the existing low trade intensities and the poor levels of infrastructure suggest that market access might not be a sufficient incentive, though this partially reflects the EU's high levels of agricultural protection and the agricultural composition of these countries' trade. Another difficulty in any negotiations with existing governments lies in the EU's demand for democratic change and a human rights agenda, demands which place the EU very often on the side of the domestic opposition – it is hard to conduct business with regimes that you would like to see overthrown.[36]

Despite the difficulties mentioned above the EU has made some considerable progress. Association Agreements have been signed with Algeria, Egypt, Israel, Jordan, Lebanon, Morocco and Tunisia, giving term duty-free access for industrial goods into EU markets. The relationships are not yet reciprocal, and many EuroMed countries also maintain non-tariff barriers. Moreover, in many cases the commitments embodied in the association agreements still need to be honoured, in both spirit and letter. The whole venture is fraught with difficulties. Yet, in economic terms, failure to conclude WTO consistent regional trade agreements will not harm the EU a great deal. The Mediterranean targets of the European Neighbourhood Policy represent together 1.8 per cent of world GDP but only 0.52 per cent of world trade. The immediate Eastern targets – Belarus, Moldova and the Ukraine are less than half their size – totalling 0.68 per cent of world GDP – but are almost equal in the share of world trade they represent, namely 0.51 per cent. Politically, however, the cost of failing to stabilise these states and to anchor them to an area of cooperation ('friendship' might be stretching ambitions too far) will be high.

ECONOMIC PARTNERSHIP AGREEMENTS: STRATEGIC PARTNERSHIP WITH RUSSIA

It is difficult to imagine a relationship more mismanaged than that between the EU and Russia. Part of the problem was that, as a former superpower, the leadership on relations with Russia was left largely to the United States. However, the roots go deeper. In the aftermath of the Cold War it is almost as though we made an artificial distinction in which Eastern Europe and the Baltic which were seen as 'victims' and the states of the former Soviet Union were identifies as the perpetrators. The fact is that these peoples, too, might have been victims of oppressive regimes. The distinction made after the Second World War between peoples and governments seems to have been lost.

Russia, too, was aware of its status and, from the start, rejected its inclusion in the European Neighbourhood Policy. As a result the EU accorded Russia the status of 'strategic partnership'. In May 2003, in St Petersburg, Russia and the EU agreed to create four separate common 'spaces':

- common economic space;
- common space for freedom, security and justice;
- common space for external security;
- space for joint research and education.[37]

Negotiations of the economic space have not progressed very far. If the construction of the economic space is to be anything similar to the 'dynamic European economic space' offered the EFTA countries in the 1980s, it is unlikely to work because Russia will be even more reluctant to accept the asymmetrical decision-making relationship than was, say, Norway. The EU has its own treaty-bound decision-making structure on questions involving the single market that leaves no room for co-decision. Meanwhile a seemingly never-ending series of disputes, squabbles and irritations have contributed to a hardening of Russia's position along a whole range of issues, including the much vaunted and much needed energy dialogue, that the EU is keen to pursue.[38]

The neglect of the EU's relations with Russia may have serious economic and political consequences. Russia's 245 million people are responsible for 2.6 per cent of world GDP and 2.4 per cent of world trade. It is a fast-growing area rich in minerals and energy resources, with a high level of human capital development and high rate of growth. It is a power factor in many of the areas in which the EU has, or aspires to have, a strategic influence, including the former Yugoslavia, the Middle East, the Caucuses and the former Soviet republics on the EU's new eastern border. There were windows of opportunity for substantial advances on both economic and political fronts but these were missed and it now remains to be seen whether the EU has the political will or flexibility to recognise and exploit new opportunities should they arise.

REGIONAL TRADE AGREEMENTS

For the duration of the Doha Round, the EU had abstained from forming new regional trade agreements and had become a champion of multilateralism. The regional trade agreements (RTAs) that it had concluded had been more for strategic reasons than for economic. In an exchange of roles, under the Bush presidency, the United States that had formerly eschewed bilateral agreements now began to pursue them with renewed vigour,[39] and the Japanese also became active in South East Asia and South America. Since the start of the Doha Round no less than 113 RTAs have been registered with the WTO (including, of course, those formed by the EU as part of the European Neighbourhood Policy and the EU enlargement treaties).[40] Realising that it was falling behind, in October 2006 the Commission signalled an important shift in the EU's priorities towards negotiating trade deals. Henceforth, the EU would take account of its own employment and growth levels in its strategy towards new RTAs. It signalled its intention of opening negotiations with ASEAN, Mercosur and South Korea. These targets all had high levels of protectionism, they all offered large markets and they were all engaged in negotiating RTAs with its competitors.[41]

In May 2007, formal talks were started with ASEAN and with South Korea. However, the idea of a free trade agreement with India stalled on Indian objections to the EU's insistence on the inclusion of a human rights clause in the agreement (which, it was feared, would open the door to non-tariff restrictions under the guise of accusations of social dumping).

CONCLUSIONS

It is difficult not to be impressed with the sheer scale of the EU's efforts to create regional trade agreements. There are 192 members of the United Nations. Twenty-seven of them are members of the European Union and until the beginning of 2007 the EU was involved in RTAs or it was actively engaged in negotiating them with a further 98 countries – over half of the UN membership. The EU (27) itself represents 21.8 per cent of world GDP and its exports amount to 39 per cent of the world total (17.8 per cent if intra-trade is discounted). The countries involved in the EU's negotiations before 2007 produced 9.7 per cent of world GDP, whilst their exports represented only 8.8 per cent of the world total. In other words, it is difficult to escape the conclusion that a large amount of diplomatic resources are being devoted to areas with relatively little economic return – the main exception is possibly the Russian Federation, but here the negotiations seem way off target. And, as we saw in the previous paragraph, the European Union has since stated its intention to open negotiations with ASEAN, Mercosur and several individual countries. This certainly represents a different order of ambition – ASEAN alone represents over 6.4 per cent of world GDP. However, it is still noticeable that the world's largest traders – the USA, Japan and China – seem to be firmly off the EU's shopping list, at least until any hope of a trade agreement within the WTO is finally extinguished.

A second point worthy of reflection is the extent to which the EU's policy mix of market access, regional integration and domestic policy reform is meeting diminishing returns. Put another way, one could question whether it can work in the absence of access to the ultimate prize, membership in the EU itself. For poorer countries the trade-off is between a new trade agreement with the EU (and the economic upheaval), and its existing concessions (and the status quo). For regimes perceived as less free and democratic, the trade-off is between a new trade agreement with the EU (and the economic upheaval) and the questionable economic benefits and social and political upheaval (revolution) aspired to by EU policy-makers. For the new areas into which the EU is advancing the trade-off may become a trade deal with the EU as opposed to a more attractive deal, with fewer strings attached, elsewhere.

POSTSCRIPT

This essay was published in Portuguese in M. Wiesebron and R.T. Griffiths (eds.), *Processos de integração regional e cooperação intercontintental desda 1989*, Posto Alegre, 2008. The world has certainly moved on since 2008. I do not think that if I were to have written it now, I would have changed the tenor of the argument, but obviously much of the detail would have changed. So allow me to run through the main differences in roughly the order they appear in the original piece.

As the tensions in the Middle East continue to bubble, especially the civil war in Syria, the geo-political importance of Turkey for EU ambitions in the area continues to grow. Yet the enlargement negotiations remain stalled over the issue of Cyprus (which is convenient since it avoids the need to voice other concerns) and the talks aimed at 'deepening' the customs union to include services and public procurement remain suspended. The progress on trade agreements with the ACP countries have resulted in agreements with the Caribbean and the Pacific, and with East and Southern Africa (Zimbabwe, Mauritius, Madagascar and Seychelles), but everywhere else progress has been uneven. Talks with regions involving Nigeria and South Africa are still proceeding.

The EuroMed situation has been transformed out of all recognition. I had written that the EU had afforded them no high priority because there were 'not caught in a process of political and social change', but that altered in the Arab Spring of 2011, which was unanticipated by EU officials and was certainly not the outcome of EU policy. And as the newly liberated citizens rather predictably chose Muslim-led governments, the animus for close(r) association with them on the part of the EU dimmed considerably, and along with it, the push for closer economic ties. On the eastern side of the EU, there are few signs of progress in its Neighbourhood Policy. The free trade agreement concluded with Ukraine in 2011 remains on ice until the necessary political reforms are introduced, and matters have not even reached that stage with Belarus, often seen as Europe's last dictatorship. And the slide backwards from democracy in Russia itself seems to have put an end to any prospects for a 'strategic partnership' in the near future.

Yet it would be unfair to suggest that the EU's policy lies in tatters. The move towards countries where agreements would offer larger benefits have been accelerating. An agreement with South Korea has been operative since June 2012 and talks with Singapore have been progressing well. In November 2012, negotiations were opened with Japan and there are reports that talks with India have revived. An ambitious agenda has been adopted for a bilateral trade and investment agreement with the United States. Several agreements in South America could soon become operational and meaningful talks with Mercosur could soon begin. Perhaps someone did read my article, after all. Of large trading partners, only China appears to be quiet.

Not too much reflective, academic work has been published since this article was written. An overview, presumably nearly as out-of-date as my own, is afforded by Jo-Ann Crawford and Roberto V. Fiorentino, 'The Changing Landscape of Regional Trade Agreements', World Trade Organization, Discussion Paper no. 8 (Geneva, 2009). Not much more recent in its coverage is Matthew Dodge, *The European Union and Interregionalism: Patterns of Engagement* (Farnham, 2012).

16
Lessons from the Euro Experience

Twenty years ago, amid a great fanfare of enthusiasm, the Treaty of Maastricht created the European Union and inaugurated the process for creating a single European currency for most of the then members (except the UK and Sweden, and later Denmark, which were given a temporary exemption) and all future members. Twenty years later, the anniversary of the treaty passed almost unnoticed.[1] On that day, however, the impact of the treaty was never far from the headlines, as had also been the case for almost every day over the previous months. The Lehman Brothers bankruptcy in September 2008 not only triggered a financial crisis that threatened to engulf the world, but it set in motion a series of shocks that have since reverberated through the euro area. It is fair to say that the crisis management has not been an example of streamlined efficiency, and there are lessons to be learned from that experience.

However, the development of the euro, and the crisis that has subsequently engulfed it, holds lessons in another direction. The European Union has long been held as a model, or an inspiration, for other experiments in regional cooperation and integration, including Mercosul, ASEAN and SADC. The model embodied a sequence of steps leading to 'ever closer union' that moved from a free trade area through a customs union and single market and culminated in economic and monetary union. With the signing and implementation of the Treaty of Maastricht, the European Union had embarked on the penultimate step in this progression. But only half of it – a monetary union without a fiscal union. The euro crisis has now called that achievement into question and, in the process, undermined the authority of those espousing a European route towards closer integration, both for themselves as well as for other nations. As a convinced federalist, myself, I would not recommend abandoning the European example altogether, but if there is a lesson to be learned from this sorry episode, it is this: 'If you are going to do it, do not do it this way.'

This essay examines the European experience with economic and monetary union from three perspectives – the design, the implementation and the management of the euro – before exploring the implications of the current crisis.

THE DESIGN

The decision to embark on the path towards economic and monetary union was taken after a period of remarkable exchange-rate stability in Western Europe. Introduced in 1979, it built on the experience of the exchange-rate mechanism (ERM) which had tied members exchange rates to a band of 2.25 per cent either side of par (except for Italy, which was given a band of 6 per cent) and which had enhanced central bank cooperation to maintain the parities. Its introduction, however, coincided with the second oil crisis and the system lurched from one crisis to the other, each being resolved by a devaluation or revaluation within the system to maintain the illusion that it remained intact.

It was similar to a 'crawling peg' arrangement, but to dignify it with this description would be to totally exaggerate the orderliness of its workings and to forget the whiff of fear surrounding its operation. Within the space of three and a half years, a gap of almost 30 per cent had opened up in the exchange rates of the strongest (German DM) and weakest (Italian lire) currencies. But then French economic policy converged with the rest, and a calm descended on the markets. The pervious turmoil was conveniently forgotten.[2] Little now seemed to disturb the serenity of European exchange rates and toward the end of the decade several non-members joined the system – Spain in June 1989, the UK in October 1990 and Portugal in April 1992. It was against this backdrop that in February 1992 the Treaty of Maastricht was signed.[3]

The design for economic and monetary union was based on five requirements that had to be met before being accepted into the single currency. First, countries had to have maintained stable exchange rates within the ERM for two years preceding membership. There then followed two fiscal targets – the stipulation that the annual government deficit should not exceed 3 per cent and that the level of sovereign debt should be no higher than 60 per cent. Presumably assuming that these requirements were met, there followed two further targets (or consequences) for the rates of inflation and for the cost of long-term borrowing. But these were given a further tweak in the direction of monetary prudence by expressing the targets not in terms of the average for the group, but in terms of the three lowest in the group, regardless of their relative size or importance. Thus inflation was not to exceed this target by more than 1.5 percentage points and long-term interest rates were not to be more than 2 percentage points higher. Generally, these requirements were at the time perceived to be deflationary and this was interpreted as a concession to German demands as the price for surrendering its own domestic currency, which had been exceptionally successful in this respect. And what was good for Germany was presumably good for the rest of us as well.[4]

Although the design has the virtue of simplicity, there are several curious deficiencies. For a start, the target for the deficit is absolute and only in one direction. It offers no opportunity for offsetting better performances (lower deficits or even surpluses) against an overshoot. If a deficit results from a recession, there is still an obligation to impose a deflationary budget. There is no scope at all for the kind of deficit financing engaged upon by the USA in the shadow of the recession following the Lehman Brothers crisis and staying within the rules. Secondly, there is an inconsistency between tolerating a government deficit, albeit 3 per cent, and the objective of holding down the level of external sovereign debt. The only way to avoid steadily accumulating a relatively greater debt is to grow faster than the 3 per cent that is added to the debt burden.[5] Growing consistently, or even sporadically, faster than 3 per cent per annum is something that the more advanced European economies have struggled to do since the first oil crisis of 1973. On the other hand, growth 'convergence' for the less advanced economies was almost a religion among European economists, as they utilised untapped productivity resources and invested the convergence or cohesion funds transferred to them from the EU budget. Unfortunately, the recipe for growth usually entailed a trade-off in terms of higher inflation.[6] This, in its turn would create a further problem. Locked first into fixed exchange rates, which precluded any currency depreciation, and later locked into a single currency and, furthermore, deprived of domestic monetary instruments, there were few options for dealing with the cumulative inflationary results. Finally, the interest rate target is an implied derivative of achieving the prescribed budget discipline and seems to be left to the mercy of the markets. This is eminently sensible, if the market is assumed to operate rationally and predictably. If it does not, however, governments are left with pitifully few short-term policy measures to alleviate the situation, and so too were the officials of the European Union. The stance of the monetary authorities became that there would be no 'bail out' of economies in difficulties and therefore there was no provision of funds to cover just such an eventuality.

IMPLEMENTATION

The Maastricht Treaty envisaged three steps whereby the new European currency would be created. In the first phase, capital controls would be removed and inter-bank cooperation would pave the way for the creation of a more central monetary authority. The second stage began with the creation of a European Monetary Institute and the five criteria agreed in Maastricht were enshrined in a Stability and Growth Pact, which was to be monitored by the European Commission. At the end of this stage, exchange rates would be locked together and the European Central Bank would be established. At this stage the euro was introduced as a means of transactions, but the launch of the currency into circulation would wait for four years.[7] That moment took place on 1 January 2002. I was in Rome that day and still remember how, at the end of the day, I examined the loose change in my pocket to discover coins minted in Germany, Ireland and the Netherlands. I should add that the novelty soon wore off. By then, however, things were already going very badly wrong.

In May 1998 eleven members of the EU were declared to have met the conditions for euro membership and became the first wave to adopt the new currency. Two other members, namely Denmark and the UK, had acquired opt-out clauses. This left only Greece and Sweden as members deemed ineligible, and Greece was admitted into the new currency in January 2001. For the record, all subsequent members of the European Union assumed the obligation to join the euro area, when conditions had been met. Slovenia did so in 2007, Cyprus and Malta joined the following year, Slovakia acceded the year after that and, finally in 2011 Estonia became a member.

But let us return to those heady halcyon days of europhoria as countries lined up to join the new currency area. One criteria was that they should have a government debt ratio of no more than 60 per cent of GDP, but if higher at the moment of entry, it should be diminishing at a 'satisfactory pace'. If we look at the statistics that policy-makers had before them at the time, in the two years before joining, three countries – Belgium, Italy and Greece – had debt ratios already towering above 100 per cent of GDP. Although they showed some decline this was at a rate that would still leave them far outside the target range two decades later. Greece too, had a debt ratio hovering around 100 per cent. Five other members – Austria, Germany, the Netherlands, Portugal and Spain – had debt ratios between 60 and 70 per cent.

TABLE 16.1: GOVERNMENT DEBT: GDP RATIO (%)

Austria		*Belgium*		*Finland*		*France*		*Germany*		*Ireland*	
1997	1998	1997	1998	1997	1998	1997	1998	1997	1998	1997	1998
66.1	65.6	124.7	121.3	59.0	57.3	57.3	58.2	61.7	61.4	65.8	59.2
Italy		*Luxembourg*		*Netherlands*		*Portugal*		*Spain*		*Greece*	
1997	1998	1997	1998	1997	1998	1997	1998	1997	1998	2000	2001
123.2	121.9	6.7	6.9	73.4	71.5	62.5	60.8	68.1	66.5	102.8	99.7

Source: European Commission, *European Economy*, Statistical Annex 1998 and 2001.

If the Maastricht Treaty had been taken seriously, the introduction of the euro in 1999 should have taken place with seven fewer members than it did, and Greece should not have been allowed to join two years later. This, of course, is where politics enters the frame. A major step forward on the road to integration without four of the six founding members of the European Union was plainly unthinkable. Equally, a monetary union comprising only Finland, France, Ireland and Luxembourg would have made no economic sense whatsoever. So, for the first time, and not for the last, the details of an agreement were pushed aside to make way for political expediency. And, having admitted Belgium and Italy with excessive sovereign debt ratios, the EU was scarcely in a position not to extend the courtesy to Greece, whose debt ratio appeared less bad than either of these. Policy-makers work with figures that they have to hand, but these figures are often revised afterwards either because the data itself is updated or because definitions have shifted. For debt ratios these revisions over time have been favourable, and would have allowed Portugal to qualify for euro membership on this criteria. For Greece, however, the situation was slightly worse.[8]

TABLE 16.2: NET GOVERNMENT BORROWING (-) OR LENDING AS % GDP

Austria		*Belgium*		*Finland*		*France*		*Germany*		*Ireland*	
1997	1998	1997	1998	1997	1998	1997	1998	1997	1998	1997	1998
-2.8	-2.6	-2.6	-2.3	-1.4	-0.2	-3.1	-3.0	-3.0	-2.6	+0.6	+1.2
Italy		*Luxembourg*		*Netherlands*		*Portugal*		*Spain*		*Greece*	
1997	1998	1997	1998	1997	1998	1997	1998	1997	1998	2000	2001
-3.0	-3.7	+1.6	+1.0	-2.1	-2.9	-2.7	-2.4	-2.9	-2.4	-2.7	-3.1

Source: European Commission, *European Economy*, Statistical Annex 1998 and 2001.

A second Maastricht criteria was that current government deficits should not exceed 3 per cent of GDP. At first sight, the record on this score was remarkably good but the results conceal a great deal of statistical and definitional creativity. Pension funds were creamed and capital assets sold and included under current revenue; parts of government debt were conveniently parked out of sight and GDP figures were massaged upwards, by as much as 10-20 per cent.[9] The impact of changes in methods and definitions in the Netherlands in 2001, for example, raised its GDP by 4.5 per cent and reduced its debt ratio from 52.95 to 50.7 per cent.[10] There was plenty of room for further revisions, if efforts were taken to include the 'black economy' in official estimates as Italy did in 1987, thereby, in one leap, overtaking the UK as the world's fifth largest economy.[11] Even so, Italy and Greece still failed to meet the Maastricht criteria on this point, but were still admitted. The reason was simple. If one was going to ignore a mountain of debt, who was going to quibble over a couple of decimal points? In this particular case, historical revision was not too kind to Portugal, Spain and Greece, all of which have now fallen above the 3 per cent range and therefore the official qualification threshold.

MANAGEMENT

Once the euro had been introduced, it was for the European Central Bank and the Eurozone ministers of finance to manage the new currency. The backbone for monetary discipline was the so-called Stability and Growth Pact that took over in their entirety all the Maastricht criteria. One of these was that budget deficits should be no higher than 3 per cent of GDP. This was first seriously challenged in 2001-2002 when a temporary recession led to a surge in budget deficits and threatened to push France, Germany, Italy and Portugal over the threshold. It was ironic that this crisis should embroil Germany since it had been largely responsible for insisting on a strict and restrictive rule in the first place. Had the rule contained some countercyclical provisions, such a development would never have caused a problem, but that was not the case. Indeed, breaching the rules could invoke sanctions in the form of fines equivalent to 0.5 per cent of GDP. But these sanctions were not automatic.

Instead of accepting the discipline of their own rules, France and Germany together began a campaign for 'easing' them. As a result of their combined pressure, a recommendation by the Commission that the two countries take immediate measures to rectify the position was overruled by the finance ministers at their meeting in November 2003.[12] In 2005 the ministers, against the misgivings of the

ECB, relaxed the rules themselves in a way that allowed the ministers to take a longer-term view of budget perspectives. It also permitted countries with a debt ratio below 60 per cent a budget deficit of 1 per cent of GDP, but held countries with a deficit of over 100 per cent to achieving a balanced budget or even generating a surplus.[13] Significantly, nothing was done to strengthen enforcement mechanisms and the new regime was repeatedly flouted by such countries as Austria, Greece, Italy and Portugal. The reason was simple. Once the rules had been bent in favour of the strong, the moral authority to impose the rules on the weak was lost, even if the inclination to do so was present.

TABLE 16.3: GOVERNMENT DEBT: GDP RATIO (%)

	99	00	01	02	03	04	05	06	07	08
Austria	-2.7	-2.9	-4.3	-2.9	-3.0	-3.4	-5.9	-4.1	-3.1	-3.5
Belgium	-0.6	0.0	+0.4	-0.1	-0.1	-0.3	-2.7	-0.1	-0.3	-1.3
Finland	+1.6	+6.8	+5.0	+4.0	+2.4	+2.3	+2.7	+4.0	+5.2	+4.2
France	-1.8	-1.5	-1.5	-3.1	-4.1	-3.6	-2.9	-2.4	-2.7	-3.3
Germany	-1.5	-1.3	-2.8	-3.7	-4.0	-3.8	-3.3	-1.6	+0.3	+0.1
Greece	-3.1	-3.7	-4.5	-4.8	-5.6	-7.5	-5.2	-5.7	-6.4	-9.8
Ireland	+2.7	+4.7	+0.9	-0.4	+0.4	+1.4	+1.6	+2.9	+0.1	-7.3
Italy	-1.7	-0.8	-3.1	-2.9	-3.5	-3.5	-4.3	-3.4	-1.5	-2.7
Luxembourg	+3.4	+6.0	+6.1	+2.1	+0.5	-1.1	0.0	+1.4	+3.7	+3.0
Netherlands	+0.4	+2.0	-0.2	-2.1	-3.1	-1.7	-0.3	+0.5	+0.2	+0.6
Portugal	-2.7	-2.9	-4.3	-2.9	-3.0	-3.4	-5.9	-4.1	-3.1	-3.5
Spain	-1.4	-1.0	-0.6	-0.5	-0.2	-0.3	+1.0	+2.0	+1.9	-4.2

Source: European Commission, *European Economy*, Statistical Annex 2011.

The 'result' of fiscal prudence should have revealed itself in two 'market' mechanisms –relatively low government borrowing costs and relatively low inflation rates. Indeed, both 'effects' were apparent. One almost immediate impact was a sharp reduction in the range of interest rates governments had to pay for long-term borrowing, which was in sharp contrast to the period leading up to the adoption of the euro.[14] What is slightly more disturbing is why this should have been so. In economic theory markets function properly when there is transparency, shared knowledge, low transaction costs and economically rational actors. Government debt should be one of the more predictable markets. Nonetheless, the rate of interest paid on the debt of a poor, debt-burdened economy renowned for its fiscal laxity (like Greece) and on that of a rich, relatively debt-light economy known for its fiscal rectitude (like Germany) was virtually identical. Few, however, remarked on the irrationality and unpredictably of capital markets. One effect was to allow countries to refinance their debts relatively cheaply, and thus removing the market penalty on persistent deficits at a time when the political sanction had also been abandoned. For the poorer economies, high government debt levels were refinanced far below those prevailing in previous decades. There was little incentive to trim excessive deficits back to the 60 per cent threshold and both Germany and France (not to mention Austria, Belgium, Greece, Italy and later Portugal) allowed themselves the luxury of higher levels of sovereign debt than that stipulated in the Stability and Growth Pact.

TABLE 16.4: GOVERNMENT DEBT: GDP RATIO (%)

	99	00	01	02	03	04	05	06	07	08
Austria	67.2	66.5	67.1	66.5	65.5	64.8	63.9	62.1	60.7	63.8
Belgium	113.7	107.9	106.6	103.5	98.5	94.2	92.1	88.1	84.2	89.6
Finland	45.7	43.8	42.5	41.5	44.5	44.4	41.7	39.7	35.2	34.1
France	58.8	57.3	56.9	58.8	62.9	64.9	66.6	63.7	63.9	67.7
Germany	60.9	59.7	58.8	60.4	63.9	65.8	68.0	67.6	64.9	66.3
Greece	94.0	103.4	103.7	101.7	97.4	98.9	100.3	106.1	105.4	110.7
Ireland	48.5	37.8	35.5	32.1	30.9	29.6	27.4	24.8	25.0	44.0
Italy	113.7	109.2	108.8	105.7	104.4	103.9	105.9	106.6	103.6	106.3
Luxembourg	6.4	6.2	6.3	6.3	6.1	6.3	6.1	6.7	6.7	13.6
Netherlands	61.1	53.8	50.7	50.5	52.0	52.4	51.8	47.4	45.3	58.2
Portugal	49.6	48.5	51.2	53.8	55.9	57.6	62.8	63.9	68.3	71.6
Spain	62.3	59.3	55.6	52.5	48.7	46.2	43.0	39.6	36.1	39.8

Source: European Commission, *European Economy*, Statistical Annex 2011.

Another result of the low prevailing interest rates was to fuel asset bubbles and the growth of speculative banking practices. But surprisingly, the impact on prices was relatively mute. No country actually breached the target, when averaged over the decade. Nonetheless, some countries were persistently higher than the three lowest and that difference, although no more than 1 to 1.5 per cent a year led to a cumulative gap in price levels of almost 20 per cent, and that inflationary gap was measured against some of the most competitive countries in Europe. As the competitiveness of Greece, Spain and Portugal gradually eroded, so their economic growth slowed and the capacity for work-creation was much reduced. The promise of convergence – high growth paid for by higher inflation – was turning into an ash of just higher inflation. If European demand were to slow, these weaknesses would be cruelly exposed.

TABLE 16.5: AVERAGE HICP INFLATION RATE OVER THE FIRST DECADE OF THE EURO

Lowest Three	*Austria*	*Belgium*	*Finland*	*France*	*Germany*
1.77	1.98	2.18	1.76	1.91	1.68
Ireland	*Italy*	*Greece*	*Netherlands*	*Portugal*	*Spain*
1.96	2.29	3.36	1.88	2.37	2.85

Source: CBS *Webmagazine*, 10.1.2012.

THE CRISIS

Few economists had anticipated the financial crisis that swept through the world economy in 2008. The signs of asset bubbles had been apparent much earlier. The ratio of real estate prices to earnings in parts of the USA and in some Mediterranean countries (as well as in Ireland and the Netherlands) had already reached levels that would prove difficult to sustain, but an adjustment need not necessarily precipitate a collapse. Ironically, it was the fact that such adjustment was underway that precipitated the crisis as people in the USA defaulted on their housing loans. This would impact directly on those financial agencies directly involved in the housing market, and it did. The Lehman Brothers, Freddie Mac and Fannie May were soon all in financial difficulties and Lehman Brothers filed for bankruptcy on 15 September 2008. What tilted a sectoral crisis into a truly global one was that Lehman Brothers had sold on the ownership of some of its mortgage assets to other banks, but in forms that made it difficult to assess the risk involved. Other banks held these poisoned assets and no one knew which banks they were and what the degree of the exposure was. Inter-bank lending, which served to lubricate the world economy, contracted virtually overnight and the impact of the resulting 'credit crunch' reverberated through the developed economies of North America and Western Europe.[15] As far as the Eurozone was concerned, attention rapidly focused on four countries, rather ungraciously known as the PIIGS – Portugal, Ireland, Italy, Greece and Spain.

TABLE 16.5: GOVERNMENT DEBT AND DEFICIT DATA FOR THE PIIGS COUNTRIES

	Portugal	*Ireland*	*Italy*	*Greece*	*Spain*
Government					
2008	-3.5	-7.3	-2.7	-9.8	-4.2
2009	-10.1	-14.3	-5.4	-15.4	-11.1
2010	-9.1	-32.4	-4.6	-10.5	-9.2
2011	-5.9	-10.5	-4.0	-9.5	-6.3
Government					
2008	71.6	44.4	106.3	110.7	39.8
2009	83.0	65.6	116.1	127.1	53.3
2010	93.0	96.2	119.0	142.8	60.1
2011	101.7	112.0	120.3	157.7	68.1

Source: European Commission, *European Economy*, Statistical Annex 2012.

Let us start with Ireland. Ireland had been almost a showcase country for the European Union. It was the 'Celtic Tiger' that, with financial support from the European Union, had transformed itself from a lesser developed part of the Continent into one that had overtaken the UK in terms of per capita national income. All of its financial indicators conformed to the targets of the Stability and Growth Pact. But none of this reflected the growing instability of the private sector. Banks had overextended themselves by borrowing cheaply on international markets and fuelling a 'property bubble' of impressive dimensions. Property prices had already begun to slide in 2007, but they collapsed as the credit crisis struck the country. To stem a possible run on overextended banks the government first guaranteed all bank deposits and, a year later, effectively nationalised the banks' bad debts. This was against the backdrop of a gathering recession that eroded government income and a programme of fiscal restraint. As the government's borrowing requirement ballooned and the level of sovereign debt soared, the credit lines began understandably to tighten.[16] In November 2010, the country accepted a 'bail out' package of €67.5 billion supplied by the IMF and the European Union (with three non-euro countries – UK, Denmark and Sweden – contributing individually) on condition that the government enact further measures to bring government spending under control.

For the purpose of this article, Italy, Portugal and Spain fall almost into the same category, though there are marked differences between them. They are all countries whose competitive positions were eroded during the years of the build-up to, and adoption of, the euro when the impact of price and inflation differentials could not be rectified by currency depreciation. Nailed to a 21st-century version of the gold-standard, economic equilibrium depended increasingly on domestic deflation (to reduce prices) or on economic reform (to increase competitiveness). When a country does neither, the foundations of economic growth erode and they become increasing vulnerable to the impact of cyclical downturns. In the case of Spain and Portugal, the situation was aggravated by a speculative property boom, similar to that which had characterised developments in Ireland. In these countries, too, when the bubble burst, the subsequent contraction of the construction sector led the slide into recession with rising unemployment and a burgeoning fiscal deficit. In Spain the impact was cushioned by the relatively low level of government debt but for Portugal the twin demands of debt roll-over and funding the current deficit stretched the confidence in the government's ability to pay.[17] In May 2011 the European Union, the ECB and the IMF (jointly known as the Troika) contributed to a Portuguese 'bail out' of €78 billion, conditional on new austerity and privatisation measures. Italy has been caught in the backwash of these developments. Although it has a relatively high level of debt, its repayment schedule is not tight and much of the debt is held domestically. Moreover, its current deficit levels are not out of line with those elsewhere in Western Europe. With markets jittery, there were doubts over Italy's ability to sustain these debt levels given the erosion of its competitiveness and growth potential and concern over the inability of the government to cut expenditure and introduce reforms. As the cost of borrowing edged ever higher, the Berlusconi government stepped down and was replaced by an emergency technocratic government deemed capable of enacting the necessary reforms.

We can now turn to Greece. The country entered the euro two years after the start because the European Commission and member states were uncertain whether it could maintain the necessary discipline. They should have stayed sceptical, but as the Greek government managed to manipulate its budget deficit to a record low of 2.7 per cent in 2000, the doubts were laid aside and euro membership was granted. The latest revised data for the year 2000 shows a deficit a full percentage point higher. Whatever the true figure, it was the best result Greece managed to achieve since thereafter the deficits annually crept ever upwards but initially, because the economy was still growing strongly on the back of cheap credit, not so the level of debt. Although successive Greek budgets became more profligate, from 2005 the debt levels did begin to respond. In that year, the Commission revealed systematic underreporting of deficits by the Greek government and it started proceedings against it. These persisted until 2007, but stopped short of applying sanctions.[18] Meanwhile, in 2006 the Greek government attempted a new approach which, had it succeeded, would have slashed the size of the deficit and weight of debt by a quarter. In September 2006 it suggested that the national income be raised by 25 per cent to include the (unreported) 'black economy'. This was rejected by Eurostat officials but they did allow an upward revision of 9.7 per cent.

The recession hit Greece hard. Competitiveness had been deteriorating and its shipping and tourism industries were particularly vulnerable to a cyclical downturn. The Greek budget forecast for 2009 was originally for a deficit of 3.7 per cent, down from the 5 per cent reported for 2008. By October of that year the two figures were revised upwards to 12.5 per cent and 7.7 per cent, respectively. The European Commission's 2010 judgement was damning. While accepting that Greek statistical recording and reporting was a mess, it also suggested that figures had been deliberately manipulated for political ends. The implications were that Greek financial reporting was uncontrolled and uncontrollable. Several months later *Der Spiegel* revealed that Goldman Sachs had connived in the underreporting of government debt by arranging currency swaps at fictitious rates that concealed the true level of government indebtedness.[19]

The spiralling levels of Greek indebtedness undermined any remaining confidence of markets in the ability of the government ever to redeem them. Interest rates on new Greek borrowing shot skywards and in April 2010 the government applied for a loan of €45 billion to cover its borrowing commitments for the rest of the year. A month later, after imposing savage budget cuts, and provoking a bitter public reaction, it received a bailout of €110 billion from the IMF, the ECB and the EU. By now, the impact of the recession, reinforced by the government's deflationary policy, were further undermining tax receipts. The Troika responded in October 2011 by offering a second bail out worth €130 billion, on condition that Greece produce a convincing and effective austerity and reform programme. At the same time, it pressured private holders of Greek debt to voluntarily to accept a debt restructuring package involving losses of up to 70 per cent on the face value of their loans, and at the same time converting them to new longer-term loans at favourable interest. It was an all-or-nothing offer, and succeeded in reducing the level of Greek debt by €105 billion. A new technocratic government, meanwhile, committed itself to bringing the level of sovereign debt back down to 120 per cent by 2020 (most recently revised to 117 per cent) – the level at which it had stood when the crisis began.

The above description of the crisis is a tidy version of events. Reality was rather different. The first problem was that Article 125 of the Maastricht Treaty specifically ruled out the option of a 'bail out' for countries with public debt problems. This position designed to eliminate the danger of what economist call 'moral hazard' whereby relief measures apparently condone and reinforce the tendency towards the deviant behaviour that had caused the problem in the first place. Thus, as the banking crisis was undermining the stability of the financial sector in various Eurozone countries, and when markets needed reassurance, the ministers of the 27 member states had to agree the basis for any intervention. Neither the framework nor the means for intervention were in place beforehand. When the means were in place, they were scarcely of the magnitude to reassure the markets. It did not take a Nobel Prize-winning economist to figure out that the size of the 'bail out' funds would be insufficient to resolve multiple concurrent crises. Moreover, as the disbursement of the funds was made conditional upon remedial measures being taken by the recipient, the entire operation doubled the causes of uncertainty, without ever resolving the essential question – would it ever be enough?

At present, in March 2012, the European Union has agreed to strengthen its financial governance. It increased the possibility of implementing an 'excessive deficit procedure' and introduced a 'reverse qualified majority voting procedure' (whereby a judgement could only be overturned by a majority against) to enable the imposition of sanctions that could amount to 0.5 per cent of GDP. A separate intergovernmental treaty would require governments to limit deficits to 0.5 per cent of GDP (1 per cent if countries had a debt level of less than 60 per cent), but with escape clauses for special circumstances. These limits should be introduced into national law. Surveillance and cooperation measures were also strengthened. At the same time, the financial instruments were strengthened. In May 2010, the EU finance ministers created a temporary funding arrangement – the European Financial Stability Facility (EFSF) with a capital commitment of €780 billion and a lending capacity of €440 billion. In December 2010, they agreed to the creation of a permanent European Stability Mechanism (ESM) with a lending capacity of €500 billion to take over from the EFSF when it lapses in July 2013. Since the EFSF has already lent €192 billion, the open question at time of writing is whether to treat the ESM additional funding, raising the total to €692 billion, or not. Whatever they decide, it will never be enough if a cataclysm does occur.

For now, the crisis has apparently subsided. Let us now briefly examine the cost and then, speculate about the future. When the crisis broke, I was in favour of the European Union maintaining its 'no bail out' stance, partly because of the moral hazard argument and partly because there was a readymade alternative in the form of the IMF. All the EU member states are individually members of the IMF and the IMF has both the mandate and the means to intervene. One argument is that the IMF might not have had the funds, but that could have been resolved by raising its capital. This need not have been difficult since the BRIC countries had wanted to do this for some time (increasing their voting power in the process) and the EU states could have contributed as well. With this resolved, the IMF could have gone into countries, bullied their governments, making itself thoroughly resented, and then left. Instead, the EU put itself into the middle of this process, despite the fact that it was not equipped for the task and that it was not a unitary actor. As a result the EU has complicated the rescue plans and heaped disapproval and resentment upon itself. This would also have been true of the IMF, but the IMF is not trying to build 'an ever closer union' as the EU is pledged to do. As distrust of Brussels institutions is rising, the EU's active involvement in various austerity programmes will damage its chances of securing referenda for any future treaty changes it requires, and moving the reform agenda outside the usual democratic circuits will only increase public disenchantment. The EU may still weather the crisis, but it could be paying the political price long after the monetary costs have been absorbed and forgotten.

But has it solved the crisis? At the moment, the markets are calm, but markets are hardly a trustworthy barometer. Despite their elevation in globalisation literature to almost omnipotent and omniscient status, markets have not performed well. In currency markets, they have presided over wild swings (both overshooting and undershooting) in exchange rates and they have long ignored blatant signs of difficulties in the capacity of debt service by certain states. They are now supposed to have been reassured by the new firmness of the EU approach, a firmness which at its first test was to give a waiver from its solemn obligations to Spain. Spain had overshot its deficit in 2011 (8.5 per cent instead of 6.0 per cent) and was given a revised target for 2012 (5.8 per cent instead of 4.4 per cent). It is good to build exceptions into legislation, but it is not good politics to begin with them. The Dutch, hitherto one of the 'best boys' in the class, has a minority government coalition in trouble over meeting the EU's criterion, and an opposition and the influential Central Planning Bureau, opposed. It may become a second country missing its obligations. And if it is not the Netherlands, there are several candidates to be next in line for special treatment.

A further problem lies in the effectiveness of the various austerity programmes. Piling deflation on economies that are already contracting usually serves to exacerbate the downward trend and could even increase the level of deficit or debt, expressed in relation to a lower GDP. The apparent immunity of deficits to the medicine prescribed may well again lead investors to question the creditworthiness of nation states, but not only them. Several countries that had experienced a credit boom in the years before the crisis also experienced inflated asset prices, which have not yet fully adjusted to the new realities. In the absence of a reappearance of sustained growth, these assets are often still lurking at inflated values on bank balance sheets. The next market attack may not be one of confidence in governments, but of confidence in banks. If, for example, housing prices do not recover in Spain, a run on Spanish banks could still occur, confronting the government with the alternatives of financial meltdown or nationalisation of bank assets. This could precipitate another 'bail out', but this time on a much larger scale than any that have gone before.[20] But even if we ride out these problems, we still have Greece. It surely stretches credulity to believe that a country where the tax system is inefficient and the population resentful, where the tax evader is a hero and the honest man a fool, is going to reduce its sovereign debt level to 120 per cent by 2020 and run a balanced budget every year, for the next ten to twenty years thereafter, until its level of debt reaches 60 per cent.

A final consideration lies in the fact that even if the EU resolves the debt/deficit issues, we have done nothing to deal with the gap in competitiveness that has emerged. It is very difficult to press a 20 per cent price differential out of the system, especially without the option of devaluation. The 'gold bloc' countries attempted this in the 1930s and failed.[21] My guess is that the Mediterranean countries, trapped within the euro and without the option of domestic protection, may find themselves left with a sound fiscal base but with a stagnant economy. The alternative of leaving the euro and adopting a new (depreciating) currency is also not an attractive option. Should the euro even survive, for them there is no happy ending inside or outside the bloc.

CONCLUSION

In May 2008 The European Commission celebrated the tenth anniversary of the start of the Eurozone (not the issue of the currency) with the publication of a commemorative volume. Writing its forward, the commissioner for economic and monetary affairs trumpeted:

> *A full decade after Europe's leaders took the decision to launch the euro, we have good reason to be proud of our single currency. The economic and monetary union and the euro are a major success. For its member countries, EMU has*

> *anchored macro-economic stability, increased cross border trade, financial integration and investment. For the EU as a whole, the euro is a keystone for further economic integration and a potent symbol of our growing political unity. And for the world, the euro is a major new pillar in the international monetary system and a pole of stability for the global economy.*[22]

It is sad to reflect now that the design was faulty, the implementation flawed, the management lax, the crisis mishandled and that the future still remains uncertain. To push forward towards even more 'European' solutions, to see the crisis as an opportunity, would at this moment be a mistake. The public is not ready for such a move, and are unlikely to forgive (yet another) attempt to do things above their heads, if not behind their backs. For the moment, it would be a considerable achievement to hold the stability of the currency area. The euro is easily salvageable, if not necessarily with its current membership. Once matters have settled, there will be the time to find structural solutions and to continue on the road of what, for all its shortcomings, has been one of the greatest achievements of post-war European history. And when we offer lessons to others, it may be with a little more modesty and humility than has often been the case in the past.

POSTSCRIPT

This essay appeared in *Austral: Brazilian Journal of Security and International Relations*, 1, 2 (2012), 15-34. Scarcely twelve months have passed since it was written and we are still lurching from periods of tranquillity following 'patch-up' solutions (that temporarily calm the markets) and renewed bursts of crisis. Anger and protest still simmer in Greece, Spain and Portugal. Italian voters showed their faith in the experiment of having an EU-favoured technocrat to lead the Italian government towards the fundamental by voting his coalition into fourth place with slightly over 10 per cent of the vote. And while the governmental process in Italy seemed paralysed, a new crisis broke out in Cyprus. This particular episode could have been seen coming for months, but when it broke, no contingency planning was in place. Although disaster was averted, yet another population was seething with anger and frustration and the rest of the world was left wondering what a 'deposit guarantee' was worth in any European bank. When, as appears increasingly necessary, the European Union implements the kind of changes that require adjustments to the existing treaties and therefore need a majority in the parliaments of each member state, can anyone be confident that the disenchanted will not seek their revenge?

17
European Identities

INTRODUCTION

The European Union is less than half the size of China in terms of population – 493 million against 1,321 million – but whilst China is governed by a single government, the European Union (EU) is fragmented into no less than 27. Many observers, not only in China, considered that decision-making in the EU, especially after the rapid expansion from 15 to 27 members, was becoming increasingly unmanageable and that some streamlining of voting procedures and further transfers of competencies to a supranational level was necessary. The 'Draft Treaty Establishing a Constitution for Europe' agreed by the member states in October 2004 was far from being a blueprint for a unitary state. Indeed, despite its 250 pages and 450 articles, it was far from being a 'constitution' either[1] but most commentators agreed that despite its unwieldy text and its pretentious title, the draft treaty represented a considerable and necessary improvement on the existing situation. Imagine the shock, therefore, when in 2005, within weeks of each other, the populations of two of the founding members of the European Union (France and the Netherlands) rejected the draft treaty.

The referendum results shattered the complacency of the Brussels elite and prompted the inauguration of a twenty-four month period of 'reflection' before deciding how to proceed further. The new treaty has made very few changes compared with the one rejected but one of the outcomes of this reflection has been to omit any reference to a European flag (twelve stars on a blue background), a European anthem (Beethoven's 'Ode to Joy') and a European motto ('Unity in Diversity') – even though all three have been in common circulation for many years. The European Union, therefore, will forego having the symbolic trappings of a state written into a formal treaty – a significant retreat in ambition but probably close to current reality.

I consider myself a 'European'. I have worked for long periods of my academic career in three different European countries. For eight years I led the research project into the History of European Integration at the European University Institute, an EU-funded post-graduate research institute in Florence. And, unusually for an Englishman, I consider myself a European federalist. I mention these facts because I wish to share with you a highly disturbing emotion I felt several years back.

I happen to be a keen follower of Rugby football. I used to play it in my youth but now my commitment is limited to the role of a supporter. I seem to be a bit of a masochist in my choice of teams. I support Wales in Rugby Internationals and the Italian team of Fiorentina in football (both teams that, over the years, have promised ecstasy but have too often delivered agony to their supporters). Thus it was that, several years ago, in my usual mixture of childish optimism tinged with a premonition of impending doom, I settled down to watch Wales' visit to Paris to face the might of France. The teams were on the pitch, the band was ready and I waited for the first chords of the Welsh national anthem 'Hen Wlad Fy Nhadau' ['Old Land of My Fathers'] to sound. Imagine then my surprise when instead the band began to play Beethoven's *Ode to Joy*. Surprise quickly turned to perplexity and then to a quiet anger, and that anger did not disappear when eventually first the Welsh and then the French anthems were played. Not even a good, hard-fought match (we lost – we usually do in Paris) restored my usual good humour. I was evidently not the only one to react negatively – the experiment was never repeated.

I reflected for some time afterwards over the source of my annoyance. Obviously, part of the reason was that playing another anthem had been so unexpected. What was the European Union doing at my rugby match? Had I known that back in the 1984-1985 the European Commission had contemplated athletes in the Olympic Games competing with a European logo on their shirts and facing a European flag at medal ceremonies,[2] I would have been less taken by surprise. And I had been only dimly aware that since 1986 the European Commission has supported an indoor tennis event, the European Community Championship, in Antwerp. Evidently someone in the Commission was trying to burnish the EU's image by association with high-level sporting achievement, though without too much success. Thus, at a deeper level my annoyance stemmed from a feeling that this type of association was artificial and inappropriate. The EU is not a nation, and had no role interfering in preparation for an *international* sporting contest. But then, I had to question why the EU did not inspire within me the same kind of identity or association I felt with my own country.

AN EU IDENTITY?

One reason why the European Union inspires a different degree of loyalty from its citizens is that it has very little actual contact with its citizens. This is ironic given the fact that nowadays well over half of domestic legislation originates in Brussels. Unlike our national governments, we do not actually choose our EU leaders. The president of the European Commission, and all the commissioners, are selected in a closed meeting of the heads of the member states. The perception that the whole deal was concluded beforehand is confirmed by the fact that there is a national quota of one commissioner for each member state. The Commission is important in the architecture of the European Union – it is the sole body able to propose legislation. Yet I doubt whether the average citizen could name more than the president of the Commission and their 'own' national commissioner, and even that is probably an optimistic assessment. It is my opinion that a directly elected president of the European Commission would significantly increase the visibility of, and citizens' identity with, the European Union as a whole. However, in all the discussions on Constitutional reform, no such change has been formally proposed. Whenever I advance the suggestion, I get one of two responses. One answer is that direct elections would make such a president too powerful vis-à-vis the member states. My response to this is that is presumably the whole point of the exercise. The second answer is that it cannot be done in a 27-country union, to which my response is that we already have EU-wide elections for the European Parliament and that such a presidential election could easily be arranged along the French two-round system. The retort to this is to question why I think a presidential election would work when the response to the elections to the European Parliament is so poor.

It is true that we elect the members of the European Parliament once every five years and that every time the voter turn-out drops even lower. In last election, in July 2004, 350 million citizens had the opportunity to cast their vote; less than half (45.7 per cent) bothered to do so. The European Parliament has a huge visibility problem. Its members remain unknown to the population at large and its debates rarely attract media attention. Even after 26 years, the elections are fought on the basis of a mixture of fairly anaemic and shapeless 'European' programs spiced up with some poignant 'national' concerns. Most of Europe's population would be hard pressed to name more than a few members of the European Parliament. Part of the problems of the European Parliament is that only recently has it begun to acquire any real power in the legislature, but those powers relate mostly to co-decision on regulations – an important role, but not headline-grabbing stuff. One reason why national parliaments attract attention is that they take (and spend) a sizeable chunk of our incomes. In most West European countries, governments dispose of 30 per cent or more of GDP and this generates considerable interest in the outcomes of policy debates, and a measure of commitment to the outcomes. By contrast, the European Union spends under 1 per cent of the EU's GDP, and 80 per cent of that is swallowed by two policy areas – the former common agricultural policy (and new rural policy) and the cohesion policy of assistance to economically backward areas. That does not leave much policy room for debate, either inside the parliament or among the electorate choosing it. Of course, not all policy discussions have to do directly with taxation or expenditure. Parliaments also discuss social issues or large questions of foreign policy. Unfortunately, at that point, the citizen discovers that most of the politically sensitive issues have been left in the hands of national governments.

A EUROPEAN IDENTITY?

Although the European Union might make European identity its concern, European identity is not concerned exclusively, or even primarily with the European Union.[3] In autumn 2005 *EuroBarometer* asked EU citizens if, in the near future, they expected to see themselves as 'European'. Only 2 per cent of those questioned answered affirmatively, though a further 7 per cent confessed to seeing themselves as 'European and French/German/British etc'.[4] The vast majority of European citizens see themselves primarily through their national identities. Even this overstates matters – there are many communities that identify themselves first and foremost in regional or provincial terms. For example, Belgians have long been split along linguistic lines between Walloons and Flemish. German reunification brought with it the division of the nation into '*Ossies*' and '*Wessies*' (former inhabitants of the GDR and the inhabitants of West Germany). Most Italians would probably identify themselves as Tuscans or Umbrians or such, before admitting to their Italian-ness. And the citizens of the Dutch province of Friesland are proud of their language and their flag. This is unsurprising. We humans are anchored in space and associate ourselves with the space in which we first lived, learned, loved and left behind our pasts. For most of us, that past lies somewhere within the frontiers of a single state or region.

However, all is not lost. It is not true that 'surveys of European public opinion reveal very little evidence of any European identity'.[5] Nor is it true that there are no equivalents to American hyphenated identities such as Irish-Americans, though it does not yet have the same resonance.[6] However, the same *EuroBarometer* of autumn 2005 revealed that a significant minority, 48 per cent, were willing to admit to a dual identity. It is true that they saw themselves *first* in national terms and only *second* as European (and not *vice-versa*). Moreover, this percentage has increased sharply since the early 1990s.[7] In fact, when adding the three degrees of European-ness together, the majority of citizens in most states admitted to some form of European identity. Only in four countries of the EU25 was there a majority of citizens with a purely national identity – Estonia, Hungary, Lithuania and the UK.

THE CONCEPT OF IDENTITY

Enough of statistics for the moment. The defeat of the Constitutional Treaty and self-denial of the trappings of supranational identity usually associated with the nation or state marks a setback in the European Union's attempt to win a more important place in the hearts and minds of its citizens. Central to these efforts is the concept of *identity*. Before continuing, it is worth considering what the concept involves. Obviously an identity involves a distinctiveness of an individual or group that has to be collectively accpeted and also, by implication, by those outsiders. Identities are socially constructed and constantly mediated (modified or reinforced) and they may exist in plural, non-exclusive forms (class, gender, religion, ethnicity, language etc.). They are most sharply defined when challenged, and in this case they are defined in relation to the 'other' that is engaged in the challenge.[8] Identity, therefore, stems from two sources. The first source of identity lies in a definition of 'self' when set against the 'other'. The second source lies in the recognition of shared values based on a common heritage and a common culture. Let us examine these in turn.

IDENTITY MEASURES AGAINST THE 'OTHER'

One of the others against which Europeans have measured themselves is 'the Americans'. Europeans are not Americans. This is at one and the same time a self-evident truth to most Europeans but it is also a puzzling one. Most Americans have their heritage in Europe and, since the 19th century, successive waves of British, Germans, Scandinavians, Italians and Eastern Europeans have made their homes in the United States. We have shared pasts, we share a religion (Christianity), we share a belief in the same values (freedom, democracy, human rights etc.), we have fought together in wars (sometimes on the same side), we are military allies (with NATO), we have together founded many of the world's global institutions (UN, World Bank, IMF, GATT/WTO etc.), we share trends in culture and clothing, we watch the same television programs and, thanks to CNN, even the same news. Europeans see themselves as Western, a characteristic that they share with Americans, but that is about as far as it goes. Anti-Americanism has a long history in Europe, but it is not a single or even a constant phenomenon. It varies between countries and between groups within countries. It is changing in intensity and focus all the time. Indeed,

> *it is the adaptive quality of the discourse, its chameleon-like ability to change colors rapidly according to its environment, that has made it so enduring. The longevity of anti-Americanism lies in its conservative outlook, which attracts followers on the left; its cultural criticism, which integrates elements of political and economic concerns; and its consistent dialectical juxtaposition with philo-Americanism, which is designed to respond to local concerns over identity, mores, and modernity.*[9]

A second route towards a European identity extends this European 'Western-ness' and projects it against a perceived non-Western-ness. This is not a new phenomenon. In the 15th and 16th centuries, the conflict with Muslims served to create a European identity within a general Christian identity. It was reinforced by the voyages of discovery that uncovered ever more others to fuel the self-identity of the European themselves and their civilising role. Finally, the Enlightenment of the 16th and 17th centuries again separated Europeans from their neighbours through its modernising discourse.[10] The post-war roots lie in the migrations into Europe to mitigate the labour shortages of the 1950s and, more noticeably, the 1960s. At that time the issue was more one of racial intolerance and a suspicion towards newcomers. The 'other' was still fragmented and localised – it might have reinforced an existing identity but it did not contribute (except with a lunatic fringe on the far right) any collective response. When to this mixture was added the economic downturn and mass unemployment of the 1970s and the continuation of immigration (mostly now through family reunification), the situation began to shift. As early as 1991 some commentators questioned whether a European identity might not be emerging 'predominantly in the direction of the idealization of "European demographic identity" conceived mainly in opposition to the "southern populations" (Turks, Arabs, Blacks)'.[11] Eight years later, two other social scientists concluded that discourses on identity were more related to 'exclusionary characteristics' than on any 'post-national' model based on personhood and territory.[12] Thus a juxtaposition between Europeans and some groups of 'non-Europeans' became increasingly accentuated long before the attack on the Twin Towers, and long before the words 'Muslim' and 'extremism/terrorism' became seemingly inextricably linked in European vocabulary. The gradual exclusion of non-European residents in Europe from the collective was accelerated by the events of 9-11 but it was now targeted not only at foreigners in our midst, but also those outside. As the nationality, ethnicity and religion of the perpetrators of successive terrorist acts became public knowledge, so the boundaries between foreigners outside and foreigners inside became increasingly blurred. It is not a pleasant process.

I live in the Netherlands, which has long been regarded as one of the more tolerant European countries as espoused by its liberal laws on soft drugs, prostitution and euthanasia. Toleration is not the same as approval. The Netherlands is a tolerant country, but also deeply conservative – the Dutch will allow certain behaviour (as long as it does not affect them) but that does not necessarily mean that they condone it. Part of this policy of toleration was a smothering of the dialogue on social issues which became literally colourless – in the official discourse social problems and crimes were seldom linked to colour or ethnicity. This taboo was broken by the populist politician Pim Fortuyn, who was murdered in May 2002. The party he had founded secured 17 per cent of the vote in the general elections held nine days after his murder. Fortuyn was an anti-establishment politician, though his politics did have a racist tinge, but the wave of frustration and discontent he harnessed and rode has since washed over the nature of public discourse, leaving a rotten debris in its wake. Turks and Moroccans inside the country, Turks wanting to join the European Union and Muslims, wherever they are, have become the stuff of a discourse that is too often bigoted and uninformed, self-opinionated and self-righteous. The heir to Fortuyn's legacy is Geert Wilders, whose party secured 6 per cent of the vote in the 2006 parliamentary elections, and who calls openly for closing Islamic schools and for banning the Koran in the Netherlands. Unfortunately, at the moment, the political elite often seems more concerned with pandering to these ideas than with trying to contain them. If this is the way towards a European identity, count me out.

IDENTITY THROUGH SHARED VALUES AND CULTURE

A more acceptable route towards the creation of an identity is through the identification and promotion of common values, based usually on a common heritage. In the debates on the draft Constitutional Treaty, before its rejection, many people argued for the inclusion in the preamble of a reference to Europe's Judeo-Christian tradition. With a history stretching back over 2000 years, this is clearly an in-depth historical and cultural appeal. Most prominent among those in favour were the Vatican and the EU Commission president at the time, Romano Prodi. Joseph Weiler also argued for its inclusion in the preamble of the treaty, not to stress the exclusive nature of a belief system, but because the preamble is the place where a reference to a common heritage most properly belongs.[13] There are two (possibly more than two) main problems with using Christianity as a point of departure and that concerns the two main ruptures that occurred within the Christian community and that still leave their marks today. The first was the split between the Latin Catholic Church and the Greek Orthodox Church in the 11th century and the second was the rift within the Catholic Church in the 16th century which gave rise to Lutheranism, Calvinism and various other Protestant Churches. It is all very well for those living in relatively secularised societies in Western Europe to deny the power of religious belief (at least within Christianity) but people have died on the borders of Christian beliefs. The most recent example has been the fighting and ethnic cleansing between Orthodox Serbs and Catholic Croats in the former Yugoslavia and it is less than ten years ago that 29 Protestants died in Omagh, Northern Ireland, in a bomb attack by the Catholic 'Real Irish Republican Army'.

Others have argued that Europe's unity is best located in its history – through its traditions of Christianity (yes – it is still there), humanism and enlightenment and through the common (elite) cultural movements that permeated much of the Continent. One could extend this shared past through social and economic history as well – a shared transformation from peasant rural society, through a more mixed society with the emergence of a mercantile class, to a largely industrial (and now post-industrial) society. Unfortunately, this common heritage has one more episodic but repetitive characteristic – an unfortunate proclivity to war, and wars in which European nations were lined up on different sides. Wars are deeply divisive not only because of the misery they create but also because of the redefinition and reinforcement of national identities that comes in their wake. It is difficult therefore to appeal to a common past that is so punctured by episodes of the shared experience of warfare in which the European nations were located on opposing sides. It is therefore interesting to note that in March 2006 a common model history textbook was launched to be used jointly in schools in France and Germany, each chapter prepared jointly by two historians, one from each country. Noticeably the first volume skipped the painful issue of European wars altogether by starting in 1945, though two volumes covering earlier periods have been promised.[14] One year later, the German education minister, Annette Schavan, proposed introducing a common history textbook throughout Europe, with the explicit intention of fostering a common European identity.[15]

If history, in its details, reminds European citizens of the worst excesses of nationalism, then European culture does the reverse. I do not share the belief that 'it is difficult to see how Europe's pronounced heterogeneity can provide for a positive cultural identification' though I would agree that it does not permeate very far.[16] In the fields of classical music and painting, in particular, the most famous composers and artists are lauded regardless of their nationalities, often without pausing to reflect on what those nationalities even are. We are, however, aware that they are European. In architecture too, the appreciation of the great medieval cathedrals and of 19th and 20th century art nouveau buildings is a shared one, and again an experience that transcends nationality but which is arguably, European. This is less the case in literature, where languages separate native from non-native speakers, though translation does allow access to some of the treasures of the literature of other European writers. The European Union has found it difficult to tap into this vein of 'high culture'. Its most enduring effort has been an initiative, launched in 1985, every year to nominate one European city (occasionally two and, in 2000, no less than nine cities) as 'cultural capital of Europe' for a year. However, the effect has been more an outpouring of local civic pride and a determined campaign to enhance tourism earnings than to enhance any European feeling of identity. Other than the local populations involved and tourists, attracted by the higher visibility of a holiday location, the entire effort leaves the population stone-cold.

Faced with these difficulties, some writers have tried to decouple the concepts of rights and identity from ethnicity and geography and link them instead to civic and political norms. Writing around the time of German reunification, and within a fierce debate on a new German identity, the political philosopher Jürgen Habermas argued that Germans were formulating a post-nationalistic (almost post-modern) identity founded on the creation of a welfare state and the acceptance of democratic constitutional principles, both of which stemmed from a desire to overcome the legacy of World War II, itself the outcome of aberrant nationalism. As he developed this argument, he suggested that Germans found their new identity outside Germany but within the European Union. In denying culture and history any role in German 'constitutional patriotism', Habermas then proceeds to transplant this bloodless form of identity onto an equally anaemic European Union. But one could question whether a weak Germanic form of national identity justified by an equally weak European identity is not, in fact, making a virtue out of necessity. It is not automatically the case that in moving towards a more globalised, liberal world, Europe no longer *needs* closed boundaries of identity. Moreover, Habermas could also be accused of projecting a peculiarly German concern onto a diverse European population where such issues are of less consequence.[17] Others have argued that a relativism from a narrow nationalist viewpoint towards a more internationalist viewpoint, does not necessarily imply the abandonment of concepts of borders or nationhood, even within the EU discourse. And post-modernist fads notwithstanding, national identity is so pervasive and so embedded in everyday discourse that it is often overlooked.[18] Still others have suggested that a Europe based on citizens' rights 'cannot be meaningfully divorced from identity and that citizenship devoid of emotion is neither feasible nor desirable' and have questioned the lack of any evidence to support the contention that this new European Man is actually emerging.[19]

It is my contention that if we are looking for a European identity, we are looking in the wrong place. Whilst racism and xenophobia tap deep roots in the consciousness of the mass of European citizens, the search for identity in history or high culture leave most of them indifferent (a painful admission for a professional historian!). The two things that have been generally overlooked in the discussion on identities are travel/tourism and sport.

At the time when the French foreign minister Robert Schuman made his call for the creation of Europe's first supranational community in May 1950, the only time that most Europeans had been abroad had been in the armed forces. However, as post-war welfare spread, holidays became more generous and rising disposable incomes made holidays away from home increasingly possible. In the UK, domestic mass tourism had started using abandoned army camps as 'holiday camps' and, at the end of the 1950s the expertise acquired was employed to foreign tourism – initially to Spain, where the summers were definitely sunnier. In Europe, the ability to afford a small car increased the ability for extended camping or caravan holidays abroad. In both cases the foreign destination was usually the focus of fellow nationals and they had the culinary infrastructure of the homeland. This began to change in the late 1960s and has been evolving ever since. For the young hitchhiking across Europe until the money ran out has been overtaken by interrailing (InterRail was started in 1972 for under-21s, though the age limit has since been abandoned), using overnight journeys to save on accommodation. I sometimes think that the InterRail Pass (a prepaid card entitling the traveller to unlimited rail travel within several European countries) is the greatest contribution to European integration. In my view, it is better than the ERASMUS programme which allows higher education students to spend time at foreign European universities, from which, at the last count, almost 200,000 students have benefited, because it is more accessible and possibly more used (since 1972, 6.8 million travellers have used the scheme). Meanwhile, the more affluent and older generations have largely abandoned 'package tours' for short weekend 'city breaks' abroad and for personally-designed vacations. Another factor whose influence should not be underestimated is that seven million EU nationals are living and working in countries other than their own. Sampling local culture, whether it be the street scenes or night clubs, the cathedrals or restaurants, has replaced the hedonistic pursuit of sunny weather. Knowing, seeing and experiencing other European peoples is breaking down national preconceptions based on ignorance and may even create an appreciation for some of the better things in life.

The writer George Orwell once said that sport was 'war without weapons' and national football teams are still fanatically supported.[20] However, we have lost most of the narrow-minded xenophobia of earlier years. I still remember the time when the English were so convinced that their domestic football was the best in the world that they did not even bother to enter the World Cup, which was seen as a competition for 'the rest'. Once they did join, in 1950, it took them sixteen years to actually win the trophy they had so despised, a feat they have managed only once. Move forward to today and look at the European Champions' League, representing all the top club teams in Europe. Most supporters can name the leading clubs of most European countries and know the best players in most of them. Many supporters follow their progress through their own national leagues and can comment, knowledgeably, on their style of play. The 2006 final was watched live throughout by an audience of 86 million people, with millions more tuning in for part of the game.

Surpassing even this, in terms of 'low culture' is the Eurovision Song Contest, which is now in its 51st year. For long it was denigrated as an international glitzy, kitsch song contest (and loved as such) but its expansion to Eastern Europe and the former Soviet Union has given it a new edge. These new countries actually seem to take it seriously and pack the voting, usually for each other (much to the chagrin of longer-standing nations, some of whom now fail even to progress beyond the preliminary rounds). The finals last year attracted a television audience of over 150 million viewers, all of whom, if only for a while, considered themselves part of Europe.

CONCLUSION

By way of conclusion, I would contend that a European identity, or an identity with Europe, is being formed. It is not particularly associated with the European Union and it is not being achieved through the routes that most politicians (and most academics) seem to consider most relevant. It percolated deeper than the elites, is held more strongly by the younger generations, and it taps levels of emotions (positive and negative) that are unrecognised by most policy-makers. This is perhaps as well, since I doubt whether the officials in Brussels would know what to do with these developments even if they were prepared to recognise them. It is not a single identity, nor usually a dominant one, but it is basically appreciative of differences in, and unity among, the subcultures represented in Europe. Actually, the proposed EU motto – 'Unity in Diversity' – captures this identity quite well. Perhaps the EU should leave it at that for the time being.

POSTSCRIPT

This essay was published in Ma Xiaoqiang and G. Ying (eds.), *The European Integration and the Sustainable Development of Northwest China*, (World Book Publishing House, 2008). The book formed the end result of a EU-China European Studies Centres Programme in which Leiden formed the European anchor of a collaborative university project to establish a centre for European Studies in North-West China. The final conference took place in Xi'an, which was the capital of the first unified kingdom. It is not difficult to feel 'European' when you are in China, but it is much more difficult to explain why there are (still) over thirty separate nations in an area with less than half of China's population. I think that they are even more perplexed by our explanation of how Europe is governed – with its different levels and separate pillars – especially when compared with the formal structure of Chinese governance. Yet, at the core of the difference lies the fact Europeans still do not feel particularly European, at least not in the way that Brussels would like them to feel. This is an area that has been neglected for too long and may now begin to impose constraints on the freedom of action that organs of the European Union have enjoyed until now. At the very moment when more coordination and cooperation is deemed necessary to resolve the contradictions that have been permitted to emerge within the euro currency area, the popular mandate for action is almost exhausted. What the Chinese readership, at whom it was aimed, made of it, I do not know. For me, it was a chance to articulate my own position as a fervent pro-European but a trenchant critic of 'Brussels'.

18

The Landscape of European Studies

I seem to have spent much of my professional life involved with European Studies. My first teaching appointment was in the European Studies department in Manchester, which stopped me settling into the 19th-century niche which my PhD research should have afforded. I was pushed firmly into the 20th century and given a whole continent to master. And there, in the UK in 1973, at the edge of history and the cusp of the future, lay the European Economic Community. In that year, in my 20th century entry course, it warranted one whole lecture to itself. It eventually expanded to three, in a schedule of twenty-four. Then, in 1980, I went to the Netherlands, by now firmly committed to 20th-century research but my work on post-war reconstruction soon brought me face-to-face with the fact that Dutch national reconstruction was impossible without European reconstruction, and so I found myself grappling with early initiatives for European integration. This was the moment that European archives were beginning to open and interest in the period as a subject for 'serious research' grew. Since the Dutch archive regime was more relaxed than that of neighbouring countries, working in the Netherlands gave me a 'competitive advantage' and I began to work closely with the research group at the European University Institute in Florence. In 1987, I was appointed to the chair of Contemporary History there and became director of its research project on the History of European Integration.

I returned to the Netherlands in 1995 as Professor of Economic and Social History at Leiden University and found myself teaching a whole range of historical periods. However, I missed teaching European history to non-historians and I brought this to the attention of the faculty. At this time, student numbers were falling, and one reason given had been the lack of connectedness with the labour market. My personal moan, therefore, coincided with a policy change already underway. As a result, I was asked to set up and direct an undergraduate 'Practical Studies' programme, which began in 2001 and which included an interdisciplinary programme in European Union Studies. A few years later, we expanded this to embrace a fully-fledged Masters degree, which I directed until September 2012, by which time it had seen over two hundred graduates pass through its doors. I no longer teach in the degree, but I still do in a similar programme at Chulalongkorn University, Bangkok.

European Studies now is an accepted part of the curriculum in many universities, and elements of EU studies are integrated into the syllabi of many, many more. But this was not always the case, and nor is it always immune from attack. It shares with other area studies recurrent attacks on its area focus (too inward looking, too narrow, insufficiently contextualised) and on its interdisciplinary nature (lacking theory, content, rigour and depth). The purpose of this article is to examine the state of European Studies undergraduate and post-graduate education in European universities and not the state of research, although in the final section I will touch on that particular discussion since it obviously impinges on course design, especially in countries outside Europe that are developing European Studies curricula. The term 'European Studies' covers a wide range of curricular designs which, in part, reflects differences in intentions but also, in part, the evolution of the object of study – i.e. Western Europe itself. Because the object of this study and its subject both alter over time, I have adopted an historical approach to this article whereby I will start with an analysis of the origins of the European Studies movement in university education. After that I will examine various course designs, drawing largely on the UK experience – partly because it was one of the earliest and partly because it is better documented. Finally, I will touch on the debate on the current state of teaching and research and the perspectives it may offer for new course design.

THE ORIGIN OF EUROPEAN STUDIES

It is difficult to separate European Studies from the study of Europe. The study of Europe has been an integral part of the university scene for most of the 20th century, if not before. European art and literature have long been recognised as pervasive influences in shaping national cultures. European history has been a staple of university history degrees; Europe has figured in international relations and comparative politics courses in Social Sciences; it has formed an integral part of international trade and finance courses in Economics departments, and it has figured heavily in international and comparative law degrees. The European continent has always provided a context for viewing national developments in most European universities and not a few universities in North America as well.

The educational innovation of studying Europe as a region, and its study across disciplinary boundaries, is far more recent phenomenon. In the study of innovation a distinction is usually made between the moment of 'invention', which is usually a matter of being first, and the process of 'diffusion', whereby the innovation spreads through society. It is only when an innovation spreads that it begins to have a real value added. Some of the earliest initiatives remain among the boldest, and possibly for that very reason, had a limited diffusion effect. This applies to most of the specifically 'European' educational institutions created since the end of the Second World War. We will examine two of these, which are closest to traditional universities, in more detail below.

TABLE 18.1: EUROPEAN INSTITUTIONS OF HIGHER EDUCATION

Year of Creation	*Institution*	*Location*
1949	College of Europe	Bruges (Belgium)
1954	International Centre for European Training	Nice (France)
1975	European University Institute	Florence (Italy)
1981	European Institute of Public Administration	Maastricht (Netherlands)
1992	Academy of European Law	Trier (France)

Source: B. Rosamond, 'The Political Sciences of European Integration', paper presented to the 10th biannual conference of the European Union Studies Association, Montreal, 17-19 May 2007.

The College of Europe was created at the Congress of Europe in the Hague in 1948, organised by the various 'European movements' at the time. It envisaged a centre where young graduates could meet and engage in research. The College started in Bruges in 1949 with 22 students. Until 1972, its first rector was the Dutch federalist Henri Brugmans. Initially, the College was little more than a federalist think-tank, but as the first supranational experiments (as the European Coal and Steel Community in 1952 and the European Economic Community and Euratom in 1958) and the Council of Europe (created in 1949) began to have an impact, so these became objects of study in their own right. The intake climbed slowly, to reach 50 by the mid-1960s, 100 by the mid-1970s, 200 by the late-1980s. Until 1992-1993 the College awarded its students a Diploma in Advanced European Studies but in that year it introduced a thesis into the course requirements and started issuing separate Masters degrees in Law, Economics, Political and

Administrative Studies, and International Relations and Diplomacy. After that, the intake climbed rapidly to reach over 400 today.

The European University Institute found its origins in the Euratom Treaty. It was intended as a large undergraduate university devoted to the cutting edge of pure and applied science, with a bit of social sciences and humanities added to inculcate some European consciousness into the students. Somewhere along the line it mutated to a small postgraduate institute with no pure science at all, but with separate faculties of Economics, History and Civilisation, Law, and Social and Political Science. It is jointly funded by the European Commission and by the member states of the European Union. Its first president was Max Kohnstamm, who worked with Monnet in the ECSC and who became secretary-general of Monnet's 'Action Committee for a United States of Europe'.[1] Originally it was not envisaged that the Institute would award its own PhD degrees but, very early in its existence, this changed. In 1992 the Robert Schuman Centre for Policy Research was established within the Institute to link academic endeavour with the policy needs of an increasingly complex European Union. At present the Institute admits about 120 students a year into its programmes.

Impressive as the achievements of these institutions may be, their organisational form was not widely adopted elsewhere in Europe. It is worth noting, in passing, that both the College of Europe and the European University Institute awarded their degrees along the traditional disciplinary lines. Although many of their graduates found careers in 'European' affairs, either through Brussels or through national ministries, many more graduates have emerged through the traditional faculties of Europe's national university systems. As we observed at the start of this section, most of these had been teaching 'European' courses within their traditional structures for the best part of the 20th century. However, in the 1960s and early 1970s, universities began to mutate to accommodate a more comprehensive approach to the study of Europe.

The European Studies movement finds its origins in the 'Area Studies movement' that started in the United States in the 1930s, initially as a reaction against the grip of esoteric 'Orientalist' research within the study and teaching on Asia. The Second World War demonstrated the limitation of America's capacity to operate militarily and diplomatically in countries outside the West. After the war, and culminating in the National Defense Education Act of 1958, the US government responded to the scarcity and diffusion of scientific expertise on the countries of the Soviet Union and Asia, by funding centres in the Humanities and the Social Sciences in major universities.[2] About the same time, in addition to worries about the relevance of university teaching geared towards the production of colonial officers in a post-colonial world, the UK government was voicing similar concerns. In 1962 the government accepted the findings of the Hayter Report to concentrate and fund a limited number of interdisciplinary, area studies centres devoted to Asia, Africa and the Soviet Union.[3]

Although the creation of Hayter Centres did not embrace Western Europe, both their interdisciplinary nature and their area approach challenged the traditional thinking on the organisation of knowledge. Their creation, in the UK, coincided with a major phase of university expansion, including the establishment of new universities which were not bound by path dependency, as were many of the more established institutions. In favour of a more interdisciplinary approach, they argued that it was paradoxical that research advances seem to be accompanied by increasing specialisation while the increasing complexity of society requires knowledge and systematic experience outside the confines of a single discipline.[4] The challenge to traditional approaches to post-secondary education was being felt by students, too, as demand for social science courses (sociology, anthropology, psychology) soared. It was not surprising, against this background, that students who wanted to pursue the study of modern languages began to demand that they could do so through the medium of contemporary politics and culture rather than through the medium of high culture and literature. The imminence of the UK's entry into the European Economic Community added to the urgency and excitement, and by the early 1970s several European Studies degrees had been established in British universities.[5] It is not true, at least at an undergraduate level, that 'the study of the European Community became a backwater of international relations, and European integration was regarded as a peripheral one-off phenomenon'.[6]

From the start the 'European Studies' label covered a wide range of undergraduate course constructions. At this point in time, in contrast with the USA, taught Masters courses were rare in the UK. All courses taught a foreign language, but with one fundamental difference – the context was not literature or poetry but newspapers, parliamentary debates and government reports. Beyond that, some of the courses resembled traditional joint degrees – language and politics or language and history, or, more modern, language and business studies – except that these focused on Europe.[7] Others were more interdisciplinary. Some attempted to be more interdisciplinary – insisting that all students follow courses in politics, economics and history as well as one course devoted to the European Communities. Finally, at the other extreme, some universities seemed to have constructed their degrees by cutting and pasting, from various university syllabi, virtually every course with a 'European' label or one linked to a foreign (European) country.[8]

At this stage, the full impact of the European Union had still to make itself felt, but that soon changed. In the UK, the continued debate over membership continuously highlighted different facets of membership – the budget, the common agricultural policy, the issue of governance and democracy, the relation to the North-South debate, etc. Moreover the (admittedly limited) theoretical foundations of the emerging communities were being refined and tested, and these too, impacted course design. In the course of the 1970s, the European Community began to figure ever more largely in these degrees – in the basic courses and in the range of specialised options. This trend accelerated in the 1980s with the European Monetary System, the Mediterranean enlargements, the emerging structural/regional policies, the moves to a single market, and the a renewed upsurge in theory-forming and conceptualisation. By this stage, some courses were self-consciously choosing labels such as 'European Integration Studies' or 'European Community Studies' to distinguish themselves from those that had remained with their joint-honours or area studies focus.

EUROPEAN STUDIES COURSES: UNDERGRADUATE

In today's university landscape, it can be seen that European Studies courses have spread across the United Kingdom and into continental Europe. The confusion over labelling and content, however, has remained. What is striking is that the link with a major foreign language component, which was almost universal in the 1970s, has been broken.

In 2001, 80 institutions offering 120 undergraduate programs under the label of 'European Studies' were registered in the UK.[9] After weeding out those which were predominantly mono-disciplinary courses focused on Europe – i.e. European Law or European Business – there remained 54 institutions offering one or more degrees with a deliberate interdisciplinary bias. These were subsequently surveyed and the information collected forms the empirical basis for this survey. Of the respondents, 84 per cent offered specific European Studies degrees. The remainder offered European Studies within a Joint Honours structure, which could be a language (but where the language would be taught independently of the European Studies syllabus) or it could be with a discipline such as History or Political Science.[10]

In contrast with the 1970s, only slightly over one-third of undergraduate degrees had a predominant focus on foreign language acquisition. Fully half were based firmly on the social sciences and a further 13 per cent linked social sciences with other disciplines (usually history and/or economics). The study of Politics was compulsory in 80 per cent of the courses, followed by History (58 per cent) and Economics (43 per cent).[11] This heavy political science bias in undergraduate courses is even more marked in British postgraduate degrees. Half of the undergraduate degrees included a compulsory year abroad (i.e. they were four-year degrees) and many of the rest had provisions for a shorter foreign experience.[12]

Finally, turning to size, the UK survey reveals a serious contraction at undergraduate level over the past decade. In terms of student enrolment, there is a wide range of experience. There are a small number of very large degrees with 14 per cent of institutions reporting an annual enrolment of over 100 students and a further 8 per cent enrolled between 40 and 100 students – the rest were lower, some significantly so.[13]

FIGURE 18.1: THE RANGE AND DISTRIBUTION OF UNDERGRADUATE EUROPEAN STUDIES DEGREES IN THE UNITED KINGDOM

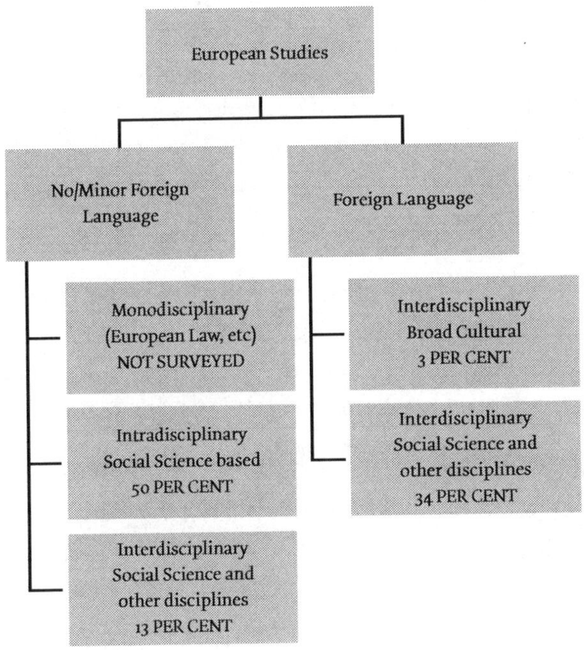

Source: M.L Smith, *The State of European Studies: Report Commissioned by the Standing Conference of Heads of European Studies* (London, 2003), 25.

A typical language-based European Studies degree would devote 50 to 60 per cent of the first two years to foreign-language acquisition. Most of the rest of the first year would follow a more or less fixed syllabus of introductory courses. Where the degree aspires to a tight link between the language and the European Studies content, there is not much choice in the second year, either. However, most courses opt for a looser structure and, while perhaps keeping one core course, will offer students various optional courses and may even offer separate tracks. At the furthest extreme, there may be little central syllabus at all with the philosophy that young minds should be left free to roam and that the brightest students would find a structure for themselves. While I have some sympathy for this approach at a Bachelors level, I have no tolerance for it at all at Masters levels. In the third year all UK language-based degrees offer students the opportunity for a year of study or work experience abroad, and most make it compulsory. In the final year, the foreign language component takes a back seat as students follow specialist courses and write an undergraduate thesis.

EUROPEAN STUDIES COURSES: POSTGRADUATE

Taught postgraduate degree programs only really took off in the UK in the 1980s and even today, certainly compared with the United States, the proportion of undergraduates continuing to a Masters is relatively low. On the other hand, throughout continental Europe, as a result of the Bologna reforms (that instituted a Bachelors/Masters/PhD cycle throughout the EU), Masters degrees are becoming more visible and are allowing a greater diversification of education at this level (including European Studies).

Of the respondents in the UK survey, half offered postgraduate degrees in European Studies. Almost half of the degrees had been created in the previous five years. In stark contrast with undergraduate degrees, the student demand seems to have been expanding[14] but the average size of intake is much smaller. Only 8 per cent of the degrees have an annual enrolment of more than 21 full-time students and 54 per cent have less than 10. If we take my own faculty's norm for 'viability' as 18 (successful) students, even taking into account part-time students (31 per cent of degrees have none at all and only 8 per cent have more than 10) most degrees seem unlikely to sustain themselves independently.[15]Many, presumably, survive by sharing modules with other masters programmes.

In the UK, the overwhelming disciplinary bias of Masters degrees is towards social science, which is basically, political science and public administration.

A full 71 per cent of degrees are based on social science alone.[16] The remainder combine social science with a language or with Business, Economics, History or Law. This does not necessarily mean that these are interdisciplinary – many degrees allow students to specialise in different tracks. Very few degrees at this level are based around a foreign language since, if one were to do so within a one-year programme, there would be little scope to do much else. Within a two-year programme (optional) language would be possible. On the other hand, it is worth observing that many students following masters programmes are actually doing so in a foreign language. In almost 80 per cent of Masters programmes, over half of the students are non-native English speakers.[17]

The structures of these UK degrees are very similar – it is the content that varies. The first semester is usually devoted to a core syllabus with at least one EU-oriented course (political theory, EU institutions, etc.) and, more often than not, a contemporary history course (usually focused on the EU). Occasionally economics and/or law is added and, depending on the room left, there may be one or more elective courses. Either in the first or the second semester, there is a compulsory course on research methods and research design. The second semester is built around a range of optional courses and the students' thesis (usually stipulated as being between 10,000 and 20,000 words). In the UK system, these second semester options are almost always based around political science, broadly defined. They may include courses on Comparative Politics, EU Decision-Making, International Relations, Policy Analysis or Political Economy. At best, such syllabi can be defined as intra-disciplinary, informed by relevant concepts and information derived from other disciplines (i.e. the remaining first semester modules).

In Leiden we have eschewed this model and have aimed at an interdisciplinary approach. To start with, we have made the focus of the degree not the EU itself, but the issue areas with which it is confronted, whether it confronts them or not. Since most of the issues are economic or political, concepts and theories from these disciplines are incorporated into the core first semester syllabus. Moreover, the EU has an impact on domestic and international law and, obviously, all the problems and the roads to their solution (or not) have their own history. Thus Law and History complete the range of core courses. In the second semester, students chose options from a wide range of specialised courses focusing on the issue areas, viewed from various disciplinary perspectives. Whilst the students may choose a single disciplinary approach in their essays, in their final theses, they have to place their findings within the relevant disciplinary frameworks of their selected topics.

Throughout this article, I have stressed that the European Studies courses taught in UK universities may not be typical for Europe as a whole, particularly in its political science bias. It is possible that multidisciplinary or interdisciplinary course structures (and we will address the difference below) may be more common elsewhere in Europe. If there is a bias in UK universities, one would expect also to find it in the distribution of its university staff and I have tried to show this by comparing the UK with five of the founding six members of the European Union.[18] One way to analyse this would be to look at the disciplines represented in national associations of European Studies. One argument against this approach is that membership composition might be a self-selecting, self-reinforcing process. Therefore, I have added to the analysis the disciplines represented in the national distribution of Jean Monnet Chairs funded by the European Union, which should reveal the collective priorities of institutes of higher education. The affiliation of the members of European Studies Associations is only surpassed in Europe by that of Denmark. And those of you who have always known that there was an Anglo-Saxon tradition of scholarship would not be surprised to learn that the political scientists made up no less than 78 per cent of membership of the USA European Studies Association. As far as the allocation of Jean Monnet Chairs is concerned, only Belgium, Denmark and Ireland approach the almost 50 per cent political science bias of the UK. Indeed, of the 705 chairs funded by the European Union only 26 per cent are in political science. Law is responsible for 41 per cent and Economics for 24 per cent. The USA only has eight chairs, which is not very representative, but seven of them are in political science – 87 per cent!

TABLE 18.2: DISCIPLINARY AFFILIATIONS OF EUROPEAN STUDIES UNIVERSITY TEACHERS (%)

Country	*Membership ES Associations*					*JM Chairs*				
	Pol. Sci.	*Law*	*Econ.*	*Hist.*	*Other*	*Pol. Sci.*	*Law*	*Econ.*	*Hist.*	*Other*
UK	50	15	20	5	10	48.5	31	17.5	2	1
Belgium	13	56	7	13	-	50	36	7	14	-
France	20	70	10	-	-	6.5	57	25	10	1.5
Germany	30	30	30	7	3	31	36	19	12.5	1.5
Italy	18	20	20	22	10	15	48	17	16	4
Netherlands	-	-	-	-	-	12	48	24	8	-

Source: Calculated from the data on membership of national ES associations at http://www.ecsanet.org and information on Jean Monnet chairs from the European Commission database at http://eacea.ec.europa.eu/llp/jeanmonnet/directory/ajmrepertoire/distrib.asp. Both sources were consulted in May 2008.

THE DEBATE ON EUROPEAN STUDIES

One of the debates on teaching and research has focused on the question of interdisciplinarity. This is not surprising since interdisciplinarity was at the core of the foundation of the European Studies movement – a 'battering ram' with which to storm the gates of an ossified academic system.[19] Before entering this discussion, it is worth clarifying the terminology, and recognising that the borders between definitions are absolute, but that there is a range of experience and ambition:

- Monodisciplinarity – the study and application of the theories and concepts of one discipline to relevant contexts
- Multidisciplinarity – the study and application of the theories and concepts of more than one discipline and applying each, in turn, to the relevant context
- Interdisciplinarity (medium definition) – the study and application of the theories and concepts of more than one discipline and applying them to the relevant context, whilst stressing their interrelationships
- Interdisciplinarity (strict definition) – the study and application of the theories and concepts of more than one discipline and applying them to the relevant context, thereby contributing to their fusion into a new conceptual framework
- Intradisciplinarity – the study and application of the theories and concepts of various approaches within a discipline and applying them to the relevant context

There are two reasons why any subject should be interdisciplinary. The first is that the complexity of subject studies requires the use of a range of disciplinary approaches to comprehend and resolve them. The second is that the theoretical and conceptual foundations of enquiry demand the use of different approaches and methods. Now, nobody claims that there is a mega-theoretical framework for the study of the European Union or contemporary Europe, and the processes that are shaping it. Part of the problem, therefore, is that for many political scientists especially, obsessed with the primacy of theory, the pragmatic approach smacks of description rather than analysis, journalism rather than science. This has led to a retrenchment as those area specialists that could do so returned to their faculty base, whilst the rest became marginalised and ghettoised.[20] Cini argues that European Studies became isolated from the discipline of politics, possibly by its interdisciplinary focus, with the result that it lost its disciplinary heritage and has even drifted towards non-disciplinarity.[21] Rosamond suggests that EU Studies is seen as little more than area studies. Critics condemn the research for being empiricist and for lacking explanatory power, or characterise it as being marked by sloppy scholarship and bad social science.[22]

Yet others argue that it is exactly the subject's attachment to political science that has been the root of the problem. Jupille, Caporaso and Checkel contend that metatheoretical debate among political scientists has hindered dialogue and fruitful empirical work. They see the EU as a 'living laboratory' within which one can study a variety of economic, social, political and institutional developments, none of which is unique to it. On this basis, they call for a refined dialogue based on empirical research to define the boundary conditions and causational spectrums (significantly, the rest of the article draws exclusively from political science publications).[23] And indeed there are signs that this is happening with a greater depth and range of scholarship being signalled in more recent literature surveys![24]

Tonra criticises EU Studies teaching (as opposed to research) for not being truly interdisciplinary but being rather a form of truncated multidisciplinarity 'where the expectation exists that students will establish their own mental synthesis after having been bombarded with different disciplinary views of the same phenomenon'.[25] My own undergraduate experience, where this is exactly what happened, would suggest that this is rather harsh, but I do agree that students would benefit from a more deliberate attempt to draw out the interrelationships.

A second debate revolves around what exactly the focus of European studies courses should be. Interestingly, this discussion gained new life through an attempt by UK political scientists to create a common core curriculum for the teaching of European Studies built around a 'hard core' of 'indispensable and fundamental components', including the history, theory, institutions and policies of the EU. In addition, the authors proposed the writing of modules that could be used in courses in various universities.[26] This initiative attracted a deluge of criticism. Some were worried that it would lead to a homogenisation of the field and, moreover, that it carried the risk that part of the syllabus would be captured by those advocating 'identity-building' for the European Union, in much the same way as nation state builders in the 19th century had done.[27] Others were worried that the common modules would lead to 'stultifying debate, boredom and sameness' and that it would freeze the study and would accentuate the trend, already present in political science-based courses, to view Europe primarily through the prism of the EU as the main actor.[28] Moreover, the creation of common core modules would downplay the diversity of national experiences within the integration process.[29]

This debate spilled over into a discussion of what exactly should be taught within the compass of European studies and, rather interestingly, dovetailed into the discussion of interdisciplinarity, or the lack of it. European Studies began as a form of area studies, linked to a concern to bring a more modern, contemporary and useful context to foreign language acquisition. As the competences of the European communities (and its membership) increased, and as theory-forming around it developed, so the focused shifted within many university courses, even to the extent, as we have seen, of losing foreign languages altogether. Many courses became European Community-oriented political science and/or pubic administration courses, whether they changed label or not. It is within this context that the discussion on the dynamism or inertia of European Studies as a field of research has taken place (few of the contributions made much mention of the work undertaken within other disciplines). Some courses, particularly those with interdisciplinary pretensions, did not take the European Union itself as a focus of study but took an approach of examining the factors behind increasing integration. Some courses went so far as to label themselves as European Integration Studies, to emphasise the difference in approach. Most of these courses were concentrated largely on Europe and in Europe. But the world has not stood still.[30]

Within the much-criticised political science literature of the European Union, there was a tendency to view the EU as a unique phenomenon and to explain the specificity of its character and development.[31] However, from the late 1970s, the scientific community and the world at large have been aware of a new phenomenon known as globalisation and it has developed new ideas, new concepts, new paradigms and a new vocabulary to analyse it. Within the globalisation literature the EU is one way of trying to manage the changes that increasingly volatile capital flows create. Another aspect of globalisation literature points out that what is seen as globalisation is, for a large part, an interlocking system of regionalisation, of which the EU is perhaps the most advanced experiment. Some authors argue that adopting these insights and applying them to the EU would enhance scholarship on the EU and provide an opportunity to introduce the EU experience into the globalisation discourse.[32]

For those planning to start European Studies degrees this turn in the debate offers new challenges and new opportunities. For one thing, seeing the EU within the context of global changes makes it more amenable to a comparative approach and, as far as that comparison stems from experience closer to home, it makes the contextualisation for non-European students easier to achieve. It also opens up a whole new research agenda where the domestic academic human capital can make an immediate impact in the discourse on regionalisation and globalisation.[33] There is no need to copy slavishly from existing models of European Studies degrees, which have their own path dependencies and meet their own societal demands. Indeed, now is the time to design exciting and relevant courses meeting today's societal demands and student interests – it is rather like being back in the early 1970s!

POSTSCRIPT

This essay is an amended version of a paper presented in Manila and published in M. Holland, S. Jora and P. Ryan (eds.), *The Future of European Studies in Asia* (Singapore, 2008). I have adapted it slightly and included it here because I am continuously frustrated by the careless way institutions treat their own history – the European Union goes to the other extreme. Since I have spent much of my career teaching and researching aspects of European integration, I felt that I should increase awareness of the development of the (sub)discipline and the challenges in teaching it at university level. One does not have to be an apologist for, or supporter of, the European Union in order to become engaged in teaching issues arising from the EU's existence. Indeed its teaching and research rewards a critical attitude and an interdisciplinary approach. But while I would argue that interdisciplinarity should anchor the core of undergraduate and postgraduate courses, it is here that the subject is most at risk. The fact that EU-based courses are being increasingly assimilated in single-disciplinary degrees is a welcome sign that the study is entering the mainstream, but is reduces the intellectual scope of enquiry. That after forty years of European Studies degrees, it still surprises me how fragile the subject remains in European universities and how defensive many of its practitioners have become. Perhaps a better awareness of the history of the discipline may encourage a more robust defence.

Notes

CHAPTER 1 (PP. 11-40)

1 The European Integration Experience, 1945-1958
The best textbook surveying the events in this chapter is Gerbet, *La Construction de L'Europe*.
2 Spaak; Monnet; Hirsch; Marjolin; Pineau and Rimbaud; Pflimlin; Uri.
3 Hoffmann.
4 See introductory chapters in Milward, *The European Rescue of the Nation State*, and Milward et al.
5 For recent surveys, see Milward, *The Reconstruction of Western Europe*, and Van der Wee.
6 Brown; Gardner.
7 See Milward, *The Reconstruction of Western Europe.*
8 The following provide different perspectives on the origins and functioning of the Marshall Plan: Carew; Ellwood; Hogan; Mee; Milward, *The Reconstruction of Western Europe*; Wexler.
9 De Long and Eichengreen; Eichengreen and Uzan; Milward, 'Was the Marshall Plan Necessary?'
10 The 'official' study is Kaplan and Schleiminger. See also Dickhaus; Diebold, *Trade and Payments in Western Europe*; Eichengreen; Milward, *The Reconstruction of Western Europe.*
11 Asbeek Brusse; Brown; Kock.
12 A classic is Brugmans. See also the four volumes in the series edited by Lipgens, as well as the voluminous works on Spinelli and the Italian federalists, but especially Pistone.
13 See the works of Preda, especially *Sulla Soglia dell' Unione*, *Storia di una speranza*, and 'De Gasperi, Spinelli e l'articolo 38 della CED'.
14 See Boekestijn; Mommens; Kersten; Meade et al.; Wiesglas.
15 Griffiths and Lynch, 'L'échec de la "Petite Europe": le Conseil Tripartite'.

16 Guillen, 'Le projet d'union économique entre la France, l'Italie et le Benelux'; Serra, 'L'union doganale italo-francese e la conferenza di Santa Margherita'.

17 Griffiths and Lynch, 'L'échec de la "Petite Europe": les négociations Fritalux/Finebel'; Guillen, 'Le projet d'union économique entre la France, l'Italie et le Benelux'.

18 Diebold, *The Schuman Plan*; Gillingham; Schwabe; Poidevin, *Robert Schuman*; Spierenberg and Poidevin.

19 For the functioning of the ECSC, see Diebold, *The Schuman Plan*; Haas; Gillingham; Palayret; Spierenberg and Poidevin.

20 There is a large literature on this topic, but see especially Vasori.

21 See Ireland; Kaplan, *The United States and NATO*; Kaplan, *NATO and the United States*; Leffler; Smith.

22 Another area with a huge literature, but see Guillen, 'Les chefs militaires français'; Melandri; Poidevin, 'La France devant le problème de la CED'; Volkmann and Schwengler.

23 Clesse; Fursdon; Köllner; Thoss and Volkmann; Volkmann and Schwengler.

24 Cardozo; Griffiths, 'Europe's First Constitution'. See also the essays in Trausch.

25 Griffiths, 'The Beyen Plan'.

26 Gerbet, *La Naissance du Marché Commun*; Küsters; and articles in Serra, *The Relaunching of Europe*.

27 Weilemann.

28 Griffiths, 'The Beyen Plan'.

29 Griffiths, *The Netherlands and the Integration of Europe*; Küsters; Milward, *The European Rescue of the Nation State*; Milward et al.; Serra, *The Relaunching of Europe and the Treaties of Rome*.

30 For the UK policy at this moment, see Burgess and Edwards; Griffiths, 'La dinamica dell'inertia politica'; Young, '"The Parting of the Ways"?'; Young, *Britain and European Unity*.

CHAPTER 2 (PP. 41-54)

1 For details of the origins of the ECSC, see Gillingham; Milward, *The Reconstruction of Western Europe*; Schwabe.

2 Brinkley and Hackett.

3 For details of the European Defence Community, see Dumoulin, *La communauté européenne de défense*; Fursdon; Volkmann and Schwengler.

4 Griffiths; Preda.

5 Asbeek Brusse.

6 Spierenburg and Poidevin.

7 For details of the relaunch and the subsequent negotiations, see Serra.

8 For an iconoclastic view, see Milward, 'The Lives and Teachings of the European Saints'.

CHAPTER 3 (PP. 55-88)

1 Speech by General George Marshall at Harvard University on 5 June 1947.
2 Speech by President Harry S. Truman to a joint session of Congress, 12 March 1947.
3 Price. See also Gomberg; Mallalieu.
4 Kindleberger.
5 Kaplan.
6 Kolko and Kolko.
7 Mastny.
8 Hogan.
9 Maier, 'The Politics of Productivity' and 'The Two Postwar Eras and the Conditions for Stability in Twentieth-Century Western Europe'.
10 Wexler. See also Mee.
11 *Foreign Relations of the United States* (FRUS), 1947, III, 204-219.
12 FRUS 1947, I, 734-750.
13 FRUS 1947, III, 220-223.
14 FRUS 1947, III, 224-230.
15 FRUS 1947, III, 230-232.
16 Hogan, 101-109.
17 Milward, 172-179.
18 Marjolin.
19 Hogan, 69-82; Milward, 80-89.
20 Spagnolo, 208-211.
21 Romero and Merli-Brandini.
22 Maier, 'The Politics of Productivity'.
23 Boel; Barjot.
24 Asbeek Brusse.
25 Diebold.
26 Dickhaus; Eichengreen, *Reconstructing Europe's Trade and Payments*; Kaplan and Schleiminger.
27 Asbeek Brusse.
28 Wexler, 148-151.
29 Cleveland.
30 Eichengreen, 'The Market and the Marshall Plan'.
31 Kindleberger.
32 Eichengreen and de Long.
33 Spagnolo, 209.

34 GNP figures in this paragraph are taken from Wexler, 251.
35 Milward.
36 Maier, 'The Two Postwar Eras and the Conditions for Stability in Twentieth-Century Western Europe', 341-342.
37 Milward, 97-98.
38 Eichengreen and Uzan, 24-26.
39 Eichengreen and de Long, 207.
40 Fodor.
41 Kindleberger.
42 Milward.
43 Maier, 'The Two Postwar Eras and the Conditions for Stability in Twentieth-Century Western Europe', 342-343, quote from p. 342.
44 Eichengreen and Uzan, 27-30.
45 Eichengreen and de Long, 209-210.
46 Milward, 101-107.
47 Kindleberger, 261-262.
48 Spagnolo, 261, 264-265.
49 Note that the low German levels come because FRG received much aid outside ERP, e.g. GARIOA aid, which had no counterpart fund arrangements attached.
50 Spagnolo, 479-495.
51 Eichengreen and Uzan, 46-47.
52 Eichengreen and Uzan, 48. See also Eichengreen and de Long, 216-217, and Casella and Eichengreen.
53 Esposito.
54 Wall.
55 Milward, 98-99.
56 Eichengreen and de Long, 6.
57 Eichengreen and de Long, 50-55.
58 Maier, 'The Politics of Productivity', 609, 614.
59 Maier, 'The Politics of Productivity', 613.
60 Maier, 'The Politics of Productivity', 615-617.
61 Maier, 'The Politics of Productivity', 624-627. For more details, see Carew; Romero.
62 Maier, 'The Politics of Productivity', 629.
63 Maier, 'The Politics of Productivity', 629.
64 Boel.
65 Wexler, 92.
66 Barjot.
67 Gimbel.
68 Milward.
69 Diebold; Milward.

70 Speech of Paul Hoffman to OEEC, 31 October 1949.

71 Asbeek Brusse.

72 Dickhaus; Kaplan and Schleiminger. For a more critical note, see Eichengreen, *Reconstructing Europe's Trade and Payments*.

CHAPTER 4 (PP. 89-112)

1 An earlier version upon which this article is based appeared in Italian in *Studi Storici*, 37, 1 (1996): 41-68. We would like to thank the editors for allowing this revised English language version to be published here. The abbreviations used in the footnotes are:
- BT – Board of Trade (see PRO)
- CAB – Cabinet (see PRO)
- NARA – National Archives and Records Administration, Washington, DC
- PRO – Public Record Office, Kew
- RG – Record Group (see NARA)

2 Porter, 663.

3 Milward; Griffiths, *Explorations in OEEC History*.

4 Edwards, 8-12.

5 Freyer, 1-4.

6 Hannah, 355-360.

7 Dell, 63-66, 114-115.

8 Swann, 115.

9 Strange, 117.

10 Haussmann, 69.

11 Ellwood,; Carew.

12 NARA, RG 469 Special Representative in Europe, Office of the General Counsel, Subject files, 1948-53, Records Pertaining to Restrictive Business Practices, 1950-53, Instruction A-252, 6.5.1950.

13 NARA, RG 469. ECA. Financial Policy and Trade Developments Division, Records Pertaining to Restrictive Business Practices, 1949-50, Country files, Trade and commercial policy working group, United Kingdom trade arrangements and controls, Cartel arrangements, patents licensing and technical assistance achievements, 17.8.1949.

14 Gillingham, 178-217.

15 NARA, RG 59, 840.054, Restrictive business practices program for enlisting labor support for the elimination of cartels and other restrictive business practices, 26.4.1950; RG 469 ECA Special Representative in Europe, Office of the General Counsel, Subject files, 1948-53, Records Pertaining to Restrictive Business Practices, 1950-1953, Possible role of information division in program against restrictive trade practices, EG/P(50)3, 29.9.1950.

16 NARA, RG 469, ECA. Financial Policy and Trade Development Division, Records Pertaining to Restrictive Business Practices, 1949-50, General records, Hoffman to American Embassy Paris, 10.3.1950.
17 Ibid., Excerpt from record of action staff meeting with the administrator, 15.8.1949.
18 Ibid., An ECA program for dealing with restrictive business practices, 20.9.1949.
19 Ibid., Address by Paul G. Hoffman, 10.11.1949 (Underlining in the original).
20 NARA, RG 469, Special Representative in Europe, Office of the General Counsel, Subject files, 1948-53, Records Pertaining to Restrictive Business Practices, 1950-53, Instruction A-252, 6.5.1950.
21 Ibidem.
22 Section 516 Mutual Security Act, 1951, quoted in NARA, RG 469 ECA. Special Representative in Europe, Office of the General Counsel, Subject files, 1948-53, Records Pertaining to Restrictive Business Practices, 1950-53, OEEC, Productivity and Applied Research Committee. Effect on Productivity of Restrictive Business Practices and Price Fixing, PRA(52)35, 6.10.1952.
23 Ibid, MSA Paris to MSA Washington, 29.8.1952.
24 Ibid., Draper to Washington and all MSA Missions, 22.8.1952.
25 Ibid., Telegram Riddleberger to Secretary of State, 4.12.1951.
26 Ibid, Memorandum ECA Activities on Restrictive Business Practices, 8.1.1951 (by A.H. Smith.).
27 Department of State (US) and Foreign Office (UK).
28 Brown, 125-131, 139-140, 222-226.
29 Brown, 130.
30 Public Record Office, Board of Trade (henceforth: PRO, BT) 64/4877, International Restrictive Business Practices, Annex to TN(56)5, 18.5.1956.
31 Lynch.
32 Gillingham, 255-261; Griffiths, 'The Schuman Plan Negotiations'.
33 Diebold, 399.
34 Spierenburg and Poidevin, 90-93.
35 Spierenburg and Poidevin, 99.
36 Spierenburg and Poidevin, 262-266.
37 Spierenburg and Poidevin, 442-445.
38 Rotthege, 218-219.
39 Wallich and Wilson, 396.
40 Rotthege, 222.
41 NARA, RG 469 SRE, OGC, Subject files, 1948-53, Restraint of Trade, 1948-53, Restrictive Business Practices in Western Germany, 27.1.1951.
42 NARA, RG 469 Agency for International Development, ECA, Financial Policy and Trade Developments Division, Records Pertaining to Restrictive Business Practices, 1949-50. Telegram, Bruce (Paris) to the State Department, no. 2469, 23.5.1950.

43 NARA, RG 469, SRE, OGC, Subject files, 1948-53, Restraint of Trade, 1948-53, Copy of inter-office memorandum, Enclosure no. 6, n.d.

44 Ibidem.

45 Ibidem.

46 Rotthege, 225-231.

47 Freyer, 228-229, 257.

48 PRO, BT 64/339, Cartel Policy: Covering Report, 8.11.1943.

49 Freyer, 244-247.

50 Stocking and Watkins, 357-362.

51 Freyer, 248-256.

52 NARA, RG 469, SRE, OGC, Subject files, 1948-53, Restraint of Trade, 1948-53, Andersen to Siegbert, 22.6.1949.

53 NARA, RG 469, FPTD, Records Pertaining to Restrictive Business Practices, 1949-50, Country files, Memorandum of Conversation, 13.12.1949.

54 NARA, RG 469, SRE, ORC, Subject files 1948-53, Restraint of Trade, 1948-53. Andersen to Siegbert, 22.6.1949.

55 Mirow and Maurer, 48-64.

56 PRO, BT 64/4882, Skene Brown to BOT, 10.8.1956; Skene Brown to BOT 28.8.1956; Monopolies Commission Inquiry into the Electrical Machinery Industry: Request for Excisions, n.d.

57 PRO, BT 64/4883 Minute Ackroyd, 4.12.1956.

58 PRO, BT 258/364, BEAMA's Overseas Agreements to Limit Price, 30.5.1957.

59 PRO, BT 258/365, Heavy Electrical Industry – Monopoly Commission Report. Brief for the President of the Board of Trade, n.d.; Eccles to Chandos, 15.7.1957.

60 Ibid., Chandos to Eccles, 19.7.1957.

61 Ibid., Note (Swindlehurst), 23.8.1957.

62 PRO, CAB 128/31, Minutes of Cabinet, 12.9.1957; CAB 129/88, Monopolies Commission Report on the Heavy Electrical Industry, Memorandum by the President of the Board of Trade, CP(57)193, 4.9.1957.

63 Kuisel, 357.

64 NARA, RG 469 ECA. Financial Policy and Trade Development Division, Records Pertaining to Restrictive Business Practices, 1949-50, General Records, Taquey to Oshine, 29.3.1950.

65 Ibid., Katz to Vienna Embassy, 10.5.1950

66 Ibid., Dowling to Department of State, dd.19.6.1950.

67 NARA, RG 469 Special representative in Europe, Office of the General Counsel, Subject files, 1948-53, Records Pertaining to Restrictive Business Practices, 1950-53, E. Flaherty to R. Blum, 11.3.1952.

68 Edwards, 28-30.

69 Mirow and Maurer, 144-147.

70 Edwards, 30.
71 *Business Week*, 16 May 1953.
72 Mirow and Maurer, 119-121.
73 Spierenburg and Poidevin.
74 Edwards, 28.
75 Mirow and Maurer, 43-46.

CHAPTER 5 (PP. 113-132)

1 The European Political Community derived its rationale and existence from the European Defence Community. The latter has been extensively researched by historians. Omitting individual articles and restricting ourselves to books, it is possible to recommend Aron and Lerner; Clesse; Fursdon; Köllner; Laird; Melandri; Riste; Thoss and Volkmann; Van der Harst; Volkmann and Schwengler; Wall.
2 Eyewitness accounts tend to skirt round the whole episode, with three exceptions: Linthorst Homan; Spaak, *Combat inachevés*; Spinelli. It is interesting to reflect that the English language version of Spaak's memoirs, *The Continuing Battle*, omits the chapter dealing with the EPC.
3 By contrast with the EDC, there is not a wealth of literature on the European Political Community and the Beyen Plan, so it is fairly easy to list all of it: Asbeek Brusse; Brizio; Cardozo; Fischer; Griffiths; Griffiths and Milward; Küsters; Lipgens; Preda, 'De Gasperi, Spinelli e l'art38 della CEA'; Preda, *Storia di una speranza.*

CHAPTER 6 (PP. 133-148)

1 This article is based a lecture I gave at the Academia Europea in Parma in June 1993. Some of the ideas have been shaped by a series of 'eyewitness' seminars Dr. Mansholt gave at the European University Institute, Florence, 17-20 April 1989. I would also like to thank my research assistant Anne Christine Knudsen for her help in its preparation.
2 The classic introductory text is Tracy.
3 Blum.
4 Barral; Lhomme; Perkins.
5 Fletcher; Olson.
6 Osterud.
7 Some of the best works were written at or close to the time. See Bacon and Schroeder; Taylor and Taylor; Timoshenko; Yates.
8 Cioccia and Toniolo.
9 Martin and Milward; Trienekens.
10 Milward, *The Reconstruction of Western Europe.*
11 Girvin and Griffiths; Milward, *The European Rescue of the Nation State*; Noel.

12 Küsters; Serra.
13 The following paragraphs have been taken from the delegation reports located in the Dutch central government archives in The Hague.
14 For accounts based on access to archives, see Von der Groeben; Burger.
15 Harris et al.; Marsh and Ritson; Fearne, 'The CAP Decision-Making Process'; Fearne, 'The History and Development of the CAP 1945-1985'; Saunders.
16 Commission of the European Communities.
17 Cited in Johnson, 48-51.
18 Mansholt; OECD; Rosenthal.

CHAPTER 7 (PP. 149-160)

1 Monnet, 353-355.
2 Milward, *The Reconstruction of Western Europe*, This builds strongly on the work of Lynch, 'Resolving the Paradox of the Monnet Plan'. For a recent survey of the entire problem, see also Gillingham; Schwabe.
3 The memorandum is published with other documents in Ziebura. When the memorandum was first published there was some discussion that it did not represent Monnet's true thinking but that it was intended to rather to provide some possible ministerial answers. See 'Diskussionsbericht zu den Referaten von Gerhard Keirsch und Christian Fenner', 211. This seems disingenuous and Schuman's biographer, Raymond Poidevin, is inclined to take it at face value. See Poidevin, 256-257.
4 See especially Barbezat 'Cooperation and Rivalry in the International Steel Cartel'; Barbezat, 'Structural Rigidity and the Severity of the Depression'.
5 Gillingham.
6 See, for example, Edwards; Mirow and Maurer.
7 Aron and Lerner; Clesse; Fursdon; Köllner; Laird; Melandri; Riste; Thoss and Volkmann; Volkmann and Schwengler; Wall.
8 Schuman, a 'European' within the ruling MRP Party, was deposed as foreign minister and replaced by his party colleague Georges Bidault, who adopted a far more patriotic line. The Socialist Party, openly 'European' on most issues, was split down the middle on this question.
9 Wiebes and Zeeman.
10 Van den Harst.
11 The socialist prime minister, Willem Drees, was as antipathetic towards supranational constructions as was his Belgian counterpart. The 'neutral' foreign minister in charge of European affairs, Johan-Willem Beyen, shared with the Calvinist economics minister, Jelle Zijlstra, a functional view of the possible uses of an economic community. The other foreign minister, Joseph Luns, treated the move towards integration with a disinterest that was later to get him into trouble with parliament.

Drees' fellow socialist and minister for agriculture, Sicco Mansholt, was the most federalist member of the cabinet and was willing to surrender virtually all Dutch positions to ensure the creation of these new communities.

12 This included Secretary of State John Foster Dulles' 'agonising reappraisal' of continuous US troop presence if Europe refused to take stronger measures in its own defence.

13 Frances Lynch suggests June 1956, when the UK first proposed an OEEC-wide free trade area (Lynch, 'Restoring France', 83-84). The problem with this is that the UK did not propose a free trade area at that time and there was no indication that any of the parties took the 'threat' that one would come as a serious challenge. Hans-Jurgen Küsters leaves the decision as late as November 1956, as part of the package announced after the Mollet-Adenauer meeting after the Suez debacle (Küsters). This places too much stress on the resolution of questions of detail and anyway the main lines of compromise were already in place before Suez. Like other meetings of great statesmen, there is a need to announce *something* afterwards.

14 Asbeek Brusse.

15 Milward, *The European Rescue of the Nation State*, 30-31.

16 See Girvin and Griffiths.

17 Milward, *The European Rescue of the Nation State*, 309-313.

CHAPTER 8 (PP. 161-176)

1 See, for example, Allison, 10-38. See also Verba. For a critical discussion, see Brennan and Pincus. The abbreviations used in the footnotes are:

- BT – Board of Trade (see PRO)
- CAB – Cabinet (see PRO)
- FO – Foreign Office (see PRO)
- MAZ – Ministerie Algemene Zaken (The Hague)
- PRO – Public Record Office, Kew
- T – Treasury (see PRO)

2 Hoffman, 35.

3 Mayer, 82, 122, 124.

4 PRO, FO 371/122034, Home to Macmillan, 3.9.1956.

5 The government received annual Economic Surveys, whose analysis was couched in these terms.

6 PRO, BT 11/5002, European Economic Integration, 20.2.1956.

7 PRO, CAB 134/1240, The TUC and Closer Economic Association with Europe, ES(E1)(56)3, 5.11.1956.

8 PRO, CAB 134/1240, Meeting of Economic Planning Board, ES(E1)(56)69, 30.10.1956.

9 PRO, FO 317/1220209, United Kingdom Initiative in Europe: Effect on United Kingdom Industry of Our Entering a Free Trade Area in Europe, 21.6.1956.

10 PRO, CAB 134/1244, Report on Duty Free Entry for Commonwealth Goods, ES(QT)(56)11, 5.5.1956.

11 Ibid., Minutes of the Subcommittee of the Committee on the Abolition of Quantitative Restrictions and Tariff Policy, 16.3.1956.

12 For the text of the declaration, see Bullen and Pelly, 723-724.

13 Among the exceptions was W. Armstrong from the Treasury. Having acknowledged that the Commonwealth represented a good thing in itself, he warned against too simplistic a consensus which might be nothing more than a silk facade. PRO, T 234/195, Evolution of the Commonwealth, 28.1.1956.

14 These developments can be traced through the archives in PRO, T 232/150.

15 PRO, FO 317/78022 Speech of Sir Stafford Cripps to Council of OEEC, 1.11.1949.

16 PRO, FO 317/16038 Wier to Coulson, 6.5.1955.

17 Ibid., Note Eden 14.5.1955.

18 PRO, CAB 134/1026 Minutes of Mutual Aid Committee, 16.6.1955.

19 PRO, CAB 128/29 Minutes of Cabinet, 30.6.1956.

20 PRO, FO 371/116042 Record of a Meeting in the Secretary of State's Room, 29.6.1955.

21 PRO, FO 371/116041 Minute Eden 11.7.1955.

22 PRO, CAB 134/1026 Minutes of Mutual Aid Committee, 15.7.1955.

23 PRO, CAB 134/1029, European Common Market: Draft Preliminary Report to Ministers MAC(55)165.

24 PRO, CAB 134/1030, The United Kingdom and a European Common Market, MAC(55) 199; The Political Implications of a European Common Market, MAC(55)200; The Economic Implication of a European Common Market, MAC(55)201.

25 PRO, CAB 134/1030, The Economic Implication of a European Common Market, MAC(55)201.

26 PRO, CAB 134/1030, The United Kingdom and a European Common Market: Report by a Working Party of Officials, MAC(55)199.

27 Ellis-Rees, head of the UK delegation to the OEEC, having outlined the success of this strategy in the past, urged adopting it once more to derail the Messina initiative. PRO, FO 317/116050 Ellis-Rees to Macmillan, 11.10.1955.

28 PRO, FO 371/116039, Messina Conference and OEEC, 16.6.1955.

29 PRO, FO 371/116040, Jebb to Macmillan, 15.6.1955.

30 PRO, FO 371/116043 Eden to de Peyter, 25.7.1955.

31 PRO, CAB 134/1044, Bretherton to Turnbull, 4.8.1955 (MASC (ECM)(55)8). This point was also echoed by another member of the UK delegation at the Brussels talks (PRO, FO 371/116045, Boothby to Coulson, 9.8.1955.).

32 PRO, CAB 134/1026, Minutes of Mutual Aid Committee, 27.10.1955. It was clear that the Treasury shared the Foreign Office view that the Six would fail. PRO, T 234/181, Note of

a Meeting Held in Sir B. Gilbert's room, 27.10.1955. See also Burgess and Edwards, 407-408; Ellison, 31-32.

33 PRO, CAB 134/889, Minutes of Economic Steering Committee, 1.11.1955. The only dissenting voice was that of Sir Frank Lee, permanent under-secretary to the Board of Trade, who felt that the economic advantage lay in joining. Since he was in a minority, he did not press his point.

34 PRO, CAB 134/1226, Minutes of Economic Policy Committee, 11.11.1955.

35 PRO, FO 371/116056, Watson to Eden, 10.11.1955.

36 PRO, T 234/181 Wright to Bretherton, 18.11.1955.

37 PRO, CAB 134/1030, Statement by Sir Hugh Ellis-Rees, 6 December 1955. This caused huge resentment among the Six and among the Benelux states in particular (ibid., Economic Cooperation in Europe – Discussion in Western European Union Council MAC(55)239 and PRO, T 234/182 Ellis-Rees to Wright 21.12.1955) and elicited a prompt response from the US State Department to desist immediately (PRO, FO 371/116056 Dulles to Macmillan 12.12.1955).

38 PRO, T 234/182, Bretherton to Wright, 22.12.1955.

39 In this context, see Allison, 67-100. For more detail, see Marsh and Simon; Marsh; Simon, *Models of Man*; Simon, *Administrative Behavior*; Marsh and Olsen.

40 The memorandum was sent on 10 May. See PRO, FO 317/16038 Warner to Coulson, 10.5.1955.

41 Griffiths.

42 See note 31.

43 PRO, FO 371/122022, Thorneycroft to Eden, 20.1.1956. See also Milward, *The European Rescue of the Nation State*, 428-429.

44 PRO, T 234/183, Minute Macmillan, 6.2.1956. Also quoted in Kaiser, 62.

45 This concern stemmed from two sources – one from the existing (and growing) imbalance of benefits to the UK arising from Commonwealth preferences and the second from the contradiction implicit in pressing for trade liberalization while maintaining a network of discriminatory trade agreements.

46 PRO, FO 371/122024, Working Group on a United Kingdom Initiative in Europe. Minutes of the Fifth Meeting, 29.3.1956.

47 PRO, FO 371/122025, T234/190, Working Group on a United Kingdom Initiative in Europe: Second Draft Report, 13.4.1956.

48 There passed a period of five weeks between the completion of the final report and the ministerial meeting that considered it. PRO, T 234/190, Record of Conclusions of a Meeting Held in the Chancellor of the Exchequer's Room, Treasury, on 31st May 1956.

49 PRO, FO 371/122029, United Kingdom Initiative in Europe: Minutes of First Meeting of Working Group held at the Treasury on 21st June 1956.

50 PRO FO 317/122032 United Kingdom Initiative in Europe. Plan G. Final Report of the Working Group 23.7.1956 EI(56)14.
51 PRO, CAB 134/1240, Note of a Meeting with TUC Representatives Held at HM Treasury on 23rd October 1956. Closer Economic Association with Europe, ES(EI)(56)63, 25.10.1956. Views of the Federation of British Industries, ES(E1)(56)74, 5.11.1956.
52 Girvin and Griffiths.
53 PRO, FO 371/122029, United Kingdom Initiative in Europe: Agricultural and Horticultural Items which Might Be Excluded from the Operation of a European Free Trade Area. Note by Tariff Division (Board of Trade), EI(56)3, 21.6.1956. PRO, T 234/196, The Relative Importance of the Increase in Trade That Might Result from Plan G. Note by the Economics Section, n.d. (probably mid-August 1956).
54 PRO, FO 371/16039 Aitken to Macmillan 8.6.1956.
55 See note 32.
56 Griffiths and Asbeek Brusse.
57 PRO, CAB 129/76 Note of a Meeting in the Chancellor of the Exchequer's Room, 21.6.1956.
58 Küsters.
59 MAZ, 351:88(4)073:32 Nederlandse Delegatie bij de Intergouvernmentele Commissie ingesteld door de Conferentie van Messina, Weekbericht Nr 2, 2 t/m 5.8.1955.
60 Ibid., Weekbericht 7, 27, t/m 30.9.1955.
61 PRO, CAB 128/30, Minutes of Cabinet, 18.9.1956. CM(56)66.
62 Ibid., Minutes of Cabinet, 14.9.1956. CM(56)65. PRO, FO 371/122033 United Kingdom Commercial Policy, 9.8.1956.
63 See note 61.
64 PRO, CAB 128/83 Plan G and the Commonwealth: Memorandum by the Secretary of State for Commonwealth Relations CP(56)267 7.9.1956. PRO, FO 371/122034 Note to Macmillan 3.9.1956.
65 See note 61.
66 PRO, CAB 129/82, United Kingdom Commercial Policy: Memorandum by the Chancellor of the Exchequer and the President of the Board of Trade, CP(56)192, 28.7.1956. CAB 129/83, *Plan G: Memorandum by the Chancellor of the Exchequer*, CP(56)208, 11.9.1956. CAB 129/84 Commercial Policy (Plan G) Memorandum by the Chancellor of the Exchequer and the President of the Board of Trade CP(56)252, 30.10.1956.
67 In his memoirs, Macmillan sees the press conference of 3 October as the decisive point in getting the plan through Cabinet (Macmillan, 85).
68 PRO, FO 371/122039 Memorandum to Ministries of Foreign Affairs, 9.11.1956.

CHAPTER 9 (PP. 177-206)

1 The best textbook surveying the events in this chapter is Gerbet, *La Construction de L'Europe*.

2 Du Bois; Camps; Griffiths, 'The Failure of the Wider European Free Trade Area'; Young.

3 Du Bois; Griffiths, 'The Importance of Fish in the Creation of EFTA'.

4 For an outline of EFTA's provisions, see Curzon; Meyer; Worswick.

5 Lindberg.

6 Barclay.

7 For archive-based studies, see Horne; Griffiths and Ward. More traditional accounts are: Beloff; Camps; Jeserich; Jouve; Kaiser; Newhouse.

8 See Griffiths and Ward; Miljan.

9 Barnavi and Friedländer; Bodenheimer; Gerbet, 'The Fouchet Plan'; Jouve; Pattison de Ménil; Silj.

10 For the record, he isolated the first Delors Commission as the second example.

11 Paxton; Swann; Von der Groeben.

12 For the List G problem, see Rhenish.

13 Casadio; Curzon and Curzon; Kock. For the first archive-based study, see Alkema.

14 Cosgrove-Twitchett; Feld; Hasenpflug; Moss.

15 The first archive-based study is Burger. See also Harris et al.; Marsh and Ritson; Fearne; Saunders.

16 Mansholt; OECD.

17 Josling and Harris.

18 Corbet and Robertson; Curzon.

19 Allen; Cairncross et al.; Davidow; Layton; Swann and McLachlan; Van Gerven.

20 Edwards.

21 Balassa; Davenport; Mayes; Sellekaerts; Verdoorn and Schwartz.

22 Verdoorn and Schwartz. See also Prewo.

23 Emminger; Kruse; Ludlow, *The Making of the EMS*; Simard; Tew; Tsoukalis.

24 For example, in 1959 P. Wigny proposed an EEC Unit of Account; in 1959 the Parliament proposed a Reserve System; in 1961 the Monetary Committee named centralization of monetary decisions a step forward and in 1962 the Commission submitted an Action Program for the second stage of the Common Market in which it dealt also with monetary integration.

25 Young; George. See also Brandt; Franck; Kolodziej.

26 *EEC Bulletin*, 1/1970.

CHAPTER 10 (PP. 207-228)

1 Abbreviations in the notes:
- BA – Bundesarchiv, Koblenz
- CAB– Cabinet (see PRO)
- DE/CE – Direction Économique, Service de Coopération Économique (see MAE)
- FO – Foreign Office (see PRO)
- HAEC – Historical Archives of the European Communities, Florence
- MAE – Ministère des Affaires Etrangères, Paris
- NARA – National Archives and Records Administration, Washington, DC
- PREM – Prime Minister's Office (see PRO)
- PRO – Public Record Office, Kew
- RG59 – Record Group 59, State Department (see NARA)
- T – Treasury (see PRO)

2 HAEC, OEEC Archives, 13/3, Cahan to Sergent, 31.12.1958.

3 It would, in a couple of years, become a cause of embarrassment for Europe as well.

4 Burgess.

5 The Six had been discussing a customs union within the context of their negotiations for a European political community. When, in the summer of 1954, these had petered out, it had been apparent that France had been resolutely opposed. Not wanting to invite a new failure at the outset of the European 'relaunch', Monnet and Spaak had originally been sceptical about including it in the Benelux memorandum. They had preferred sticking to their original plan of extending the ECSC to cover atomic energy, a field that they knew interested the French.

6 PRO, FO 371/116038, Ellis-Rees to FO, 7.6.1955.

7 The government sanctioned an OEEC heads of delegation meeting to make the announcement. To the fury of the Benelux countries, in particular, Ellis-Rees used the occasion to brand the initiative as premature and to accuse the Six of attempting to divide Europe into two camps. PRO, CAB 134/1030, Statement by Sir Hugh Ellis-Rees, 6 December 1955.

8 PRO, FO 371/122022, Thorneycroft to Eden, 20.1.1956.

9 PRO, T 234/190, Record of Conclusions of a Meeting held in the Chancellor of the Exchequer's Room, Treasury, on 31st May 1956.

10 Chancellor of the Exchequer and the President of the Board of Trade.

11 PRO, CAB 129/82, Organisation for European Economic Cooperation and Tariffs, Memorandum by the Chancellor of the Exchequer and the President of the Board of Trade, CP(56)172, 9.7.1956; CAB 128/30, Minutes of Cabinet, 12.7.1956.

12 PRO, T 234/195, Bretherton to Cohen, 23.7.1956. This account is somewhat at odds with the upbeat account in Macmillan's memoirs. See Macmillan, 79.

13 OEEC, *Report on the Possibility of Creating a Free Trade Area in Europe.*

14 PRO, T 234/375, Projet français associant à la Communauté Économique européenne les autres pays européens au sein d'une Union Européenne de Coopération Économique.
15 *Foreign Relations of the United States*, 1955-1957, IV, 450-453
16 NARA, RG59/440.002/1853, Department of State Instruction, 31.1.1958, 13.2.1958.
17 NARA, RG59/440.002/1853, Paris to Secretary of State, 19.2.1958; Luxembourg to Secretary of State, 26.2.1958; RG59/440.002/1854, Paris to Secretary of State, 1.3.1958.
18 Figures taken from *Survey of Current Business, 1968*, and converted into the earlier system of categorisation up until 1965. The American practice of including short-term capital is not common in Europe. However, in this case the figure is extremely small and does not distort the overall picture.
19 NARA, RG59/440.002/1853, State Department Circular, 20.2.1958; RG59/440.002/1854, State Department Circular, 20.3.1958.
20 PRO, FO 371/134528, Foreign Office to OEEC Delegation, 4.7.1958.
21 PRO, PREM 11/2532, Maudling to Macmillan, 30.9.1958.
22 MAE, DE/CE 754, Note 6.10.1958. This position was greeted with frank incomprehension by the British (PRO, T 234/378, Record of a Meeting Held in the Paymaster General's Office [...] Tuesday 14th October 1958) and it was also raised in the Maudling Committee later that month.
23 NARA, RG59/440.002/1855, Paris to Department of State, 30.10.1958.
24 MAE, DE/CE 754, Alphand to MAE, 31.10.1958; NARA 59/440.002/1855, Department of State Circular, 3.11.1958. The following day, the French embassy sought clarification of the US priorities, that the USA had no intentions to intervene, that it only supported an OEEC solution 'if possible'.
25 Quoted in Macmillan, 457-458.
26 NARA, RG59/440.002/1855, State Department Circular, 8.11.1958.
27 NARA, RG59/440.002/1855, Paris to Secretary of State, 18.11.1958; Luxembourg to Secretary of State, 19.11.1958.
28 Many French and Italian tariffs would have had to come down eighteen months later as part of the realignment to the new common external tariff (CET), so the concession was not as great as it seemed. Moreover, the mutual concessions on the Benelux tariffs that lay below the CET were not globalised.
29 HAEC, OEEC Archives, 24/3(80), Council 423rd session, 15.12.1958.
30 The problem was resolved when, at the end of December, France returned to 90 per cent liberalisation as part of a sweeping package of economic reform that included a second devaluation, the restoration of convertibility and the full acceptance of EEC obligations.
31 Compare the European data in OEEC, *Twelfth Annual Economic Review*, 185, with the data for the USA in Hieronymi, 119.
32 See Griffiths.

33 BA, B 136, 2598, Vialon to Adenauer, 28.1.1959; MAE, DE/CE 745, CIE Note a.s. politique commerciale extérieure de la CEE, 30.1.1959. HAEC, Premier mémorandum de la Commission de la Communauté Économique Européenne au Conseil des Ministres de la Communauté en exécution de la decision du 3.12.198 relatif aux problèmes posés par la création d'une Association économique européenne, 26.2.1959, COM(59)18 Rev 2.

34 Marjolin's rationalisation of the Commission's report to Butterworth carefully mirrored all the American sensibilities. See NARA, RG59/440.002/1856, Brussels to Secretary of State, 4.3.1959.

35 NARA, RG59/440.002/1858, Brussels to Secretary of State, 10.9.1959; Paris to Secretary of State, 24.9.1959; London to Secretary of State, 24.9.1959; RG59/840.00/4395, Luxembourg to Secretary of State, 25.9.1959.

36 NARA, RG59/440.002/1858, Department of State Memorandum of Conversation, 28.9.1959. Similar conversations were held with Lange, Luns and Segni.

37 Pinay made this statement in his budget speech on 6 November. He called for the quick removal of all quota discrimination against dollar goods (placing a two-year limit on quotas on manufactures), the reduction of the EEC's external tariff on the basis of reciprocity and an early start to GATT negotiations.

38 NARA, RG59/440.002/1858, Department of State Circular, 13.10.1959.

39 NARA, RG59/440.002/1858, Department of State to London, rpt, 19.10.1959.

40 Senate Resolution 19.3.1959 introduced by Humphrey, Clifford Case, Cooper and Kefauver (S.Con.Res 17). Identical resolutions were tabled in the House of Representatives by Morgan, Carnahan and Zablocki (H.Con Res.146, 107, 108).

41 NARA, RG59/740.5/3159, Roper to Herter, 21.4.1959: '[W]e have tried to get the document to correspond with what Clifford Case said you thought advisable. Maybe we're on the road to a convention that will show as much imagination in facing up to the problems of government in the twentieth century as another convention showed once in facing up to the problems in the eighteenth century.'

42 NARA, RG 59/740.5/3159, Merchant to Secretary of State, 4.5.1959.

43 This was a privately sponsored and privately directed event attended by some 600 citizens from fourteen of the fifteen NATO states; Iceland refused to attend such a meeting in London because of the 'cod war' between itself and the UK.

44 *The Times*, 6.6.1959, p. 7. The petition included such names as former President Truman, Adlai Stevenson, W. Averell Harriman, and future under-secretary of state, Chester Bowles. The full list of signatories and the text of the petition are in NARA, RG59/740.5/3160, Declaration of Atlantic Unity.

45 HAEC, OEEC Archives, Secrétaire Général, Réorganisation de l'OECE, 12/III, Cahan to Sergent, 16.6.1959.

46 NARA, RG59/750.5/3160, Paris to Secretary of State, *The Atlantic Congress, London, June 5-10, 1959*, 26.6.1959.

47 U.S.News and World Report, 13 July 1959

48 NARA, RG59/440.002/1857/, Birgfield to State Department, 3.8.1959. Tuthill to Acting Secretary of State, 11.9.1959.

49 NARA, RG59/440.002/1858, Memorandum of Conversation, 5.10.1959.

50 NARA, RG59/440.002/1858, Burgess to Secretary of State, 22.10.1959.

51 NARA, RG59/740.5/3162, Kohler to Under Secretary, 18.11.1959 and accompanying documentation.

52 NARA, RG59/750.5/3162, Herter to Burgess and Tuthill, 9.12.1959.

53 NARA, RG59/750.5/3163, NATO Parliamentarians' Conference, Report of the Economic Committee and Economic Committee Resolutions, November 1959.

54 NARA, RG59/440.002/1858, Memorandum for the President. Subject: Proposed United States Initiative to Mobilize Free World Resources for Development and to Strengthen Trade Relations, Proposal for US Membership in a Reorganized OEEC, 24.11.1959. These documents are reproduced in US Department of State, *Foreign Relations of the United States, 1958-1960, Vol. 4, Foreign Economic Policy*, 58-62.

55 PRO, T 234/717, Mr. Dillon's Visit, Sixes and Sevens: Record of a Meeting Held in the Foreign Office at 3 pm on December 8, 1959.

56 PRO, T 234/718, Memo from Clarke to Treasury Officials; *Europe*, 4.1.1960.

57 An account of this meeting was given by a French official to Ellis-Rees, who duly communicated developments to the Treasury. PRO, T 234/721, Ellis-Rees to Clarke, Note for the Record: Dillon Proposals, 17.12.1959.

58 PRO, FO 371/150094, Harpham to Jackling, 5.5.1960. For Dillon's account of the events see NARA, RG 59/750.5/3612, Memorandum for the Secretary, 13.12.1959.

59 NARA, RG59/840.00/4397, Dillon (eyes only) to Herter, 15.12.1959.

60 NARA, RG59/840.00/4397, Dillon to Eisenhower, 16.12.1959.

61 NARA, RG59/440.002/1859, Herter to State Department, 19.12.1959.

62 The communiqué called for an informal meeting to be held in Paris with the object of 'furthering the development of the less developed countries', and 'pursuing trade policies directed to the sound use of economic resources and the maintenance of harmonious international relations' (Burgess).

63 Cahan had become increasingly impatient of French manoeuvring. For example, he condemned the French proposals in March 1958 as 'the most selfish, the most hypocritical and the most unrealistic approach to an international problem that I have ever seen in a document prepared by the government of a civilised country' (HAEC, OEEC Archives, 13/3, Cahan to Sergent, 24.3.1958). Later, he described their attitude as 'the negation of co-operation' (ibid., Cahan to Sergent, 23.6.1958).

64 PRO, FO 371/150076, Crawford to FO, 30.1.1960, reporting a conversation with Valery.

65 PRO, FO 371/142463, Ellis-Rees to Gore-Booth, 12.9.1959.

66 They were Ellis-Rees, Valery, Ockrent and Werkmeister.

67 PRO, FO 371/142463, Ellis-Rees to Gore-Booth, Note for the Record, 21.9.1959, 22.9.1959.

68 PRO, FO 371/150079, Ellis-Rees to FO, 16.01.1960.

69 For practical reasons, the meeting was not attended by all twenty OEEC member and associate countries, but by a cross-section of thirteen countries to represent the various interests. Most of these countries were from the EEC and EFTA, but Greece attended as a representative of the 'peripherals'. The thirteen countries were Belgium, Canada, France, Denmark, Germany, Greece, Italy, The Netherlands, Sweden, Switzerland, Portugal, the United Kingdom, the United States and a representative of the Commission of the EEC. PRO, FO 371/150091, Ellis-Rees to Gore-Booth, Note for the Record, 21.4.1960.

70 PRO, T 234/719, Paul Gore-Booth, Paris Economic Meetings, January 11-15 1960; Some Diplomatic Notes.

71 NARA, RG 59/840.00/4392, Legal Implications of US Accession to OEEC Convention, (Department of State Legal Advisor), 10.12.1959. Background Brief for Dillon by Button, 13.12.1958.

72 NARA, RG59/840.00/4396, Butterworth to Secretary of State, 18.11.1959, 11.12.1959.

73 PRO, FO 371/150076, Gore Booth to FO, 29.1.1960; FO 371/150077, Second Meeting of the Group of Four on Economic Organisation, Centre des Conférences internationales (Paris), January 29, 1960.

74 PRO, CAB 134/1819, Re-organisation of the OEEC. Memorandum by the Chancellor of the Exchequer, EQ(60)5, 8.2.1960.

75 PRO, FO 371/150091 Gore-Booth to FO, GOFEO: Comments by the UK Member on Report and Draft Convention, 20.4.1960.

76 A preference for the continuation of trade functions in the new organisation was expressed in varying degrees by the EFTA countries, the Benelux, Germany, Greece and Spain. PRO, FO 371/150079-81.

77 PRO, FO 371/150091, Gore Booth to FO, GOFEO: Comments by the UK member on Report and Draft Convention, 20.4.1960.

78 PRO, FO 371/150077, Twelfth Meeting, Centre International de Conférences, Paris, 8 February 1960; FO 371/150078 Gore-Booth to FO, 9.2.1960.

79 PRO, FO 371/150091, Gore Booth to FO, *GOFEO*: Comments by the UK Member on Report and Draft Convention, 20.4.1960.

80 PRO, FO 371/150093, Laver to Holliday, 4.5.1960.

81 PRO, FO 371/150094, Cullen to Holliday, 9.5.1960.

82 PRO, FO 371/150093, Gore-Booth to FO, 11.5.1960.

83 PRO, FO 137/150092 Ellis-Rees to Jackling, 26.4.1960.

84 PRO, FO 371/150094, Future of the Organisation for European Economic Cooperation. Paper Approved by the Minister of State, Foreign Office, 11.5.1960.

85 HAEC, OEEC Archives, 13/3, Cahan to Sergent, 31.12.1958.

86 PRO, FO 371/150079, Twenty-Third Meeting. Centre Internationale des Conférences, Paris, 22 February 1960, GF/CR/23.

87 PRO, FO 371/150094, Harpham to Jackling, 5.5.1960.

88 PRO, FO 371/150093, Gore-Booth to FO, 3.5.1960.
89 These fears were conveyed through numerous sources, including the German delegate to the OEEC, Werkmeister, and the German Commercial Counsellor in London. PRO, FO 371/150094, Hankey to Gore-Booth, 12.5.1960.
90 PRO, FO 371/150093, Kirk to Holliday, 29.4.1960.
91 PRO, FO 371/150095, Notes on the Swiss Draft Convention, 16.5.1960.
92 These fears had been expressed earlier within Arnold France's 'inner group' in the Treasury dealing with European economic cooperation. PRO, FO 371/150094, Rich to FO, 16.5.1960.
93 PRO, FO 371/150097, Hankey (OEEC) to FO, 24.5.1960.
94 PRO, FO 371/150098, Hankey to Selwyn Lloyd, 1.6.1960.
95 PRO, FO 371/150104, Hankey to Home, Ministerial Conference on the Proposed Organisation for Economic Cooperation and Development, 4.8.1960.
96 HAEC, OEEC Archives, 12/3, Cahan to Sergent, 24.12.1959.

CHAPTER 11 (PP. 229-242)

1 For recent archive-based studies see: Burgess and Edwards; Bullen; Young; Griffiths, 'La dinamica dell'inertia politica'; Griffiths, 'The British Attitude towards European Integration'. Abbreviations used in the notes are:
- BT – Board of Trade (see PRO)
- CAB – Cabinet (see PRO)
- FO – Foreign Office (see PRO)
- NARA – National Archive and Records Administration (Washington, DC)
- PRO – Public Record Office, Kew
- RG – Record Group (see NARA)
- T – Treasury (see PRO)

2 PRO, FO 371/122022, Thorneycroft to Eden, 20.1.1956.
3 PRO, T 234/190, Record of Conclusions of a Meeting held in the Chancellor of the Exchequer's Room, Treasury, on 31st May 1956.
4 PRO, T 234/190, Initiative in Europe, Memorandum by the President of the Board of Trade, 22.5.1956.
5 PRO, CAB 129/82, United Kingdom Commercial Policy CP(56)191, 27.7.1956; ibid., United Kingdom Commercial Policy. Memorandum by the Chancellor of the Exchequer and the President of the Board of Trade CP(56)192, 28.7.1956.
6 PRO, CAB 128/30, Minutes of Cabinet, 20.11.1956.
7 The classic of this genre remains Camps, *Britain and the European Community*. See also Camps, *European Common Market and Free Trade Area*; Camps, *The European Free Trade Association*; Benoit; Kaiser, *EWG und Freihandelszone*.
8 A thorough treatment from the English position is Macmillan, 61-88, 431-459.

9 Charlton; Du Bois and Hurni.

10 PRO, T 234/720, Free Trade Area Negotiations: Post Mortem (Figgures), 17.7.1959; Note (Clarke), 21.7.1959; Thoughts in Retrospect on the Free Trade Area Negotiations: 1956-1959 (Clarke) 18.1.1960.

11 PRO, CAB 134/1030, Statement by Sir Hugh Ellis-Rees, 6 December 1955. For the furious reaction of the Benelux countries in the WEU see Ibid., Economic Cooperation in Europe – Discussion in the Western European Council.

12 PRO, T 234/200, Macmillan to Heads of Government of the Six, 28/29.11.1956. At the time the Six were anxious to complete the treaty while there was still a French government in power willing to ratify it. Also West German elections were due.

13 PRO, CAB 134/1855, Meetings of Subcommittee on Closer Economic Association with Europe, 17.4.1957, 29.4.1957. CAB 134/1859, The Customs Union and the Free Trade Area. Next Steps. Report by Officials, ES(EI)(57)119 Final, 30.4.1957.

14 PRO, CAB 134/1859, Meeting of the Anglo-French Economic Committee Meeting in Conference Room A, Cabinet Office, on 16 April 1957, ES(EI)(57)118, 15.4.1957.

15 PRO, FO 371/128343, Record of Conversation between the Secretary of State and M. Pineau in Bonn on Friday May 3rd. FO 371/128344, The Rome Treaties and the Free Trade Area. Discussions with the German Government.

16 National Archives and Records Administration, Washington, (NARA), Record Group 59, 440.02/1850, Adams to Department of State, 29.5.1957.

17 PRO, Prime Minister's Office (PREM) 11/2531, Note by the Prime Minister in His Discussion on the European Free Trade Area with Mr. Maudling on March 17; Record of Conversation at the Hotel Matignon after Dinner on June 29.

18 PRO, T 234/720, Free Trade Area Negotiations: Post Mortem (Figgures), 17.7.1959; Wright to Clarke, 27.8.1959.

19 PRO, FO 371/116038, Ellis-Rees to Foreign Office, 7.6.1955.

20 Asbeek Brusse, 183-229. This was based upon a 'common list' of products in which trade was predominantly intra-European. Tariffs on these items were to be cut by 25 per cent and the reduction was to be extended to other GATT members via the MFN clause.

21 PRO, CAB 129/82, Organisation for European Economic Cooperation and Tariffs. Memorandum by the Chancellor of the Exchequer and the President of the Board of Trade, CP(56)172, 9.7.1956. See also PRO, CAB 128/30, Minutes of Cabinet, 12.7.1956, which approved these steps without discussion.

22 PRO, T 243/195, Bretherton to Cohen, 23.7.1956.

23 PRO, T 234/720, Free Trade Area Negotiations: Post Mortem (Figgures), 17.7.1959; Coulson to Clarke, 1.9.1959; Gore-Booth to Clarke, 1.9.1959.

24 PRO, T 234/720, Gore-Booth to Clarke, 1.9.1959.

25 PRO, FO 371/128343, Record of Conversation between the Secretary of State and M. Spaak in Bonn on Friday, May 3; see also FO 371/128344, Visit of Baron Snoy on 13 May.

26 PRO, T 234/720, Thoughts in Retrospect on the Free Trade Area Negotiations: 1956-1959 (Clarke) 18.1.1960.
27 PRO, CAB 128/30, Minutes of Cabinet, 18.9.1956.
28 PRO, T 234/196, The United Kingdom Commercial Policy (Butler), 9.8.1956. See also CAB 128/30, Minutes of Cabinet, 14.9.1956.
29 PRO, FO 371/122034, Home to Macmillan, 3.9.1956.
30 PRO, CAB 128/30 Minutes of Cabinet, 18.9.1956.
31 PRO, PREM 11/2136, Stuart to Eden, 14.9.1956.
32 PRO, T 234/720, Free Trade Area Negotiations: Post Mortem (Figgures), 17.7.1959; Note (Clarke), 21.7.1959; Gore-Booth to Clarke, 1.9.1959; Thoughts in Retrospect on the Free Trade Area Negotiations: 1956-1959 (Clarke) 18.1.1960.
33 PRO, T 234/201, Clarke to Ellis-Rees, 17.5.1957. See also CAB 134/1855, Meeting of the Subcommittee on Closer Economic Association with Europe, 14.5.1957.
34 PRO, CAB 128/89, European Free Trade Area: Agriculture C(57)219, 4.10.1957.
35 PRO, CAB 134/1861, Record of Conversation between Mr. Maudling and Mr. Gaillard ES (EI)(57)224.
36 PRO, T 234/720, Free Trade Area Negotiations: Post Mortem (Figgures), 17.7.1959; Note (Clarke), 21.7.1959; Gore-Booth to Clarke, 1.9.1959; Thoughts in Retrospect on the Free Trade Area Negotiations: 1956-1959 (Clarke) 18.1.1960; Bretherton to Clarke, 3.2.1960.
37 PRO, T 234/375, Note for the Record (Figgures), 18.4.1958.
38 PRO, T 234/375, Ellis-Rees to Foreign Office, 2.4.1958.
39 OEEC Group of Trade Experts. Report on the Proposals by Mr. Carli 25.3.1958 CIG(58)33 (HMG Negotiations for a European Free Trade Area 153-163) OEEC, Proposals by Mr. Carli. Report by the Steering Board for Trade 29.3.1958 CIG(58)35 (ibid., 163-164).
40 PRO, CAB 129/93, European Free Trade Area: Origin Problems. Note by the Paymaster-General C(58)110, 16.5.1958.
41 PRO, CAB 123/130, Minutes of cabinet committee for a free trade area 15.5.1958 GEN 580/4th Meeting. The full cabinet was subsequently informed of this decision, CAB 129/93 European Free Trade Area: Origin Problems. Memorandum by the Chancellor of the Exchequer 20.5.1958 C(58)114.
42 PRO, CAB 123/130, European Free Trade Area Negotiations. Memorandum by the Paymaster General GEN 580/9, 19.7.1958.
43 PRO, CAB 129/94, European Free Trade Area. Note by the Paymaster-General C(58)184, 9.9.1958.
44 PRO, T 234/720, Free Trade Area Negotiations: Post Mortem (Figgures), 17.7.1959.
45 PRO, T 234/720, Free Trade Area Negotiations: Post Mortem (Figgures), 17.7.1959; Note (Clarke), 21.7.1959; Wright to Clarke, 27.8.1959; Gore-Booth to Clarke, 1.9.1959; Thoughts in Retrospect on the Free Trade Area Negotiations: 1956-1959 (Clarke) 18.1.1960.
46 In addition to the literature cited in notes 8-10, see, for a first archive-based account, Griffiths, 'The Importance of Fish for the Creation of EFTA'.

47 PRO, T 234/720, Thoughts in Retrospect on the Free Trade Area Negotiations: 1956-1959 (Clarke), 18.1.1960.

CHAPTER 12 (PP. 243-266)

1 On the European side this article is based on: (1) the official reports of the EC finance ministers meetings, the discussion papers and the somewhat less full Dutch delegation reports, (2) the Dutch delegation reports of the EC monetary committee, the discussion papers and the official reports (which are more often than not useless), (3) the Dutch delegation reports of meetings of the G10 deputies and the less informative official reports and (4) the Dutch delegation reports of OECD WP3. American material has been obtained from the John F. Kennedy Library. Unfortunately, the Dillon and Roosa papers were inaccessible because they are still awaiting classification. The abbreviations in the archives are:

- DGES – Directorate-generaal voor Economische Samenwerking (MBZ)
- GT BBV – Generale Thesaurie, Buitenlandse Betalingsverkeer (MF)
- JFKL – John F. Kennedy Library, Boston
- POF/DA – President's Office Files, Departments and Agencies (JFKL)
- MBZ – Ministerie van Buitenlandse Zaken, The Hague
- MF – Ministerie van Financieen, The Hague
- NSF – National Security Files (JFKL)

2 MF, GT BBV 215, Code telegram van Roijen to Min. BZ 10.3.1961.

3 Figures taken from *Survey of Current Business, 1968*, and converted into the earlier system of categorization used until 1965. The American practice of including short-term capital is not common in Europe.

4 MBZ, DGES 996.27, Verslag van de vierentwintigste zitting van het Monetair Comite van de EEG te Brussel op 13 en 14 november 1960.

5 Ibid., Verslag van de vijfentwintigste zitting van het Monetair Comite van de EEG te Brussel op 13 en 14 december 1960.

6 Germany was contemplating an early repayment of $500 million, possibly in return for deblocking $200 million of 'enemy assets'. The EC-MC deplored the idea that such conditions become general. Ibid., Verslag van de zesentwintigste zitting van het Monetair Comite van de EEG te Brussel op 10 januari 1961.

7 Germany announced removing some quota restrictions and $600-700 million early repayment of US debt. There were also negotiations in progress on sharing local defence costs, but these were not expected to yield much of a dollar saving. Carli, the Italian Central Bank president, observed that although the conditions within Italy led many to consider capital exports '*comme une crime*', these had nonetheless increased so that in 1960 they had totalled $492 million.

8 MF, GT BBV 215, CEE Projet de procès-verbal de la sixième réunion des ministres des finances de la C.E.E. tenue a la Haye les 13 et 14 janvier 1961, II/507/61-F.

9 MF, GT BBV 147, Verslag van de twintigste zitting van het Monetair Comite van de E.E.G. te Brussel op 21 juni 1960. Projet de Compte Rendu de la Vingtieme session du Comite Monetaire (tenue le 21 juin 1960), 4.7.1960, II/3817/60-F.

10 MF, GT BBV, 215, CEE Projet de procès-verbal de la cinquième réunion des ministres des finances de la C.E.E. tenue a Luxembourg les 24 et 25 octobre 1960, II/6297/60-F.

11 MBZ, DGES 996.27, Verslag van de vijfentwintigste zitting van het Monetair Comite van de EEG te Brussel op 13 en 14 december 1960.

12 MF, GT BBV 215, CEE Projet de procès-verbal de la sixième réunion des ministres des finances de la C.E.E. tenue a la Haye les 13 et 14 janvier 1961, II/507/61-F. The UK replied affirmatively three days after receiving the letter. MF, GT BBV, 215, Zijlstra to Selwyn Lloyd, 17.1.1961, Selwyn Lloyd to Zijlstra, 21.1.1961.

13 MBZ, DGES 996.27, Verslag van de negenentwintigste zitting van het Monetair Comite van de EEG te Brussel op 14 en 15 april 1961. Emminger explained that a 7 per cent revaluation had been considered but the acceleration in wages, which at 9.5 per cent in 1960 had outstripped productivity, had made that impossible.

14 MF, BBV GT 215, CEE, Document de travail établi en vue de la session de Mars de la Conférence des Ministres des Finances, 10.3.1961, II-6/FBGms/10.III.

15 JFKL, White House Central Subject File, 242/FO4, also POF/DA, 73 (CEA), Memorandum for the President, International Monetary Reform and Related Problems (Heller), 18.3.1961.

16 Strange, 84-85. The operation to prop up sterling continued to the end of the year. The most outstanding had been £325 million, but during the crisis the UK had also borrowed £536 million from the IMF and arranged a standby credit of £179 million. The swap agreements were not used again until February and March 1963. Again the UK was the beneficiary. Tew, 136.

17 Strange, 107-109.

18 MBZ, DGES 996.27, Verslag van de achtentwintigste zitting van het Monetair Comite van de EEG te Brussel op 1 maart 1961.

19 MF, GT BBV 215, CEE, Procès verbal de la septième réunion des ministres des finances de la C.E.E. tenue a Dusseldorf les 20 et 21 mars 1961, II/2487/61-F.

20 JFKL, POF/DA 73 (CEA), Memorandum for the President, Paris Report No3: International Monetary Developments and French Recalcitrance (Heller), 16.5.1961.

21 Strange, 108-109.

22 JFKL, POF/DA 89 (Treasury), Memorandum for the President, (Dillon), 5.7.1961. This was to be borrowed (on the basis of art VII of its Statutes) for 3 to 5 years and was to be denominated in creditor currency. It would be repaid either in gold or in the creditor's currency, thus guaranteeing the loans against the effects of any devaluation.

23 MF, GT BBV 215, Procès-verbal de la huitième réunion des ministres des financies des pays de la C.E.E. tenue a Ostende les 17 et 18 juillet 1961, 12.9.1961, II/5409/61-F. Verslag van de achtse Conferentie van de Ministers van Financien van de landen van de Europese Economische Gemeenschap gehouden op 17 en 18 juli 1961 te Ostende.

24 MF, GT BBV 216, Dillon to Zijlstra 22.8.1961.

25 Ibid., Procès-verbal de la neuvième réunion des ministres des finances des pays de la C.E.E. tenue a Bad Godesberg le 5 septembre 1961, 28.11.1961, II/6130/61-F. Verslag van de negende Conferentie van de Ministers van Financien van de landen van de Europese Economische Gemeenschap gehouden op 5 septembre 1961 te Bad-Godesberg.

26 Ibid., Statement Relating to Creation of Special Resources for use by Participating Countries through the International Monetary Fund, Draft Decision of Executive Directors on General Arrangements to Borrow, n.d. end November 1961. See also Horsefield, I, 510-511.

27 JFKL, NSF/DA 289, Memorandum for the President (Dillon), 25.9.1961.

28 MF, GT BBV 216, Projet de Procès-verbal de la dixième réunion des ministres des finances des pays de la C.E.E. tenue a Paris le 1er decembre 1961, 6.1.1962, II/8910/61-F. Verslag van de tiende Conferentie van de Ministers van Financien van de landen van de Europese Economische Gemeenschap gehouden op 1 december 1961 te Parijs.

29 Strange, 112-113; Tew, 129-130.

30 JFKL, POF/DA 89a (Treasury), Memorandum for the President (Dillon), 20.7.1962. and enclosure International Liquidity (Roosa), n.d.

31 Ibid., Memorandum for the President, (Dillon), and enclosure The New Convertible Gold-Dollar System (Roosa), 9.8.1962.

32 MBZ, DGES 996.231.1, Van Roijen to MBZ, 20.10.1961, conveying text of letter Roosa to Van Lennep.

33 Ibid., Verslag van de Vijfde Zitting van Werkgroep-Van Lennep op 25 en 26 oktober 1961. France had loans of $1,400 million outstanding, Italy $250 million, Germany $200 million and Netherlands $170 million. Verslag vergadering Werkgroep 3 van de Economic Policy Comitee v/d OECD (betalingbalansevenwicht), 19.1.1962.

34 In 1962 the plan was to halve the deficit, including short-term capital movement, from $2,250 million in 1961.

35 There were plans before Congress to offset 8 per cent of investment costs against company taxation.

36 US interest rate policy had been heavily criticized by Emminger, Cairncross and Posthuma.

37 MBZ, DGES 996.231.1, Verslag van de zesde Zitting van Werkgroep-Van Lennep op 12, 13 en 14 december 1961.

38 JFKL, POF/DA 89 (Treasury), Memorandum for the President, Gold Flows (Dillon), 31.8.1961.

39 Ibid., Roosa to Dillon, Paris Meetings on the United States Balance of Payments, 18.12.1961.

40 JFKL, POF/DA 74 (CEA), Note for the Files, Highlights of Financial Summit Meeting – January 18 (Tobin), 1.2.1962.

41 JFKL, POF/DA 89 (Treasury), Memorandum for the President (Dillon), 28.3.1962.

42 MBZ, DGES 996.221.1, Verslag van de Veertiende Zitting van Werkgroep 3 van de OESO (Werkgroep-Van Lennep) op 12 en 13 december 1962. See also A Note on US Views, prepared by Ralph Young of the Federal Reserve Board, circulated at the meeting.

43 MBZ, DGES 996.231.1, Verslag van de Zestiende Zitting van Werkgroep 3 van de OESO (Werkgroep Van Lennep) op 25 en 26 februari 1963.

44 MF, GT BBV 146, Verslag van de negenenveerstigste zitting van het Monetair Comite van de E.E.G. te Brussel op 5 April, Projet de Compte Rendu de la Quarante-neuvième session du Comité Monetaire (5 avril 1963), 9.4.1963, 3969/II/63-F.

45 MBZ, DGES 996.231.1, Verslag van de Zeventiende Zitting van Werkgroep 3 van de OESO (Werkgroep Van Lennep) op 29 en 30 april 1963.

46 MF, GT BBV 217, Projet de Procès-verbal de la quinzième réunion des ministres des finances des pays de la C.E.E. tenue a Spa le 10 et le 11 juin 1963, 1.8.1963, 7754/II/63-F. Verslag van de vijftiende conferentie van de Ministers van Financien van de landen van de E.E.G. op 10 en 11 juni 1963 te Spa.

47 MBZ, DGES 996.231.1, Verslag van de 19e Zitting van Werkgroep 3 van de OESO (Werkgroep Van Lennep) op 12 juli 1963.

48 JFKL, White House Files, JK Galbraith 77, Memorandum for the President, Interest Rates and Your Meeting Tomorrow with the Banking Svengalis, (Galbraith), 16.2.1961.

49 JFKL, POF/DA 73 (CEA), Memorandum for the President, The Future of the Dollar, (Heller), 15.9.1961.

50 Ibid., Memorandum for the President, The Balance of Payments Dilemma (Heller), 22.11.1961.

51 Official foreign holdings of dollars amounted to $10.3 billion and private holdings to a further $10.8 billion. Against this the USA held $16.8 billion in reserves, of which $11.4 billion was frozen to provide cover for domestic currency. Its free reserves, therefore, were $5.4 billion. Ten years previously they had been $11.7 billion as opposed to total foreign dollar holdings of $9.1 billion. JFKL, POF/DA 74 (CEA), Memorandum for the President, Gold and Domestic Policy (Tobin), 5.5.1962. In a similar vein, see also ibid., Memorandum for the President, Government Overseas Programs and the Balance of Payments (Heller, Gordon, Tobin), 27.6.1962, and Memorandum for the President, Visit of Giscard d'Estaing (Heller), 16.7.1962.

52 JFKL, POF/DA 89a (Treasury), Memorandum for the President, Gold Guarantees (Kaysen and Gordon), 18.7.1962.

53 Ibid., An Interim International Monetary Agreement (Leddy), 9.8.1962.

54 JFKL, POF/DA 75 (CEA), Memorandum for the President, Why We Need an Interim International Monetary Agreement (Heller), 9.8.1962.

55 JFKL, POF/DA 89a (Treasury), Memorandum for the President (Dillon), 20.7.1962. and enclosure International Liquidity (Roosa), n.d.

56 Ibid., Memorandum for the President (Dillon) and enclosure The New Convertible Gold-Dollar System (Roosa), 9.8.1962.

57 Ibid., Memorandum for the President (Dillon) and enclosure Appraisal of Problems in the Proposal for an 'Interim International Monetary Arrangement', 16.8.1962, and Treasury Program for further International Monetary Action, 16.8.1962.

58 Ibid., Commentary on 'An Interim International Monetary Agreement (Martin), 20.8.1962.

59 Ibid., Memorandum for the Secretary of the Treasury etc. (Kennedy), 24.8.1962.

60 JFKL, POF/DA 90 (Treasury), Memorandum for the President (Dillon), Report on Measures to Improve the Balance of Payments, 9.10.1962.

61 Ibid., Memorandum for the President The Mutual Financial and Economic Potential to Exert Pressures – US and France (Dillon), 24.1.1963.

62 Ibid., Memorandum for the President (Dillon), 11.2.1963; POF/DA 75a (CEA), Tobin to Acheson 20.2.1963 and enclosure.

63 JFKL, POF/DA 75a (CEA), Tobin to Acheson, 20.2.1963 and enclosure.

64 JFKL, POF/DA 90 (Treasury), The Balance of Payments, 28.8.1963.

65 Ibid., The Galbraith Proposals (Tobin), 11.9.1963.

66 JFKL, POF/DA 76 (CEA), Memorandum for the President, *The Balance of Payments* (Tobin), 11.10.1963.

67 Horsefield, I, 541-544.

68 MF, GT BBV A2320, Verslag van de vierde zitting van de Plaatsvervangers van de Ministers en Centrale Bank-Presidenten van de Groep van Tien gehouden te Parijs op 5 en 8 november in het Franse Ministerie van Financien, Informal Record of Meetings. Paris, 5th and 8th November, 21.11.1963, X/DEL/17. The Role of Reserve Currencies: Analysis of Deputies' Papers (Note of the Secretariat), n.d., X/DEP/26 (Rev).

69 JFKL, POF/DA 91 (Treasury), Memorandum for the President (Dillon), 14.11.1963.

70 JFKL, White House Files, JK Galbraith 76, Galbraith to Kennedy, 15.11.1963.

CHAPTER 13 (PP. 267-292)

1 Hirschman.

2 Weiler, 'The Transformation of Europe', 2426.

3 Weiler, 'The Community System', 292.

4 Burley and Mattli, 42.

5 Alter, 462.

6 Weiler, 'The Transformation of Europe', 2435.

7 Ludlow, *The Making of the European Monetary System*, 11-25.
8 George, 49.
9 Baker and Seawright, 17.
10 HMSO White paper, 1970, para. 44
11 David Colman mentions that the government estimated an overall balance-of-payments deterioration somewhere between £100-1,100 million in the 1970 white paper, but it is not clear how he obtained these numbers.
12 Young, 36.
13 Young, 3.
14 1975 white paper, 5.
15 Baker and Seawright, 17.
16 Young, 113.
17 Swann, 78.
18 Allen, 212.
19 Pinder, 16.
20 Williamson.
21 The 1973 Thompson Report on the Regional Problems of the Enlarged Community concluded that even the most prosperous region in the United Kingdom lay below the Community average!
22 George, 56.
23 Under the Commission's plans Germany would contribute 28 per cent of the cost in return for only 8 per cent of the benefits.
24 Baker and Seawright, 20-21.
25 Tsoukalis, 169.
26 Padoa-Schioppa, 241-242.
27 Oppenheimer, 23.
28 Marsh, 19.
29 Story, 149.
30 Ludlow, 'An Opportunity or a Threat?', 3.
31 Loedel; Heisenberg.
32 Aldcroft, 188.
33 Aldcroft, 206-207.
34 Cairncross, 6.
35 Boskin, 18.
36 Dinan, 66.
37 Holmes and Kempton, 302.

CHAPTER 14 (PP. 293-308)

1 In 1975, EFTA decided to support democracy in Portugal by creating a fund to promote industrial development. Assistance would be in the form of low interest loans which, when repaid, could be reallocated to other projects. The Fund began its work in 1977 with a capital of $100 million and in its first 12 years it extended loans of almost twice that amount. Pintado.

2 *EFTA Bulletin*, 14, 5, 1973, 7-9.

3 *EFTA Bulletin*, 14, 1, 1973, 10-11.

4 *EFTA Bulletin*, 14, 8, 1973, 4-6.

5 *EFTA Bulletin*, 16, 2, 1975, 3-5; ibidem.,16, 9, 1975, 15-16; ibidem, 17, 7, 1976, 15-16.

6 *EFTA Bulletin*, 18, 5, 1977, 4-6.

7 Senti.

8 Norway and Sweden were the worst offenders, with subsidies equivalent to over 10 per cent of wage costs in some sectors of manufacturing. They were followed by Austria and Finland, with equivalent figures of 6 and 3 per cent, respectively. Wiesner, 14.

9 These also affected 45 per cent of Portugal's textile exports to Western Europe. *EFTA Bulletin*, 25, 3, 1984, 4-5.

10 In 1983-1986 alone, anti-dumping or equivalent measures had been taken by the EC on EFTA exports of ferro-silicon, ferro chromium, wooden clogs, fibre building board, hardboard and silicon carbide. Norberg, 7.

11 *EFTA Bulletin*, 24, 4, 1983, 15-18.

12 Sapir.

13 *EFTA Bulletin*, 25, 2, 1984, 6-7.

14 Senti; Lindström.

15 Brunner.

16 Hurni.

17 Laursen, 317.

18 See Nell, 352.

19 Krugman.

20 Sapir, 385-386.

21 *EFTA Bulletin*, 30, 2, 1989, 1.

22 *EFTA Bulletin*, 30, 2, 1989, 4-7.

23 For an excellent description of the negotiations, see Gstöhl.

24 Interestingly, absorbing EFTA into the single market would, in terms of GDP, be like adding France to the EC. Or, another analogy, EC exports to EFTA were equivalent to those to the USA and Japan combined.

25 Kobach, 194-195.

26 See Kostrzewa and Schlieding; Dezseri; Neumann, esp. 373-375; Baldwin, 10-11.

CHAPTER 15 (PP. 309-328)

1 The European Union has undergone several metamorphoses since its inception. What started as the European Economic Community (EEC) in 1957 became the European Communities or Community (EC) in 1967 when the executives of the EEC, the European Coal and Steel Community and Euratom were fused. With the Treaty of Maastricht in 1992, it reinvented itself again, this time as the European Union (EU). In this chapter we have used the name and the abbreviation employed at time of the events described.

2 Meunier and Nicolaïdis, 907.

3 Manners; Bicchi.

4 Sjursen.

5 Young and Peterson.

6 Diez.

7 Bicchi.

8 Grabbe.

9 The GDP calculations are derived from Penn World Tables 6.1. The trade figures are calculated from GATT, *International Trade 89-90*, Volume II, GATT Secretariat: Geneva, 1990, Table A3.

10 The data for RTAs comes from the WTO website.

11 Pedersen.

12 The relationship was a somewhat uneven one. On the one hand, the EFTA states absorbed 10.3 per cent of the EEC's exports and supplied 9.2 per cent of its imports; on the other hand, 56.4 per cent of EFTA's exports were destined for the EEC and it derived 61.8 per cent of its imports from there.

13 Montana.

14 Aristotolous; Barbarinde and Faber; Cosgrove.

15 Calculated from Maddison.

16 Ackerhof, Rose, Yellen and Hessenius.

17 Hughes Hallett and Ma.

18 Friis.

19 The GDP data is derived from IMF *World Economic Outlook*, April 2007, and the trade data from WTO, *International Trade Statistics*, 2006.

20 The actual free trade agreements did not come into force until February 1994 for Hungary and Poland, and a year later for the latter two. De Benedictis, De Santis and Vicarelli. All agreements are listed in Appendix 1 of Spies and Marques.

21 European Council in Copenhagen. 21-22 June 1993, Conclusions of the Presidency, http://ue.eu.int/ueDocs/cms_Data/docs/pressdata/en/ec/72921.pdf.

22 O'Brennan.

23 The World Bank's Governance Indicators are available for 1996-2005 at their interactive website and are accessible through http://web.worldbank.org.

24 In May and June 2005 the French and Dutch electorates rejected the Draft Constitutional Treaty in their respective referenda. Caution over past and future enlargement played an important role in the defeats.
25 Several books appreared as the opening of negotiations appeared imminent. See Carkoglu and Rubin; Griffiths and Özdemir; Netherlands Council for Scientific Research.
26 Carkoglu and Rubin, ch. 1; Griffiths and Özemir, ch. 1.
27 In March 2004 four commuter trains in Madrid were ripped apart by explosions, killing 200 people. In July 2005 three London underground trains and a bus were bombed, with a death toll of 56 people. Both attackes were associated with 'Islamic terrorists'.
28 The fast changing scene on EU enlargement can be followed form the European Commission's own site: http://ec.europa.eu/enlargement/index_en.htm.
29 The EC had removed frontier barriers to trade among the members in the 1960s and had extended this to the EFTA states in the 1970s. However, the recession following the oil crisis ushered in a new range of protectionism, including product definition, technical regulations, state subsidies, anti-dumping regulations and voluntary export restraints, to name but a few.
30 Pedersen; Gstöhl.
31 Stevens, McQueen and Kennan; Panagariya.
32 Babarinde and Faber.
33 Candau and Jean; Hinkle and Schiff; Milner, Morrissey and McKay.
34 Statement made by Peter Mandelson in Brussels, 25 May 2007, http://trade.ec.europa.eu/doclib/docs/2007/may/tradoc_134747.pdf.
35 Jones and Emerson, 19-20.
36 Declour; Magan; Milcher, Slay and Collins.
37 Hughes.
38 Declour, 133-136.
39 Ahearn, 3. In 1999, the trade coverage of the EU's RTAs was three times larger than that of the USA with its bilateral partners.
40 See the WTO RTA database.
41 Ahearn, 3-4.

CHAPTER 16 (PP. 329-344)

1 European Policy Centre.
2 Jordan-Wagner.
3 Issing.
4 Garrett.
5 Buiter, Corsetti and Roubini.

6 Fingleton; Leonardi.
7 Issing.
8 European Commission, *European Economy*.
9 Bos, fn. 15.
10 CBS.
11 Siesto.
12 Collignon.
13 Fischer, Jongun and Larch.
14 Ehrmann, Fratzscher, Gürkaynak and Swanson.
15 Eichengreen, Mody, Nedeljkovic and Sarno.
16 Lane.
17 Blundell-Wignall and Slovik.
18 European Commission, *Report on Greek government Deficit and Debt Statistics*.
19 Balzli.
20 McRae.
21 Eichengreen and Irwin.
22 European Commission, *The EMU@10*, iii.

CHAPTER 17 (PP. 345-356)

1 Klabbers and Leino.
2 Shore, 28.
3 Schild.
4 *EuroBarometer* 64, 2005, 46.
5 Carey, 388.
6 Delanty, *Inventing Europe*, 12-13.
7 Cirtin and Sides, 168-171.
8 Mayer and Palmowski, 576-577.
9 Gienow-Hecht, 1089-1090.
10 Delanty, *Inventing Europe*.
11 Balibar and Wallerstein, 105.
12 Jacobs and Maier.
13 Cited in Delanty, *Inventing Europe*, 14.
14 Braun, Bernlochner, Boesenberg and Henri.
15 BBC News, 2.3.2007.
16 Mayer and Palmowski, 581-583; quotation on p. 583.
17 Turner, 303.
18 Simonson, 359.
19 Shore, 27, 35-38.
20 Levermore and Millward.

CHAPTER 18 (PP. 357-370)

1 Palayret.
2 Lewis and Wigen, 163-164.
3 Phillips.
4 Holt.
5 Milward.
6 Hooghe and Marks, 110.
7 Holt.
8 Milward; Smith, 'Creating a New Space', 21-24.
9 Smith, 'Creating a New Space', 21-24.
10 Smith, *The State of European Studies*, 11-12.
11 Smith, *The State of European Studies*, 25, 27.
12 Smith, *The State of European Studies*, 35-38.
13 Smith, *The State of European Studies*, 39-42.
14 Smith, *The State of European Studies*, 13, 47.
15 Smith, *The State of European Studies*, 43.
16 Smith, *The State of European Studies*, 25.
17 Smith, *The State of European Studies*, 44.
18 Rosamond, 'European Integration and the Social Science of EU Studies', 235.
19 Tonra, 2-3.
20 Bates; Katzenstein.
21 Cini.
22 Rosamond, 'Globalization' 30.
23 Jupille, Caporasso, and Checkel.
24 Jupille; Murray.
25 Tonra, 6.
26 EPSNet.
27 Bache, 240-242.
28 Rumford and Murray, 'Do We Need a Core Curriculum for European Studies?'.
29 Field.
30 Murray.
31 Rosamond, 'European Integration and the Social Science of EU Studies'; Warleigh.
32 Rosamond, 'Globalisation'; Rumford and Murray, 'Do We Need a Core Curriculum for European Studies?'.
33 Warleigh-Lack, Robinson, Rosamond and Rosamond.

Bibliography

1 The European Integration Experience, 1945-1958

Asbeek Brusse, W., *West European Tariff Plans, 1947-1957: From Study Group to Common Market*, PhD thesis, European University Institute, Florence, 1991. Subsequently published as *Tariffs, Trade and European Integration, 1947-1957: From Study Group to Common Market*, New York, 1997.

Boekestijn, A.J., 'The Formulation of Dutch Benelux Policy' in R.T. Griffiths (ed.), *The Netherlands and the Integration of Europe, 1945-1957*, Amsterdam, 1989.

Brown, W.A., *The United States and the Restoration of World Trade: An Analysis and Appraisal of the ITO Charter and the General Agreement on Tariffs and Trade*, Washington, DC, 1950.

Brugmans, H., *Prophètes et fondateurs de l'Europe*, Bruges, 1974.

Burgess, S. and E. Edwards, 'The Six plus One: British Policy-making and the Question of European Economic Integration, 1955', *International Affairs*, 64, 3 (1988): 393-413.

Cardozo, R., 'The Project for a Political Community (1952-54)' in R. Pryce (ed.), *The Dynamics of European Union*, London, 1987, 49-77.

Carew, A., *Labour under the Marshall Plan: The Politics of Productivity and the Marketing of Management Science*, Manchester, 1987.

Clesse, A., *Le projet de C.E.D. du Plan Pleven au 'crime' du 30 août: Histoire d'un malentendu européen*, Baden-Baden, 1989.

De Long, J.B. and B. Eichengreen, 'The Marshall Plan: History's Most Successful Structural Adjustment Program' in R Dornbush et al. (eds.), *Postwar Economic Reconstruction and Lessons for the East Today*, Cambridge, 1993, 189-230.

Dickhaus, M., '"It Is Only the Provisional That Lasts": The European Payments Union' in R.T. Griffiths (ed.), *Explorations in OEEC History*, Paris, 1994, 183-200.

Diebold, W., *The End of the ITO*, Princeton, 1952.

Diebold, W., *Trade and Payments in Western Europe: A Study in Economic Cooperation, 1947-1951*, New York, 1952.

Diebold, W., *The Schuman Plan: A Study in Economic Cooperation, 1950-1959*, New York, 1959.

Dinan, D., *Europe Recast: A History of European Union*, Houndmills, 2004.

Eichengreen, B., *Reconstructing Europe's Trade and Payments: The European Payments Union*, Manchester, 1993.

Eichengreen, B. and M. Uzan, 'The Marshall Plan: Economic Effects and Implications for Eastern Europe and the Former USSR', *Economic Policy*, 14 (1992): 13-76.

Ellwood, D.W., *Rebuilding Europe: Western Europe, America and Postwar Reconstruction*, London, 1992.

Fursdon, E., *The European Defence Community: A History*, London, 1979.

Gardner, R., *Sterling-Dollar Diplomacy: Anglo-American Collaboration in the Reconstruction of Multilateral Trade*, Oxford, 1956.

Gerbet, P., *La Construction de L'Europe*, 2nd ed., Paris, 1994.; 4th ed., Paris, 2004.

Gerbet, P., *La Naissance du Marché Commun*, Brussels, 1987.

Gilbert, M., *European Integration: A Concise History*, Lanham, 2011.

Gillingham, J., *Coal, Steel, and the Rebirth of Europe, 1945-55*, Cambridge, 1991.

Griffiths, R.T., 'The Beyen Plan' in R.T. Griffiths (ed.), *The Netherlands and the Integration of Europe, 1945-1957*, Amsterdam, 1990, 165-182.

Griffiths, R.T., 'La dinamica dell'inertia politica. La partecipazione ed il ritiro del Regno Unito nella conferenza Spaak, 1955-1956' in E. Decleva and A. Magliazza (eds.), *Diplomazia e storia delle relazioni internazionali. Studi in onore di Enrico Serra*, Milan, 1991, 677-697.

Griffiths, R.T., 'Europe's First Constitution: The European Political Community, 1952-1954' in S. Martin (ed.), *The Construction of Europe: Essays in Honour of Emile Noël*, Dordrecht, 1994, 17-39.

Griffiths, R.T., *History of the European Union: An Audio Course on the Development of the EU*, Home Academy, The Hague, 2004.

Griffiths, R.T. (ed.), *The Netherlands and the Integration of Europe, 1945-1957*, Amsterdam, 1990.

Griffiths, R.T. and F.M.B. Lynch, 'L'échec de la "Petite Europe": le Conseil Tripartite, 1944-1948', *Revue d'Histoire de la Deuxième guerre mondiale et des Conflicts Contemporains*, 152 (1988): 39-62.

Griffiths, R.T. and F.M.B. Lynch, 'L'échec de la "Petite Europe": les négociations Fritalux/Finebel, 1949-1950', *Revue Historique*, 274 (1985): 159-189.

Guillen, P., 'Les chefs militaires français: Le réarmement de Allemagne et la CED, 1950-1954', *Revue d'histoire de la deuxième guerre mondiale*, 33, 129 (1983): 3-33.

Guillen, P., 'Le projet d'union économique entre la France, l'Italie et le Benelux' in R. Poidevin (ed.), *Origins of the European Integration, March 1948-May 1950*, Brussels, 1986.

Haas, E., *The Uniting of Europe: Political, Social and Economic Forces, 1950-1957*, Stanford 1958.

Hirsch, E., *Ainsi va la vie*, Lausanne, 1988.

Hoffmann, S., 'Obstinate or Obsolete? The Fate of the Nation State and the Case of Western Europe', *Daedalus*, 95, 3 (1966): 863-915.

Hogan, M.J., *The Marshall Plan: America, Britain, and the Reconstruction of Western Europe, 1947-1952*, New York, 1987.

Ireland, T.P., *Creating the Entangling Alliance: The Origins of the North Atlantic Treaty Organisation*, Westport, 1981.

Kaplan, J. and G. Schleiminger, *The European Payments Union: Financial Diplomacy in the 1950s*, Oxford, 1989.

Kaplan, L.S., *NATO and the United States: The Enduring Alliance*, Boston, 1988.

Kaplan, L.S., *The United States and NATO: The Formative Years*, Lexington, 1984.

Kaiser, W. and A. Vasori (eds.) *European Union History: Themes and Debates*, Houndmills, 2010.

Kersten, A.E., *Maken drie kleinen een grote? De politieke invloed van Benelux 1945-1955*, Bussum, 1982.

Kock, K., *International Trade Policy and the GATT, 1947-1967*, Stockholm, 1969.

Köllner, L. (ed.), *Anfänge westdeutscher Sicherheitspolitik 1945-1956: Die EVG-Phase*, Munich, 1990.

Küsters, H.-J., *Die Gründung der europäischen Wirtschaftsgemeinschaft*, Baden-Baden, 1982. (French edition, 1990).

Leffler, M.P., *A Preponderance of Power: National Security, the Truman Administration and the Cold War*, Stanford, 1992.

Lipgens, W. (ed.), *Documents on the History of European Integration*, Berlin, 1985-1991.

Marjolin, R., *Le travail d'une vie*, Paris, 1986.

Meade, J.E. et al., *Case Studies in European Economic Union: The Mechanics of Integration*, London, 1962.

Mee, C.L., *The Marshall Plan: The Launching of the Pax Americana*, New York, 1984.

Melandri, P., 'Les États-Unis et le plan Pleven: Octobre 1950 – Juillet 1951', *Relations Internationales*, 11 (1977): 201-229.

Milward, A.S., *The European Rescue of the Nation State*, London, 1992.

Milward, A.S., *The Reconstruction of Western Europe, 1945-51*, London, 1984.

Milward, A.S., 'Was the Marshall Plan Necessary?', *Diplomatic History*, 13, 2 (1989): 231-253.

Milward, A.S. et al., *The Frontiers of National Sovereignty*, London, 1993.

Mommens, T.E., 'Agricultural Integration in Benelux' in R.T. Griffiths (ed.), *The Netherlands and the Integration of Europe, 1945-1957*, Amsterdam, 1989

Monnet, J., *Mémoires*, Paris 1976.

Palayret, J.-M., 'Jean Monnet, la haute Autorité de la CECA face au problème de la reconcentration de la sidérurgie dans la Ruhr (1950-1958)', *Revue d'Histoire Diplomatique*, (1991): 308-348.

Pflimlin, P., *Mémoires d'une Européen, de la IVe à la Ve République*, Paris, 1991.

Pineau, C. and C. Rimbaud, *Le grand pari, l'aventure du traité de Rome*, Paris, 1991.

Pistone, S. (ed.), *L'idea dell'unificazione europea dalla prima alla seconda guerra mondiale*, Turin, 1975

Poidevin, R., 'La France devant le problème de la CED: incidences nationales et internationales, été 1951 à été 1953', *Revue d'histoire de la deuxième guerre mondiale*, 33, 129 (1983): 35-57.

Poidevin, R., *Robert Schuman, homme d'État 1886-1963*, Paris, 1986.

Preda, D., 'De Gasperi, Spinelli e l'articolo 38 della CED' in *Il Politico*, 4 (1989).

Preda, D., *Storia di una speranza. La battaglia per la CED e la Federazione Europea nella carte della delegazione italiana (1950-1952)*, Milan, 1990.

Preda, D., *Sulla Soglia dell' Unione*, Milan, 1994.

Schwabe, K. (ed.), *The Beginnings of the Schuman-Plan*, Brussels, 1988.

Serra, E., 'L'union doganale italo-francese e la conferenza di Santa Margherita' in *Italia e Francia, 1946-1954*, Milan, 1989, 73-114.

Serra, E. (ed.), *The Relaunching of Europe and the Treaties of Rome*, Milan, 1986.

Smith, J. (ed.), *The Origins of NATO*, Exeter, 1990.

Spaak, P.-H., *Combats inachevés*, 2 vols, Paris, 1970-1971.

Spierenberg, D. and R. Poidevin, *Histoire de la Communauté européenne du charbon et de l'acier, une expérience supranationale*, Brussels, 1993.

Thoss, B. and H.E. Volkmann (eds.), *Sicherheits- und Deutschlandpolitik der Bundesrepublik im Maechtesystem der Jahre 1953-1956*, Boppard am Rhein, 1988.

Trausch, G. (ed.), *Die europäische Integration vom Schuman-Plan bis zu den Verträgen von Rom: Pläne und Initiativen, Enttäuschungen und Misserfolge: Beiträge des Kolloquiums in Luxemburg, 17-19 Mai 1989/The European Integration from the Schuman-plan to the Treaties of Rome: Projects and Initiatives, Disappointments and Failures: Contributions to the Symposium in Luxembourg, May 17-19, 1989*, Baden-Baden, 1993.

Uri, P., *Penser pour l'action: un fondateur de l'Europe*, Paris, 1991.

Van der Wee, H., *Prosperity and Upheaval: The World Economy, 1944-1980*, Berkeley, 1987.

Vasori, A., *Il Patto di Bruxelles (1948): tra integrazione europea e alleanza atlantica*, Rome, 1990.

Volkmann,V.E. and W. Schwengler (eds.), *Die Europäische Verteidigungsgemeinschaft: Stand und Probleme der Forschung*, Boppard am Rhein, 1985.

Weilemann, P., *Die Anfaenge der Europeische Atomgemeinschaft: zur Gruendungsgeschichte von EURATOM, 1955-1957*, Baden-Baden, 1983.

Wexler, I., *The Marshall Plan Revisited: The European Recovery Programme in Economic Perspective*, Westport, 1983.

Wiesglas, M., *Benelux. van nabuurstaten tot uniepartners*, Amsterdam, 1949.

Young, J.W., *Britain and European Unity, 1945-1992*, London, 1993.

Young, J.W., '"The Parting of the Ways"?: Britain, the Messina Conference and the Spaak Committee, June-December 1955' in M. Dockrill and J.W. Young (eds.), *British Foreign Policy, 1945-56*, Basingstoke, 1989, 197-224

2 The Founding Fathers

Asbeek Brusse, W., *Tariffs, Trade, and European Integration, 1947-1957. From Study Group to Common Market*, New York, 1997.

Brinkley, D. and C. Hackett, *Jean Monnet: The Path to European Unity*, New York, 1991.

Dûchene, F., *Jean Monnet, the First Statesman of Interdependence*, New York, 1995.

Dumoulin, M., *Spaak*, Brussels, 1999.

Dumoulin, M. (ed.), *La communauté européenne de défense, leçons pours demains?* Berne, 2000.

Dumoulin, M. (ed.), *The European Commission: History and Memories*, Brussels, 2007.

Fursdon, E., *The European Defence Community: A History*, London,1980.

Gerbet, P., G. Bossuat and T. Grobois (eds.), *Dictionnaire historique de l'Europe unie*, Brussels, 2009.

Gillingham, J., *Coal, Steel and the Rebirth of Europe, 1945-1955*, Cambridge, 1991.

Griffiths, R.T., *The European Political Community, 1952-1954: Europe's First Federal Constitution*, London, 2000.

Jones, E., A. Menon and S. Weatherill, *The Oxford Handbook on the European Union*, Oxford, 2012.

Milward, A.S., 'The Lives and Teachings of the European Saints' in A.S. Milward, *The European Rescue of the Nation State*, London, 1992, 318-344.

Milward, A.S., *The Reconstruction of Western Europe, 1945-51*, London, 1984.

Monnet, J., *Mémoires*, Paris, 1976.

Pistone, S. (ed.), *Altiero Spinelli. Una strategia per gli Stati Uniti d'Europa*, Bologna, 1989.

Poidevin, R., *Robert Schuman, homme d'État, 1886-1963*, Paris, 1986.

Preda, D., *Sulla soglia dell'unione:la vicenda della Communita Politica Europea (1952-1954)*, Milan, 1993.

Schirmann, S. (ed.), *Robert Schuman et les Pères de l'Europe*, Brussels, 2008.

Schwabe, K.(ed.), *Die Anfänge des Schuman-Plans 1950/51: The Beginnings of the Schuman Plan*, Baden-Baden, 1988.

Schwarz, H.-P., *Adenauer*, 2 vols, Stuttgart, 1986 and 1991.

Serra, E., *Il Rilancio dell'Europa e i Tratti di Roma. La Relance Européenne et les traités de Rome. The Relaunching of Europe and the Treaties of Rome*, Brussels, 1989.

Spaak, P.-H., *Combat inachevés*, 2 vols, Paris, 1969.

Spierenburg, D. and R. Poidevin, *Histoire de la Haute Autorité de la Communauté du charbon et de l'acier, une expérience supranationale*, Brussels, 1993.

Volkmann, H.E. and W. Schwengler (eds.), *Die Europäische Verteidigungsgemeinschaft: Stand und Probleme der Forschung*, Boppard am Rhein, 1985.

Weenink, W., *Bankier van de wereld. Bouwer van Europe. Johan Willem Beyen, 1897-1976*, Amsterdam, 2005.

3 The Marshall Plan and Western European Reconstruction

Agnew, J. and J. Nicholas Entrikin, *The Marshall Plan Today: Model and Metaphor*, London, 2004.

Asbeek Brusse, W., 'Regional Plans for European Trade' in R.T. Griffiths (ed.), *The Economic Development of the EEC*, Cheltenham, 1997, 57-63.

Barjot, D., *Catching up with America: Productivity Missions and the Diffusion of American Technological Influence after the Second World War*, Paris, 2002.

Boel, B., *The European Productivity Agency: Politics of Productivity and Transatlantic Relations, 1953-1961*. PhD thesis, University of Copenhagen, 1998. Subsequently published as *The European Productivity Agency and Transatlantic Relations, 1953-1961*, Copenhagen, 2003.

Carew, A., *Labor under the Marshall Plan: The Politics of Productivity and the Marketing of Management Science*, Manchester, 1987.

Casella, A. and B. Eichengreen, 'Halting Inflation in Italy and France after World War II' in M.D. Bordo and F. Capie (eds.), *Monetary Regimes in Transition*, Cambridge, 1993, 312-45.

Cleveland, H., 'If There Had Been No Marshall Plan...' in S. Hoffman and C. Maier (eds.), *The Marshall Plan: A Retrospective*, Boulder, 1984, 59-64.

Dickhaus, M., '"It Is Only the Provisional That Lasts": The European Payments Union' in R.T. Griffiths (ed.), *Explorations in OEEC History*, Paris, 1997, 183-200.

Diebold, W., *Trade and Payments in Western Europe: A Study in Economic Cooperation, 1947-1951*, New York, 1952.

Eichengreen, B., 'The Market and the Marshall Plan' in M. Schain (ed.), *The Marshall Plan: Fifty Years After*, New York, 2001, 136-139.

Eichengreen, B., *Reconstructing Europe's Trade and Payments: The European Payments Union*, Manchester, 1993.

Eichengreen, B. and J.B. de Long, 'The Marshall Plan: History's Most Successful Structural Adjustment Programme' in R. Dornbush et al. (eds.), *Postwar Economic Reconstruction and Lessons for the East Today*, Cambridge, 1993.

Eichengreen, B. and M. Uzan, 'The Marshall Plan: Economic Effects and Implications for Eastern Europe and the Former USSR', *Economic Policy*, 14 (1992): 13-76.

Esposito, C., *America's Feeble Weapon: Funding the Marshall Plan in France and Italy, 1949-1950*, Westport, 1994.

Fauri, F. and P. Tedeschi (eds.), *Novel Outlooks on the Marshall Plan: American Aid and European Re-industrialization*, New York, 2011.

Fodor, G., 'Why Did Europe Need a Marshall Plan in 1947?', EUI Working Paper, European University Institute, Florence, 1985.

Gimbel, J., *The Origins of the Marshall Plan*, Stanford, 1976.

Gomberg, W., 'Labor's Participation in the European Productivity Program: A Study in Frustration', *Political Science Quarterly*, 74, 2 (1959): 240-255.

Hogan, M.J., *The Marshall Plan: America, Britain and the Reconstruction of Western Europe, 1947-1952*, Cambridge, 1987.

Kaplan, J. and G. Schleiminger, *The European Payments Union: Financial Diplomacy in the 1950s*, Oxford, 1989.

Kaplan, L. S., *The United States and NATO: The Formative Years*, Lexington, 1984.

Killick, J., *The United States and European Reconstruction, 1945-1960*, Edinburgh, 1998.

Kindleberger, C.P., *Marshall Plan Days*, Boston, 1987.

Kolko, J. and G. Kolko, *The Limits of Power: The World and United States Foreign Policy, 1945-54*, New York, 1972.

Maier, C.S., 'The Politics of Productivity: Foundations of American International Economic Policy after World War II', *International Organization*, 31, 4 (1977): 607-633. Reprinted in C.S. Maier (ed.), *In Seach of Stability: Explorations in Historical Political Economy*, New York, 1987.

Maier, C.S., 'The Two Postwar Eras and the Conditions for Stability in Twentieth-Century Western Europe', *American Historical Review*, 86, 2 (1981): 327-352. Reprinted in C.S. Maier (ed.), *In Seach of Stability: Explorations in Historical Political Economy*, New York, 1987.

Mallalieu, W.C., 'The Origins of the Marshall Plan: A Study in Policy Formation and Political Leadership', *Political Science Quarterly*, 73 (1958): 481-504.

Margairaz, M., 'Entre Plan Marshall et Plan Monnet' in R. Girault and M. Levy-Leboyer (eds.), *Le Plan Marshall et le Relèvement Économique de l'Europe. Colloque tenu à Bercy les 21, 22, 23 mars 1991*, Paris, 1993.

Marjolin, R., *Le travail d'une vie*, Paris, 1986.

Mastny, V., *The Cold War and Soviet Insecurity:Tthe Stalin Years*, Oxford, 1996.

Mee, C.L., *The Marshall Plan: The Launching of the Pax Americana*, New York, 1984.

Milward, A.S., *The Reconstruction of Western Europe, 1945-51*, London, 1984.

Price, H.H., *The Marshall Plan*, New York, 1955.

Romero, F., *The United State and the European Trade Union Movement, 1941-1951*, Chapel Hill, 1989.

Romero, F., and P. Merli-Brandini, *Gli Stati Uniti e il sindacalismo europeo: 1944-1951*, Rome, 1989.

Sorel, E. and P.C. Padoan (eds.), *The Marshall Plan: Lessons Learned for the 21st century*, Paris 2008.

Spagnolo, C., *The Marshall Plan and the Stabilization of Western Europe*, PhD thesis, European University Institute, 1998. Subsequently published as *La stabilizzazione incompiuta: Il piano Marshall in Italia, 1947-1952*, Rome, 2002.

Wall, I.M., *The United States and the Making of Postwar France, 1945-1954*, Cambridge, 1991.

Wexler, I., The *Marshall Plan Revisited: The European Recovery Programme in Economic Perspective*, Westport, 1983.

4 The Management of Markets: Business, Governments and Cartels in Post-war Europe

Brown, W.A., *The United States and the Restoration of World Trade*, Washington, DC, 1950.

Carew, A., *Labour under the Marshall Plan: The Politics of Productivity and the Marketing of Management Science*, Manchester, 1987.

Dell, S., *Trade Blocs and Common Markets*, London, 1963.

Department of State (US) and Foreign Office (UK), *Proposals for Consideration by an International Conference on Trade and Employment: As Transmitted by the Secretary of State of the United States of America to His Majesty's Ambassador at Washington, 6th December, 1945*, London, 1945

Diebold, W., *The Schuman Plan: A Study in Economic Cooperation, 1950-1959*, New York, 1959.

Edwards, C.D., *Control of Cartels and Monopolies: An international Comparison*, New York, 1967.

Ellwood, D., *Rebuilding Europe: Western Europe, America and Postwar Reconstruction*, London, 1992.

Freyer, T., *Regulating Big Business: Antitrust in Great Britain and America, 1880-1990*, Cambridge, 1992.

Gillingham, J., *Coal, Steel and the Rebirth of Europe, 1945-1955: The Germans and French from Ruhr Conflict to Economic Community*, Cambridge, 1991.

Gowan, L., *The Antitrust Revolution in Europe: Exploring the European Commission's Cartel Policy*, Cheltenham, 2010.

Griffiths, R.T., 'The Schuman Plan Negotiations: The Economic Clauses' in K. Schwabe (ed.), *Die Anfänge des Schumanplanes 1950/51: The Beginnings of the Schuman Plan*, Baden-Baden, 1988.

Griffiths R.T. (ed.), *Explorations in OEEC History*, Paris, 1997.

Hannah, L., 'Economic Ideas and Government Policy on Industrial Organization in Britain since 1945' in M. Furner and B. Supple (eds.), *The State and Economic Knowledge: The American and British experiences*, Cambridge, 1990, 354-379.

Haussmann, F., *Der Wandel des internationalen Kartellbegriffs. Amerikanische Kartelldoktrin und World Trade Charter*, Bern, 1947.

Kuisel, R.F., 'The Marshall Plan in Action: Politics, Labor, Industry and the Program of Technical Assistance' in R. Girault and M. Levy-Leboyer (eds.), *Le Plan Marshall et le*

Relèvement Économique de l'Europe. Colloque tenu à Bercy les 21, 22, 23 mars 1991, Paris, 1993.

Lynch, F.M.B., 'Resolving the Paradox of the Monnet Plan: National and International Planning in French Reconstruction', *Economic History Review*, 37, 2 (1984): 229-243.

Maddox, R.F., *The War within World War II: The United States and International Cartels*, Westport, 2001.

Mercer, H., *Constructing a Competitive Order: The Hidden History of British Antitrust Policies*, Cambridge, 2009.

Milward, A.S., *The Reconstruction of Western Europe 1945-51*, London 1984.

Mirow, K.R. and H. Maurer, *Webs of Power: International Cartels and the World Economy*, Boston, 1982.

Porter, M.E., *The Competitive Advantage of Nations*, New York, 1990.

Rotthege, G., *Die Beurteilung von Kartellen und Genossenschaften durch die Rechtswissenschaft. Eine rechtshistorische Analyse von Hypothesen über Kooperationswirkungen und deren Bewertung*, Tübingen, 1982.

Spierenburg, D. and R. Poidevin, *The History of the High Authority of the European Coal and Steel Community. Supranationality in Operation*, London, 1994.

Stocking, G.W. and M.W. Watkins, *Cartels or Competition? The Economics of International Controls by Business and Government*, New York, 1948.

Strange, S., *States and Markets*, 2nd ed., London, 1994.

Swann, D., *The Economics of the Common Market*, 6th ed., London, 1988.

Wallich, H.C. and J.F. Wilson, 'Economic Orientations in Postwar Germany: Critical Choices on the Road towards Convertibility', *Zeitschrift für die gesammte Staatswissenschaft*, 137, 3 (1981): 390-406.

5 Europe's First Constitution: The European Political Community, 1952-1954

Aron, R. and D. Lerner, *La querelle de la C.E.D.: Essais d'analyse sociologique*, Paris, 1956.

Asbeek Brusse, W., *West European Tariff Plans, 1947-1957: From Study Group to Common Market*, PhD thesis, European University Institute, Florence, 1991. Subsequently published as *Tariffs, Trade and European Integration, 1947-1957: From Study Group to Common Market*, New York, 1997.

Bousuat, G., *Émile Noël, premier secrétaire général de la Commission européenne*, Brussels, 2011.

Brizio, F., *La Communita politica europea: saffronto tra dui progetti*, PhD thesis, Turin, 1990.

Burgess, M., *Federalism and the European Union: The Building of Europe, 1950-2000*, London, 2000.

Cardozo, R., 'The Project for a Political Community (1952-54)' in R. Pryce (ed.), *The Dynamics of European Union*, London, 1987, 49-77.

Clesse, A., *Le projet de C.E.D. du Plan Pleven au 'crime' du 30 août: Histoire d'un malentendu européen*, Baden-Baden, 1989.

Fischer, P., 'Das Projekt der europäischen politischen Gemeinschaft (1952-1954)' in L. Herbst et al. (eds.), *Vom Marshall-Plan zur EWG. Die Eingliederung der Bundesrepublik Deutschland in die Westliche Welt*, Munich, 1990, 279-299.

Fursdon, E., *The European Defence Community: A History*, London, 1979.

Griffiths, R.T., 'The Beyen Plan' in R.T. Griffiths (ed.), *The Netherlands and the Integration of Europe, 1945-1957*, Amsterdam, 1990, 165-182.

Griffiths, R.T. and A.S. Milward, *The Beyen Plan and the European Political Community*, EUI Working Paper no. 85/199, European University Institute, San Domenico (Firenze), 1985. (Also published in W. Maihofer (ed.), *Noi si mura: Selected Working Papers of the European University Institute*, European University Institute, Florence, 1986, 595-621.)

Köllner, L. (ed.), *Anfänge westdeutscher Sicherheitspolitik 1945-1956: Die EVG-Phase*, Munich, 1990.

Küsters, H.J., *Die Gründung der europäischen Wirtschaftsgemeinschaft*, Baden-Baden, 1982. (French edition, 1990).

Laird, R.F. (ed.), *French Security Policy: From Independence to Interdependence*, Boulder, 1986.

Linthorst Homan, J., *Wat zijt gij voor een vent: Levensherinneringen*, Assen, 1974.

Lipgens, W., 'EVG und Politische Foederation: Protokolle der Konferenz der Aussenminister der an den Verhandlungen über eine europaeische Verteidigungsgemeinschaft beteiligten Laender am 11. Dezember 1951', *Vierteljahreshefte für Zeitgeschichte*, 32 (1984): 637-688.

Melandri, P., *Les États-Unis face l'unification de l'Europe*, Paris, 1980.

Preda, D., 'De Gasperi, Spinelli e l'art38 della CEA' *Il Politico*, 4 (1989): 641-650.

Preda, D., *Storia di una speranza. La battaglia per la CED e la Federazione Europea nella carte della delegazione italiana (1950-1952)*, Milan, 1990.

Riste, O. (ed.), *Western Security. The Formative Years: European and Atlantic Defence, 1947-1953*, New York, 1985.

Spaak, P.-H., *Combat inachevés*, Paris, 1969.

Spaak, P.-H. *The Continuing Battle: Memoirs of a European*, London, 1971.

Spinelli, A., *Diario europeo, 1948-1969*, Bologna, 1989.

Thoss. B. and H.E. Volkmann (eds.), *Sicherheits- und Deutschlandpolitik der Bundesrepublik im Maechtesystem der Jahre 1953-1956*, Boppard am Rhein, 1988.

Trausch, G. (ed.), *Die europäische Integration vom Schuman-Plan bis zu den Verträgen von Rom: Pläne und Initiativen, Enttäuschungen und Misserfolge: Beiträge des Kolloquiums in Luxemburg, 17-19 Mai 1989/The European Integration from the Schuman-plan to the Treaties of Rome: Projects and Initiatives, Disappointments and Failures: Contributions to the Symposium in Luxembourg, May 17-19, 1989*, Baden-Baden, 1993.

Van der Harst, J., *European Union and Atlantic Partnership: Political, Military and Economic Aspects of Dutch Defence, 1948-1954, and the Impact of the European Defence Community,*

PhD thesis, European University Institute, Florence, 1987. Subsequently published as *The Atlantic Priority: Dutch Defence Policy at the Time of the European Defence Community*, Florence, 2003.

Volkmann, H.E. and W. Schwengler (eds.), *Die Europaeische Verteidigungsgemeinschaft: Stand und Probleme der Forschung*, Boppard am Rhein, 1985.

Wall, I.M., *L'influence americaine sur la politique française, 1945-1954*, Paris, 1989.

6 Agricultural Pressure Groups and the Origins of the Common Agricultural Policy

Bacon, L.B. and F.C Schroeder, *World Trade in Agricultural Products*, Rome, 1940

Barral, P., 'La politique agricole française au temps de Méline', *Revue Économique et Politique*, 79, 2 (1969): 506-512.

Blum, J., *The End of the Old Order in Rural Europe*, Princeton, 1977.

Burger, A., *Voor Boerenvolk en Vaderland. De vorming van het EEG beleid, 1959-1966*, Amsterdam, 1993.

Cioccia, P. and G. Toniolo (eds.), *L'economia italiana nel periodo fascista*, Bologna, 1976.

Commission of the European Communities, *The Situation in Agriculture*, Brussels, Annual.

Farqueson, J.E., *The Plough and the Swastika: The NSDAP and Agriculture in Germany, 1928-1945*, London, 1976.

Fearne, A., 'The CAP Decision-Making Process' in C. Ritson and D.R. Harvey (eds.), *The Common Agricultural Policy and the World Economy: Essays in Honour of John Ashton*, Oxford, 1991.

Fearne, A., 'The History and Development of the CAP 1945-1985' in C. Ritson and D.R. Harvey (eds.), *The Common Agricultural Policy and the World Economy: Essays in Honour of John Ashton*, Oxford, 1991.

Fletcher, T.W., 'The Great Depression of English Agriculture, 1873-1896' *Economic History Review*, 13, 3 (1961): 417-432.

Girvin, B. and R.T. Griffiths (eds.), *European Integration, the Green Pool and the Origins of the Common Agricultural Policy*, London, 1995.

Griffiths, R.T., 'Waarom kunnen wij het GLB niet hervormen?' in W. Asbeek Brusse et al. (eds.), *De Toekomst van het Europese Gemeenschappelijk Landbouwbeleid*, Utrecht, 2002, 49-62.

Harris, S., A. Swinbank and G. Wilkinson, *The Food and Farm Policies of the European Community*, Chichester, 1983.

Johnson, D.G., *World Agriculture in Disarray*, London, 1973.

Knudsen, A.-C.L., *Farmers on Welfare: The Making of Europe's Common Agricuctural Policy*, Ithaca, 2009.

Küsters, H.J., *Die Gründung der europäischen Wirtschaftsgemeinschaft*, Baden-Baden, 1982.

Lhomme, J., 'La crise agricole à la fin du XIXe siècle en France', *Revue Économique*, 21, 4 (1970): 521-553.

Mansholt, S., 'The Promised Land for a Community' in C. Barber (ed.), *European Community, Vision and Reality*, London, 1973.

Marsh, J. and C. Ritson, *Agricultural Policy and the Common Market*, London, 1971.

Martin, B. and A.S. Milward (eds.), *Agriculture and Food Supply in the Second World War*, Ostfildern, 1985.

Milward, A.S., *The European Rescue of the Nation State*, London, 1992.

Milward, A.S., *The Reconstruction of Western Europe, 1945-1950*, London, 1983.

Noel, G., *Du Pool Vert à la politique agricole commune. Les tentatives de Communauté agricole européenne entre 1945 et 1955*, Paris, 1988.

OECD, *Agricultural Policy of the EEC*, Paris, 1974.

Olson, M., 'The United Kingdom and the World Market in Wheat and Other Primary Products, 1885-1914', *Explorations in Economic History*, 11, 4 (1974): 325-355.

Osterud, O., *Agrarian Structure and Peasant Politics in Scandinavia*, Oslo, 1978.

Perkins, J.A., 'The Agricultural Revolution in Germany, 1850-1914', *Journal of European Economic History*, 10, 1 (1981): 71-118.

Rosenthal, G.G., *The Men behind the Decisions: Cases in European Policy-making*, Lexington, 1975.

Saunders, C., 'The CAP and Intra-EC Trade' in C. Ritson and D.R. Harvey (eds.), *The Common Agricultural Policy and the World Economy: Essays in Honour of John Ashton*, Oxford, 1991.

Serra, E. (ed.), *Il rilancio dell'Europa e i Trattati di Roma*, Brussels, 1989.

Taylor, H.A. and A.D. Taylor, *World Trade in Agricultural Products*, New York, 1943.

Thiemeyer, G., *Vom 'Pool Vert' zur Europäischen Witrschaftgemeinschaft. Europäische Integration. Kalter Kreig und die Anfänge der Gemeinsamen Europäischen Agrarpolitik, 1950-1957*, Munich, 1999.

Timoshenko, V.P., *World Agriculture and the Depression*, Ann Arbor, 1953.

Tracy, M., *Government and Agriculture in Western Europe, 1880-1988*, London, 1989.

Trienekens, G.T.M., *Tussen ons Volk en de Honger. De voedselvoorziening, 1940-1945*, Utrecht, 1985.

Van Merriënboer, J., *Mansholt: A Biography*, Brussels, 2011.

Van Zanden, J.L., *De economische ontwikkeling van de Nederlandse landbouw in de negentiende eeuw, 1800-1914*, Utrecht, 1985.

Von der Groeben, H., *Aufbaujahre der europaeischen Gemeinschaft: Das Ringen um den Gemeinsamen Markt und die Politische Union, 1955-1966*, Baden-Baden, 1982.

Yates, P.L., *Food Production in Western Europe*, London, 1940.

7 'Thank You M. Monnet; I'll Take Care of That': Some Counterfactual Reflections on Institutional Creation and the Origins of European Integration

Aron, R.and D. Lerner, *La querelle de la C.E.D.: Essais d'analyse sociologique*, Paris, 1956.

Asbeek Brusse, W., *West European Tariff Plans, 1947-1957: From Study Group to Common Market*, PhD thesis, European University Institute, Florence, 1991. Subsequently published as *Tariffs, Trade and European Integration, 1947-1957: From Study Group to Common Market*, New York, 1997.

Barbezat, D.,'Cooperation and Rivalry in the International Steel Cartel, 1926-1933' *Journal of Economic History*, 49, 2 (1989): 435-447.

Barbezat, D.,'Structural Rigidity and the Severity of the Depression: The AVI and the German Steel Cartels, 1929-1939', *Explorations in Economic History*, 31 (1994): 479-500.

Clesse, A., *Le projet de C.E.D. du Plan Pleven au 'crime' du 30 août: Histoire d'un malentendu européen*, Baden-Baden, 1989.

Cowley, R. (ed.), *The collected What If?*, New York, 2001.

'Diskussionsbericht zu den Referaten von Gerhard Keirsch und Christian Fenner' in *Politische Grundströmungen im europäischen Integrationsprozess*, Baden-Baden, 1982.

Edwards, C.D., *Cartelization in Western Europe*, Washington, DC, 1964.

Eichengreen, B. and A. Boltho 'The Economic Impact of European Integration', CEPR Discussion Paper no. 6820, 2008.

Fursdon, E., *The European Defence Community: A History*, London, 1979.

Gillingham, J.R., *Coal, Steel and the Rebirth of Europe, 1945-1955*, Cambridge, 1991.

Girvin, B.and R.T.Griffiths (eds.), *The Green Pool and the Origins of the Common Agricultural Policy, 1950-1955*, London, 1995.

Köllner, L. (ed.), *Anfänge westdeutscher Sicherheitspolitik 1945-1956: Die EVG-Phase*, Munich, 1990.

Küsters, H.J., *Die Gründung der europäischen Wirtschaftsgemeinschaft*, Baden-Baden, 1982.

Laird, R.F. (ed.), *French Security Policy: From Independence to Interdependence*, Boulder, 1986.

Lynch, F.M.B., 'Resolving the Paradox of the Monnet Plan: National and International Planning in French Reconstruction', *Economic History Review*, 37, 2 (1984): 229-243.

Lynch, F.M.B., 'Restoring France: The Road to Integration' in A.S. Milward, F.M.B. Lynch, F. Romero, R. Ranieri and V. Sorensen, *The Frontiers of National Sovereignty: History and Theory, 1945-1992*, London, 1993

Melandri, P., *Les États-Unis face l'unification de l'Europe*, Paris, 1980.

Milward, A.S., *The European Rescue of the Nation State*, London, 1992.

Milward, A.S., *The Reconstruction of Western Europe, 1945-1952*, London, 1984.

Milward, A.S., F.M.B. Lynch, F. Romero, R. Ranieri and V. Sorensen, *The Frontiers of National Sovereignty: History and Theory, 1945-1992*, London, 1993.

Mirow, K.R. and H. Maurer, *Webs of Power: International Cartels and the World Economy*, Boston, 1982.

Monnet, J., *Mémoires*, Paris, 1976.

Poidevin, R., *Robert Schuman: Homme d'état*, Paris, 1986.

Riste, O. (ed.), *Western Security: The Formative Years: European and Atlantic Defence, 1947-1953*, New York, 1985.

Schwabe, K. (ed.), *The Beginnings of the Schuman Plan*, Baden-Baden, 1988.

Thoss, B.and H.E. Volkmann (eds.), *Sicherheits- und Deutschlandpolitik der Bundesrepublik im Maechtesystem der Jahre 1953-1956*, Boppard am Rhein, 1988.

Van den Harst, J., *European Union and Atlantic Partnership: Political, Military and Economic Aspects of Dutch Defence, 1948-1954 and the Impact of the European Defence Community*, PhD thesis, European University Institute, Florence, 1988. Subsequently published as *The Atlantic Priority: Dutch Defence Policy at the Time of the European Defence Community*, Florence, 2003.

Van der Meer, Tom (ed.), *Wat als ... Pim Fortuyn niet was vermoord? Dertien alternatieve geschiedenissen van het Koninkrijk Nederland*, Amsterdam, 2011.

Volkmann, H.E.and W. Schwengler (eds.), *Die Europaeische Verteidigungsgemeinschaft: Stand und Probleme der Forschung*, Boppard am Rhein, 1985.

Wall, I.M., *L'Influence americaine sur la politique française, 1945-1954*, Paris, 1989.

Wiebes, C. and B. Zeeman, 'The Origins of Western Defence: Belgian and Dutch Perspectives, 1940-1949' in E. Di Nolfo (ed.), *The Atlantic Pact Forty Years Later: A Historical Reappraisal*, Berlin, 1991.

Ziebura, G., *Die deutsch-französischen Bezichungen seit 1945. Mythen und Realitäten*, Pfullingen, 1970.

8 The Dynamics of Policy Inertia: The UK's Participation in and Withdrawal from the Spaak Negotiations

Allison, G.T., *The Essence of Decision: Explaining the Cuban Missile Crisis*, Boston, 1971.

Brennan, G. and J. Pincus, 'Rational Actor Theory in Politics: A Critical Review of John Quiggin', *Economic Record*, 63, 180 (1987): 22-32.

Bullen, R. and M.E. Pelly (eds.), *Documents on British Policy Overseas, Series II, Volume I: The Schuman Plan, the Council of Europe and Western European Integration, 1950-1952*, London, 1986.

Burgess, S. and E. Edwards, 'The Six plus One: British Policy-making and the Question of European Economic Integration, 1955', *International Affairs*, 64, 3 (1988): 393-413.

Ellison, J., *Threatening Europe: Britain and the Creation of the European Community, 1955-58*, London, 2000.

Girvin, B. and R.T. Griffiths (eds.), *The Green Pool and the Origins of the Common Agricultural Policy*, London, 1995.

Griffiths, R.T., *Europe's First Constitution: The European Political Union, 1952-1954*, London, 2000.

Griffiths, R.T. and S. Ward (eds.), *Courting the Common Market: The First Attempt to Enlarge the EC, 1961-63*, London, 1996.

Griffiths, R.T. and W. Asbeek Brusse, 'The Dutch Cabinet and the Rome Treaties' in E. Serra (ed.), *Il rilancio dell'Europa e I trattati di Roma*, Milan, 1989.

Hoffman, S., 'Reflections on the Nation State in Western Europe Today', *Journal of Common Market Studies*, 31, 1 (1982).

Kaiser, W., *Using Europe, Abusing Europeans: Britain and European Integration, 1945-63*, London, 1996.

Küsters, H.-J., *Die gründung der europäischen Wirtschaftsgemeinschaft*, Baden-Baden, 1982.

Ludlow, N.P., *Dealing with Britain: The Six and the UK's First Application to the EEC*, Cambridge 1997.

Macmillan, H., *Riding the Storm, 1956-1959*, London, 1981.

Marsh, J.G., *Handbook of Organizations*, Chicago, 1965.

Marsh, J.G. and H.A. Simon, *Organizations*, New York, 1958.

Marsh, J.G. and J.P. Olsen, *Ambiguity and Choice in Organizations*, Bergen, 1976.

Mayer, F.V., *United Kingdom trade with Europe*, London, 1957.

Milward, A.S., *The European Rescue of the Nation State*, London, 1992.

Milward, A.S., *The Rise and Fall of a National Strategy, 1945-1963*, vol. 1 of *The United Kingdom and the European Community*, London 2002.

Simon, H.A., *Administrative Behavior: A Study of Decision-making Processes in Administrative Organization*, 3rd ed., New York, 1976.

Simon, H.A., *Models of Man*, New York, 1957.

Verba, S., 'Assumptions of Rationality and Non-Rationality in Models of the International System' in J.N. Rosenau (ed.), *International Politics and Foreign Policy*, New York, 1969, 217-231.

9 The European Integration Experience, 1958-1973

Alkema, Y. 'European-American Trade Policies, 1961-1963' in D. Brinkley and R.T. Griffiths (eds.), *John F. Kennedy and Europe*, Louisiana State University Press, Baton Rouge, 1999.

Allen, D., 'Managing the Common Market: The Competition Policy' in H. Wallace, W. Wallace and C. Webb (eds.), *Policy Making in the European Community*, Chichester 1977.

Balassa, B. (ed.), *European Economic Integration*, Amsterdam, 1975.

Barclay, G.St.J., *Commonwealth or Europe*, Quebec, 1970.

Barnavi, E. and S. Friedländer, *La Politique étrangère du général de Gaulle*, Geneva, 1985.

Beloff, N., *The General Says No: Britain's Exclusion from Europe*, London, 1963.

Bitsch, M.-T. and G. Bossuat (eds.), *L'Europe Unie et l'Afrique. De l'idée d'Eurafrique à la convention de Lomé I*, Baden-Baden, 2005.

Bodenheimer, S.J., *Political Union: A Microcosm of European Politics, 1960-1966*, Leiden, 1967.

Brandt, W., *Aussenpoltik, Deutschlandpolitik, Europapolitik*, Berlin, 1968.

Brinkley, D. and R.T. Griffiths (ed.), *Kennedy and Europe*, New Haven, 1995.

Burger, A., *Voor Boerenvolk en Vaderland. De vorming van het EEG-landbouwbeleid, 1959-1966*, Amsterdam, 1993.

Camps, M., Britain and the European Community, 1955-1963, London, 1964.

Cairncross, A. et al., *Wirtschaftspolitik fuer Europa*, Munich, 1974.

Casadio, G.P., *Transatlantic Trade: USA-EEC Confrontation in the GATT Negotiations*, Dordrecht, 1973.

Corbet, H. and D. Robertson, *Europe's Free Trade Area Experiment: EFTA and Economic Integration*, Oxford, 1970.

Cosgrove-Twitchett, C., *Europe and Africa*, Farnborough, 1978.

Curzon, G. and V. Curzon, 'The Management of Trade Relations in the GATT' in A. Shonfield (ed.), *International Economic Relations of the Western World, 1959-1971*, London, 1976.

Curzon, V., *The Essentials of Economic Integration: Lessons of EFTA Experience*, London, 1974.

Davenport, M., 'The Economic Impact of the EEC' in A. Boltho (ed.), *The European Economy*, Oxford, 1982.

Davidow, J., 'EEC Fact Finding Procedures in Competition Cases' *Common Market Law Review*, 14 (1977): 175-189.

Deighton, A. and A. Milward (eds.), *Widening, Deepening and Acceleration: The European Economic Community, 1957-1963*, Baden-Baden, 1999.

Du Bois. P. (ed.), *EFTA from Yesterday to Tomorrow*, Geneva, 1987.

Edwards, C.D., *Control of Cartels and Monopolies: An International Comparison*, New York, 1967.

Emminger, O., *DM, Dollar, Waehrungskrisen*, Stuttgart, 1986.

Fearne, A., 'The CAP Decision-Making Process' in C. Ritson and D.R. Harvey (eds.), *The Common Agricultural Policy and the World Economy: Essays in Honour of John Ashton*, Oxford, 1991.

Feld, W., *The European Community in World Affairs*, New York, 1976.

Franck, C., 'New Ambitions: From The Hague to Paris Summits (1969-72)' in R. Pryce, *The Dynamics of European Union*, London, 1989.

Friedländer, S., *La Politique étrangère du général de Gaulle*, Geneva, 1985.

Gehler, M. (ed.), *Vom gemeinsamen Markt zur europäischen Unionsbildung. 50 Jahre Römische Verträge, 1957-2007*, Vienna, 2009.

George, S., *An Awkward Partner: Britain in the European Community*, Oxford, 1990.

Gerbet, P., 'The Fouchet Plan' in R. Pryce, *The Dynamics of European Union*, London, 1987.

Gerbet, P., *La Construction de L'Europe*, 2nd ed., Paris, 1994.

Griffiths, R.T., 'The Failure of the Wider European Free Trade Area', *EFTA Bulletin* 3/91 (1991).

Griffiths, R.T., 'The Importance of Fish in the Creation of EFTA', *EFTA Bulletin*, 1/92 (1992).

Griffiths, R.T. and S. Ward (eds.), *Courting the Common Market: The First Membership Applications and the French Veto*, London, 1995.

Harris, S. et al., *The Food and Farm Policies of the European Community*, Chichester 1983.

Hasenpflug, H., 'Ausgestaltung und handelspolitische Wirkungen der EG-Assoziierungs- und Praeferenzpolitik' in T.M. Loch (ed.), *Die Assoziierungs- und Praeferenzpolitik der EG*, Bonn, 1974.

Horne, A. *Macmillan, 1957-1986*, London, 1989.

Jeserich, W., *Die Konflikt zwischen EWG und EFTA: Ein Kapitel aus Grossbritanniens Europapolitik*, Cologne, 1963.

Josling, T. and S. Harris, 'Europe's Green Money', *The Three Banks Review*, 109 (1976): 57-72.

Jouve, E., *Le Général de Gaulle et la construction de l'Europe, 1940-66*, Paris, 1967.

Kaiser, K., *EWG und Freihandelszone, England und der Kontinent in der europaeischen Integration*, Leiden, 1963.

Kock, K., *International Trade Policy and the GATT, 1947-1967*, Stockholm, 1969.

Kolodziej, E.A., *French International Policy under De Gaulle and Pompidou: The Politics of Grandeur*, Ithaca, 1974.

Kruse, D.C., *Monetary integration in Western Europe. EMU, EMS and Beyond*, London, 1980.

Layton, C., *Cross-Frontier Mergers in Europe*, Bath, 1971.

Lieshout, R.H., M.L.L. Segers and A.M. van der Vleuten, 'De Gaulle, Moravcsik, and *The Choice for Europe*: Soft Sources, Weak Evidence', *Journal of Cold War Studies*, 6, 4 (2004): 89-139.

Lindberg, L., *The Political Dynamics of European Economic Integration*, Stanford, 1963.

Loth, W. (ed.), *Crises and Compromises: The European Project, 1963-1969*, Baden-Baden, Brussels, 2001.

Ludlow, N.P., 'The Making of the CAP: Towards a Historical Analysis of the EU's First Major Policy' *Contemporary European History*, 14, 3 (2005): 347-371.

Ludlow, P. *The Making of the EMS: A Case Study of the Politics of the EC*, London, 1982.

Mansholt, S., 'The Promised Land for a Community' in C. Barber (ed.), *European Community, Vision and Reality*, London, 1973.

Marsh, J. and C. Ritson, *Agricultural Policy and the Common Market*, London, 1971

Mayes, D.G., 'The Effects of Economic Integration on Trade', *Journal of Common Market Studies*, 17, 1 (1978): 1-25.

Meyer, F.V., *The Seven: A Provisional Appraisal of the European Free Trade Association*, London, 1960.

Miljan, T., *The Reluctant Europeans: The Attitudes of the Nordic Countries towards European Integration*, London, 1977.

Moravcsik, A., 'De Gaulle between Grain and Grandeur: The Economic Origins of French EC Policy, 1958-1970' *Journal of Cold War Studies*, 2, 2 (2000) and 2, 3 (2000).

Moss, J., *The Yaounde Convention, 1964-75*, PhD thesis, New School for Social Research, 1978.

Newhouse, J., *De Gaulle and the Anglo-Saxons*, London, 1970.

Nuenlist, C., A. Locher, and G. Martin (eds.), *Globalizing De Gaulle: International Perspectives on French Foreign Policies, 1958–1969*, Lanham, 2011.

OECD, *Agricultural Policy of the EEC*, Paris, 1974.

Pattison de Ménil, L., *Who Speaks for Europe? The Vision of Charles de Gaulle*, London, 1977.

Paxton, J., *The Developing Common Market*, London, 1976.

Prewo, W.E., 'Integration Effects in the EEC: An Attempt at Quantification in a General Equilibrium Framework', *European Economic Review*, 5, 4 (1974): 379-405.

Rhenish, T., *Die Deutsche Industrie und die gruendung der Europaeischen Wirtschaftsgemeinschaft*, PhD thesis, European University Institute, Florence, 1994.

Ritson, C. (ed.), *The Common Agricultural Policy and the World Economy*, Oxford, 1991.

Saunders, C., 'The CAP and Intra-EC Trade' in C. Ritson and D.R. Harvey (eds.), *The Common Agricultural Policy and the World Economy: Essays in Honour of John Ashton*, Oxford, 1991.

Seidel, K., 'Taking Farmers off Welfare: The EEC Commission's Memorandum "Agriculture 1980" of 1968', *Journal of European Integration History*, 16, 2 (2010): 237-255.

Sellekaerts, W., 'How Meaningful Are Empirical Studies on Trade Creation and Trade Diversion?', *Weltwirtschaftliches Archiv*, 109, 4 (1973): 519-553.

Silj, A., *Europe's Political Puzzle: A Study of the Fouchet Negotiations and the 1963 Veto*, Harvard, 1967.

Simard, D., *La France et la remise en cause du système Bretton Woods 1945-71. Colloque Ministère de l'économie, des finances et du budget*, Paris, 1992.

Swann, D., *The Economics of the Common Market*, London, 1970.

Swann, D. and D.L. McLachlan, *Competition Policy in the European Community*, London, 1967.

Tew, B., *The Evolution of the International Monetary System, 1945-77*, London 1977.

Tsoukalis, L., *The Politics and Economics of European Monetary Integration*, London, 1977.

Van der Harst, J. (ed.), *Beyond the Customs Union: The European Community's Quest for Deepening, Widening and Completion, 1969-1975*, Brussels, 2007.

Van Gerven, W., '12 years EEC Competition Law (1962-1973) Revisited', *Common Market Law Review*, 11, 1 (1974): 38-61.

Varsori, A. (ed.), *Inside the European Community: Actors and Policies in the European Integration from the Rome Treaties to the Creation of the "Snake" (1958-1972)*, Baden-Baden, 2005.

Verdoorn, P.J. and A. Schwartz, 'Two Alternative Estimates of the Effects of EEC and EFTA on Patterns of Trade', *European Economic Review* (1972).

Von der Groeben, H., *Aufbaujahre der Europaeischen Gemeinschaft – Das Ringen um den Gemeinsamen Markt und die Politische Union (1958-1966)*, Baden-Baden, 1982.

Wall, S., *The Official History of Britain and the European Community, Volume II: From Rejection to Referendum, 1963-1975*, London, 2013.

Wilkes, G. (ed.), *Britain's Failure to Enter the European Community 1961-63: The Enlargement Negotiations and Crises in European, Atlantic and Commonwealth Relations*, London, 1997.

Worswick, G.D.N. (ed.), *The Free Trade Proposals*, Oxford, 1960.

Young, J.W., *Britain and the Unity of Europe*, London, 1993.

10 'An Act of Creative Leadership': The End of the OEEC and the Birth of the OECD

Burgess, W.R., *A Remodelled Economic Organisation: A Report by the Group of Four Established by the Resolution of 14th January 1960 of the Twenty Governments and the Commission of the European Economic Community*, Paris, 1960.

Chancellor of the Exchequer and the President of the Board of Trade, *A European Free Trade Area: United Kingdom Memorandum to the Organisation for European Economic Co-operation*, London, 1957.

Griffiths, R.T., 'The Importance of Fish for the Creation of EFTA', *EFTA Bulletin*, 1/92 (1992): 34-40.

Hieronymi, O., *Economic Discrimination against the United States in Western Europe (1945-1958)*, Geneva, 1973

Macmillan, H., *Riding the Storm, 1956-1959*, London, 1971.

Mahon, R. and S. McBride (eds.), *The OECD and Transnational Governance*, Vancouver, 2008.

OEEC, *Report on the Possibility of Creating a Free Trade Area in Europe*, Paris, 1957.

OEEC, *Twelfth Annual Economic Review*, Paris, 1961.

US Department of State, *Foreign Relations of the United States, 1955–1957: Western European Security and Integration, Volume IV*, Washington, DC, 1988

US Department of State, *Foreign Relations of the United States, 1958-1960, Vol. 4, Foreign Economic Policy*, Washington, DC, 1992.

11 The United Kingdom and Free Trade Area: A Post Mortem

Asbeek Brusse, W. *West European Tariff Plans, 1947-1957: From Study Group to Common Market*, PhD thesis, European University Institute, Florence, 1991.

Benoit, E., *Europe at Sixes and Sevens: The Common Market, the Free Trade Association and the United States*, New York, 1961.

Bullen, R. 'Britain and 'Europe', 1950-1957' in E. Serra (ed.), *Il rilancio dell'Europa e i Trattati di Roma*, Brussels, 1989, 315-338.

Burgess, S. and E. Edwards, 'The Six plus One: British Policy-making and the Question of European Economic Integration, 1955', *International Affairs*, 64, 3 (1988): 393-413.

Camps, M., *Britain and the European Community*, London, 1964.

Camps, M., *European Common Market and Free Trade Area*, Princeton, 1957.

Camps, M., *The European Free Trade Association: A Preliminary Appraisal*, London, 1959.

Charlton, M., *The Price of Victory*, London, 1983.

Du Bois, P. and B. Hurni, *L'AELE d'hier à Demain*, Geneva, 1987.

Griffiths, R.T., 'The British Attitude towards European Integration', *EFTA Bulletin* 2/91 (1991): 17-22.

Griffiths, R.T., 'La dinamica dell'inertia politica. La partecipazione ed il ritiro del Regno Unito nella conferenza Spaak, 1955-1956' in E. Decleva and A. Magliazza (eds.), *Diplomazia e storia delle relazioni internazionali. Studi in onore di Enrico Serra*, Milan, 1991.

Griffiths, R.T., 'The Importance of Fish for the Creation of EFTA', *EFTA Bulletin* 1/92 (1992): 34-40.

Griffiths, R.T., 'The Origins of EFTA' in K. Bryn and G. Einarsson (eds.), *EFTA 1960-2010: Elements of 50 Years of European History*, Geneva, 2010.

Griffiths, R.T. and S. Ward (eds.), *Courting the Common Market: The First Attempt to Enlarge the EC, 1961-63*, London, 1996.

Kaiser, K., *EWG und Freihandelszone: England und der Kontinent in der Europäischen Integration*, Leiden, 1963.

Kaiser, W., *Using Europe, Abusing the Europeans: Britain and European Integration, 1945-1963*, London, 1996.

Macmillan, H., *Riding the Storm, 1956-1959*, London, 1971.

Milward, A.S., *The Rise and Fall of a National Strategy, 1945-1963*, vol. 1 of *The United Kingdom and the European Community*, London, 2002.

Olesen, T.B. (ed.), *Interdependence versus Integration: Denmark, Scandinavia and Western Europe, 1949-1960*, Odense, 1995.

Tratt, J., *The MacMillan Government and Europe*, London, 1996.

Young, J.W., '"The Parting of the Ways"?: Britain, the Messina Conference and the Spaak Committee, June-December 1955' in M. Dockrille and J.W. Young (eds.), *British Foreign Policy, 1945-56* Basingstoke, 1989, 197-224.

12 'Two Souls, One Thought'? The EEC, the USA amd the Management of the International Monetary System

Bordo, M.D., O.F. Humpage and A. J. Schwartz, 'U.S. Intervention during the Bretton Woods Era, 1962-1973', NBER Working Paper no. 16946, 2011.

Chivvis, C.S., 'Charles de Gaulle, Jacques Rueff and French International Monetary Policy under Bretton Woods', *Journal of Contemporary History*, 41, 4 (2006): 701-720.

Horsefield, J.K., *The International Monetary Fund*, 3 vols., Washington, DC, 1969.

O'Hara, G., *Governing Post-War Britain: The Paradoxes of Progress, 1951-1973*, London, 2011.

Strange, S., *International Monetary Relations*, Oxford, 1976.

Tew, B., *The Evolution of the International Monetary System, 1945-77*, London, 1977.

Zimmermann, H., *Money and Security: Troops, Monetary Policy and West Germany's Relations with the United States and Britain, 1950-1971*, Washington, DC, 2002.

13 A Dismal Decade? European Integration in the 1970s

Aldcroft, D.H., *The European Economy, 1914-2000*, 4th ed., New York, 2001.

Allen, D., 'Cohesion and Structural Funds: Transfers and Trade-offs,' in H. Wallace and W. Wallace (eds.), *Policy-making in the European Union*, 4th ed., Oxford, 2001.

Alter, K.J., 'The European Court's Political Power', *West European Politics*, 19 (1996): 458-487.

Baker, D. and D. Seawright, *Britain for and against Europe: British Politics and the Question of European Integration*, Oxford, 1998.

Boskin, M.J., *Reagan and the Economy: The Successes, Failures, and Unfinished Agenda*, San Francisco, 1987.

Burley, A.-M. and W. Mattli, 'Europe before the Court: A Political Theory of Legal Integration', *International Organization* 47 (1993): 41-76.

Cairncross, A., *The British Economy since 1945: Economic Policy and Performance, 1945-1990*, Oxford, 1992.

Dinan, D., *Ever Closer Union: An Introduction to European Integration*, 2nd ed., London, 1999.

Gehler, M. (ed.), *Vom gemeinsamen Markt zur europäischen Unionsbildung. 50 Jahre Römische Verträge, 1957-2007*, Vienna, 2009

George, S. *An Awkward Partner: Britain in the European Community*, Oxford, 1998.

Godley, W., 'The United Kingdom and the Community Budget' in W. Wallace (ed.), *Britain in Europe*, London, 1980.

Heisenberg, D., *The Mark of the Bundesbank: Germany's Role in European Monetary Cooperation*, Boulder, 1999.

Hirschman, A.O., *Exit, Voice and Loyalty: Responses to Decline in Firms, Organizations and States*, Cambridge, 1970.

Holmes, P. and J. Kempton, 'The EU in the Global Economy' in D.A. Dyker, *The European Economy*, 2nd ed., New York, 1999.

HMSO *White Paper. Britain and the European Communities*, London, 1970.

Johnson, C., *The Economy under Mrs. Thatcher, 1979-1990*, London, 1991.

Loedel, P., *Deutsche Mark Politics: Germany in the European Monetary System*, Boulder, 1999.

Ludlow, N.P., *The Making of the European Monetary System: A Case Study of the Politics of the European Community*, London, 1983.

Ludlow, N.P., 'An Opportunity or a Threat? The European Commission and the Hague Council on December 1969', *Journal of European Integration History*, 9, 2 (2003): 11-25.

Marsh, D., *The Bundesbank: The Bank That Rules Europe*, London, 1993.

Membership of the European Community: Report on Renegotiation, London, 1975.

Oppenheimer, P., 'Monetary Union: A Survey of the Main Issues', *The Economist*, 122 (1994): 23-48.

Padoa-Schioppa, T., *The Road to Monetary Union in Europe: The Emperor, the Kings, and the Genies*, Oxford, 1994.

Pinder, P., *Regional Economic Development and Policy: Theory and Practice in the European Community*, London, 1983.
Story, J., 'The Launching of the EMS: An Analysis of Change in Foreign Economic Policy', *Political Studies*, 36, 3 (1988): 390-420.
Swann, D., *The Economics of the Common Market*, 6th ed., Suffolk, 1988.
Tsoukalis, L., *The Politics and Economics of European Monetary Integration*, London, 1977.
Ungerer, H., *A Concise History of European Monetary Integration: From EPU to EMU*, Westport, 1997.
The United Kingdom and the European Communities, London, 1971.
Wall, S., *The Official History of Britain and the European Community, Volume II: From Rejection to Referendum, 1963-1975*, London, 2013
Weiler, J.J., 'The Community System: The Dual Character of Supranationalism', *The Yearbook of European Law* 1, 1 (1981): 267-306.
Weiler, J.J., 'The Transformation of Europe', *Yale Law Journal*, 100 (1990-1991): 2403-2483.
Williamson, J., 'The Implications of European Monetary Integration for Peripheral Areas' in L. Needleman (ed.), *Economic Sovereignty and Regional Policy*, Dublin, 1975.
Young, J.W., *Britain and European Unity, 1945-1999*. New York, 2000.

14 EFTA and European Integration, 1973-1994: Vindication or Marginalisation?

Baldwin, R., 'An Eastern Enlargement of EFTA', *EFTA Bulletin*, 33, 3-4 (1992): 10-11.
Brunner, H., 'The Rules of Origin in the Free Trade Agreement between Switzerland and the EC', *EFTA Bulletin*, 14, 2 (1973): 3-6.
Dezseri, K., 'Hungarian Orientation toward Western Europe. Will It Be to the EC and\or to the EFTA?', *Soviet and Eastern European Foreign Trade*, 26, 4 (1990-1991): 50-64.
Gstöhl, S., 'EFTA and the European Economic Area or the Politics of Frustration' *Cooperation and Conflict*, 29, 4, 1994, 333-366.
Hurni, B., 'The Rules of Origin: How Important Are They Today?' *EFTA Bulletin*, 27, 1 (1986): 15-16.
Kobach, K.W., 'Spurn Thy Neighbour: Direct Democracy and Swiss Isolationism', *West European Politics*, 20, 3 (1997): 185-211.
Kostrzewa W. and H. Schlieding, *Die EFTA-Option fur Osteuropa: Eine Chance zur wirtschaftlichen Reintegration des Kontinents*, Keiler Diskussionbeitrage, no. 154 (1989).
Krugman, P., 'EFTA and 1992', EFTA Occasional Paper no. 23, 1988.
Laursen, F., 'The Community's Policy towards EFTA: Regime Formation in the European Economic Space (EES)', *Journal of Common Market Studies*, 28, 4 (1990): 303-325.
Lindström, S.-G., 'A Simplification of Border Formalities in Europe?' *EFTA Bulletin*, 27, 2 (1986): 8-9.
Nell, P.G., 'EFTA in the 1990s: The Search for a New Identity', *Journal of Common Market Studies*, 28, 4 (1990): 327-358.

Neumann, I.B., 'The European Free Trade Association: The Problem of an All-European Role', *Journal of Common Market Studies*, 28, 4 (1990): 359-377.

Norberg, S., 'Price Competition in the European Free Trade Area: Anti-dumping Law or Competition Law', *EFTA Bulletin*, 28, 2 (1987): 7-9

Pintado, V.X., 'A Continuing Commitment: The EFTA Fund for Portugal', *EFTA Bulletin*, 30, 2 (1989): 12-16.

Sapir, A., 'Domino Effects in Western European Regional Trade, 1960/1992', *European Journal of Political Economy*, 17, 2 (2001): 377-388.

Senti, R., 'New Protectionism in Foreign Trade: Forms and Causes', *EFTA Bulletin*, 26, 4 (1984): 14-16.

United Nations, *International Trade Statistics*

Wiesner, T., 'Government Aids to Industry in EFTA' *EFTA Bulletin*, 28, 2 (1987): 13-15.

15 The Concentric Circles of the European Union's Trade Regime, 1989 to the Present

Ackerhof, G.A., A.K. Rose, J.L.Yellen and H. Hessenius, 'East Germany in from the Cold: The Economic Aftermath of Currency Union', *Brookings Papers on Economic Activity*, 1, 1 (1991).

Ahearn, R.J., *Europe's New Trade Agenda*, CRS Report to Congress, Washington, DC, December 2006, http://fpc.state.gov/documents/organization/77701.pdf.

Aristotolous, K., 'European Union and Africa: Two Decades of Lomé', *International Advances in Economic Research*, 2, 1 (1996): 21-33.

Barbarinde O. and G. Faber, 'From Lomé to Cotonou: Business as Usual?', *European Foreign Affairs Review*, 9, 1 (2004): 27-47.

Bicchi, F., '"One Size Fits All": Normative Power Europe and the Mediterranean', *Journal of European Public Policy*, 13, 2 (2006): 286-303.

Candau, F. and S. Jean, 'What Are EU Trade Preferences Worth for Sub-Saharan Africa and Other Developing Countries?', CEPII Working Paper 2005-19, 2005, www.cepii.fr/anglaisgraph/workpap/pdf/2005/wp05-19.pdf.

Carkoglu, A. and B. Rubin (eds.), *Turkey and the European Union: Domestic Politics, Economic Integration and International Dynamics*, London, 2003.

Cosgrove, C. 'Has the Lomé Convention Failed ACP Trade?', *Journal of International Affairs*, 42, 1 (1994): 225-249.

Crawford, J.-A., and R.V. Fiorentino, 'The Changing Landscape of Regional Trade Agreements', World Trade Organization, Discussion Paper no. 8, Geneva, 2009.

De Benedictis, L., R. De Santis and C. Vicarelli, 'Hub-and-Spoke or Else? Free Trade Agreements in the "Enlarged" European Union', Instituto di Studie e Analisi Economica, Working Paper no. 52, 2005, http://www.isae.it/Working_Papers/WP_DeBenedictis_n52_2005.pdf.

Declour, L., 'Does the European Neighbourhood Policy Make a Difference? Policy Patterns and Reception in Ukraine and Russia', *European Political Economy Review*, 7 (Summer 2007): 118-155.

Diez, T., 'Europe's Other and the Return of Geo-politics', *Cambridge Review of International Affairs*, 17, 2 (2006): 319-335.

Dodge, M., *The European Union and Interregionalism: Patterns of Engagement*, Farnham, 2012.

Friis, L.. '... And Then They Were 15: The EU's EFTA-Enlargement Negotiations', *Cooperation and Conflict*, 33, 1 (1998): 81-107.

Grabbe, H., *The EU's Transformative Power: Europeanization through Conditionality in Central and Eastern Europe*, Basingstoke, 2005.

Griffiths, R.T. and D. Özdemir (eds.), *Turkey and the EU Enlargement: Processes of Incorporation*, Istanbul, 2004.

Gstöhl, S., 'EFTA and the European Economic Area or the Politics of Frustration', *Cooperation and Conflict*, 29, 4 (1994): 333-366.

Hinkle, L.E. and M. Schiff, *Economic Partnership Agreements between Sub-Saharan Africa and the EU: A Development Perspective of Their Trade Components*, Draft Africa Region Working Paper, World Bank, February 2004, www.unige.ch/ses/ecopo/demelo/Cdrom/RIA/Readings/EU_SSA_EPA.pdf.

Hughes, J., 'EU Relations with Russia: Partnership or Asymmetric Interdependency?' in N. Casarini and C. Muzu (eds.), *The EU's Foreign Policy in an Evolving International System: the Road to Convergence*, London, 2006.

Hughes Hallett, A.J., and Y. Ma, 'East Germany, West Germany, and Their Mezzogiorno Problem: A Parable for European Economic Integration', *Economic Journal*, 103 (1993): 416-428.

Jones, S. and M. Emerson, 'European Neighbourhood Policy in Mashreq Countries', CEPS Working Document 229, September 2005.

Maddison, A., *The World Economy: Historical Statistics*, Paris, 2003.

Magan, A., 'The Shadow of Enlargement: Can the European Neighbourhood Policy Achieve Compliance?', CDDRL Working Paper 68, August 2006.

Manners, I., 'Normative Power Europe: A Contradiction in Terms', *Journal of European Public Policy*, 40, 2 (2002): 235-258.

Meunier, S. and K. Nicolaïdis, 'The European Union as a Conflicted Trade Power', *Journal of European Public Policy*, 13, 6 (2006): 906-925.

Milcher, S., B. Slay and M. Collins, 'The Economic Rationale of the "European Neighbourhood Policy"' in A. Åslund and M. Ðrowski (eds.), *Europe after Enlargement*, Cambridge, 2007, 165-188.

Milner, C., O. Morrissey, and A. McKay, 'Some Simple Analytics of the Trade and Welfare Effects of Economic Partnership Agreements', *Journal of African Economies*, 14, 3 (2005): 327-358.

Montana, I.M., 'The Lomé Convention from Inception to the Dynamics of the Post-Cold War, 1957-1990s', *African and Asian Studies*, 2, 1 (2003): 63-97.

Netherlands Council for Scientific Research, *The European Union, Turkey and Islam*, Amsterdam, 2004.

O'Brennan, J., *The Eastern Enlargement of the European Union*, London, 2006.

Panagariya, A., 'EU Preferential Trade Agreements and Developing Countries', *The World Economy*, 25 (2002): 1415-1432.

Pedersen, T., *European Union and the EFTA Countries: Enlargement and Integration*, New York, 1994.

Sjursen, H. 'The EU as a Normative Power: How Can This Be?', *Journal of European Public Policy*, 13, 2 (2006): 235-251.

Spies, J. and H. Marques, 'Trade Effects of the European Agreements', Hohenheimer Diskussionsbeiträge no. 274, 2006, http://www.auwi.uni-hohenheim.de/forsch/downs/DP274-2006.pdf.

Stevens, C., M. McQueen and J. Kennan, *After Lomé IV: A Strategy for EU-ACP Relations in the 21st Century*, Commonwealth Secretariat, Institute for Development Studies, December 1998.

Young, A.R., and J. Peterson, 'The EU and the New Trade Politics', *Journal of European Public Policy*, 13, 6 (2006): 795-814.

16 Lessons from the Euro Experience

Balzli, B., 'Greek Debt Crisis: How Goldman Sachs Helped Greece to Mask its True Debt', *Spiegel Online*, 2 August 2010, http://www.spiegel.de/international/europe/0,1518,676634,00.html.

Blundell-Wignall A.and and P Slovik, 'A market perspective on the european sovereign debt and banking crisis'. *OECD Journal: Financial Market Trends*, 2 (2011): 1-28.

Bos F. *Use of National Accounts: History, International Standardization and Applications in the Netherlands*, MPRA Paper 9387, 2008, http://mpra.ub.uni-muenchen.de/9387/1/MPRA_paper_9387.pdf.

Buiter, W., G. Corsetti and N. Roubini (1993) 'Excessive deficits: Sense and Nonsense in the Treaty of Maastricht', *Economic Policy*, 8, 16 (1993): 57-100.

CBS, Press release, 1.6.2005

Collignon, S., 'The End of the Stability and Growth Pact?', *International Economics and Economic Policy*, 1, 1 (2004): 15-19.

Ehrmann, M., M. Fratzscher, R.S. Gürkaynak and E.T. Swanson, 'Convergence and Anchoring of Yield Curves in the Euro Area', *Review of Economics and Statistics*, 93, 1 (2011): 350-364.

Eichengreen, B., A. Mody, M. Nedeljkovic and L. Sarno, *How the Subprime Crisis Went Global: Evidence from Bank Credit Default Swap Spreads*, NBER Working Paper no. 14904, 2009.

Eichengreen, B. and D.A. Irwin, 'The Slide to Protectionism in the Great Depression: Who Succumbed and Why?', *Journal of Economic History*, 70, 4 (2010): 871-897.

European Commission, *The EMU@10: Successes and Challenges after Ten Years of Economic and Monetary Union*, Brussels, 2008.

European Commission, *European Economy*, Statistical Annex 2011.

European Commission, *Report on Greek Government Deficit and Debt Statistics*, 8 January 2010.

European Policy Centre, *The Maastricht Treaty – 20 Years Later*, Event Report, 16 February 2102.

Eurostat, *Report by Eurostat on the Revision of the Greek Government Deficits and Debt Figures*, 4 November 2004.

Fingleton, B., 'Estimates of Time to Economic Convergence: An Analysis of Regions of the European Union', *International Regional Science Review*, 22, 1 (1999): 5-34.

Fischer, J., L. Jonggun and M. Larch, '101 Proposals to Reform the Stability and Growth Pact: Why So Many?', *European Economy: Economic Papers*, no. 267, Brussels, 2006.

Garrett, G., 'The Politics of Maastricht', *Economy and Politics*, 5, 2 (1993): 105-123.

Issing, O., *The Birth of the Euro*, Cambridge, 2008.

Jordan-Wagner, J., 'A Historical Analysis of ERM Realignments', *Essays in Economic and Business History*, 12 (1994): 31-47.

Lane, P., *The Irish Crisis*, CEPR Discussion Paper no. DP8287, 2011.

Leonardi, R., *Convergence, Cohesion and Integration in the European Union*, New York, 1995.

McRae, H., 'Why Spain Is Odds-on for a Bailout by the End of the Year', *The Independent*, 29 February 2012.

Siesto, V., 'Concepts and Methods Involved in the Last Revision of Italy's GDP', *Labour*, 1, 3 (1987): 181-200.

17 European Identities

Balibar, E. and I. Wallerstein, *Race, Nation, Class: Ambiguous Identities*, London, 1991.

Braun, M., L. Bernlochner, L. Boesenberg, and D. Henri, *Manuel d'Histoire franco-allemand Tles L-ES-S: L'Europe et le monde depuis 1945*, Paris, 2006.

Bruter, M., *Citizens of Europe?: The Emergence of a Mass European Identity*, Basingstoke, 2005.

Carey, S., 'Undivided Loyalties: Is National Identity an Obstacle to European Integration?', *European Union Politics*, 3, 4 (2002): 387-413.

Cirtin, J. and J. Sides, 'More Than Nationals: How Identity Choice Matters in the New Europe' in R.K. Herrmann, T. Risse and M.B. Brewer (eds.), *Transnational Identities: Becoming European in the EU*, Lanham, 2004, 161-185.

Delanty, G., *Inventing Europe: Idea, Identity, Reality*, London, 1995.

Delanty, G., 'What Does It Mean to be a "European"?', *Innovation*, 18, 1 (2005): 11-22.

Delgado-Moreira, J.M., 'Cultural Citizenship and the Creation of European Identity', *Electronic Journal of Sociology*, 2, 3 (1997), http://www.sociology.org/content/vol002.003/delgado.html.

EuroBarometer 64 (December 2005).

Gienow-Hecht, J.C.E., 'Always Blame the Americans: Anti-Americanism in Europe in the Twentieth Century', *American Historical Review*, 111, 4 (2006): 1067-1091.

Hand, D. and E. Crolley, *Football and European Identity: Historical Narratives through the Press*, London, 2006.

Hooghe, L. and G. Marks, 'Calculation, Community and Cues: Public Opinion on European Integration', *European Union Politics*, 6, 4 (2005): 419-443.

Jacobs, D. and R. Maier, 'European Identity: Construct, Fact or fiction' in M. Gastelaars and A. de Ruijter (eds.), *A United Europe: The Quest for a Multifaceted Identity*, Maastricht, 1998, 13-34.

Klabbers, J. and P. Leino, 'Death by Constitution? The Draft Treaty Establishing a Constitution for Europe', *German Law Journal*, 4, 12 (2003): 1293-1305.

Levermore, R. and P. Millward, 'Using Sport as a Vehicle to Help Build a Pan-European Identity?', paper presented at the 'Europe in the World' conference, University of Liverpool, July 2004.

Mayer, F.C. and J. Palmowski, 'European Identities and the EU: The Ties that Bind the Peoples of Europe', *Journal of Common Market Studies*, 42, 3 (2004): 573-599.

Rich, P., 'European Identity and the Myth of Islam: A Reassessment', *Review of International Studies*, 25, 3 (1999): 435-451.

Risse, T., 'European Institutions and Identity Change: What Have We Learned?' in R. Herrmann, M. Brewer and T. Risse (eds.), *Transnational Identities: Becoming European in the EU*, Lanham, 2004, 247-270.

Schild, J., 'National versus European Identities? French and German in the European Multi-Level System' in *Journal of Common Market Studies*, 39/2, 2001, 331-351.

Shore, C., 'Whither European Citizenship?: Eros and Civilization Revisited', *European Journal of Social Theory*, 7, 1 (2004): 27-44.

Simonson, K.F., '"Europe", National Identities and Multiple Others', *European Urban and Regional Studies*, 11, 4 (2004): 357-362.

Turner, C., 'Jürgen Habermas: European or German', *European Journal of Political Theory*, 3, 3 (2004).

18 The Landscape of European Studies

Bache, I., 'The Europeanization of Higher Education: Markets, Politics or Learning' *Journal of Common Market Studies*, 44, 2, 2006, 231-248.

Bates, R.H., 'Area Studies and the Discipline: A Useful Controversy?' *Political Science and Politics*, 30, 2 (1997): 166-169.

Cini, M., 'The "State of the Art" in EU Studies: From Politics to Interdisciplinarity (and Back Again?)', *Politics*, 26, 1 (2006): 38-46.

EPSNet, *Teaching Europe: A Core Curriculum on European Integration*, 2002, http://www.epsnet.org/project/teaching/core.htm.

Field, H., 'European Integration Curricula and "Europeanization": Alternative Approaches and Critical Appreciation', Paper presented to the Seventh ECSA Bienniel Conference, 31 May-2 June 2001, Madison, Wisconsin.

Holt, S., 'Interdisciplinarity and European Studies', *Studies in Higher Education*, 2, 2 (1997): 161-166.

Hooghe, L. and G. Marks, 'European Union?' *West European Politics*, 31, 1 (2008): 108-129.

Jupille, J., 'A Thousand Flowers Blooming? Methodological Practices in European Union Studies', *ESP Newsletter* (Spring/Summer 2005), 2-6.

Jupille, J., J.A. Caporaso, and J.T. Checkel, 'Integrating Institutions: Radicalism, Constructivism and the Study of the European Union', *Comparative Political Studies*, 36, 1-2 (2003): 7-40.

Katzenstein, P.J., 'Area and Regional Studies in the United States,' *Political Science & Politics*, 34, 4 (2001): 789-791.

Lewis, M.W. and K. Wigen, 'A Maritime Response to the Crisis in Area Studies', *Geographical Review*, 89, 2 (1999): 161-168.

Manners, I., 'European Studies', *Journal of Contemporary European Studies*, 11, 1 (2003): 67-83.

Milward, A.S., 'The European Studies Movement: What's in a Name?', *Journal of Common Market Studies*, 14, 1 (1975): 69-80.

Murray, P., 'Setting Agendas in European Studies: Some Reflections', paper presented at a national workshop on 'European Studies in Australia: Setting Further Agendas', 24 August 2007, University of Melbourne.

Palayret, J.-M., *A University for Europe: Prehistory of the European University Institute in Florence (1948-1976)*, Rome, 1996.

Phillips, C.H., 'Modern Asian Studies in the Universities of the United Kingdom', *Modern Asian Studies*, 1, 1 (1967): 1-14.

Rosamond, B., 'European Integration and the Social Science of EU Studies: The Disciplinary Politics of a Subfield', *International Affairs*, 83, 1 (2007): 231-252.

Rosamond, B., 'Globalization, the Ambivalence of European Integration and the Possibilities for a Post-Disciplinary EU Studies', *Innovation*, 18, 1 (2005): 23-43.

Rosamond, B., 'The Political Sciences of European Integration', paper presented to the 10th biannual Conference of the European Union Studies Association, Montreal, 17-19 May 2007.

Rumford, C. and P. Murray, 'Do We Need a Core Curriculum for European Studies?', *EPS*, 3, 1 (2003): 85-92.

Rumford, C. and P. Murray, 'Globalization and the Limitations of European Integration Studies: Interdisciplinary Considerations', *Journal of Contemporary European Studies*, 11, 1 (2003): 85-93.

Smith, M.L., 'Creating a New Space: UK European Studies Programmes at the Crossroads', *Journal of Contemporary European Studies*, 11, 1 (2003): 21-34.

Smith, M.L. *The State of European Studies: Report Commissioned by the Standing Conference of Heads of European Studies*, London, 2003.

Tonra, B. 'Interdisciplinarity in European Studies: Core Value or Side Payment?', paper presented at the ECPR General Conference, Marburg, 18-21 September 2003.

Warleigh, A. 'Learning from Europe? EU Studies and the Re-thinking of International Relations', *European Journal of International Relations*, 12, 1 (2006): 31-51.

Warleigh-Lack, A., N. Robinson, N. Rosamond and B. Rosamond, *New Regionalism and the European Union: Dialogues, Comparisons and New Research Directions*, Basingstoke, 2011.

Publications of Richard T. Griffiths

Books

Industrial Retardation in the Netherlands, 1830-1850, The Hague, 1979.

Achterlijk, Achter of Anders? Aspecten van de economische ontwikkeling van Nederland in de 19e eeuw, Amsterdam, 1980.

(with J.L. van Zanden) *De economische geschiedenis van Nederland in de twintigste eeuw 1920-1985*, Utrecht, 1989.

Europe's First Constitution: The European Political Union, 1952-1954, London, 2000.

(with V. Sergeev) *Economic Reconstruction: A Comparison of Post-war Europe and Post-Soviet Russia*, Moscow, 2003. (In Russian)

Edited Books

Government, Business and Labour in European Capitalism, London, 1977.

The Economy and Politics of the Netherlands since 1945, The Hague, 1980.

(with H.W. von der Dunk et al.) *Wederopbouw, welvaart en onrust. Nederland in de jaren vijftig en zestig*, Houten, 1986.

The Netherlands and the Gold Standard, 1931-1936: A Study in Policy Formation and Policy, Amsterdam, 1987.

The Netherlands and the Integration of Europe, 1945-1957, Amsterdam, 1990.

Socialist Parties and the Question of Europe in the 1950's, Leiden, 1993.

The Green Pool and the Origins of the Common Agricultural Policy, London, 1995.

(with S. Ward) *Courting the Common Market: The First Attempt to Enlarge the European Community and the French Veto, 1961-1963*, London, 1996.

Explorations in OEEC History, Paris, 1997.

(with P.A. Schregardus, G.J. Telkamp and L.W.M. Timmermans) *Van strohalm tot strategie: het Marshall-plan in perspectief*, Assen, 1997.

The Economic Development of the EEC, London, 1997.

(with D. Brinkley) *John F. Kennedy and Europe*, Baton Rouge, 1999.
(with T. Tachibanaki) *From Austerity to Affluence: The Transformation of the Socio-Economic Structure of Western Europe and Japan*, Macmillan, London, 2000.
(with W. Asbeek Brusse and J. Bouma) *De toekomst van het Europese Gemeenschappelijk Landbouwbeleid. Actuele vraagstukken en perspectieven voor Nederland*, Utrecht, 2002.
(with W. Asbeek Brusse and D. Broeders) *Immigratie en asiel in Europa. Een lange weg naar gemeenschappelijkheid?*, Utrecht, 2004.
(with D. Özdemir) *Turkije in Europa. Turkije en Lidmaatschap van de Europese Unie*, Utrecht, 2004. English edition with Bilgi University Press, Istanbul, 2004.
(with M. Wiesebron) *Processos de integração regional e cooperação intercontintental desda 1989*, Posto Alegre, 2008.

Articles, Contributions to Books etc.

'De Nederlandse Handel Maatschappij en calicotweverijen in 1847', *Textielhistorische Bijdragen*, 14 (1972): 80-100.
'Iets meer over de Haarlemse Katoenfabrieken', *Textielhistorische Bijdragen*, 15 (1973): 38-58.
'Introduction' in R.T. Griffiths (ed.), *Government, Business and Labour in European Capitalism*, London, 1977, 13-22.
'Techniques of Macro-economic management in the Netherlands' in *ibidem*, 135-151.
'Eyewitness at the Birth of the Dutch Cotton Industry, 1832-1839', *Economisch- en Sociaal-Historisch Jaarboek*, 40 (1977): 113-181.
'The Role of Taxation in Wage Formulation in the Dutch Economy in the First Half of the Nineteenth Century' in *Ondernemende Geschiedenis; 22 opstellen bij het afscheid van Mr. H. van Riel als voorzitter van de vereniging Het Nederlandsch Economisch Historisch Archief*, Martinus Nijhoff, The Hague, 1977, 260-271.
'The Netherlands Central Planning Bureau' in R.T. Griffiths (ed.), *The Economy and Politics of the Netherlands since 1945*, The Hague, 1979, 135-161.
'The Netherlands and the European Communities', *ibidem*, 277-303. Also published in C. and K.J. Twitchett (eds.), *Building Europe: Britain's Partners in the EEC*, London, 1981, 119-144.
'Ambacht en Nijverheid in de Noordelijke Nederlanden, 1770-1844' in *Algemene Geschiedenis der Nederlanden*, vol. 10, Haarlem, 1981, 219-252, 495-496.
'The Creation of a National Dutch Economy, 1795-1909', *Tijdschrift voor Geschiedenis*, 95, 4 (1982): 513-537.
with J.M.M. de Meere, 'The Growth of the Dutch Economy in the Nineteenth Century – Back to Basics?', *Tijdschrift voor Geschiedenis*, 96, 4 (1983): 563-572.
'Economic Reconstruction Policy in the Netherlands and its International Consequences, May 1945 – March 1951', EUI Working Paper no. 76, European University Institute, San Domenico (Firenze), 1984.

with F.M.B. Lynch, 'L'échec de la 'Petite Europe'? Les négoçiations Fritalux/Finebel, 1949-1950', *Revue historique*, 274 (1985): 159-193.

'Het Nederlandse economische wonder' in H. von der Dunk et al. *Wederopbouw, welvaart en onrust. Nederland in de jaren vijftig en zestig*, De Haan, Houten 1986, 147-167, 180-181. Also published in *Bijdragen en Mededelingen betreffende de geschiedenis der Nederlanden*, 101, 1 (1986): 95-109. English version in J.L. van Zanden (ed.), *The Economic Development of the Netherlands since 1870*, Cheltenham, 1996, 173-186.

'Enkele kanttekeningen bij de eerste industrialisatie nota's van Dr. J.R.M. van den Brink', *Bijdragen en Mededelingen betreffende de geschiedenis der Nederlanden*, 101, 1 (1986): 110-117, 128.

with J.I. Israel and M.J. Wintle, 'Select Bibliography of Works in English on the Economic History of the Netherlands from the Sixteenth to the Nineteenth Century', *Dutch Crossing: A Journal of Low Country Studies*, 30 (1986): 112-127.

with A.S. Milward, 'The Beyen Plan and the European Political Community' in W. Maihofer (ed.), *Noi si mura: Selected Working Papers of the European University Institute*, European University Institute, Florence, 1986, 595-621.

'Economy and Politics' in R.T. Griffiths (ed.), *The Netherlands and the Gold Standard 1931-1936: A Study in Policy Formation and Policy*, Amsterdam, 1987, 1-18.

'The Policy-Makers', *ibidem*, 165-192.

with M.E. de Vries, 'The Agricultural Lobby', *ibidem*, 47-62.

with E. Schoorl, 'The Single-Issue Pressure Groups', *ibidem*, 139-164.

'De eerste fase van de Westeuropese eenwording' in T.P.W.M. van der Krogt et al. (eds.), *Big Is Beautiful? Schaalproblemen in de overheid en samenleving*, VUGA, The Hague 1987, 435-453.

'De economische ontwikkeling van industrieel Europa' in F. van Besouw et al. (eds.), *Balans en perspectief. Visies op de geschiedwetenschap in Nederland*, Groningen, 1987, 147-165.

'The Schuman Plan Negotiations: The Economic Clauses' in K. Schwabe (ed.), *Die Anfänge des Schumanplanes 1950/51: The Beginnings of the Schuman Plan*, Baden-Baden 1988, 35-71. Reprinted in B. Eichengreen (ed.), *The Reconstruction of the International Economy, 1945-1960*, Cheltenham, 1996, 435-471.

'The Abortive Dutch Assault on European Tariffs, 1950-52' in M. Wintle (ed.), *Modern Dutch Studies: Essays in Honour of Peter King*, London 1988, 186-208.

with F.M.B. Lynch, 'L'échec de la "Petite Europe"? Le Conseil Tripartite, 1944-1948', *Guerres mondiales et conflits contemporains*, 252 (1988): 39-62.

with J.J. Seegers, 'Spreken(-de) Cijfers? Een beschouwing en vergelijking van het nationaal inkomen in de prestatistische periode', *N.E.H.A. Bulletin* (1988): 67-76.

with W. Asbeek Brusse, 'The Dutch Cabinet and the Rome Treaties' in E. Serra (ed.), *Il Rilancio dell'Europa e i trattati di Roma*, Milan 1989, 461-493.

'The Stranglehold of Bilateralism' in R.T. Griffiths (ed.), *The Netherlands and the Integration of Europe 1945-1957*, Amsterdam, 1990, 1-26.

'The Mansholt Plan', *ibidem*, 93-112.

'The Schuman Plan', *ibidem*, 113-135.

'The Beyen Plan', *ibidem*, 165-182. Reprinted in R.T. Griffiths (ed.), *The Economic Development of the EEC*, London, 123-140.

'The Common Market' in R.T. Griffiths (ed.), *The Netherlands and the Integration of Europe 1945-1957*, Amsterdam, 1990 183-208. Reprinted in R.T. Griffiths (ed.), *The Economic Development of the EEC*, London, 183-226.

'Die Benelux Staaten und die EGKS' in L. Herbst et al. (eds.), *Vom Marshall-Plan zur EWG. Die Eingliederung der Bundesrepublik Deutschland in die Westliche Welt*, Munich 1990, 263-278.

'The Exploitation of the Dutch Economy 1940-1945' in J.P.G. Jonker et al. (eds.), *Vijftig jaar na de inval. Geschiedsschrijving en tweede wereldoorlog*, The Hague 1990, 115-124, 212-213.

'Macro-economic Planning in the Netherlands (1945-1958)' in E. Aerts and A.S. Milward (eds.), *Economic Planning in the Post-1945 Period*, Leuven, 1990, 52-60.

'A la recherche des débuts de l'intégration européenne', *Revue de synthèse* IV, 3 (1990): 235-252.

'La Dinamica delle Inertia Politica. La partecipazione ed il ritiro del Regno Unito nella confernza Spaak, 1955-1956' in E. Decleva and A. Magliazza (eds.), *Diplomazia e storia delle relazioni internazionali. Studi in onore di Enrico Serra*, Milan, 1991, 677-697.

'De economische achtergronden van de Europese integratie 1945-1957' in W.A.F. Camphuis and C. Wilderboer Schut (eds.), *Europese eenwording in historische perspectief*, Zaltbommel, 1991, 206-222.

'Between Market and Planning: The Origins of Indicative Planning in the Netherlands 1945-1951' in H. Lademacher and J. Bosmans (eds.), *Tradition und Neugestaltung. Zu Fragen des Wiederaufbaus in Deutschland und den Niederlanden in der fruehen Nachkriegzeit*, Munster, 1991, 121-157.

'The Changing Concept of Europe', *EFTA Bulletin* 1/91 (1991): 2-5.

'The British Attitude towards European Integration', *EFTA Bulletin* 2/91 (1991): 17-22.

'The Failure of the Wider Free Trade Area', *EFTA Bulletin* 3/91 (1991): 15-20.

with W. Fritschy, 'Il bloco continentale: il caso dei Paesi Bassi' in E. Castelnuovo and V. Castronovo (eds.), *Europa 1700-1992. L'età delle rivoluzioni*, Milan, 1991, 237-244.

'The Importance of Fish for the Creation of EFTA', *EFTA Bulletin* 1/92 (1992): 34-40.

'Free Traders in a Protectionist World: The Foreign Economic Relations of the Netherlands 1930-1950' in S. Groenveld and M. Wintle (eds.), *State and Trade: Government and the Economy in Britain and the Netherlands since the Middle Ages*, vol. 10 of *Britain and the Netherlands*, Zutphen, 1992, 152-168.

'De Benelux Landen en het Schuman Plan' in E.S.A. Bloemen (ed.), *Het Benelux-effect. Belgie, Nederland en Luxembourg en de Europese integratie, 1945-1957*, Amsterdam, 1992, 71-88.

with D. Barbezat, 'The European Integration Experience' in Global Coalition for Africa, Commission of the European Community and European University Institute, *Workshop on the Promotion of Regional Cooperation and Integration in Sub-Saharan Africa, Brussels*, 1992, 85-101. (Also in French)

'European Utopia or Capitalist Trap? The Socialist International and European Unity' in R.T. Griffiths (ed.), *Socialist Parties and the Question of Europe in the 1950's*, Leiden, 1993, 9-25.

with D. Barbezat, 'Western European Recovery and the Lessons for Bulgaria' in I. Petkova (ed.), *The Problem of the Relations between Bulgaria and the European Community*, Bucharest 1993, 5-26. (Original Bulgarian)

'The Origins of the Common Agricultural Policy' in J. Cheng, *The Common Agricultural Policy of the European Community*, Nanking, 1994, 1-33. (Original Chinese)

'Die deutsch-französische Achse und der Ursprung der europäischen Integration' in *Historicum* (Spring 1994): 18-23.

'Europe's First Constitution: The European Political Community, 1952-1954' in S. Martin (ed.), *The Construction of Europe: Essays in Honour of Emile Noël*, Kluwer, Dordrecht, 1994, 19-39.

'Op weg naar Europese economische integratie' in J.J. van Dijk and E. Heres (eds.), *Werken aan Europa*, Kampen, 1994, 15-22.

'Agricultural Pressure Groups and the Origins of the Common Agricultural Policy' in *The European Review*, 3, 3 (1995): 233-242.

'The European Integration Experience, 1945-1958' in K. Middlemas, *Orchestrating Europe: The Informal Politics of the European Union, 1973-95*, London, 1995, 1-36, 699-702.

'The European Integration Experience, 1958-1973' in *ibidem*, 37-70, 702-705.

'The Dynamics and Stages of European Integration, 1945-1995' in European Union, Southern-African Development Community, *Seminar on the Regional Integration Process, Brussels and Paris, 12-15 June 1995*, Caen, 1995, 65-84.

'The National and International Ramifications of Post-war Reconstruction' in T.B. Olesen (ed.), *Interdependence versus Integration: Denmark, Scandinavia and Western Europe, 1949-1960*, Odense, 1995, 24-39.

'The United Kingdom and the Free Trade Area: A Post Mortem' in *ibidem*, 167-181.

'The Green Pool Negotiations, 1953-1955' in R.T. Griffiths and B. Girvin (eds.), *The Green Pool and the Origins of the Common Agricultural Policy, 1950-1955*, London, 1995, 21-50.

with B. Girvin, 'The Origins of the Common Agricultural Policy' in *ibid*, vi-xl.

with F. Guirao, 'The First Proposals for a European Agricultural Community: The Pflimlin and Mansholt Plans' in *ibid*, 1-20.

with H.O. Pharo, 'Small States and European Integration – Literature Survey and Analysis', ARENA Working Paper no. 19, Oslo, 1995.

'Desenvolvimento Agricola e Comércio Agricola, 1945-1973' in *Portugal e a Europa, 50 anos de integraçao*, Lisbon, 1996, 143-163. Translation (plus notes) printed in R.T. Griffiths (ed.), *The Economic Development of the EEC*, London, 350-364.

with Y. Alkema, 'Hollowing-out in the Past: Historical Parallels: The Dutch Republic (1670-1790) and the United Kingdom (1850-1970)', *EXIM Review*, 16, 1 (1996): 67-99.

with W. Asbeek Brusse, '"L'European Recovery Program" e i cartelli: una indagine preliminare', *Studi Storici*, 37, 1 (1996): 41-68.

with E.S.A. Bloemen, 'La storia industriale dell'Olanda nel XIX e nel XX secolo' in A. Giuntini (ed.), *Memoria di un Mondo che Scompare. Un builancio storiografico sull'avvento, gli sviluppi e il diclino dell'industria meccanizzata in tredici paesi della rivoluzione industriale a oggi*, Bari, 1996, 167-188.

with B. Lie 'Portugal e a EFTA, 1959-1973' in *Portugal e a Europa, 50 anos de integraçao*, Lisbon, 1996, 185-206.

with D.-J. Noordam 'De overheid en de economische en sociale ontwikkelingen van 1780 tot 1830' in W. Fritschy and J. Toebes (eds.), *Het ontstaan van het moderne Nederland. Staatsvorming en natievorming tussen 1780 en 1830*, Nijmegen, 1996, 157-184.

with S. Ward, '"The End of a Thousand Years of History": The Origins of Britain's Decision to Join the European Community, 1955-61' in R.T. Griffiths and S. Ward, *Courting the Common Market: The First Attempt to Enlarge the European Community and the French Veto, 1961-1963*, London, 1996, 7-37.

'"An Act of Creative Leadership": The End of the OEEC and the Birth of the OECD' in R.T. Griffiths (ed.), *Explorations in OEEC History*, Paris, 1997, 235-256.

'Het jaar 1947' ['The Year 1947'] in R.T. Griffiths et al. (eds.), *Van strohalm tot strategie: het Marshall-plan in perspectief*, Van Gorcum, Assen, 1997, 5-15.

'Het Marshall-Plan: kan de geschiedenis ons nog iets leren?' in *ibid*, 123-134.

'How Should We Look at Marshall Aid?' in H. Labohm, *The Fiftieth Anniversary of the Marshall Plan in Retrospect and in Prospect*, Clingendael, 1997, 15-17.

'A Slow One Hundred and Eighty Degree Turn: British Policy towards the Common Market, 1955-1960' in G. Wilkes (ed.), *Britain's Failure to Enter the European Community, 1961-63: The Enlargement Negotiations and the Crises in European, Atlantic and Commonwealth Relations*, London, 1997, 35-50.

'The Creation of Europe's Supranational Institutions, 1945-1958' in K. E. Jørgensen (ed.), *Reflective Approaches to European Governance*, London, 1997, 87-106.

'The Economic Development of the EEC' in R.T. Griffiths (ed.), *The Economic Development of the EEC*, London, 1997, xii-xxii.

with W. Asbeek Brusse, 'Exploring the OEEC's Past: The Potentials and Sources' in R.T. Griffiths (ed.), *Explorations in OEEC History*, Paris, 1997, 15-32.

with W. Asbeek Brusse, 'The Management of Markets: Business, Governments and Cartels in Post-war Europe' in U. Olsson (ed.), *Business and European Integration since 1800: Regional, National and International Perspectives*, Göteborg, 1997, 162-188.

with W. Asbeek Brusse, 'Early Cartel Legislation and Cartel Policy in the Netherlands. In Memoriam: The Economic Competition Act (1956-1997)' in *Acta Politica*, 32, 4 (1997): 375-405.

'De institutionele benadering van de Marshall-hulp' in *Het Marshall Plan in hedendaags perspectief*, Atlantisch Onderwijs Paper 17, 1997, 14-25.

with W. Asbeek Brusse, 'The Incidence of International Manufacturing Cartels in Post-war Europe' in C. Morelli (ed.), *Cartels and Market Management in the Post-war World*, LSE Business History Unit Occassional Paper, 1997/1, 78-117.

'In Search of Renewal: Contemporary Economic History at a Juncture' in Lars Herlitz (ed.), *Mellon konomi og Historie*, Aalborg 1998, 11-27.

'"Dank U mijnheer Monnet; Ik zal er voor zorgen." Enige contrafactuele beschouwingen over het oprichten van organisaties en de oorsprong van de Europese integratie' in M.P. Bossenbroek, M.E.H.N. Mout and C. Musterd (eds.), *Met de Franse Slag. Opstellen voor H.L. Wesseling*, Leiden, 1998, 107-122. Also in Thai in *Journal of European Studies* (Chulalongkorn University), 6, 1 (1998): 81-99.

with W. Asbeek Brusse, "Paradise Lost or Paradise Regained?' Cartel Policy and Cartel Legislation in the Netherlands' in S. Martin (ed.), *Competition Policy in Europe*, Amsterdam, 1998, 15-39.

'Verloren toekomsten. Economische voorspellingen sinds de Tweede Wereldoorlog' in *Internationale Spectator*, 53, 1 (1999): 12-17.

'"Two Souls, One Thought"? The EEC, the USA and the Management of the International Monetary System' in D. Brinkley and R.T. Griffiths (eds.), *John F. Kennedy and Europe*, Louisiana State University Press, Baton Rouge, 1999, 189-211.

with T. Tachibanaki, 'From Austerity to Affluence: The Turning-point in Modern Societies' in R. T. Griffiths and T. Tachibanaki (eds.), *From Austerity to Affluence: The Transformation of the Socio-Economic Structure of Western Europe and Japan*, Macmillan, London, 2000, 1-24.

'Economic Growth and Overfull Employment in Western Europe' in *ibidem*, 60-81.

'Nice: Another Step Forward?' *The Parliament*, December 2000.

'Reflections after Another IGC: Was There Ever an Alternative?' *The Parliament*, January 2001.

'Reflections on the History of European IGCs' in Martyn Bond and Kim Feus (eds.), *The Treaty of Nice Explained*, London, 2001, 57-74. Also published in slightly revised form as 'Failure or Success? Reflections on the History of IGCs, 1951-2001', *Leidschrift*, 19, 1 (2004).

'Stalin's Modernisation', *Kleio*, 8 (2001): 9-13.

with J. de Jong, 'De maat genomen: de Nederlandse economie in de 19e eeuw', *BMGN*, 117, 3 (2002): 352-363.

with E.S.A. Bloemen, 'Resisting Revolution in the Netherlands' in D. Barjot (ed.). *Catching up with America: Productivity Missions and the Diffusion of American Economic and Technological Influence after the Second World War*, Paris, 2002, 113-121.

'The Foundations of European Integration', *Polis*, 4/2002 (2002): 135-145. (In Russian)

'Waarom kunnen wij het GLB niet hervormen?' in W. Asbeek Brusse et al., *De Toekomst van het Europese Gemeenschappelijk Landbouwbeleid*, Utrecht, 2002, 49-62.

with W. Asbeek Brusse and J. Bouma, 'Inleiding' and 'Besluit' in *ibidem*, 11-13 and 155-164.

with W. Asbeek Brusse, 'Europees landbouwbeleid op de helling? Anatomie van beleidsinertie en hervormingsdruk' *Openbaar Bestuur* (June/July 2003).

with W. Asbeek Brusse, 'De poreuze muren van het Fort Europa. De EU en de illegale grensmigratie' in W. Asbeek Brusse, D. Broeders and R.T. Griffiths (eds.), *Immigratie en asiel in Europa. Een lange weg naar gemeenschappelijkheid*, Utrecht, 2004, 81-100.

'Turks lidmaatschap: implicaties voor het EU-begrooting' in R.T. Griffiths and D. Özdemir (eds.) *Turkije in Europa. Turkije en Lidmaatschap van de Europese Unie*, Utrecht, 2004, 177-192. Also in English in R.T. Griffiths and D. Özdemir (eds.), *Turkey and the European Enlargement: Processes of Incorporation*, Istanbul, 2004, 171-188.

(with W. Asbeek Brusse) 'Goede bedoelingen en onuitgesproken motieven. De relaties tussen de EU en Turkije in historisch perspectief' in R.T. Griffiths and D. Özdemir (eds.), *Turkije in Europa. Turkije en Lidmaatschap van de Europese Unie*, Utrecht, 2004, 21-32. Also in English R.T. Griffiths and D. Özdemir (eds.), *Turkey and the European Enlargement: Processes of Incorporation*, Istanbul, 2004, 13-27.

'EU Studies in European and in ASEAN Universities' in *Proceedings: First Asean-EU Rectors' Conference: Higher Education and Sustainable Development*, Kuala Lumpur, 2004, 77-82.

with Ida Petter, 'Financiële euroscepsis in Nederland' in B. Boer and H. Vollaard (eds.), *Euroscepsis in Nederland*, Utrecht, 2005, 45-69.

"A Dismal Decade?' European Integration in the 1970s' in D. Dinan (ed.), *Origins and Evolution of the European Union*, Oxford, 2006, 169-190.

with G.C. Quispel, 'When Borders Move: An agenda for Historical Research', *EuroLimes*, 1, 1 (2006): 34-45.

'Waarom is het gemeenschappelijke landbouwbeleid totstandgekomen?' in G. Verburg et al. *Vijftig jaar verdrag van Rome. De betekenis van landbouw voor één Europa*, Den Haag, 2007, 14-20.

'Os Círculos Concêntricos do Regime Comercial da União Européia de 1989 até os dias de hoje' in M. Wiesebron and R.T Griffiths (eds.), *Processos de integração regional e cooperação intercontintental desda 1989*, Posto Alegre, 2008, 109-129.

'European Identities' in Ma Xiaoqiang and G. Ying (eds.), *The European Integration and the Sustainable Development of Northwest China*, X'ian, 2008, 3-16.

'Development Aid: Some Reference Points for Historical Research' in H. Pharo and M. Pohle (eds.), *The Aid Rush: Aid Regimes in Northern Europe during the Cold War*, Olso, 2008.

'The Landscape of European Studies in European Universities' in M. Holland, S. Jora and P. Ryan (eds.), *The Future of European Studies in Asia*, Singapore, 2008.

'The Development of Development Economics' in M. Dierikx, *Diplomacy and Development: Proceedings of the 10th International Conference of Editors of Diplomatic Documents*,The Hague, 2010, 9-22.

'The Origins of EFTA' in K. Bryn and G. Einarsson (eds.), *EFTA 1960-2010: Elements of 50 Years of European History*, University of Iceland Press, Reykjavik, 2010, 43-60

'EFTA and European Integration, 1973-1994: Vindication and Marginalisation' in K. Bryn and G. Einarsson (eds.), *EFTA 1960-2010: Elements of 50 Years of European History*, Reykjavik, 2010, 145-158.

'The Founding Fathers' in E. Jones, A. Menon and S. Weatherill (eds.), The *Oxford Handbook on the European Union*, Oxford, 2012, 181-192.

'The Lessons from the Euro Crisis', *Austral: Brazilian Journal of Security and International Relations*, 1, 2 (2012): 15-34.